Ultimate Biography®

Ultimate

Biography

Inside the Lives of the World's
250 Most Influential People

LONDON, NEW YORK, MUNICH,
MELBOURNE, and DELHI

DK PUBLISHING
Project Editor Barbara Berger
Senior Art Editor Michelle Baxter
Creative Director Tina Vaughan
Editorial Director Chuck Wills
Jacket Art Director Dirk Kaufman
Publisher Chuck Lang
Production Manager Chris Avgherinos
DTP Designer Russell Shaw

First American Edition, 2002
2 4 6 8 10 9 7 5 3
Published in the United States
by DK Publishing, Inc.
375 Hudson Street
New York, New York 10014

produced by AVALON PUBLISHING GROUP, INC.
Executive Editor Thomas Dyja
Editor Clint Willis
Photo Editor Tracy Armstead
Designer Lisa Vaughn
Contributors Mark Klimek, Nate Hardcastle, Taylor D. Smith,
March Alex Truedsson, John Patrick Bishop,
Amrita Narayanan Bruce, Nathaniel Knaebel

**Director of Consumer Products Licensing,
A&E Television Networks** Carrie Trimmer

DK Publishing, Inc. offers special discounts for bulk purchases
for sales promotions or premiums. Specific, large-quantity needs
can be met with special editions, including personalized
covers, excerpts of existing guides, and corporate imprints.
For more information, contact
Special Markets Department, DK Publishing, Inc.,
375 Hudson Street, New York, NY 10014 Fax: 212-689-5254

Cataloging in Publication data is available from the
Library of Congress

Reproduced by Colourscan, Singapore
Printed in the United States by R. R. Donnelley & Sons, Ohio

see our complete product line at
www.dk.com

CONTENTS

HUMAN ACHIEVEMENT

HUMAN SPIRIT

WORLD HISTORY

INTRODUCTION

Since premiering in April of 1987, *Biography*®, has profiled an amazing array of more than 1,000 people, from Albert Einstein to Lucille Ball, Winston Churchill to Michael Jackson. To mark the fifteenth anniversary of *Biography*, A&E Television Networks teamed up with Dorling Kindersley to develop this book. *Ultimate Biography* covers 250 of the world's most important, most influential, most beloved, and even most infamous personalities.

Ultimate Biography is as entertaining to read as the Biography program is to watch: it is a thorough reference that not only entertains and informs but offers a novel way to look at The People You Thought You Knew™.

Ultimate Biography weaves a tapestry of the life lived and the backdrop of world events and milestones to fill out each life's story. The stories told range across time and place—from Spiritual Teachers to Talk Show Hosts; from the Founding Fathers to Giants of Jazz; from Conquerors to the Creators of Rock & Roll.

On some pages you can't help but be uplifted. Artists such as Michelangelo, Camille Pissarro and Zora Neale Hurston gave their entire lives to the pursuit of truth and beauty, while Martin Luther King, Jr., Mohandas Ghandi, and Nelson Mandela each wielded the powerful weapon of non-violence to raise up their peoples and find justice. There are explorers such as Magellan and Shackleton, who tested the limits of human endurance; Einstein and Newton, who tested the limits of our knowledge. Men and women who went into space, tended the sick, made our hearts flutter, our toes tap, our nations what they are today. You'll find here restless imaginations, deep passions, spiritual light and the

"There is properly no history; only biography."

RALPH WALDO EMERSON

knack for making people laugh. To read *Ultimate Biography* is to be inspired by the wonders of humanity; the awesome power we have in us to conquer continents, crack codes and split atoms, our constant desire over the centuries to bring peace and healing, the buildings we've built, the paintings we've painted, the stars to which we've aspired.

But many of history's most important people were despicable, depraved. Adolf Hitler, Joseph Stalin and Ivan the Terrible all made their marks on history and their stories must be told here. Reading of the foolish arrogance of Marie Antoinette, the genocidal plan of Pol Pot, the rapaciousness of Napoleon Bonaparte and Genghis Khan reminds us of the destructive power contained within the human drive to rule.

Getting down to 250 subjects was no easy task, and by no means does it mean that these are the only people who have changed the world. You'll find throughout the book short lists of other memorable people related to the subjects at hand. If you don't

want to start at page one, take a look at the index, which includes every person named in *Ultimate Biography*. From Aaron to Emile Zola, you'll see hundreds of people who fit into the vast puzzle of human history and you'll soon be flipping back to see exactly where.

—**Harry Smith, for Biography**

HARRY SMITH, HOST
OF "BIOGRAPHY"

SPIRITUAL TEACHERS

THROUGHOUT HISTORY, CERTAIN GIFTED AND INSPIRED INDIVIDUALS HAVE helped human beings develop their notions of the divine. Their lives, experiences, and teachings have given us humanity's best-known stories, and have guided and shaped civilizations.

Tradition has it that Moses led the Hebrews on a 40-year exodus from enslavement in Egypt to the promised land, introducing them to God's commandments along the way—the founding of Judaism. Chinese politician and philosopher Confucius left his government office to wander the countryside, preaching what became known as Confucianism, a philosophy of social reform and individual conduct. In a kingdom near the Himalayas, Prince Gautama Siddartha renounced his worldly status to achieve enlightenment. In what is today Israel, Jesus Christ taught divinely inspired compassion; his teachings led to the formation of Christianity. And while walking in the hills of what is now Saudi Arabia, the merchant Muhammad received the vision that grew into Islam.

△ MOSES READS THE TEN COMMANDMENTS *to the Israelites. The Old Testament tells how Moses climbed to the top of Mount Sinai and received two tablets from God inscribed with the commandments or laws.*

JESUS CHRIST
(c. 4 B.C.–A.D. 29)

TWENTY CENTURIES after the birth of Jesus Christ, more than a third of the Earth's people consider themselves his followers. His brief life has possibly had a greater impact on human history than any other before or since.

THE SON OF GOD

Tradition says that Jesus' mother, Mary, was a virgin when she encountered an angel who told her that she was to bear the Son of God. Around 4 B.C. Mary and her husband, Joseph, traveled to Bethlehem, where she gave birth to Jesus. The family then fled to Egypt for a time to escape persecution by King Herod.

At the age of 30, Jesus met John the Baptist, who recognized him as the "Messiah," or "Christ," the second coming of God prophesized in the Old Testament. Jesus then spent 40 days and nights fasting and praying in the wilderness, and chose 12 apostles (followers) to help spread his message of brotherly love and devotion to God. According to the Gospels—four accounts of Jesus life,

△ THE CROSS *symbolizes the crucifixion of Jesus Christ and represents the religion that grew out of his teachings.*

all written after his death—he traveled the countryside with his followers, ministering to the people and performing miracles. Jesus claim to be the Son of God, his criticism of the Jewish religious establishment, and the rapid growth of his following worried the Roman authorities who controlled the area. Judas Iscariot, one of his apostles, betrayed him after a Passover dinner in Jerusalem. He was arrested, and, following a hasty trial, Roman governor Pontius Pilate sentenced him to death by crucifixion. Christians believe that after dying on the cross, he returned to earth for 40 days, then ascended into Heaven. His life story and teachings, as recorded in the New Testament, form the basis of the Christian religion.

▷ DESPITE THE COMMON *image of Jesus, no contemporary portraits of him exist.*

△ A LARGE WRAPPING *cloth known as the Shroud of Turin is believed by some to miraculously hold the image of Jesus, though scientific investigation casts doubt on that claim.*

◁ CHRIST HEALS A BLIND *man's sight. His miracles included healing the sick, turning water into wine at a wedding feast, and raising his friend Lazarus from the dead.*

Did you know?

■ Some 22,000 separate churches, sects, and denominations make up the Christian faith today.

■ Aside from the New Testatament, references to Christ appear in works by Pliny the Younger, the Roman Jewish philosopher Josephus, and the Roman historian Seutonius.

△ ROMAN CATHOLICS *believe that during the sacrament of the Eucharist, bread and wine are transubstantiated into— literally become   the body and blood of Jesus Christ.*

Influential Apostles

ST. PETER (c. A.D. 1–64)
Regarded as the first pope.

JUDAS ISCARIOT
(c. 4 B.C.–A.D. 29)
Betrayed Christ to the Roman authorities.

ST. JOHN (c. A.D. 1–100)
Evangelist and author of fourth gospel and the Book of Revelation.

▽ THE FIRST CELEBRATION *of the Eucharist, the ritual meal reenacted at every Catholic Mass, was at the Last Supper, a Passover seder shared between Christ and his disciples the night before his execution.*

△ THE TOMB OF KONG FU ZE
in Qufu, in the Shandong province.

KONG FU ZE
(551–479 B.C.)

THE TEACHINGS OF CHINESE PHILOSOPHER Kong Fu Ze, or Confucius, have attracted more followers over a longer period of time than those of any other spiritual leader.

MASTER KONG

Born to a family of minor aristocracy in the state of Lu (modern Shandong), Kong mastered various arts, including music, history, poetry, and arithmetic, and became one of China's first professional teachers. Kong later entered politics. His efforts for social reform were heralded by the masses but scorned by the imperial government, which dismissed him. For the next 12 years Kong roamed the countryside looking for work and teaching to a loyal following of students.

After his death at age 73, Kong's followers compiled a collection of his sayings and pronouncements in a book entitled the *Analects*. This treatise outlines the tenets of his doctrine, including the improvement of human beings through learning, veneration of the past, and the importance of ritual and proper conduct.

△ KONG FU ZE TAUGHT *that the individual should focus on public virtue and traditional codes of conduct, inspired and guided by the study of the worthy kings, their rituals, and music.*

Did you know?

■ Although Confucianism has become a religious path, Kong himself never wrote about God.

■ Some scholars believe that Kong had a brief and contentious meeting at the Imperial Court with Lao Ze, founder of Taoism.

■ Confucianism forms the ethical underpinning of Chinese culture.

▽ AFTER KONG *and his disciples wandered for years in search of a government willing to adopt Confucian tenets, they returned to his hometown, where Kong was later named a provincial governor.*

▷ KONG HOLDS THE FIVE CLASSICS *in this 18th-century painting, although these texts on his tenets did not exist while he was alive (they were compiled c. 500).*

MUHAMMAD
(A.D. 570–632)

In 612, Muhammad, the orphaned son of a poor Arabian merchant, was visited by the Angel Gabriel, who told him that he was the messenger of God. Thus began the religion of Islam—a faith that shares roots with Judaism and Christianity, but worships a god that cannot be personified, and reveres Muhammad as the last of the prophets.

△ WHILE MEDITATING IN A CAVE *of Mt. Hira, Muhammad heard a voice order him to begin reciting what would later be called the Koran, or "The Recitation," the revelation of Allah's truth.*

THE MESSENGER

Born in the city of Mecca, Saudi Arabia, Muhammad led trading caravans in his youth. He met and married a wealthy woman named Khadija and became a successful and esteemed merchant in Mecca. When he was around 40 years old, he received visions that proclaimed him to be a prophet of *Allah* (God).

Muhammad called for his followers to purify the tradition taught by Abraham, to lead pious, moral lives, and pray to God. The former merchant's following grew rapidly when he began to preach—arousing the anger of Mecca's ruling class, who cast him out of the city. He lived for the next eight years in the neighboring city of Medina, expanding his influence and carrying out a series of successful military campaigns against Mecca. His efforts eventually unified the Arabian Peninsula under Islam. Muhammad fell ill and died in the city of Medina in June 632.

△ MUHAMMAD CLAIMED THAT *the angel Gabriel visited him a year before he left Medina, and took him on a journey to Jerusalem during which they also ascended into heaven.*

Islamic spirituality

EL-GHAZALI (1056–1111) Mystic and intellectual, influenced St. Francis of Assisi.

RUMI (1207–1273) Sufi poet, founder of the Whirling Dervishes.

Did you know?

■ The revelations that make up the Koran came to Muhammad over the course of 23 years.

■ Muslims pray facing their holy city of Mecca five times a day, repeating a prescribed set of ritual postures and prayers.

■ "Islam" is an Arabic word that means submission and surrender to the will of God, so that one can find peace.

▷ THE KA'BA *in Mecca is believed to be the original site of a shrine built by Abraham and his son Ishmael, the father of the Arabs. Islam requires faithful Muslims to make a pilgrimage to the site, called a hajj, at least once in their life.*

MOSES
(b. c. 1250 B.C.)

PROPHET, LIBERATOR, LAWGIVER, AND TEACHER, Moses is the greatest figure in the history of the Jewish faith, and he is revered by Christians and Muslims as well.

THE LAWGIVER

Born while the Egyptians held the Hebrew people in captivity, the infant Moses was adopted and raised in the house of the Pharaoh, Egypt's supreme ruler. He later learned of his Hebrew identity and fled to the land of Midian. There, Moses was commanded by God to liberate his people. The Pharaoh initially rejected Moses' appeals for the Israelites' freedom, but relented after Egypt suffered the ten plagues of Exodus, which included the water of the Nile turning to blood, and plagues of frogs, gnats, and flies. Moses then led the Hebrews across the desert toward Canaan, the land promised them by God, a journey that according to tradition lasted close to 40 years. Along the way, Moses ascended Mount Sinai and received from God the Ten Commandments, which established the moral principles for the Israelite nation. Moses died east of the Jordan River, before the Hebrew people entered the Promised Land.

△ MOSES SPENT FORTY DAYS *on top of Mount Sinai, receiving the ten commandments from God on two engraved stone tablets, while the Israelites waited below. Upon returning to his people, Moses found that they had turned away from God, and smashed the tablets in anger.*

"Let my people go."

MOSES AS QUOTED IN EXODUS 5:1

△ MOSES WAS GOD'S *intermediary; he negotiated God's covenant or law code with the Israelites. This 12-century French bible illumination shows Moses (right) before God.*

◁ MOSES WAS SUPPOSEDLY *found by Egyptian royalty in a reed basket floated on the River Nile by his mother. Pharoah had issued a law that any male infant born to an Israelite was to be killed.*

Did you know?

■ The Torah—the first five books of the Old Testament—is also known as the Five Books of Moses.

■ Moses anointed his brother Aaron as one of the first priests of the Jewish religion.

BUDDHA
(c. 560–480 B.C.)

THE TEACHINGS OF GAUTAMA SIDDHARTHA, who founded Buddhism in the 6th century B.C., are followed by more than 300 million adherents who believe, among other things, in the ability of the individual to achieve liberation from suffering.

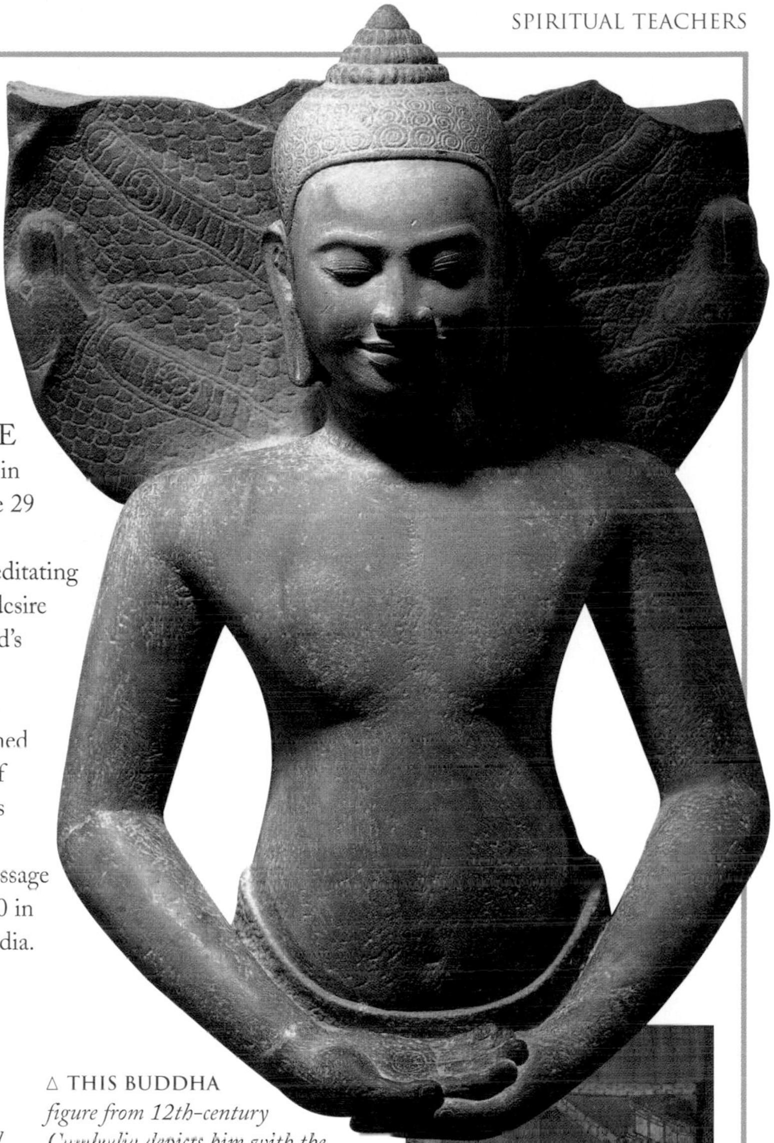

THE ENLIGHTENED ONE

Born a prince in the town of Lumbiri, in Southwestern Nepal, Siddhartha at age 29 renounced his courtly life to become a wandering ascetic. At age 35, while meditating under a tree, Siddhartha realized that desire and ignorance are the cause of mankind's suffering, and that everything in life is transitory. With this understanding, he became a buddha—meaning "enlightened one" in Sanskrit, the sacred language of ancient India. He began preaching his discoveries, and soon had a core of disciples who helped spread his message throughout Asia. He died at age 80 in the present-day town of Kasia, India.

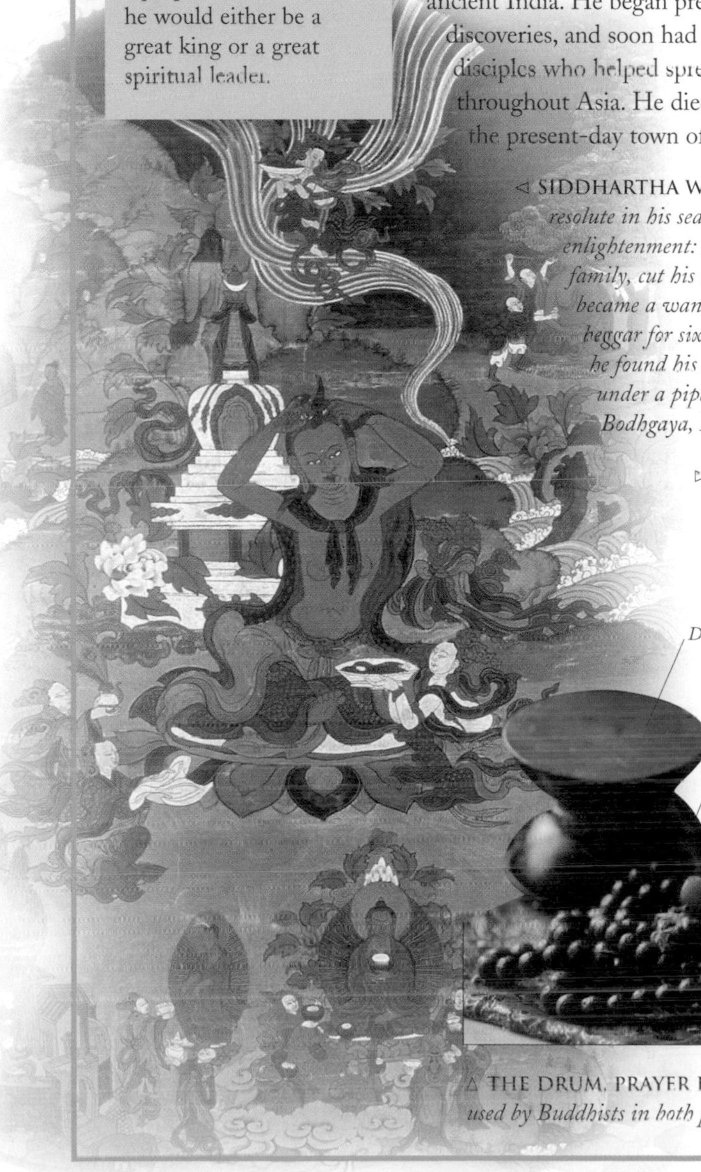

◁ SIDDHARTHA WAS *resolute in his search for enlightenment: he left his family, cut his hair, and became a wandering beggar for six years until he found his answers under a pipal tree near Bodhgaya, India.*

△ THIS BUDDHA *figure from 12th-century Cambodia depicts him with the Naga, a serpent deity said to hold certain teachings before they were liberated by a later Buddhist master.*

▷ SIDDHARTHA MET FOUR MESSENGERS—*an old man, a sick man, a dead man, and a monk—through whom he began to learn the nature of suffering.*

Drum

Bell

Cup

Prayer beads

△ THE DRUM, PRAYER BEADS, CUP, AND BELL *are all symbolic objects used by Buddhists in both personal and ritual meditation, worship, and prayer.*

CONQUERERS

HUMANS ARE TERRITORIAL ANIMALS. IT IS NOT ONE OF OUR BETTER ATTRIBUTES. AT ITS MOST BENIGN, this trait manifests itself as an urge to put up fences and set boundaries, but at its worst, the taste for more land and power creates conquerors who will stop at nothing to get what they desire.

In the name of policy, ideology, or ego, these five people laid waste to many miles of land so they could rule. Alexander the Great was 25 when his final triumph at Guagamela in 331 B.C. won him the throne of the Persian Empire. In the fifth century Attila the Hun repeatedly broke treaties with Roman emperors—taking their tribute money and then attacking their lands. As Emperor of the West in the eighth century, Charlemagne spread Christian rule throughout western Europe and began the Carolingian Renaissance. Mongol Genghis Khan succeeded in establishing perhaps history's largest land empire, and Napoleon Bonaparte became dictator of France, eventually dominating Europe.

△ THIS LANCET WINDOW, *created in the 13th century for Chartres Cathedral in France, depicts Charlemagne leaving for his Spanish Crusade with Roland and Archbishop Turpin of Reims.*

NAPOLEON BONAPARTE
(1769–1821)

NAPOLEON BONAPARTE—military genius, political visionary, despot—changed the map of Europe.

NAPOLEON'S HAT

FRENCH DICTATOR

Born in Corsica, Bonaparte led the French artillery at the 1793 siege of Toulon and in 1795 put down a royalist revolt in Paris. Made commander of France's army in Italy, he captured Mantua in 1797, then marched on Vienna and signed the Treaty of Campo Formio with Austria. Returning to France a hero, Bonaparte next sought to drive the British navy from the Mediterranean. In July 1798 he defeated Turkish forces at the Battle of the Pyramids, but British Admiral Nelson destroyed the French fleet a month later at Aboukir Bay.

Bonaparte then backed a successful coup in 1799 that named him first consul for life—in effect the dictator of France. His power unchecked, he established the legal Code Napoléon and crowned himself emperor in 1804. With France under his control, he took on the rest of Europe, defeating Austria, Russia, and Sweden. When Russia refused to obey his Continental System, which forbade trade with England, Bonaparte invaded. Approximately 500,000 troops entered Russia in June 1812, but difficult fighting and bitter cold forced a disastrous retreat. In 1813 the War of Liberation began. A coalition consisting of Russia, Prussia, Britain, Sweden, and Austria defeated Bonaparte at Leipzig, but he refused their treaty so they marched on Paris in 1814. Bonaparte abdicated and was exiled to the Mediterranean island of Elba. He returned in 1815, rallied France behind him, and began his rule of the Hundred Days until his defeat at Waterloo. Bonaparte died in exile on St. Helena.

▷ NAPOLEON PLACES THE CROWN *of the Holy Roman Empire on his own head in* The Crowning of Napoleon *(1804), by French neoclassic painter Jacques-Louis David.*

◁ THIS VELVET BOUND COPY OF *the Napoleonic Code is embellished with gold thread and features Napoleon's coat of arms.*

> "I should have conquered the world."
>
> NAPOLEON

ALEXANDER THE GREAT
(356–323 B.C.)

ALEXANDER THE GREAT CONQUERED the Persian Empire and much of the known world of his time, spreading Greek culture in his wake.

△ ALEXANDER'S *clean-shaven jaw was a novelty at the time, though many followed in the conqueror's style.*

LORD OF ASIA

The son of King Philip II of Macedonia, Alexander grew up in the royal court at Pella and was tutored by the philosopher Aristotle. He studied Homer and modeled himself after the hero Achilles. When his father was assassinated in 336 BCE, he ascended the throne, and soon demonstrated his military genius by putting down rebellions in Thrace, Illyria, and Thebes. With an allied Greek army, he began a war against King Darius III of Persia, fighting battles at Granicus, Issus, and Guagamela. Alexander chased Darius to Bactria (now Afghanistan), conquering lands and taking slaves along the way. Darius was finally killed in Bactria, and Alexander became ruler of the Persian Empire. Growing ever more despotic, Alexander marched on to India, where he defeated the Punjabs. By now he had conquered much of the known world, and the Greek culture he spread profoundly influenced these regions during the following centuries. Eager to return to Greece, his men turned back, reaching Susa in Persia in 324. Alexander died there in 325, probably from illness made worse by heavy drinking.

△ ALEXANDER BOWS *to the mother of Darius upon entering her tent with his companion Hephaestion—the day after they stormed Darius's camp and captured his entire family .*

△ ALEXANDER'S FATHER, PHILLIP II, *built this temple, the Temple of Athena Palias, in what is now Priene, Turkey, in 340 B.C.*

Did you know?

■ After conquering Persia, Alexander adopted Persian royal dress and ordered 80 of his generals to take Persian wives.

■ Alexander named a city "Bucephalus" in honor of his dead horse.

■ Although married to two women, Alexander is believed by some to have had a homosexual relationship with his best friend Hephaestion.

ATTILA THE HUN
(c. 406–453)

ATTILA THE HUN devastated the lands from the Black Sea to the Mediterranean, inspiring fear through the late Roman Empire.

THE SCOURGE OF GOD

Born in what is now Hungary, Attila and his brother Bleda, whom he murdered in 445, were named co-rulers of the Huns in 434. Attila united the tribes of the Hun kingdom and was said to be a just ruler to his own people. In 434, Roman emperor Theodesius II paid a tribute—in essence, protection money—to Attila, but Attila broke the peace treaty and in 441 invaded the Balkans. When Theodosius begged for terms, Attila's tribute was tripled, but in 447 he struck the empire again and negotiated yet another new treaty. When the new Eastern Roman emperor, Marcian, and Western Roman emperor, Valentinian III, refused to pay tribute, Attila amassed an army of half a million men and invaded Gaul (now France). He was defeated at Chalons in 451 by Aetius, who had banded together with the Visigoths. Attila invaded northern Italy in 452, but spared the city of Rome thanks to the diplomacy of Pope Leo I and the rough shape of his own troops. Attila died the next year, before he could try once again to take Italy.

△ **ATTILA'S FIERCE GAZE** *was notorious; according to historian Edward Gibbon, he always rolled his eyes "as if to enjoy the terror he inspired."*

Did you know?

■ Attila reputedly scared others by claiming to own the actual sword of Mars, the Roman god of war.

■ Legend has it that St. Peter and St. Paul appeared to Attila, threatening to strike him dead if he did not settle with Pope Leo I.

> "There, where I have passed, the grass will never grow again."
>
> ATTILA THE HUN

△ **TO DEFEND AGAINST ATTILA,** *Theodosius II built these walls in present-day Istanbul. Consisting largely of horsemen, Atilla's army could not take the fortified city.*

CHARLEMAGNE
(ca. 742-814)

BY CONQUERING MOST of Christian western Europe, Charlemagne brought unity to the region for the first time since the collapse of the Roman Empire.

THE CAROLINGIAN RENAISSANCE

After the death of his father, Pepin the Short, Charlemagne shared the Frankish throne with his brother Carloman. Following Carloman's death in 771, Charlemagne annexed Carloman's lands and disinherited his young sons. In collusion with Pope Adrian I, he conquered the Lombards in 773. For more than thirty years, Charlemagne struggled to conquer and control most of Europe. He invaded Spain, annexed Bavaria, and waged war against the Avars (a Central Asiatic nomadic tribe) and the Slavs. He fought the Saxons for 32 years before finally conquering them in 804. In 800, Pope Leo III legitimized his rule over western Europe by crowning him Holy Roman Emperor, causing a split between the Roman and the Byzantine Empires. Christianity, the arts, education, trade, and agriculture all flourished during Charlemagne's reign. He died of a fever in 814.

△ **A GOTHIC RELIQUARY** *depicting Charlemagne*

△ **THE EPIC POEM** The Song of Roland *recounts a battle against the Basques during Charlemagne's unsuccessful invasion of Spain, begun in 778.*

△ CHARLEMAGNE HOLDS A SWORD AND CROSS *in this 16th-century portrait by Albrecht Durer, illustrating his role as a champion of Christendom. The emperor was also a champion of progress: he set up diplomatic councils, stimulated foreign trade, established schools, and preserved classical literature.*

Did you know?

■ Charlemagne refused to let his daughters marry, but did not object to them having illegitimate children.

■ Napoleon called himself Charlemagne's successor.

■ To honor his Frankish forebears, Charlemagne often wore the common dress of the Franks, and led a frugal life.

GENGHIS KHAN

(c. 1167–1227)

RUTHLESS WARRIOR-EMPEROR Genghis Khan unified the nomadic tribes of Mongolia and created an empire stretching from the Pacific coast of China to the Adriatic Sea.

UNIVERSAL MONARCH

Originally named Temujin, Genghis was orphaned at age nine and succeeded his father as ruler of a Mongol tribe. As a young man he was kidnapped and imprisoned by another tribe but managed to escape. Mongol princes in 1206 named him the leader of a Mongolian confederacy and gave him the title Genghis Khan, meaning "Universal Monarch." Genghis then turned to foreign conquest. His army breached China's Great Wall in 1213, and by 1215 the Mongols stormed the capital, conquering the mighty Chin dynasty. Genghis led his army west for the next ten years, ruthlessly rolling through Central Asia, finally pushing as far as modern-day Hungary. He returned to Mongolia in 1225, and died on a campaign in 1227.

Other key invaders

JULIUS CAESAR (100–44 B.C.) Creator of the Roman Empire.

ALARIC (370–410) Goth destroyer of Rome.

HERNAN CORTES (1485–1547) Conqueror of Aztecs in Mexico.

△ GENGHIS *developed a fierce military style based on a hard-hitting mounted army.*

Did you know?

■ In 1202 Genghis began a campaign against the Tatars, the tribe that had murdered his father, which resulted in the near extinction of the Tatar people.

■ While Genghis was escaping from the Taichi'ut tribe, a Taichi'ut discovered him, but was so impressed by his determination that he helped Genghis escape.

◁ GENGHIS KHAN *instituted a legal code called the* Great Yasa, *which provided for such punishments as flogging.*

THE CIVIL RIGHTS ERA

THE AMERICAN CIVIL RIGHTS MOVEMENT BEGAN IN THE 1950S AS MEN AND WOMEN used nonviolent means to win the most groundbreaking equal-rights legislation for African-Americans since Reconstruction.

In the 1950s, much of the South was segregated under the protection of the US Supreme Court's 1896 decision to allow "separate but equal" public facilities for blacks and whites. The movement began in earnest after the Supreme Court's 1954 *Brown vs. Board of Education* ruling declaring segregated public schools inherently unequal.

The brave act of Rosa Parks, who refused to give up her seat to a white passenger on a bus in Montgomery, Alabama, and the leadership of Martin Luther King, Jr., in the boycott that followed, ignited the struggle against segregation and its defenders such as Alabama governor George Wallace. Malcolm X injected a militant voice into the Civil Rights Movement, which soon broadened to encompass related struggles, including labor activist Cesar Chavez's efforts to win protection for migrant farm workers.

△ THE FIRST "JIM CROW" LAWS—*legalizing segregation in the South— were enacted during Reconstruction, but such legislation spread rapidly throughout the region in the early 20th century and soon became the norm.*

MALCOLM X
(1925–1965)

MILITANT BLACK MUSLIM MALCOLM X rejected nonviolence and promoted African-American pride, separatism, and self-reliance.

BY ANY MEANS NECESSARY

Born Malcolm Little in Omaha, Nebraska, his father supported Marcus Garvey's back-to-Africa movement. Racist attacks often forced the family to move. When Malcolm's father was murdered, his mother was institutionalized, and her eight children were sent to foster homes. Malcolm drifted from Boston to New York and was arrested for burglary in 1946. While in prison, Malcolm converted to the Black Muslim faith and changed his name to Malcolm X to symbolize the African name his ancestors had lost to slavery. Released in 1952, he became the protégé of Nation of Islam leader Elijah Muhammad and distinguished himself as the Nation's most powerful organizer and speaker. As his popularity grew, however, his relations with the group became strained. In 1963, he called President Kennedy's assassination a case of "the chickens coming home to roost," which led Muhammad to ban him from speaking for the Nation. Malcolm left the organization and, after making the ritual Muslim journey to Mecca, began supporting more orthodox views of unity.

△ THE JOURNAL *in Malcolm X's pocket when he was assassinated, and notes from his speech*

On February 21, 1965, he was assassinated by Black Muslim gunmen at a rally in Harlem.

△ ALTHOUGH MALCOLM X'S *approach was in conflict with the nonviolent tactics advocated by Martin Luther King, Jr., Malcolm X eventually came to appreciate King's philosophy.*

MARTIN LUTHER KING, JR.

(1929-1968)

AMERICAN BAPTIST MINISTER and activist Martin Luther King, Jr.'s nonviolent leadership was the driving force behind the American Civil Rights Movement.

THE PACIFIST LEADER

King was born the son of a Baptist minister in Atlanta. He entered Morehouse College at the age of 15, then went on to study at Crozer Theological Seminary and at Boston University, where he met and later married Coretta Scott. The couple moved to Montgomery, Alabama, where King became pastor of the Dexter Avenue Baptist Church. On December 1, 1955, King was chosen to lead a successful year-long boycott against the city's bus system after an African-American woman, Rosa Parks, was arrested for refusing to give up her seat to a white passenger. Capitalizing on this victory, King formed the Southern Christian Leadership Conference. In 1960 he moved back to Atlanta where he was arrested, along with 33 others, for protesting segregation at a department store. In 1963 King was jailed again during a protest in Birmingham, Alabama, and thrust into the national spotlight. His eloquent letter from the Birmingham jail garnered more support for his cause, and after his release King joined the March on Washington, D.C., demanding civil rights. There, on August 28, 1963, at the Lincoln Memorial, King delivered the "I have a dream" speech that galvanized the movement. Congress in 1964 passed the Civil Rights Act authorizing the federal government to enforce desegregation and King was awarded the Nobel Peace Prize later that year. King led other actions across the country, notably in Selma, Alabama, and Chicago. As he was beginning to broaden his cause by opposing the Vietnam War and improving the lives of the nation's poor, King was assassinated by James Earl Ray on April 4, 1968, in Memphis, Tennessee.

△ KING SPEAKS AT A PRESS CONFERENCE *after a 1963 rights march in Birmingham. His philosophy of nonviolence was deeply influenced by Mohandas Gandhi, whose example was the guiding light of King's strategy against racism.*

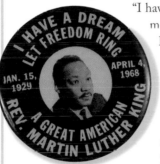

PIN FROM 1968 KING MEMORIAL SERVICE

Did you know?

■ In 1958, King was nearly assassinated in Harlem by a woman who stabbed him in the chest as he was signing copies of his book *Stride Toward Freedom.*

■ After King received the Nobel Peace Prize, FBI chief J. Edgar Hoover called him "the most notorious liar in the country."

■ Dr. King's family later supported James Earl Ray's claims that King's assassination was part of a conspiracy.

△ AFTER BEING EXPELLED *from the Nation of Islam and making his hajj to Mecca, Malcolm X founded the Organization of Afro-American Unity in 1964.*

Did you know?

■ In 1958, Malcolm X named his first daughter Attilah, after Attila the Hun, who sacked Rome.

■ After his trip to Mecca, Malcolm X took the name El-Hajj Malik El-Shabazz.

■ Alex Haley, author of *Roots,* worked with him on *The Autobiography of Malcolm X.*

◁ IN MEMPHIS *to support striking sanitation workers, King was assassinated just moments after this photo was taken at the Lorraine Motel.*

GEORGE WALLACE
(1919–1998)

ALABAMA GOVERNOR GEORGE CORLEY WALLACE led the South's fight against federally mandated integration in the 1960s.

RESISTING CHANGE

Born in Clio, Alabama, Wallace put himself through college as a professional boxer. After serving in World War II, he returned to Alabama to practice law, later becoming a judge and then member of the state legislature. Elected governor on a segregationist platform in 1962, one year later he thrust himself into the struggle against civil rights by blocking the University of Alabama entrance against two African-American students; he backed down only after President Kennedy sent in the National Guard.

△ **WALLACE CLAIMED** *he was not a racist; he merely opposed federal control.*

Wallace ran unsuccessfully as a presidential candidate with the American Independent party in 1968, though he won 13 percent of the vote—carrying five Southern states—and helped begin the political realignment of the South. Reelected to a second term as governor in 1970, he was shot by a mentally unstable man named Arthur Bremer in an assassination attempt two years later and became partially paralyzed. Although wheelchair bound, he was reelected in 1974, and made an unsuccessful bid for the Democratic presidential nomination in 1976. By now he had begun to soften his segregationist stance and by 1982 he had fully renounced his past hard-line positions in an effort to reach out to African-Americans. He was again elected governor, this time with substantial support from African-American constituents. He retired from politics in 1987.

IT · TAKES COURAGE !
WALLACE
HAS IT! DO YOU ?
Stand Up for America!

WALLACE CAMPAIGN POSTER

Did you know?

■ Wallace was legally ineligible to succeed himself as governor in 1966, so his wife, Lurleen, ran and won. She died in office two years later.

△ **WALLACE DEFIANTLY BLOCKED THE ENTRANCE** *to the University of Alabama against James Hood and Vivian Malone. Running for governor in 1962, he had proclaimed, "Segregation now, segregation tomorrow, segregation forever."*

CESAR CHAVEZ
(1927–1993)

LABOR LEADER CESAR ESTRADA CHAVEZ practiced a program of nonviolent activism to achieve higher wages and improved conditions for migrant farm workers in the United States.

Did you know?

■ Chavez attended 65 different elementary schools and never finished high school.

■ Three hunger strikes during the course of his career may have contributed to his death.

■ Chavez fought bitterly against Teamsters Union attempts to sign migrant workers to their union.

THE VOICE OF MIGRANT LABOR

Chavez was born in Yuma, Arizona, to a migrant farming family, and received little education. After two years in the US Navy during World War II, Chavez became a migrant worker in Arizona and California. He started organizing with the Community Services Organization; in 1958 Chavez became its director. He resigned four years later to start the National Farm Workers Association, and in 1965 began a successful campaign for better pay and working conditions from California table and wine grape growers that included a five-year strike and a boycott of their grapes. The NFWA in 1966 merged with the AFL-CIO to become the United Farm Workers Organizing Committee, and Chavez expanded his efforts . While leading a boycott of the use of dangerous pesticides, he weakened during a 36-day fast and died. In 1994 he was posthumously awarded the Presidential Medal of Freedom.

△ **OTHER CIVIL RIGHTS LEADERS** *such as Coretta Scott King (left) joined Chavez's call for justice through economic pressure.*

◁ AS LEADER OF THE UFW, *Chavez never earned more than $5,000 a year.*

ROSA PARKS
b. 1913

ROSA LOUISE MCCAULEY PARKS'S act of civil disobedience on a segregated bus helped ignite the struggle for racial equality in the United States.

RACIST WAITING ROOM SIGN

SHE WOULD NOT BE MOVED

Parks attended Alabama State College before marrying her husband, Raymond, in 1932. Both were active in civil rights efforts, and in 1943 Rosa was elected secretary of the Montgomery branch of the National Association for the Advancement of Colored People (NAACP). On December 1, 1955, she boarded a segregated bus on her way home from her job as a seamstress. When asked to give up her seat for a white passenger, she refused and was arrested. Parks's case became the focus of the civil rights struggle and brought out the leadership ability of the young Martin Luther King, Jr. The ensuing Montgomery Bus Boycott lasted for more than a year, but the Supreme Court ultimately ruled the segregated seating unconstitutional. Parks moved to Detroit in 1957 and once again took up work as a seamstress though she was much in demand as a speaker. In later years she has remained active in civil rights.

> ### "All I was doing was trying to get home from work."
> ROSA PARKS

▽ ROSA PARKS IS ARRESTED *and fingerprinted in Montgomery on February 22, 1956, two months after refusing to give up her seat on a bus.*

Did you know?

■ Parks sued the rap group OutKast for using her name in a song without her consent. She lost the case.

■ In 1999 Parks received the Congressional Gold Medal—the country's highest civilian honor.

■ Parks was an assistant to US Representative John Conyers of Michigan during the mid-1960s.

△ BY 1975, A REPORTED *17 million Americans were honoring Chavez's boycott against California table and wine grape growers.*

Other Rights Activists

JESSE JACKSON b.1941 Founder of PUSH (People United to Save Humanity) and the Rainbow Coalition.

RALPH ABERNATHY (1926–1990) King's chosen successor.

HUEY NEWTON (1945–1989) With Bobby Seale, the founder of the Black Panther Party.

> ### "There is no such thing as defeat in nonviolence."
> CESAR CHAVEZ

IMPRESSIONISTS

ORIGINATING IN LATE-19TH-CENTURY FRANCE, THE IMPRESSIONIST MOVEMENT influenced artists across the globe and paved the way for the modern art movements of the 20th century.

Impressionism grew out of a friendship among painters Claude Monet, Pierre-Auguste Renoir, Alfred Sisley, and Frédéric Bazille. Rejecting the contemporary dogma that art's role was to portray only historical, religious, or mythological subjects, they met with like-minded artists such as Camille Pissarro and Edgar Degas to develop their own style, based upon a more truthful reproduction of light and nature and a personal approach to their subject matter. Mary Cassatt, the first American Impressionist, helped seed the movement across the Atlantic. Although the title "Impressionists" was originally meant to be derogatory, the name proved to be an accurate description of their intentions: to convey visual "impressions" of images in light. Today, the paintings of the Impressionists are among the most-loved and highly valued in the world.

△ CAFÉS, CABARETS, PERFORMERS, *and everyday scenes were favorite Impressionist subjects. This famous painting by Pierre-Auguste Renoir,* Lunch of the Boating Party *(1879), depicts a festive group of diners.*

CLAUDE MONET
(1840–1926)

A PAINTER WHO INSPIRED ARTISTS from Van Gogh to Jackson Pollock, Claude Monet was a founding father of Impressionism.

THE MASTER OF LIGHT AND COLOR

In 1845 Monet's family moved from his birthplace in Paris to the seaside town of Le Havre. As a youth Monet gained a reputation as a talented caricaturist. His work was included in a group exhibition where he met the landscape painter Eugene Boudin, who introduced him to outdoor painting, soon the cornerstone of Monet's work. In Paris, he was

MONET'S GLASSES

strongly influenced by the paintings of the Barbizon school and studied at the Academie Suisse, where he met Pissarro. After serving in the military in Algeria from 1861 to 1862, he returned to Paris to enter the studio of Charles Gleyre, there befriending Renoir and Sisley. At the outbreak of the Franco-Prussian War in 1870, Monet left for London, where he met up with Pissarro and art dealer Paul Durand-Ruel. After returning to Argenteuil in 1872, he began to develop his own technique. To evoke the fleeting light and colors of nature, he painted with short strokes full of individual colors, in contrast to the blended colors and evenness of classical art. Monet began to exhibit with the Impressionists at their first show in 1874 and continued into the 1880s. In 1883 he moved to his final home, Giverny. He gained financial and critical success during the late 1880s and 1890s, and started his serial paintings, repeating scenes such as haystacks and the Rouen Cathedral at different times of day. By 1899 Monet had begun painting his gardens at Giverny. He developed cataracts in his right eye in 1912. By 1923 both eyes were seriously affected and he was nearly blind, yet he continued working until his death.

△ DISPLAYED IN THE FIRST IMPRESSIONIST EXHIBITION *in 1874, Monet's* Impression: Sunrise *(1872) lent its name to the movement when a French journalist began to refer to the exhibiting artists derisively as "impressionists."*

> "Color is my day-long obsession, joy, and torment."
> CLAUDE MONET

What Came Next

PAUL GAUGUIN (1839–1906) His abstracted approach to line and brushstroke presaged the Cubists.

VINCENT VAN GOGH (1853–1890) Tortured genius of *Starry Nights* and *Sunflowers*

PABLO PICASSO (1881–1973) The titan of modern art; with Braque the creator of Cubism.

△ FOUR MONTHS BEFORE *his death in 1926 and nearly blind, Claude Monet sits by the pond in his garden at Giverny.*

△ MONET COMPLETELY ELIMINATED FIGURES *from his later works; they were pure landscapes, almost abstract in their bold representation of nature. This groundbreaking style evolved due to his failing sight, which prompted a more physical approach to painting, involving long brushes that allowed him to stand far back from the canvas. But perhaps an even more compelling motivation for change was Monet's desire to transcend impressionistic depictions and capture the memories and emotions inspired by nature, as seen above in* Waterlily Pond in Green *(1899).*

MONET'S PALETTE AND BRUSH

Did you know?

■ Monet attempted suicide in 1868, one year after his first child was born.

■ In 1918, Monet donated twelve Waterlillies paintings to the nation of France to celebrate the Armistice.

■ Though they became friends in later life, Monet claimed in an interview that Eduoard Manet at first hated him because people confused their names.

△ MONET ATTEMPTED *not to simply represent nature with his paintings, but to paint as a force of nature himself.*

△ IN 1900, MONET BOUGHT *the house in Giverny that he had been renting for ten years. Since 1980 it has housed the Claude Monet Foundation.*

CAMILLE PISSARRO
(1830–1903)

CAMILLE PISSARRO PLAYED A CRUCIAL ROLE in the emergence of Impressionism, through both his own work and his support of young artists such as Monet and Renoir.

THE FATHER OF IMPRESSIONISM

Born in St. Thomas, West Indies, Pissarro studied in Paris as a young man, and showed promise as an artist. He returned to St. Thomas to work in the family store, and in 1855 he finally gained his parents' permission to live in Paris and become a painter. He was inspired by the sense of realism and the direct observation of nature in the landscapes of Courbet and Corot. During the Franco-Prussian War (1870–71) Pissarro went to London where he and Monet were influenced by the landscape paintings of John Constable and J.M.W. Turner. Pissarro's work gradually evolved into use of pure color, the play of light on various objects, and the observation of atmosphere and movement. His greatest impact on Impressionism may have been his work as an organizer. In 1874, after the government-sponsored Salon again rejected their work, Pissarro encouraged his colleagues to join him in mounting an independent exhibition, the *Salon des Refuses*—the first Impressionist show in Paris. Seven more followed through 1886, and in 1892 a large retrospective exhibition of his work won him the international acclaim and financial stability that had eluded him for so long.

△ THIS SELF-PORTRAIT BY PISSARRO *was done in 1873, one year before the first Impressionist Salon. The oldest member of the group, he had a warm, generous nature, and was dearly loved by his fellow artists.*

▷ PISSARRO POSES FOR A PORTRAIT WITH CÉZANNE *(on left). Pissarro was not only the founding father of Impressionism, but he also influenced the future of painting as the teacher of Paul Gauguin, Paul Cézanne, and Georges Seurat.*

Did you know?

■ Pissarro was the only artist represented in all eight Impressionist exhibitions.

■ At one point, Pissarro's wife, Julie Vellay, was so overwhelmed by their poverty that she considered drowning herself and their two children as an option.

■ Breaking with tradition, which called for painting in a studio, Pissarro painted outside, even in the middle of winter.

"One must be sure of success to the very end, for without that there is no hope!"

CAMILLE PISSARRO

△ PISSARRO PAINTED MANY RURAL SCENES, *such as* Young Peasant Girl with a Stick *(1881); although he was also known for his cityscapes and tropical landscapes.*

EDGAR DEGAS

(1834–1917)

ONE OF THE MOST SUCCESSFUL and influential artists of his time, Hilaire Germaine Edgar Degas fused Impressionism with classical art.

DEGAS'S PALETTE

THE MASTER OF MOTION

Born into a wealthy Parisian banking family, Degas abandoned the study of law to attend the Ecole des Beaux-Arts. After studying the work of the Renaissance masters in Italy, his early work was historical and based on the styles of Mantegna, Bellini, and Ingres. He returned to Paris in 1861 and met Manet, who steered him to contemporary images such as the ballet, the racetrack, brothels,and cafés. He continued these themes throughout the 1870s and 1880s, his work reflecting his interest in interior light and in compositions that took advantage of advances in photography. He captured his subjects in natural poses, emphasizing their relationship to interior settings. After 1890, his eyesight began to fail, and he focused almost exclusively on pastels and sculpture.

△ **UNLIKE MOST OF THE IMPRESSIONISTS**, *Degas worked often in the studio, valuing the classical discipline of Jean-Auguste Ingres more than the effects of natural light that preoccupied his contemporaries.*

"Only when he no longer knows what he is doing does the painter do good things."

EDGAR DEGAS

Did you know?

■ Degas served in an artillery division of the French National Guard during the Franco-Prussian War.

■ Strongly influenced by by photography, Degas experimented with photographic techniques such as unusual cropping and skewed perspective to aid in composition design.

■ Degas never faced poverty, unlike many of his contemporaries.

▷ **PERHAPS DEGAS'S MOST FAMOUS SCULPTURE**, The Little Dancer, Aged 14 (1881), *was astonishingly realistic for its time—he "dressed" the bronze in actual clothes.*

△ **ALMOST HALF OF DEGAS'S 2,000 WORKS** *concern dance, as in* The Dance Class *(1874).*

MARY CASSATT
(1844–1926)

TRANSCENDING CONVENTIONAL VIEWS OF WOMEN in the 19th century, Mary Cassatt became one of the most important artists of her time; through her work and her promotion of other artists, she introduced Impressionism to America.

THE AMERICAN IMPRESSIONIST

Though her wealthy parents wished her to pursue a more conventional life, Cassatt instead left her home in Pennsylvania for Paris in 1866 to take painting lessons and study the masterpieces at the Louvre.

In 1868 Cassatt entered one of her paintings into the prestigious Paris Salon; the piece was accepted, as were more of her paintings in the Salons of 1872, 1873, and 1874, establishing her reputation as a talented artist. But Cassatt began to be disillusioned with the constraints of the conservative Salon. She met Degas, becoming his devoted disciple. He convinced her to exhibit eleven of her works in an 1879 Impressionist exhibition. The show was a success, as were later shows in 1880, 1881, and 1886. Her works were known for their focus on motherhood and their pleasant simplicity and color. By 1900 she began to focus on promoting the work of other artists, encouraging wealthy Americans to buy Impressionist works. She began to lose her sight in 1900, and by 1915 had stopped working.

△ **THE BOLD DEFTNESS OF CASSATT'S** *Self-Portrait (1880) demonstrates why Cassatt was the only American painter invited to exhibit with the Impressionists.*

In much of Cassatt's work, the background draws attention away from the subjects, creating a tension that heightens the viewer's appreciation of both.

Women Artists

BERTHE MORISOT (1841–1995) Impressionist painter and sister-in-law of artist Edouard Manet.

GEORGIA O'KEEFFE (1887–1986) Colorful explorations of the American West and female sensuality.

FRIDA KAHLO (1907–1954) Surreal visions of Mexican mysticism and her own emotional and physical pain.

Cassatt liked to portray women performing everyday tasks; she also explored the special intimacy between mothers and their children .

Did you know?

■ As a child, Cassatt and her family lived in France and Germany for four years, exposing her to the arts. This led her to move to Paris in her 20s.

■ France awarded Cassatt the Legion of Honor in 1904.

■ During a 1910 visit to Egypt, Cassatt was so amazed by ancient art that she temporarily lost confidence in her work.

"I have not done what I wanted to, but I tried to make a good fight."

MARY CASSATT

△ **LIKE HER FRIEND DEGAS**, *Mary Cassatt was greatly influenced by the strong colors of Japanese woodblock prints, first seen in Paris in the 1850s, and their flat surfaces.*

PIERRE-AUGUSTE RENOIR
(1841–1919)

WITH HIS USE OF VIBRANT COLORS and his portrayal of everyday life, French painter Pierre-Auguste Renoir was a central figure in Impressionism.

THE PLEASURES OF LIFE

Early in life, Renoir exhibited a talent for drawing, and at age 13 found work painting plates in the Limoges porcelain factory. In 1862 he began painting lessons in the Paris studio of leading Swiss painter and teacher Charles Gleyre, where he became friends with other founders of Impressionism, including Alfred Sisley, Claude Monet, and Frédéric Bazille. The 1870s proved to be a fruitful decade for Renoir. He participated in the first Impressionist exhibition in 1874, and painted some of his most famous works, including *Moulin de la Galette* (1876) and *Madame Charpentier and Her Children* (1878). Renoir used small, multicolored strokes to communicate flickering light falling on human subjects enjoying the pleasures of life. More so than his fellow Impressionists, Renior applied Impressionism to the human form; he produced some of the genre's most celebrated paintings. He traveled in the 1880s to Algeria and Italy, entering a "dry" period that produced what are generally considered to be his least important paintings as he tried to move beyond Impressionism. At the end of his life, by then world-renowned, he focused on intimate, full-figured nudes and portraits of young girls.

Did you know?

■ Renoir once said: "Why shouldn't art be pretty? There are enough unpleasant things in the world."

■ For a time, Renoir lived in artist Frédéric Bazille's house with Monet.

■ In 1907 Renoir bought an estate at Cagnes on the Riviera, his final home.

▷ DANCING COUPLES *were the subject of three life-size Renoirs; his friend Paul Lhote is in all three.* Dance in the Country *(1883), right, also features his wife, Aline Charigot.*

◁ AT THE END *of his life, Renoir suffered from rheumatoid arthritis. He continued to paint, however, with a brush tied to his crippled hand.*

▷ RENOWNED FILMMAKER *Jean Renoir, director of works such as* La Marseillaise *and* Grand Illusion, *was the son of Pierre Auguste Renoir.*

THOSE WHO TOUCHED THE SKY

ON THE FACE OF THINGS, IT MIGHT SEEM THAT WE WERE NEVER MEANT TO FLY. Too ungainly, not blessed by nature with feathers or wings, humans make unlikely candidates for flight.

And yet man has not been deterred, finding instead another set of gifts that has allowed us take to the skies.

The curiosity of the 18th-century Montgolfier brothers, stirred by wood chips rising over a fire at their family's paper factory, led them to investigate the power of heat, which in time let humans rise off the ground for the first time. The genius of another pair of brothers, the Wrights, channeled the urge to fly into a reliable means of transportation with creativity and inventiveness. In the 1920s and 30s, the courage of pilots Charles Lindbergh and Amelia Earhart to make airborne journeys once unthinkable eventuallly inspired millions to consider flying as natural an act as walking. And the wild, daredevil courage of test-pilot Chuck Yeager took us to the outskirts of the stars, testing the limits of what man can achieve.

△ THE DREAM OF FLYING *has always stirred the human imagination, from the Greek legend of Icarus to the sometimes wild inventions of those who aspire to touch the sky.*

AMELIA EARHART
(1897–1937)

AMELIA EARHART WAS THE FIRST woman to fly solo across the Atlantic, but she is most remembered for her mysterious disappearance as she attempted to fly around the world.

△ LIKE LINDBERGH, *Earhart became a celebrity once she flew over the Atlantic.*

THE LOST "AVIATRIX"

Born in Atchison, Kansas, Earhart worked as a nurse in Canada and as a social worker in Boston after World War I. She began taking flight lessons in 1920 after visiting an air show. A quick learner, she bought her first plane in 1922 and by age 23 had made her first solo flight. In 1928 Earhart became the first woman to fly across the Atlantic (she went as a passenger to demonstrate the safety of flight, with two male pilots). A few months later, Earhart made a solo flight across the US, and in 1932, she made the first solo flight across the Atlantic by a woman, also setting a speed record. She became a celebrity, and toured the country making public appearances. In 1937 Earhart and a navigator attempted to fly around the globe. The plane completed the first 22,000 miles, then vanished in the South Pacific. Neither the plane nor the bodies were found, and no cause for the disappearance has ever been established.

△ EARHART CELEBRATES WITH HER MOTHER, AMY, *after returning to the States from her historic 1932 solo Atlantic flight. She received a tickertape parade in New York, among many other honors.*

JOSEPH-MICHEL MONTGOLFIER (1740–1810)
JACQUES-ETIENNE MONTGOLFIER (1745–1799)

THE MONTGOLFIER BROTHERS became pioneers in the world of aviation with their invention of the hot-air balloon in 1783. Their achievement eventually enabled scientists to begin exploring the earth's upper atmosphere.

CAPTURING THE POWER OF HEAT

The two Montgolfier brothers were born in Annonay, near Lyons, to a prosperous paper-making family. Inspired by watching a wet shirt billow over a fire and wood scraps rise in a chimney, the scientifically inclined brothers conceived of a hot-air balloon. They began developing it in 1782, and the following year gave the first public demonstration in their hometown: fueled by burning straw and wool, the balloon rose some 6,000 feet, stayed aloft for ten minutes, and traveled more than a mile and a half. Three months later, the Montgolfiers repeated the experiment at Versailles for King Louis XVI, this time sending up a rooster, a sheep, and a duck. The first manned flight followed in November 1783.

Did you know?

■ King Louis XVI wanted two prisoners to take the first flight, and was prepared to pardon them if they survived.

■ Joseph also invented a calorimeter, the hydraulic ram, and a method for making vellum paper.

■ The brothers' first balloon, the *Seraphina*, was made of paper, fabric, and over 2,000 buttons.

△ EARHART POSES *for a publicity photo during a lecture tour for her book,* 20 Hours, 40 Minutes, *after her 1928 solo flight across the US.*

Did you know?

■ Rumors abound over Earhart's disappearance. Some historians believe she was sent to spy on the Japanese and was shot down, while others think she survived and spent the rest of her life on an island in the Pacific.

■ Amelia married publisher George Palmer Putnam in 1931, but kept her original name.

■ In 1964, Geraldine Mock successfully flew around the world using Earhart's planned route.

△ AN ENGRAVING *of Jacques-Etienne, known as "Etienne."*

△ JOSEPH *was the first brother to experiment with air; he tried to fill an envelope with steam.*

△ THE MONTGOLFIERS *did not take part in the first manned balloon ascent. Only Joseph ever went up, and he did so only once.*

WILBUR WRIGHT (1867–1912)
ORVILLE WRIGHT (1871–1948)

THE WRIGHT BROTHERS made the first controlled, sustained flight of a motor-driven aircraft, near Kitty Hawk, North Carolina.

△ IN 1905, ORVILLE AND WILBUR *(left, right) tried to sell their plans to the US government, but were turned down.*

FIRST IN FLIGHT

As young boys, the Wrights showed exceptional mechanical skills. Orville built a printing press and published a newspaper in high school. The brothers opened a bicycle shop in 1892, and were soon making their own bicycles. Fascinated by a helicopter-like toy that their father brought home from a trip, and influenced by the German engineer Otto Lilienthal's glider flights, the pair became obsessed with flight, and in 1900 they built their first glider. From 1900 through 1903, they used their shop to experiment with aircraft construction, conceiving of movable wing structures and pioneering the physics of wind pressure. Orville designed an engine that they attached to a glider, and their experimentation resulted in 1903 in the first true airplane flight, which lasted 12 seconds. The brothers won a contract for the first US military plane in 1908, and later started an airplane manufacturing firm. Wilbur died of typhoid in 1912, but Orville went on to serve on the National Advisory Committee for Aeronautics.

Did you know?

■ Wilbur and Orville were practically inseparable, and both remained bachelors their entire lives.

■ Wilbur was injured in a skating accident in 1886, interfering with his plans to attend college.

▽ **THOUGH OTHERS HAD** *put flying machines into the air for a few seconds, the great achievement of the Wright Brothers was sustained, controlled flight. On December 1903, in Kittyhawk, Orville flew their glider 120 ft (40m) while Wilbur (at far right) watched.*

CHARLES LINDBERGH
(1902–1974)

CHARLES LINDBERGH—a man whose name is virtually synonymous with aviation—made the first nonstop solo flight across the Atlantic.

THE SPIRIT OF ST. LOUIS

Born in Detroit, Michigan, Lindbergh studied mechanical engineering in college, but left after two years to attend flight school. During the early- and mid-'20s he worked as a barnstormer, or daredevil stunt pilot, and as an airmail pilot on the St. Louis-to-Chicago route; he also served in the US Air Service Reserve.

Lindbergh achieved worldwide fame in 1927 with his solo Atlantic crossing. In his airplane, the *Spirit of St. Louis*, he completed the 3,600-mile journey from New York City to Paris in 33.5 hours. Lindbergh then worked in the aviation industry and promoted the airplane as a means of transportation. In 1929 he married Anne Morrow, daughter of an American ambassador. Three years later, their 20-month-old son was kidnapped and killed in what was then called the "Crime of the Century." Controversy followed Lindbergh: in 1939 he spoke out against US intervention in World War II. Though some Americans accused him of anti-Semitism and Nazi sympathies, he flew combat missions in the Pacific once the US entered the war. In 1954 he was named a brigadier general in the Air Force Reserve, and in the 1960s became active in environmental causes. He died of lymphatic cancer in Hawaii.

Aviation Pioneers

MERYL BARKHAM (1902–1986) Colorful pilot and writer who lived in 1930s Africa.

BENJAMIN DAVIS, JR. b. 1912 Leader of the Tuskegee Airmen.

HUGO JUNKERS (1859–1934) Pioneer German aviation designer.

△ ANNE MORROW AND BABY CHARLES *in 1930. A carpenter, Bruno Hauptman, was executed for kidnapping and murdering the Lindbergh boy in 1932.*

▷ AFTER HIS HISTORIC FLIGHT *Lindbergh received the Congressional Medal of Honor, as well as decorations from nations around the world.*

▽ LINDBERGH POSES in front of the *Spirit of Saint Louis*, which he helped design; it was built with financial assistance from nine St. Louis businessmen.

"Where am I?"

CHARLES A. LINDBERGH, UPON ARRIVAL IN PARIS

Did you know?

■ In the 1930s Lindbergh collaborated on inventing an "artificial heart"—a pump that kept organs alive outside the body during surgery.

■ His wife, Anne Morrow, was an accomplished author of both poetry and prose.

■ Lindbergh won a Pulitzer Prize for his autobiography, *The Spirit of St. Louis*.

CHUCK YEAGER
b. 1923

AVIATOR CHUCK YEAGER is best known as the first man to fly a plane faster than the speed of sound.

THE FIRST SUPERSONIC PILOT
Born in Myra, West Virginia, Yeager joined the US Army Air Force shortly after finishing high school, in September 1941. As a fighter pilot stationed in England, he flew 64 missions and shot down 13 German aircraft during World War II. When his plane was shot down over France, he evaded capture with the help of the French resistance.

He became a test pilot after the war and was chosen to fly the experimental Bell X-1 aircraft, which he used on October 14, 1947, to become the first man to break the sound barrier, flying more than 660 mph. He continued to make test flights, and set a world speed record of 1,650 mph in 1953, flying an X-1A rocket plane. Yeager served in a number of Air Force positions during the next 20 years, teaching many future astronauts how to fly. He retired from the Air Force as a brigadier general in 1975, and published his best-selling autobiography, *Yeager*, in 1985.

△ CHUCK YEAGER'S BELL X-1A, *the first plane to break the sound barrier.*

△ YEAGER *has received every major award in the field of flight.*

Did you know?

■ When Yeager broke the sound barrier, he had a cracked rib due to a horseback riding accident that had occurred several days before his flight.

■ During one of Yeager's flights, the X-1A spun about all three axes and plummeted for more than 40,000 feet before he regained control.

■ Yeager appears in Tom Wolfe's book, *The Right Stuff*, and was played by Sam Shepard in the movie.

△ YEAGER TESTED THIS SUPERSONIC JET IN 1949, *and countless others during his 34 years in the Air Force. In 1976, President Gerald Ford awarded him the Congressional Gold Medal, and President Ronald Reagan honored him with the Presidential Medal in 1985.*

THOSE WHO REACHED THE STARS

WHILE THE SKIES HAVE ALWAYS TEMPTED US, FOR MOST OF HUMAN HISTORY, we could only dream of the stars. But in the late 20th century, the stars were suddenly within reach.

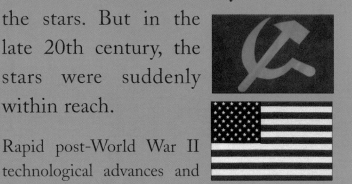

SOVIET EMBLEM AND AMERICAN FLAG

Rapid post-World War II technological advances and competition between the United States and the Soviet Union turned the exploration of space into a beachhead of the Cold War. In 1961, four years after the Soviet Union had launched Sputnik, the first artificial satellite, cosmonaut Yuri Gagarin became the first person to enter space. The race was on. That year, President John F. Kennedy set a goal for the United States to send a man to the moon by 1970, and the next year, John Glenn became the first American in space. The Soviets countered with Valentina Tereshkova, the first female space explorer. The race continued through the decade, each nation going a little farther until July 1969, when Neil Armstrong and his *Apollo 11* crew realized Kennedy's goal. The US space program shifted focus to the Space Shuttle, and Sally Ride became the first American woman in space.

△ A TOTAL OF TWELVE ASTRONAUTS *walked on the Moon in seven missions. The last was Eugene Cernan, on December 14, 1972.*

NEIL ARMSTRONG
b. 1930

AMERICAN ASTRONAUT Neil A. Armstrong became an international hero as commander of the *Apollo 11* mission, and the first man to step on the moon.

THE MAN ON THE MOON

Fascinated by aviation from childhood, Armstrong began studying for his pilot's license at 14. In 1947 he became a naval air cadet. He was studying aeronautical engineering at Purdue University when the Korean War disrupted his education in 1950. After receiving his degree in 1955, Armstrong worked as a test pilot for the National Committee for Aeronautics, flying more than 1,100 hours in supersonic fighters. He joined NASA in 1962, and in 1966, while piloting the Gemini-Titan 8, he performed the first space-docking procedure while in orbit. A malfunctioning thruster forced Armstrong and his fellow astronauts to make an emergency splashdown in the Pacific Ocean, but Armstrong's grace under pressure earned him the respect of NASA officials. Armstrong was chosen to command the first crewed lunar expedition, *Apollo 11*. He set off for the moon on July 16, 1969, with fellow astronauts Edwin "Buzz" Aldrin and Michael Collins. Three days later, television viewers around the world watched Armstrong step onto the moon's surface. He and Aldrin took photographs, collected samples, and released scientific instruments. They returned to the command module 21 hours later and began their voyage home. After an 18-day quarantine, they embarked on a world tour, during which they were hailed as heroes. Armstrong retired from NASA in 1971 and became a professor at the University of Cincinnati.

△ ARMSTRONG (LEFT) AND BUZZ ALDRIN (RIGHT) *manned the lunar module* Eagle *on July 19, 1969, while Michael Collins (center) orbited the moon in the command module.*

▽ ARMSTRONG *was the youngest pilot in his Korean War squadron and received three Air Medals.*

VALENTINA TERESHKOVA
b. 1937

RUSSIAN COSMONAUT Valentina Vladimirovna Tereshkova was the first woman to travel into space. She later became a leading spokesperson for Soviet feminism.

THE FIRST WOMAN IN SPACE

Tereshkova was born in a small village named Maslennikovo and worked in a textile factory. She had no previous experience as a pilot, but her 126 jumps as an amateur parachutist gained her a position as a cosmonaut in 1962. As the chief pilot of the *Vostok VI,* Tereshkova rode into space on June 16, 1963, and made 48 orbits of the earth in 70 hours and 50 minutes, proving that women could endure the physical and mental stress of space travel, though she was not allowed to fly the spacecraft manually. Upon her return she was declared a Hero of the Soviet Union and decorated with the Order of Lenin and the Gold Star Medal. She then toured the world promoting Soviet women's equality. She was named head of the Soviet Women's Committee (1977), headed the USSR's International Cultural and Friendship Union (1987–1991), and beginning in 1991, the Russian Association of International Cooperation.

Women in Space

SHANNON LUCID b.1943 Woman with most hours logged in space.

CHRISTA MCAULIFFE (1948–1986) Teacher, died in *Challenger* disaster.

EILEEN COLLINS b.1956 First woman to command Space Shuttle.

Did you know?

■ While orbiting Earth, the *Vostok VI* came within 3.1 miles of the *Vostok V,* launched two days earlier.

■ Tereshkova's father was a tractor driver and her mother worked in a textile mill. Tereshkova did not begin school until she was eight, then quit when she was 16 to go to work herself.

■ The next woman to go into space was another Soviet—Svetlana Savitskaya, who was aboard the *Soyuz T-7* 19 years later.

> "That's one small step for [a] man, one giant leap for mankind."

NEIL ARMSTRONG

Did you know?

■ The plaque Armstrong and Aldrin planted read: "Here men from the planet Earth first set foot upon the Moon. We came in peace for all mankind."

■ Richard Nixon had prepared a letter to be read if Aldrin and Armstrong did not return from the moon.

△ TERESHKOVA HAD THE RADIO NAME "Chaika," *which means "seagull" in Russian. She was chosen for the flight after Khrushchev saw a letter she had written praising the Soviet space program.*

∧ IN 1963, TERESHKOVA *married fellow Soviet cosmonaut Andrian Nikolayev. Doctors studied their daughter Yelena to determine whether her parents' space exposure had harmed her. They found no problems. The couple divorced in 1980.*

YURI GAGARIN
(1934–1968)

RUSSIAN COSMONAUT Yuri Gagarin was the first person to travel into space and the first to orbit the Earth.

THE FIRST MAN IN SPACE

The son of a carpenter on a collective farm, Gagarin was born in Gzhatsk, joined the Soviet Air Force in 1957, and in 1959 became a cosmonaut.

On April 12, 1961, Gagarin's spacecraft, *Vostok I*, was launched to a maximum altitude of 187 miles and orbited the Earth once. Gagarin's flight lasted only 108 minutes, but proved that man could endure the rigors of space travel while operating the craft. He returned to Earth as an international hero, and was awarded the Order of Lenin and named a Hero of the Soviet Union and Pilot Cosmonaut of the Soviet Union.

Gagarin, who never returned to space, died in the crash of a training flight in 1968.

△ SINCE NO ONE KNEW *how a man would react in space,* Vostok I *was controlled entirely from the ground. Gagarin had no control over the ship, save for a manual overdrive meant only for an emergency.*

Did you know?

■ When asked how he could sleep the night before the launch, he responded: "It was my duty to sleep so I slept."

■ Gagarin's hometown of Gzhatsk was renamed Gagarin after his death.

■ His fellow cosmonauts voted Gagarin to be the first in space.

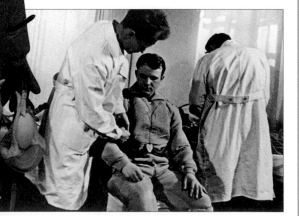

▽ PREFLIGHT TESTS *were extensive even though Gagarin's flight was less than two hours.*

◁ THE SUIT GAGARIN *wore over 40 years ago has evolved to accomodate a wide range of activities both inside and outside the orbiter.*

JOHN GLENN
b. 1921

ASTRONAUT John Herschel Glenn, Jr,. was the first American to orbit the Earth, and, at the age of 77, the oldest man to travel into space. In 1974 he was elected senator in Ohio.

FROM SPACE TO THE SENATE

Glenn was born in Cambridge, Ohio. He joined the Marine Corps in 1943 and was a highly successful pilot in World War II and the Korean War, earning five Distinguished Flying Crosses and 19 Air Medals. After serving as a test pilot from 1954 to 1959, Glenn was one of seven pilots selected for Project Mercury, America's first manned space flights. On February 20, 1962, Glenn completed three orbits of the Earth in the *Friendship 7*.

In 1964 Glenn retired from the space program and the Marine Corps, entering the private sector where he was an executive with Royal Crown Cola. A staunch Democrat, he became a close friend of Robert Kennedy and ran unsuccessfully for the Senate in 1970. Four years later he was elected to the US Senate from Ohio and had a few brushes with higher office: For a time Jimmy Carter considered him for the vice presidency in 1976, and he briefly ran for president in 1983. After leaving the Senate in 1998, he returned to the space program to join shuttle mission STS-95, where he participated in experiments studying the effects of weightlessness on older bodies.

△ THE FLIGHT *of* Friendship 7 *was not without problems. The autopilot failed, forcing Glenn to fly the capsule manually, and the heat shield intended to protect him during reentry came loose.*

△ JOHN GLENN *was 77 years old when he took part in the STS-95 mission. He gave 17 blood samples while in orbit, and then took part in three weeks of follow-up tests on aging and space.*

Did you know?

■ Glenn piloted the first nonstop supersonic flight from Los Angeles to New York in 1957.

■ Glenn authored the Nuclear Nonproliferation Act of 1978, which prohibits the sale of nuclear equipment to nations without nuclear weapons.

■ Glenn was the oldest of the seven *Mercury* astronauts.

▽ THIS PATCH COMMEMORATES *the first manned orbital mission of the United States, the* Mercury-Atlas 6, *piloted by John Glenn.*

SALLY RIDE
b. 1951

SALLY RIDE was the first American woman to journey into space, paving the way for future female astronauts.

AMERICA'S FIRST WOMAN ASTRONAUT

Sally Ride was born in Encino, California, to an adventurous and scholarly family. A Ph.D candidate in laser physics at Stanford in 1978, Ride was selected by NASA as one of the first six potential female astronauts. By August 1979 she had earned her Ph.D, obtained a pilot's license, and completed her NASA training to become a shuttle mission specialist. On June 18, 1983, in the shuttle *Challenger,* Ride became the first American woman to journey into space. She returned on another mission in 1984, and was preparing for a third mission when *Challenger* exploded in 1986. Appointed to the presidential commission investigating the explosion, she shifted her workplace to NASA headquarters in Washington, D.C. Two years after Ride retired from NASA in 1987, she was named director of the California Space Institute and became a physics professor at the University of California, San Diego.

△ THE SPACE SHUTTLE Challenger *lifted off from Kennedy Space Center on June 18, 1983, with a five-person crew, the largest up to then.*

Did you know?

■ Ride's childhood friend Kathryn Sullivan was the first American woman to walk in space.

■ To protest its military use, Soviets fired a laser at the shuttle during Ride's second flight.

■ Ride dropped out of Swarthmore College to pursue a career as a pro tennis player.

△ RIDE SPECIALIZED IN OPERATING *the remote manipulator arm used to move payloads such as satellites in and out of the space shuttle.*

KINGS & QUEENS OF ENGLAND

OTHER EUROPEAN MONARCHIES MAY HAVE BEEN WEALTHIER OR MORE POWERFUL in their days; some may have been more colorful. But none has matched the English throne for longevity and legend.

The kings and queens of England, from the infancy of the country to the present day, guided the fate of what for a time was the most powerful empire on earth. The beautiful Eleanor of Aquitaine used her position, charm, and intelligence to become Europe's most influential woman. Richard III resorted to intrigue and violence to secure the throne. Shakespeare portrayed him as a hunchbacked villain, but Richard's true character remains a mystery. Henry VIII butted heads with the Roman Catholic Church over his many marriages and divorces (which often resulted in imprisonment or death for his wives). George III's policies angered colonists in the New World and helped ignite the American Revolution, while Queen Victoria presided over the Victorian Age, known for its strict moral values, social reforms, and technological advances.

△ THE TOWER OF LONDON *was begun in 1078. Since then it has seen the end of many royal enemies as a prison and place of execution. The Tower currently holds the Crown Jewels of Great Britain.*

HENRY THE VIII
(1491–1547)

Henry VIII, King of England from 1509 to 1547, was an egotist and unpredictable despot; yet he was also a savvy ruler who ushered in the English Reformation and founded the Church of England.

A KING OF GREAT APPETITES

Born in Greenwich, England, Henry ascended the throne after the death of his father, Henry VII. In 1512 Henry joined his father-in-law, Ferdinand II of Aragon, in a war against France in support of Pope Clement VII. In 1521, Henry published a pamphlet against Martin Luther, prompting the pope to give him the title "Defender of the Faith." Six years later, wishing to divorce his wife, Catherine of Aragon, who was also his brother's widow, he asked Clement to support his move. When refused, he privately married Anne Boleyn in 1533. A year later he decreed his marriage to Catherine invalid because she was his sister-in-law, and broke from Rome by setting up the Church of England. Catherine died in 1536, and Henry had Anne executed for infidelity. Ten days later he married Jane Seymour, who died giving birth to Edward VI. Henry then married—and quickly divorced—Anne of Cleves. He next wed Catherine Howard, in 1540 but ordered her executed for infidelity in 1542. His last marriage was to Catherine Parr, in 1543. From 1542 to 1546, he again waged war against France and Scotland, with ruinous effects on the English economy. After years of failing health, he died in 1547.

HENRY VIII'S SWORD OF STATE

△ AS PORTRAYED BY HANS HOLBEIN THE YOUNGER IN 1540, *Henry VIII had already begun a descent into paranoia and gluttony.*

▽ THESE COINS *were salvaged from the wreck of the* Mary Rose, *Henry VIII's flagship, which sank in 1545.*

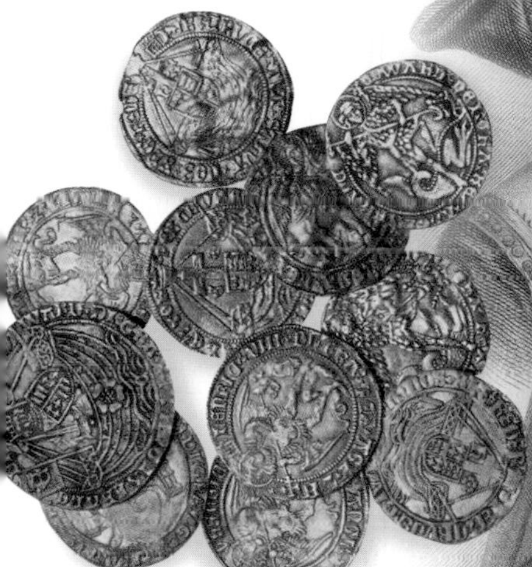

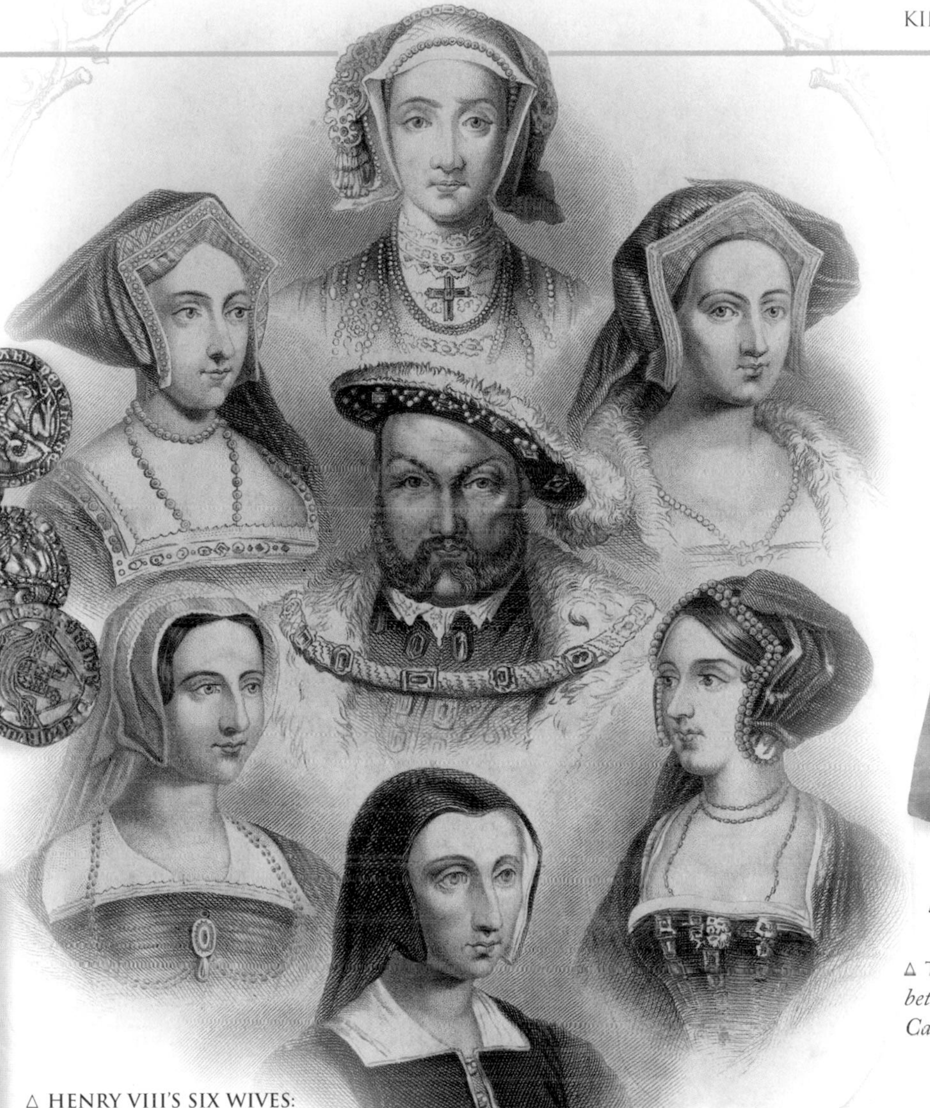

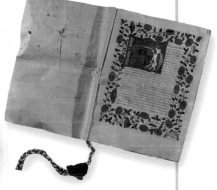

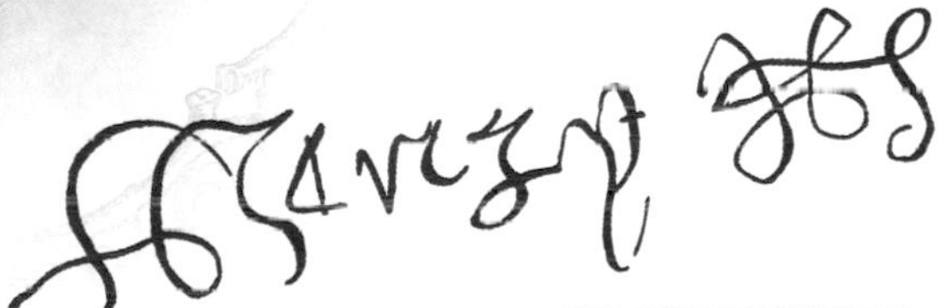

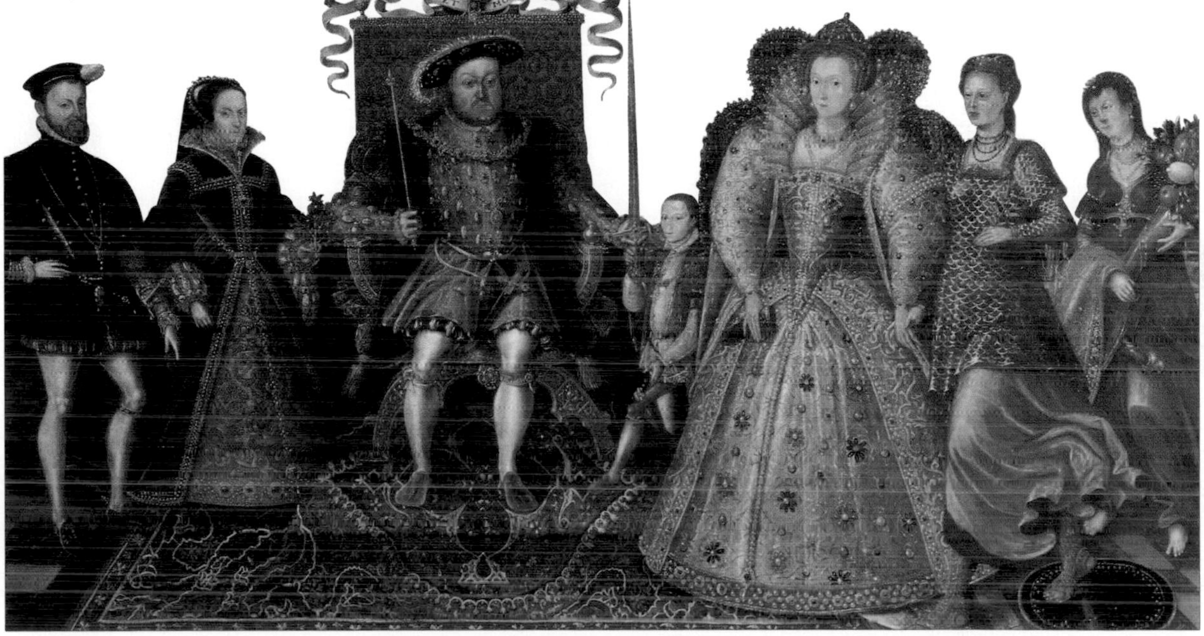

△ HENRY VIII'S SIX WIVES: *Clockwise, from top, Anne of Cleves (#4), Katherine Howard (#5), Anne Boleyn (#2), Catherine of Aragon (#1), Catherine Parr (#6), and Jane Seymour (#3).*

Key Contemporaries

SIR THOMAS MORE (1478–1535) English statesman and scholar, executed for not recognizing Henry as head of the English church, now a saint.

THOMAS WOLSEY (1471–1530) Archbishop of York and Henry VIII's chancellor.

△ THE MARRIAGE AGREEMENT *between Henry VIII and Catherine of Aragon.*

HENRY'S SIGNATURE

Did you know?

- Henry's fourth wife, Anne of Cleves, was chosen by his brilliant advisor Thomas Cromwell in the hopes of a northern European alliance against France. Henry reportedly hated the sight of Anne, and divorced her almost immediately.
- Several songs and poems have been attributed to Henry. The first English Renaissance king, he set an example for later court poets such as Wyatt and Surrey.

▷ THE TUDOR SUCCESSION, *illustrated in this allegorical painting, shows Henry VIII sitting on the throne with his daughter, Elizabeth, at his left, and his son and immmediate successor, Edward VI, at his right.*

QUEEN VICTORIA
(1819–1901)

VICTORIA, QUEEN of the United Kingdom of Great Britain and Ireland and Empress of India, enjoyed a 64-year reign, the longest (thus far) of any British monarch.

THE QUEEN OF EMPIRE

Born in London, Victoria became Queen of England in 1837, at the age of 18. Her prime minister, Lord Melbourne, advised her on constitutional principles and the scope of her power. In 1840 she married her German cousin, Prince Albert of Saxe-Coburg-Gotha, who became the dominant influence in her life, diverting her from the somewhat conservative ideals Lord Melbourne had encouraged. The couple had nine children. Victoria was grief-stricken at Albert's death in 1861, and during her 25 years of mourning was widely criticized for neglecting her political duties. Victoria's stern views on morality, and the preeminence of Britain on the world stage under her rule, helped define the age that bears her name. Beloved by the time of her diamond jubilee in 1897, she was hailed as an exemplary monarch at her death in 1901.

Eminent Victorians

CHARLES DICKENS (1812–1870) Epic novelist and social critic.

GEN. CHARLES GORDON (1833–1885) His loss at Khartoum began the Empire's end.

THOMAS ARNOLD (1795–1842) Champion of the English public school.

△ DURING HER GOLDEN JUBILEE, *Victoria visited France, the first English monarch to do so since 1431.*

▷ VICTORIA'S MARRIAGE *to Prince Albert Saxe-Coburg-Gotha was very much a love match.*

Did you know?

■ In her later years, Victoria did not permit knocking at her bedroom door. Family members announced their presence by a gentle scratching.

■ Victoria was strongly opposed to new technology, even though her age was defined in part by the development of the railway and telegraph.

■ She hated childbearing, which she called "the shadow side of marriage."

△ A STRICT GRANDMOTHER, *Queen Victoria poses with Prince Arthur and Princess Margaret of Connaught in 1886.*

RICHARD III
(1452–1483)

RICHARD III, THE LAST YORKIST KING of England, was a controversial figure who has been depicted in history and literature as a villain.

◁ RICHARD III'S *education included the use of the sword and dagger, as well as singing, dancing, and playing the harp.*

THE KING OF CONTROVERSY

Born in Northamptonshire, England, Richard Plantagenet became Duke of Gloucester at age nine when his elder brother Edward overthrew Henry VI to become king of England as Edward IV. When Edward IV died in 1483, Richard assumed the protection of Edward's 12-year-old son and successor. However, Richard quickly declared Edward IV's marriage invalid and his children illegitimate, and named himself Richard III, King of England. The two sons soon disappeared and historians still debate whether Richard had them killed. His power, though, built on this shaky foundation, was unstable. A rebellion by his associate Henry Stafford, Duke of Buckingham, was quelled, but served to erode Richard's legitimacy. Henry Tudor, Earl of Richmond and claimant to the throne, returned from exile in France to engage Richard's forces in battle. Many of Richard's men defected at the last minute, and he died fighting at Bosworth Field on August 22, 1485.

"He was malicious, wrathful, envious"
MEDIEVAL HISTORIAN SIR THOMAS MORE
IN THE HISTORY OF KING RICHARD THE THIRD

◁ THE NEGATIVE IMAGE *of Richard III began with Sir Thomas More's* History of King Richard III, *published in 1543, which blamed the murder of "the little princes" on Richard, whom More alleges ordered their deaths.*

△ THE LAST OF THE PLANTAGENET LINE, *Richard III was the only king of England to die on the field of battle. After his death, Henry took the throne, ending the Wars of the Roses.*

GEORGE III

(1738–1820)

A MEMBER OF THE Hanover dynasty that ruled England for almost two centuries, George III was King of Great Britain during some of the nation's most tumultuous years, including those of the American Revolutionary War (1775–1783).

FARMER GEORGE

Born in London, George William Frederick was slow to develop mentally. He was crowned at age 12, in the middle of the Seven Years War (1756–63), which pitted Great Britain and Prussia against France, Austria, and Russia. The young George left political decisions to his mentor and prime minister, John Stuart, third Earl of Bute— until Bute's resignation amid political turmoil. George and his new minister, Lord North, restored a stable government, but neither could prevent the loss of the American colonies in 1783, a war that George himself continued to back, even after support for it had ebbed in Parliament. Shortly after the end of the American Revolution, George had a breakdown and was declared insane by his doctors. He recovered briefly in 1789 but relapsed, and the anxious Parliament enacted the regency of his son. George remained ill, with periods of lucidity, until his death in 1820. He left behind 15 children.

△ ON AUGUST 2, 1786, *the deranged Margaret Nicholson attempted to assassinate George III at the Garden Entrance of St. James's Palace. When she was caught, the King (who would one day go insane himself) said, "Pray do not harm the poor woman!"*

Kings of War

HENRY V (1387–1422) Shakespeare's hero, the victor at Agincourt.

GEORGE V (1865–1936) Queen Victoria's son, he sat on the throne during World War I.

GEORGE VI (1895–1952) Britain's monarch through World War II.

Did you know?

■ George III took a keen interest in agriculture, particularly on his estates at Richmond and Windsor, and was known as "Farmer George."

■ Modern medical research suggests that George III's "madness" may actually have been due to porphyria, an inherited metabolic condition that produces the kind of pain, hyperactivity, paralysis, and delirium that plagued the king.

△ DURING GEORGE III'S REIGN, *Parliament took on the responsibility of paying the costs of government from the Crown.*

"Nothing of consequence happened today."

KING GEORGE III
TO HIS DIARY ON JULY 4, 1776

▷ WHILE HIS REPUTATION *has been marred by the loss of the American colonies and his mental breakdowns, George III was deeply involved in political affairs during his reign and brought a high level of culture to the throne.*

△ **THIS PAINTING** *of Eleanor of Aquitaine is one of several royal effigies at Fontevrault Abbey in southewestern France.*

ELEANOR OF AQUITAINE
(c. 1122-1204)

ELEANOR OF AQUITAINE, queen consort to Louis VII of France and, subsequently, of Henry II of England, was one the most powerful women in 12th-century Europe.

THE LIONESS OF EUROPE

Eleanor was the daughter of William X, Duke of Aquitaine and Count of Poitiers. In 1137 she married Louis VII, becoming, at age 15, the French queen. Her beauty and charm helped give her a substantial role in public affairs, and she accompanied her husband on the second Crusade to protect Jerusalem from the Turks. Her personal conduct, however, aroused her husband's jealousy, and their marriage was annulled in 1152. Eleanor took possession of Aquitaine, and married England's Henry II. Eleanor's sons revolted against their father in 1173, and Henry II imprisoned her as a conspirator. Released following her husband's death in 1189, Eleanor continued to play a role in politics, frequently governing the realm on behalf of her sons, King Richard I and King John.

Did you know?

■ Eleanor brought 300 women with her on the Second Crusade. Though they never fought, all of them wore armor and carried lances—much to the distress of the other Crusaders.

■ Many believed that Eleanor, Henry II's senior by 11 years, harbored resentment of her husband's many infidelities and instigated her sons' rebellion.

▽ **ELEANOR OF AQUITAINE** *is entombed between her husband Henry II and her son Richard the Lionhearted in Fontevrault Abbey. She had often taken shelter there during her tumultuous life.*

△ **PART OF ELEANOR'S FORTUNE** *came from the Duchy of Aquitaine, a great fiefdom on the border between France and Spain. During her reign the arts flourished, she welcomed Moorish culture, and promoted the musical artistry of the troubadors.*

SCIENTISTS

SCIENTISTS HAVE ARGUABLY DONE MORE THAN ANY OTHER GROUP to radically change our understanding of the universe and to alter our daily lives.

Louis Pasteur's work taught 19th-century physicians and food producers how to sterilize their instruments, advancing both medicine and public health. He also developed cures for anthrax and rabies, two of the world's most destructive diseases. Almost 100 years later, J. Robert Oppenheimer led the US government's program to develop the atomic bomb. The destructive result ended World War II, but also created the threat of nuclear conflict. In 1953 James Watson and Francis Crick determined the structure of DNA and its method of replication, proving that it held the secrets to our genetic inheritance. Craig Venter and Francis Collins followed that discovery with a race to blueprint our genetic material. Stephen Hawking, meanwhile, looked up to the stars to posit the existence of black holes and increased popular understanding of physics through his writings.

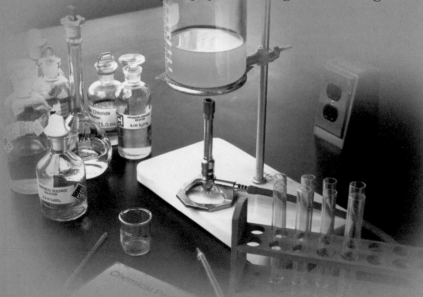

△ AS LOUIS PASTEUR SAID, *"Chance favors the prepared mind." Great scientists follow this dictum every day with careful, precise experimentation that allows the chance elements of nature to reveal themselves.*

STEPHEN HAWKING
b. 1942

STEPHEN HAWKING HAS BECOME one of the major theoretical physicists of the past century, as well as its greatest popularizer, despite suffering from a crippling neuromuscular disease.

BLACK HOLES

Hawking was born in Oxford, England. He attended St. Alban's school and then University College at Oxford, his biologist father's alma mater, where he studied physics. He earned a first-class honors degree in natural science after three years. In 1962 he left Oxford for Cambridge to study cosmology. In 1963 he was diagnosed with Amyotrophic Lateral Sclerosis (ALS, also known as Lou Gehrig disease), a degenerative neuromuscular disease .

△ HAWKING *continues to write, helping to keep the study of the universe in the public eye.* The Universe in a Nutshell *was published in 2001.*

His symptoms worsened, eventually confining him to a wheelchair and shutting down almost all of his physical activity. Hawking continued with his work despite these obstacles, and in 1966 earned his Ph.D.

Hawking stayed at Cambridge as a research fellow, and since 1979 has held the post of Lucasian Professor of Mathematics—the same chair once held by Newton. He has expanded on Einstein's General Theory of Relativity, showing, with Roger Penrose, that the theory implied that space and time began in the Big Bang and would end in black holes. He has worked since then on creating a unified theory of the universe, incorporating both general relativity and quantum theory. In 1985 Hawking nearly died from pneumonia. An operation saved his life but cost him his voice. Since then he has communicated by switching a lever with his one working finger to activate a voice-simulator. He published A *Brief History of Time* in 1986 to explain his theories to a wide audience. The book, an instant best-seller, made him a global celebrity. The father of three, he continues to lecture extensively, and work on his unified theory.

▷ HAWKING *has actually ascribed some of his success to his ailment, saying that it allows him time to think.*

JAMES WATSON b. 1928
FRANCIS CRICK b. 1916

JAMES D. WATSON AND FRANCIS CRICK discovered the double-helix structure of deoxyribonucleic acid (DNA), described how the genetic material replicates, and confirmed the theory that DNA carries an organism's hereditary information.

THE DOUBLE HELIX

Watson was born in Chicago and studied under geneticist Hermann J. Muller. He later earned a research fellowship in Copenhagen, where he studied DNA in viruses. Crick was born in Northampton, England, and studied at London's University College and Cambridge University's Cavendish Laboratory. Watson went to Cambridge in 1951 and with Crick began studying DNA using X-ray diffraction photographs taken by Maurice Wilkins and Rosalind Franklin. Watson and Crick's research was aided by the animosity between Wilkins and Franklin: Wilkins secretly showed Watson one of Franklin's best, and then unpublished, DNA photographs. Watson and Crick used it and large cardboard replicas of DNA to discover the "complementarity" of its four major components—adenine, thymine, guanine, and cytosine—and to show that combinations of these hold all genetic information. Watson, Crick, and Wilkins shared the 1962 Nobel Prize for medicine.

Geneticists

GREGOR MENDEL (1822-1884) Monk whose experiments proved how heredity works.

WILLIAM BATESON (1861-1926) Father of the science of genetics.

△ THE FOUR COMPONENTS *of DNA combine to form long, ladderlike strings that replicate by zipping apart.*

△ NOBEL PRIZE WINNERS *Crick (second from left) and Watson (far right) in Stockholm, Sweden, 1962.*

"We have found the secret of life."
JAMES WATSON

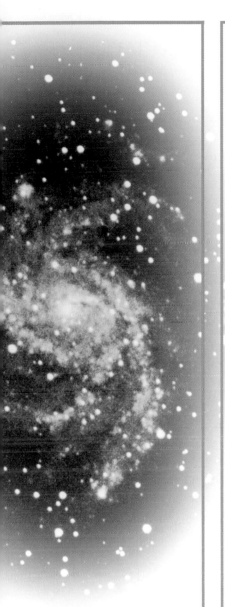

△ SPIRAL GALAXY NGC6946. *As Hawking has gone further back in his studies of the nature of the universe and its beginnings, he has come closer to offering theories that are as much philosophical in their nature as they are scientific.*

Did you know?

■ Stephen Hawking was born exactly 300 years after the death of Galileo.

■ He is a fan of *The Simpsons, Star Trek,* and Formula One car racing.

■ It takes Hawking about 40 hours to prepare one 45-minute lecture.

Did you know?

■ Personality clashes between Watson and Crick ended their work together in 1956.

■ Watson began as an ornithologist. At the time of their joint discovery of the structure of DNA Crick had not earned a doctorate.

■ Franklin died in 1958, four years before Wilkins, Watson, and Crick won the Nobel Prize, which is not awarded posthumously.

△ THE COMPETITIVE SPIRIT *that Watson (left) and Crick (right) displayed in their pursuit of DNA—and that Watson portrayed in his outspoken book* The Double Helix—*revealed that science was no longer the province of selfless academicians.*

J. CRAIG VENTER b. 1946
FRANCIS COLLINS b. 1950

J. CRAIG VENTER AND FRANCIS COLLINS led rival teams that both succeeded in sequencing the 3 billion components of the human genome. Their success is expected to revolutionize medicine by allowing researchers to identify genetic causes of, and cures for, disease.

J. CRAIG VENTER

MAPPERS OF THE HUMAN GENOME

The two men are a study in contrasts. Venter was a rebellious youngster: He barely graduated from high school, and afterward surfed on southern California's beaches instead of attending college. The Navy drafted him for Vietnam, where he served as a medical corpsman. After the war Venter enrolled at the University of California, San Diego, where he earned a Ph.D in physiology and pharmacology. Collins, a devout Christian, grew up on a small farm in Virginia and was home-schooled through the fifth grade. He earned a chemistry degree from the University of Virginia, a Ph.D in physical chemistry from Yale, and a medical degree from the University of North Carolina, where he first worked on medical genetics. Both men worked for the National Center for Human Genome Research. Collins now heads the organization, while Venter in 1994 left to start a private research firm, the Institute for Genomic Research. Venter in 1998 founded Celera Genomics and announced his goal of sequencing the human genome by 2001—several years before the target set by Collins. Their competition has benefited science: Both succeeded in mapping the human genome in 2000, almost five years ahead of the Genome Project's original schedule.

FRANCIS COLLINS

Did you know?

■ Venter's 1998 claim that Celera would sequence the human genome by 2001 led to a war of words between the two scientists. Collins claimed Celera's gene map would read "like *Mad* magazine." Venter responded by calling the Genome Project "the liar's club."

■ While he was in Vietnam, Venter was jailed twice for not following orders.

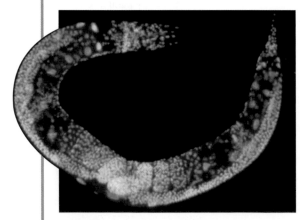

△ IN 1998, THE LOWLY ROUNDWORM, Caenorhabditis elegans, *was the first animal to have its entire genetic structure mapped.*

"This is an adventure into ourselves, to read our own blueprint."

FRANCIS COLLINS

J. ROBERT OPPENHEIMER (1904–1967)

J. ROBERT OPPENHEIMER IS OFTEN CALLED "the father of the atomic bomb" for leading the Manhattan Project, the program that developed the first nuclear weapon during World War II.

Atomic Scientists

ENRICO FERMI (1901–1954) First to split atoms.

MARIE CURIE (1867–1934) Radiation pioneer.

NIELS BOHR (1885–1962) Atomic structure theorist with Manhattan Project.

THE BOMB

Oppenheimer was born in New York City to German Jewish immigrants. He attended Harvard University, and began his atomic research in 1925. A year later he teamed with Max Born to develop the "Born-Oppenheimer method," an important contribution to quantum molecular theory. Oppenheimer became politically active in the 1930s, and agreed with Albert Einstein and Leo Szilard that the Nazis could develop a nuclear weapon. In 1942 he led the scientific end of the Manhattan Project in Los Alamos, New Mexico. The project culminated in August 1945, when the military successfully detonated the first nuclear device over Hiroshima, Japan. After seeing the bomb's devastation, Oppenheimer argued against its further development and was stripped of his security clearance by the Atomic Energy Commission in 1953 amid accusations that he was a communist. He died of throat cancer in 1967.

△ OPPENHEIMER SERVED AS *chairman of the General Advisory Committee of the Atomic Energy Commission and supported international control of atomic energy.*

▽ THIS EARLY TEST BLAST *was observed by marines, under order of the US military, even though the effects of radiation were far from clear.*

LOUIS PASTEUR
(1822–1895)

LOUIS PASTEUR PIONEERED human understanding of the causes and prevention of disease, creating specific ways to prevent and defeat it.

△ **LOUIS PASTEUR** *is depicted in his laboratory, searching for a cure for rabies, in a print published in 1895.*

MICROBE HUNTER

Pasteur was born in Dole, France, and earned a doctorate in crystallography. Conducting experiments examining the relationship between certain crystals and mold led him to study why food products such as wine, beer, and vinegar sometimes spoiled. During this work Pasteur discovered the biological causes of fermentation, and proved that screening or heating methods could destroy microorganisms and prevent spoilage. Together, these discoveries allowed him to invent a process that would help preserve food longer, a process now called pasteurization. He also demonstrated the then-controversial idea that certain microbes thrive in the absence of oxygen. In 1881 Pasteur ended Europe's anthrax epidemic by developing the first vaccine against the disease, based on the work of a veterinary doctor named Toussant. Three years later he developed the first rabies vaccine for animals, and in 1885 successfully tested it on humans, although some scientists today question the risks to which he exposed these first subjects. When he died in 1895, France buried him as a national hero.

> "I am become death, the destroyer of worlds."

OPPENHEIMER, QUOTING FROM THE BHAGAVAD-GITA

▽ "LITTLE BOY," *the first nuclear weapon used in warfare, exploded over Hiroshima, Japan, on the morning of August 6, 1945.*

Did you know?

■ Oppenheimer allied himself with communists during the Spanish Civil War, but later severed all ties to the Communist party to protest the mistreatment of Russian scientists by Stalin.

■ Shaken by the death toll caused by the atomic bombs, Oppenheimer opposed the development of more powerful nuclear weapons.

Did you know?

■ Pasteur suffered a cerebral hemorrhage in 1868 that left parts of his left arm and leg permanently paralyzed.

■ One of the men who guarded Pasteur's Paris tomb during World War II was Joseph Meister, the first person to be saved by Pasteur's rabies vaccine. In 1940 German soldiers demanded that he open Pasteur's crypt, and Meister committed suicide rather than comply with their orders.

◁ PASTEUR, *c. 1875. The loss of three of his children to typhoid fever drove Pasteur to solve the puzzle of how disease spreads.*

CREATORS OF ROCK 'N' ROLL

IN THE MID-1950S, A NEW SOUND BEGAN TO POUR out of radios and record players.

Characterized by driving rhythms, electrified guitars, and lyrics that touched on the risqué and the raucous, the personal and the political, the new music drew listeners from across racial, economic, and gender lines at a time when integration and equality were hot topics. Disc jockey Alan Freed helped bring diverse segments of society together through his radio broadcasts and his famous rock 'n' roll dance parties, staged at venues around the country. Chuck Berry and Bo Diddley changed the rules for the guitar, bringing the instrument into the spotlight with their highly charged styles. Buddy Holly's accessible sound belied his thoughtful and innovative synthesis of country, blues, and pop. And Elvis Presley successfully melded the diverse sounds of his southern upbringing into a potent form that crowned him the undisputed king of rock 'n' roll. Together, these pioneers left a legacy that continues to influence rock musicians today.

△ WHEN ELVIS PRESLEY *appeared on* The Ed Sullivan Show *in 1956, an astonishing 82 percent of American televisions tuned in to witness his racy pelvic gyrations.*

ELVIS PRESLEY
(1935–1977)

ELVIS PRESLEY DID MORE than any other performer in the world to popularize rock 'n' roll, becoming an American icon.

THE KING

Elvis Presley spent his early years in Tupelo, Mississippi, singing in church choirs and teaching himself to play guitar, before moving with his family at age 13 to Memphis, Tennessee. There, he was drawn to country music, the gospel singing at his church, and the blues of Beale Street. While working as a truck driver, he made a record at Memphis's Sun Studios as a present for his mother. On his next trip to Sun, Presley met the owner, Sam Phillips. Teamed with a bassist and a guitarist, in 1954 he recorded his first single, "That's All Right, Mama," which became a local success. Presley gained national attention in 1955 with his *Mystery Train* album, and with the help of his aggressive manager, "Colonel" Tom Parker, moved to the larger RCA label. Elvis recorded nine number-one hits during the next two years, before being drafted into the Army in 1958. Returning to the US in 1960, he spent much of the next decade making a string of undistinguished but popular films. His last visit to the top of the charts was with "Suspicious Minds" in 1969. He continued to tour and record for the next eight years, but destructive personal habits took a toll; he died on August 16, 1977 at his mansion, Graceland.

△ ELVIS STARRED *in 31 films between 1956 and 1969, including four made in one year—1964.*

△ ON DECEMBER 21, 1970, *Presley visited President Richard Nixon in the White House, who named him a "Federal Agent-at-Large."*

△ ELVIS *always wore his hair long and slicked back, a style that became inseparable from his image, and which was widly imitated by his fans.*

> "I don't know anything about music. In my line you don't have to."
>
> ELVIS PRESLEY

Did you know?

- Elvis had an identical twin brother, Jesse, who died at birth.
- By the time he was 40, Elvis had earned, and spent, $100 million.
- An estimated one billion Elvis Presley records have been sold throughout the world.

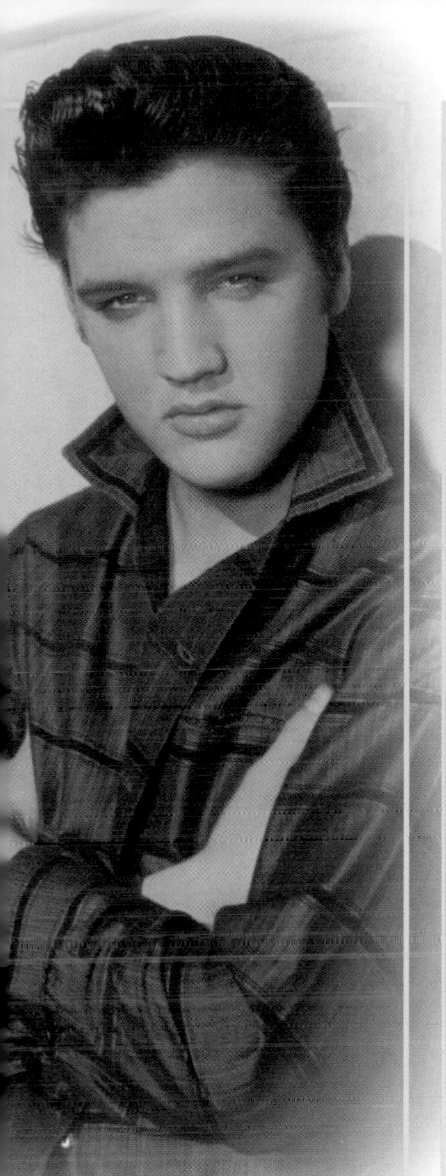

CHUCK BERRY

b. 1926

CHUCK BERRYwas a rock 'n' roll innovator and a major influenceon many of rock's greatest musicians.

THE ETERNAL TEENAGER

Born in St. Louis, Berry served a term in jail for armed robbery at the age of 18 before beginning his career as a musician. In 1955, legendary blues musician Muddy Waters helped introduce St. Louis native Berry to Chess Records owner Leonard Chess, who offered Berry a record deal. His first single, "Maybellene," quickly reached number five on the charts and helped introduced Berry's distinctive vocal and guitar styles to American audiences. A string of hits during the next five years cemented his reputation as one of rock 'n' roll's major figures.

A 1961 conviction for transporting a 14-year-old girl across state lines for "licentious purposes" resulted in a jail sentence and clouded Berry's popular image. When he was released from prison in 1963, Berry found a music scene ruled by British bands influenced by his early recordings. He continued to tour and record, reaching number two on the charts—his biggest hit—with the bawdy "My Ding-a-Ling" in 1972. Today, he still enjoys success as a performer, not just internationally, but universally—a copy of his classic "Johnny B. Goode" was sent into space on the Voyager 1 spacecraft as a symbol of American culture.

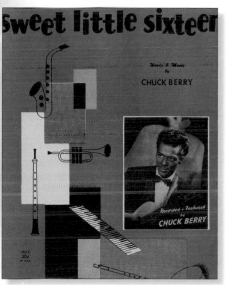

△ THOUGH BEST KNOWN FOR HIS *groundbreaking music, Berry's lyrics, with their insight into the lives of teens, also contributed to the freshness and popularity of his work.*

Did you know?

- According to Berry, his now-famous "duck walk"—moving around the stage with his knees bent and neck bobbing—was born in 1956 out of an attempt to hide wrinkles in his rayon suit.
- Before becoming a full-time musician, Berry studied to become a hairdresser.

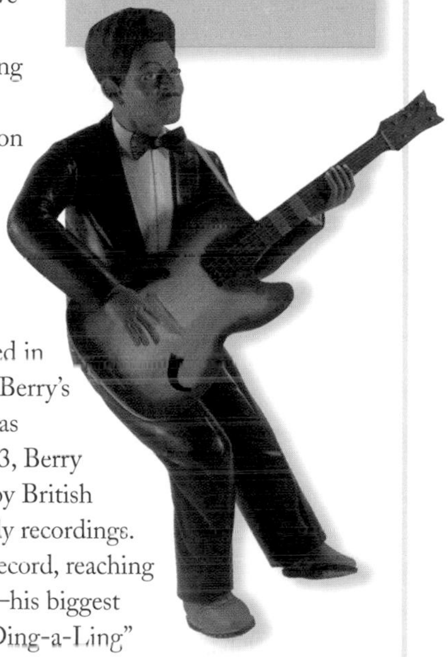

△ AN ICON *of modern music, Berry is a charter member of the Rock and Roll Hall of fame.*

Other Key Players

JERRY LEE LEWIS
b. 1935 His "Great Balls of Fire" burned pianos

LITTLE RICHARD
b. 1932 Over-the-top early mover and shaker

BILL HALEY
(1925–1981) Taught teens to "Rock around the Clock" with his Comets

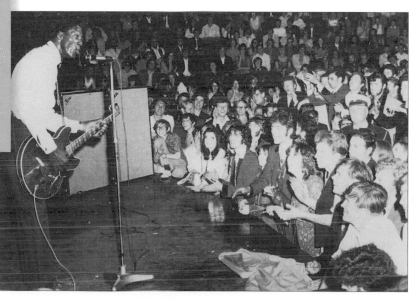

▷ WHILE BERRY *started as a blues musician, his sudden and immense popularity with white teenagers helped him not only cross over into mainstream music, but created the entire genre of rock 'n' roll.*

BUDDY HOLLY
(1936–1959)

BUDDY HOLLY'S INNOVATIVE MIX of country and rock 'n' roll rhythms and bluesy lyrics helped change the face of rock 'n' roll forever—and he did it in just two years.

△ HOLLY DIED IN A PLANE *crash at the age of 22.*

THE DAY THE MUSIC DIED

Born Charles Hardin Holley in Lubbock, Texas, Holly grew up playing piano, fiddle, and steel guitar. He was a seasoned performer by age 16, and as a teenager played a weekly radio gig. His performance as an opening act for Bill Haley and the Comets led to a recording contract with Decca Records in 1956. Early the next year, Buddy Holly and the Crickets, Holly's three-piece backing band, recorded its first number-one hit, "That'll Be the Day." The following two years saw a string of chart successes that included "Peggy Sue" and "Rave On." Chronic tour-bus problems during the winter of 1959 led Holly to charter a plane to the next show for himself, J. P. Richardson ("The Big Bopper"), and Ritchie Valens, following a show in Green Bay, Wisconsin. The plane flew only eight miles before crashing in a cornfield, killing all aboard. Holly was 22 years old.

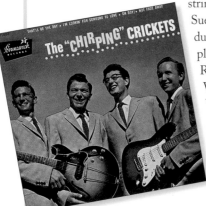

△ HOLLY'S UNIQUE "CHIRPING" *vocal style, with its leaps and pauses, gave rise to the name The Crickets.*

Did you know?

■ Singer/songwriter Don McLean's 1972 hit "American Pie" was a remembrance of the fateful plane crash as "the day the music died."

■ The Cricket's sound made bookers at the Apollo Theater in Harlem think they were African-American. Booed at first, they soon won over the crowd.

△ THE CRICKETS *pose in a promotional photograph. From top to bottom: Jerry Allison (drums), Buddy Holly (vocals, acoustic guitar), and Joe Mauldin (bass).*

BO DIDDLEY
b. 1928

BO DIDDLEY'S INFECTIOUS and inventive guitar rhythms influenced generations of musicians, and shaped the early style of rock 'n' roll.

THE ORIGINATOR

Born Otha Ellas McDaniel, Diddley began playing guitar at age ten. As a teen he became a street-corner gospel and blues singer, and by the time he was in his early twenties, he was regularly booked in the clubs of Chicago's South Side. In 1955, Diddley was signed by blues label Checkers Records, a subsidiary of the legendary Chess Records. Only a handful of Diddley's songs cracked the charts, but his recordings found strong support among his musical peers. Many bands during the early 1960s adopted his African-influenced rhythms, helping to popularize rock 'n' roll with a wide audience. He gained popularity as a touring act and on programs such as *The Ed Sullivan Show.* His touring and recording slowed by the 1970s, but Diddley remains a member of rock 'n' roll royalty.

△ DIDDLEY'S *true success came as an R&B act. Only "Say Man" in 1959 crossed over to the pop charts.*

> "Don't let your mouth write no check that your tail can't cash."

BO DIDDLEY

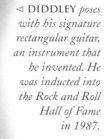

◁ DIDDLEY *poses with his signature rectangular guitar, an instrument that he invented. He was inducted into the Rock and Roll Hall of Fame in 1987.*

ALAN FREED
(1921–1965)

WITH HIS RADIO SHOWS and live revues, Alan Freed became one of the most influential figures in the popularization of rock 'n' roll.

THE DISC JOCKEY

Born Albert Freed in Johnstown, Pennsylvania, Freed worked his way up on local radio shows until July 11, 1951, when he began hosting a rhythm-and-blues program on WJW in Cleveland, Ohio, using the name "Moondog." Through his radio shows, he introduced rock 'n' roll music, whose appeal had previously been limited to a primarily African-American audience, to a huge new national audience that was made up of young listeners both black and white. This widespread exposure helped establish rock 'n' roll as an important development in popular music. His popularity increasing, Freed joined New York radio station WINS in 1954. He continued to host high-profile, racially integrated rock 'n' roll shows, which quickly ignited controversy. A 1958 Boston concert that ended in violence led to charges that Freed had incited a riot, and he was dropped from WINS. In 1959 he was also indicted for allegedly taking record company payoffs to promote artists during his radio shows. He pleaded guilty to the charges three years later, and his career never recovered. He bounced from station to station and began drinking heavily, eventually dying in Palm Springs, California, of cirrhosis of the liver.

△ FREED'S CONCERTS, *like the one advertised in the above flyer, played a vital role in breaking down racial barriers in the music world.*

Did you know?

■ Freed's 1957 television show featured African-American performer Frankie Lymon dancing with a white girl, which drew furious reactions from affiliates, resulting in its cancellation.

■ In high school, Freed had a band named The Sultans of Swing.

Did you know?

■ Bo Diddley's name reportedly came from the diddley bow, a one-stringed African instrument.

■ The rhythm Diddley was credited with popularizing was dubbed the "hambone," or "shave and a haircut—two bits."

◁ THOUGH DIDDLEY *is not known for the blues like B.B. King (right), he grew up playing them in Chicago and provided a bridge to rock 'n' roll.*

△ ONE OF FREED'S SHOWS *in March 1952 in Cleveland is regarded as the first rock concert.*

◁ FREED *in a 1950s promo photo. In 1958 he was indicted by a Massachusetts grand jury for inciting a rock 'n' roll riot in Boston.*

NATIVE AMERICANS

WHILE NO ONE KNOWS EXACTLY HOW the first humans arrived in North America, it is believed they crossed a land bridge over the Bering Strait connecting present-day Russia and Alaska some 12,000 years ago.

These first Americans spread across a continent remarkable for its richness. While they developed different cultures and tribal systems, they all held in common a deep reverence for the land and all that it offered them. The arrival of permanent European settlers in the 17th century altered the fine balance the Native Americans had created. While men such as Squanto and Sequoyah cooperated with the new arrivals, exchanging information that helped both Native Americans and settlers survive, such tolerance was short-lived. By the late 19th century, leaders like Crazy Horse, Chief Joseph, and Sitting Bull led the final resistance against "Manifest Destiny"—US continental expansion—and the bitter fate it portended for the true discoverers of America.

△ THE MIGRATION *of European Americans began pushing the Native Americans westward from the 17th century on. Faced with the loss of their ancestral lands and their resources, many Native Americans fought back.*

SITTING BULL
(c. 1831–1890)

ONE OF THE MOST CELEBRATED and feared Native American leaders, Sitting Bull spent his life fighting against white efforts to steal tribal land. As a Sioux chief, he united other Sioux in their struggles against whites, and commanded several tribes during the famous and bloody battle at the Little Bighorn.

SIOUX WARRIOR AND CHIEF

Sitting Bull was born near Grand River in the Dakota Territory, and was heralded as a courageous warrior and wise leader from early on. He joined his first war party at age 14 and helped lead the Strong Heart warrior society. He fought in several battles against the US cavalry, and was elected chief of the Sioux nation in 1867. The following year, Sitting Bull made peace with the US government after it promised the Sioux its own large reservation. But the discovery of gold in the Black Hills in the 1870s caused a surge in white settlers on the land. Determined to fight, Sitting Bull brought the Sioux, Cheyenne, and some Arapaho to his camp in Montana Territory, where together the tribes defeated General George Crook at the Battle of Rosebud. The Indians then moved into the Little Bighorn River Valley. Here, in 1876, the united warriors overwhelmed Custer and his troops in one of the most famous battles in US history. Faced with a rapidly declining buffalo population due to over-hunting by whites, Sitting Bull led the hungry Sioux to Canada in 1877. Famine eventually forced Sitting Bull to surrender to US authorities in 1881. After serving a two-year prison sentence, he gained fame as a member of Buffalo Bill's Wild West show. He returned to activism in 1889 through his support of the Ghost Dance movement, which predicted that an Indian revival would wipe out the white race. Police arrested Sitting Bull, who was shot during the arrest.

◁ SITTING BULL SHARES A PEACE PIPE *with a friend. When he gave up his gun to US authorities, he said, "I wish it to be remembered that I was the last man of my tribe to surrender my rifle."*

CHIEF JOSEPH
(c.1835–1904)

CHIEF JOSEPH, the chief of the Nez Percé tribe, led his people in legendary battles against the US Army during a failed attempt to escape to Canada.

THUNDER ROLLING DOWN THE MOUNTAIN

Joseph was born in what is now Oregon. His father, a tribal leader who initially cooperated with whites, refused to move the Nez Percé to an Idaho reservation after the US government seized much of the tribe's land in 1863. Tensions with whites peaked after Chief Joseph was elected leader. Faced with a likely attack, he agreed to transport his tribe to Idaho in 1877. Before the move could take place, though, Nez Percé warriors killed several white settlers. Joseph, fearing retaliation, led his 700 followers on a three-month, 1,400-mile march to Canada, fighting US soldiers along the way. Chief Joseph finally surrendered within just 40 miles of the Canadian border, and the tribe was relocated to reservations in Kansas and Oklahoma. Through his efforts, in 1885 some tribal members were able to return to an area not far from their home valley. However, Joseph and others were placed on a reservation away from the rest of their people. He spent his later years speaking out against US government policy toward Native Americans.

△ **GENERAL NELSON MILES** *was the nation's foremost soldier in the West, subjugating not just Chief Joseph, but Geronimo's Apaches and the Montana and Dakota Sioux.*

> "Hear me my chiefs! I am tired. My heart is sick and sad. From where the sun now stands I will fight no more forever."

CHIEF JOSEPH'S SPEECH OF SURRENDER, OCTOBER 5, 1877

△ **CHIEF JOSEPH DAM**, *the second largest hydroelectric dam in the nation, sits across Washington's Columbia River, not far from the city of Bridgeport. The chief is buried in Nespelem, Washington, in a Native American cemetery.*

△ **SITTING BULL'S** *Sioux name*, Tatanka Iyotanka, *means "a buffalo sitting on its haunches, unable to be moved," a name befitting his lifelong stance of resistance.*

Did you know?

■ Sitting Bull quit Buffalo Bill's Wild West show after four months.

■ Sitting Bull had a vision shortly before the Battle of the Little Bighorn in which he saw soldiers falling into his camp "like grasshoppers from the sky."

■ There is some debate as to whether Sitting Bull ran away during the Battle of Little Bighorn, although most scholars think he stayed to lead his men.

Did you know?

■ His tribal name, *Hin-mah-too-yah-lat-kekt*, means "Thunder Rolling Down the Mountain." He became known as Joseph because his father took that name when he was baptized a Christian.

■ Joseph may have had little influence on the tribe's fighting tactics. His brother Olikut actually led the warriors while Joseph guarded the camp.

∧ **CALLED BY THE** *American press "The Red Napoleon" for his masterful retreat to Canada, Chief Joseph died in 1904 in exile in Washington State from what his doctor termed "a broken heart."*

SQUANTO
(c. 1580–1622)

A PAWTUXET INDIAN who was fluent in English, Tisquantum or "Squanto" is best remembered for serving as an interpreter and guide for the Pilgrim settlers at Plymouth in the 1620s.

THE PILGRIMS' HELPER

Historians know little about Squanto's early life. Born in present-day Massachusetts, he is believed to have been captured along the Maine coast in 1605 and brought to England. He returned to his homeland in 1614 with English explorer John Smith, possibly acting as a guide, but was captured again by another British sailor and sold into slavery in Spain. Squanto escaped, lived with monks for a few years, and eventually returned to North America in 1619, only to find his entire Patuxet tribe dead from smallpox. He went to live with the nearby Wampanoags.

In 1621, Squanto was introduced to the Pilgrims at Plymouth, and acted as an interpreter between Pilgrim representatives and Wampanoag chief Massasoit. He deepened the Pilgrims' trust by helping them find a lost boy in 1622 and assisted them with planting and fishing. Embroiled in the politics emerging between the settlers and the local tribes, he died of a fever while acting as a guide for Governor William Bradford.

△ **THE PILGRIMS AND WAMPANOAGS** *celebrated the first Thanksgiving after reaping a successful crop in fall 1621.*

Did you know?

■ George Weymouth, the first captain to capture Squanto, did so because he thought his financial backers in Britain might want to see some Indians.

■ In England, Squanto lived with Sir Ferdinando Gorges, owner of the Plymouth Company. He taught Squanto English, and hired him to be an interpreter and guide.

◁ **SQUANTO'S** *unique knowledge of the English language and English ways gave him power. He abused his power by threatening his people that he would tell the Pilgrims to "release the plague" if they did not do what he wanted.*

CRAZY HORSE
(c. 1842–1877)

OGLALA SIOUX CHIEF CRAZY HORSE was the defining symbol of Sioux resistance to the white man's expansion into Native American homelands on the Great Plains during the 1800s.

Native Voices

BLACK ELK (1863–1950) Popular spiritual guide.

LOUISE ERDRICH b. 1954 Elegaic chronicler of Native American life.

SHERMAN ALEXIE b. 1966 Author and filmmaker.

THE WARRIOR

Born near the Black Hills of what is now South Dakota, Crazy Horse was a natural hunter and fighter. He took part in all major Black Hills military campaigns, including Oglala chief Red Cloud's three-year war against Wyoming settlers (1865–68), and the annihilation of Captain William J. Fetterman and his 80 troops at Fort Phil Kearny in 1867. Admired for his regal bearing and good looks, he was named Oglala chief in 1876, and that June, along with Sitting Bull, defeated General George Crook's forces at the Battle of Rosebud. His most famous battle was at the Little Bighorn, where he and Sitting Bull led the bloody victory over General George Custer. Relentlessly pursued following Little Bighorn, and facing starvation, he surrendered to US forces in 1877 and was killed, unarmed, during a scuffle with soldiers taking him to a guardhouse.

> "It is a good day to fight —it is a good day to die."

CRAZY HORSE'S RALLYING CRY

△ **THE GUARDHOUSE** *at Fort Robinson State Park near Crawford, Nebraska, where Crazy Horse was stabbed from behind by a soldier. His last words were, "Let me die fighting!"*

△ CASIMIR ZIOLOWSKI *continues the work started by his father Korczak in 1948 on a massive sculptue of Crazy Horse in the Black Hills of South Dakota. The head alone is 90 feet high.*

△ VICTOR MATURE, *a Caucasian, was Crazy Horse in this 1955 film, unusual at the time for its sympathetic portrayal of Native Americans.*

SEQUOYAH
(1776–1843)

SEQUOYAH INVENTED the Cherokee writing system, which fostered literacy among thousands of Cherokee Indians.

TALKING LEAVES

Born in Tuskeegee, Tennessee, son of Nathaniel Gist, a British trader, and Wut-the, the daughter of a Cherokee chief, Sequoyah was often called George Gist or Guess by his white contemporaries. He became an accomplished silversmith, he also fought the British and Creek Indians in the War of 1812, under the command of Andrew Jackson. He recognized the importance of literacy for the Cherokee, believing that the ability to read and write would allow his people to record their history and also prevent their exploitation by their white neighbors.

Sequoyah met a wealthy Georgia landowner named Charles Hicks who showed him the English alphabet. Sequoyah spent more than a decade developing a Cherokee writing system—one of the first for any American Indian language. Incorporating letters from English, Greek, and Hebrew, the system of 85 or 86 characters was technically a syllabary: Each symbol represented a syllable in the Cherokee language. When he introduced the syllabary to other Cherokee in 1821, they quickly began teaching it in their schools and using it to print books and newspapers. In his later years Sequoyah worked as a miner and was active in politics.

△ WOODEN BUST OF SEQUOYAH, *17th century. During the 1820s Sequoyah taught thousands of Cherokee to read and write.*

▷ SEQUOYAH *called his letters "talking leaves." He first demonstrated their value when he settled a dispute by reading information from a piece of paper in a Cherokee court.*

WILD WEST

DURING THE MID-TO-LATE 1800S, THE PEOPLE OF THE UNITED STATES BEGAN TO migrate into the vast territories west of the Mississippi River.

A new frontier with a populace as varied—and often as tough—as the land, the American West became a wild place, full of outlaws who took advantage of the rough terrain and relative lawlessness of the territory. Butch Cassidy and the Sundance Kid pulled off some of the most daring train and bank robberies of their day. Billy the Kid's death at the age of 21 ended the short life of one of America's most infamous outlaws. Meanwhile, lawmen such as Wyatt Earp and "Wild Bill" Hickok brought peace to some of the Wild West's rowdiest outposts. The expansion west also brought to a head the bloody conflict between Europeans and the indigenous people of North America. While the defeat of George Custer at the Little Bighorn found the Native Americans victorious, it was the beginning of the end of their hold on the West.

COWBOY HAT

△ THE LORE OF THE WILD WEST *endures in American memory, and is kept alive not just in popular culture, but in towns such as Tombstone, Arizona, where the gunfights and swagger of the frontier are reenacted.*

GEORGE A. CUSTER
(1839–1876)

DESPITE HIS MANY heroic exploits during the Civil War, George Custer will forever be remembered for his fatal miscalculation as the commander of the US troops at the Battle of the Little Bighorn.

THE LAST STAND

Born in New Rumley, Ohio, Custer enlisted in the Union army after graduating from West Point, and quickly distinguished himself as a gutsy, though flamboyant, soldier, rising to the rank of brigadier general by the end of the Civil War. In 1866 he headed to the Western frontier as a lieutenant colonel of the 7th Cavalry, a regiment created to help control the volatile situation between white settlers and the Native Americans of the Great Plains. His troops in November 1868 surprised a Cheyenne encampment on the Washita River, near what is now Cheyenne, Oklahoma. The 7th Cavalry destroyed the village, driving the surviving Cheyenne into the winter cold without food or, in many cases, adequate clothing. The attack was deemed a great success, but raised ethical questions: The tribe was located within a designated Cheyenne reservation, and a white flag was flying above Chief Black Kettle's tepee.

The discovery of gold in the Black Hills of the Dakota Territory by a Custer-led expedition pushed tribes of Sioux out of their sacred hunting ground. Led by Sitting Bull and Crazy Horse, many of these tribes gathered at a spring camp on the Little Bighorn River, Montana Territory. As the 7th Cavalry searched for this encampment, Custer and his troops were sent ahead as scouts. Upon discovering the tribes at the Little Bighorn on June 24, 1876, Custer decided to attack and split his company into three columns. Underestimating the number of warriors camped on the river, he led more than 200 men straight into the camp, where they were quickly annihilated. His mutilated body was buried at West Point.

△ CUSTER COULD HAVE *taken a Gatling gun (an early-model machine gun) and four more companies with him, but chose not to, believing they would slow his progress into the Little Bighorn Valley.*

"Like a circus rider gone mad!"

A FELLOW OFFICER COMMENTING ON CUSTER'S FLAMBOYANT APPEARANCE

Wild Westerners

ANNIE OAKLEY (1860–1926) Beloved Wild West sure-shot.

JESSE JAMES (1847–1882) Gunslinger and bankrobber.

CALAMITY JANE (1852–1903) Cowgirl on the rough frontier.

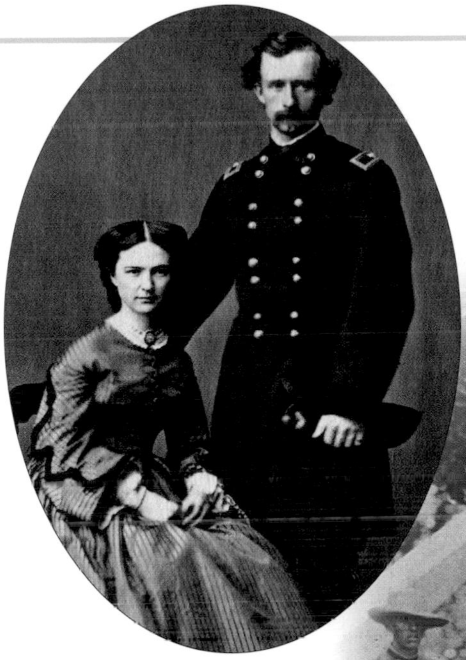

△ PORTRAIT OF CUSTER AND HIS WIFE ELIZABETH, *taken by Matthew Brady on October 23, 1864. Custer was 25 when he was promoted to major general.*

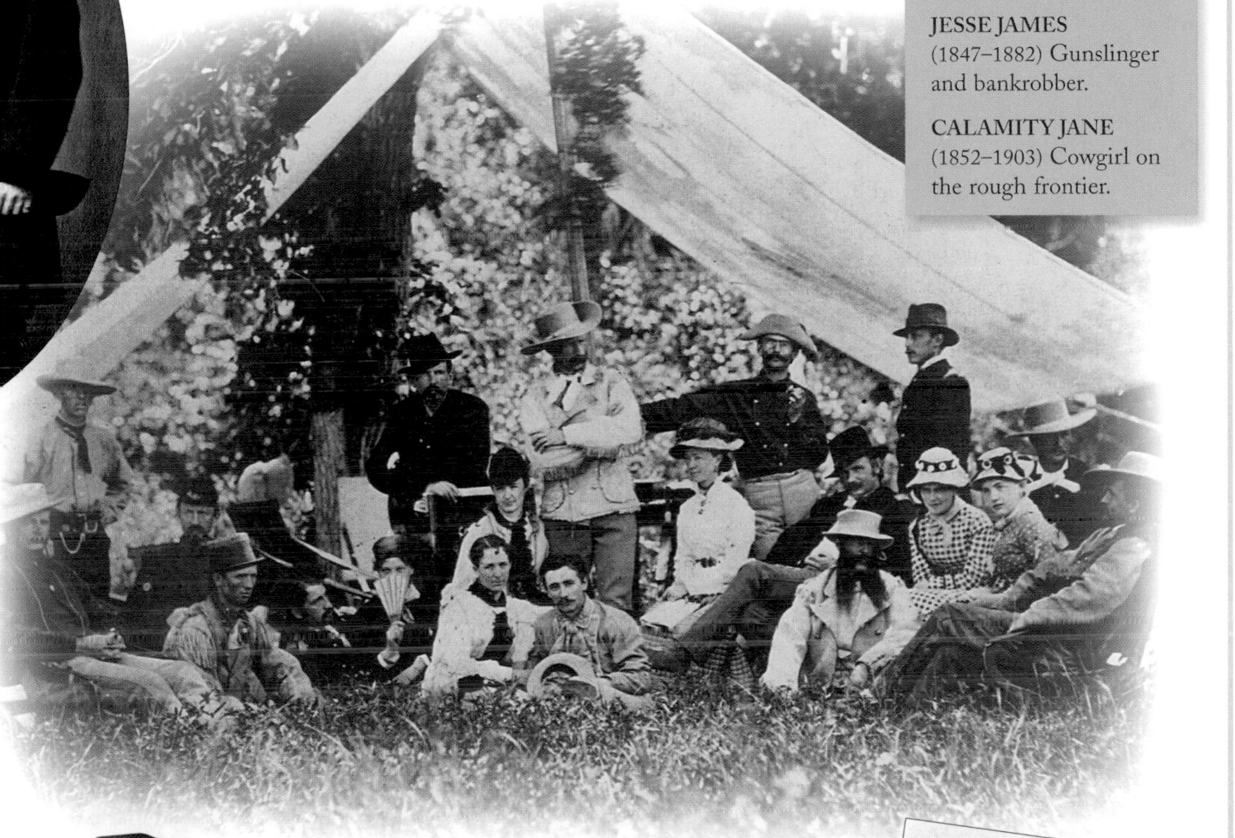

△ CUSTER STANDS *at the center of a hunting and camping party of guests he invited and took out to the Little Heart River in the Dakota Territory in 1875.*

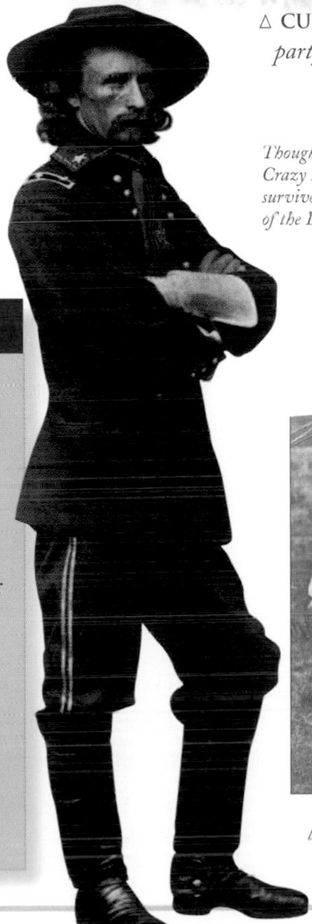

▷ A DASHING FIGURE, *Custer was not loved by the 7th Cavalry (due to his mistreatment of his men in several instances)—and the feeling seems to have been mutual.*

Did you know?

- Custer graduated last in his West Point class.
- During the Civil War, Custer was promoted to the rank of brigadier general at the age of 23—the youngest soldier to reach that rank.
- In 1867, Custer was court-martialed for visiting his wife without leave. He was suspended from duty without pay for one year, but was reinstated.

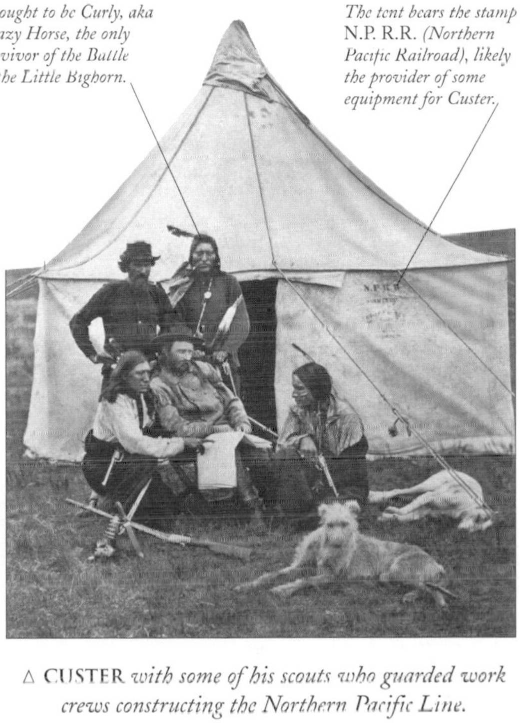

Thought to be Curly, aka Crazy Horse, the only survivor of the Battle of the Little Bighorn.

The tent bears the stamp N.P. R.R. (Northern Pacific Railroad), likely the provider of some equipment for Custer.

△ CUSTER *with some of his scouts who guarded work crews constructing the Northern Pacific Line.*

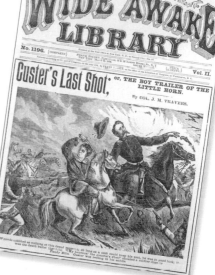

△ CUSTER'S LAST STAND *became the stuff of legends in years to come, as celebrated in this 1894 dime novel. Rather than discuss Custer's tactical blunder, though, popular writers of the time tended to present the battle as proof of Native American "savagery."*

BILLY THE KID

(1859–1881)

THE INFAMOUS OUTLAW Billy the Kid, son of Irish immigrants, was born William H. Bonney in the Bowery section of New York City.

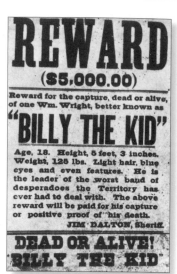

△ A $5,000 REWARD POSTER *for Billy's capture, dead or alive. Billy was one of the leaders of the Regulators, a vigilante faction in the New Mexico cattle wars. On the other side was the Murphy Gang, who ran the county.*

THE GUNFIGHTER

Bonney was brought west by his mother Catherine in 1865. By the age of 13 he was already breaking laws in the Kansas Territory, and when his mother died two years later, Bonney was on his own in the Wild West. Legend has it that he got his name in 1877, when a man in a bar called the teen "Billy the Kid Goat." Billy then shot him. He met his mentor, J. H. Tunstall, while working as a cowboy in Lincoln County, New Mexico. Tunstall had begun to direct Billy toward a legitimate living, but in 1878 he was murdered by rival cattlemen, setting off the Lincoln County War. Billy vowed to kill everyone involved in his mentor's death and joined a vigilante group. When he killed Sheriff William Brady and his deputy, though, Billy became the target. A posse organized to hunt Billy surrounded the outlaw and his men in a Lincoln mansion. After a three-day standoff, Billy miraculously escaped. He offered to turn evidence against one of Tunstall's murderers, but changed his mind and escaped. In 1880, Lincoln County sheriff Pat Garrett finally caught Billy, who was tried and sentenced to death. Billy escaped once more, but Garrett overtook him on July 14, 1881, in Fort Sumner, in New Mexico Territory, shooting him to death in an ambush. Billy died at just 21 years of age.

△ BILLY THE KID'S FIRST *victims were two Native Americans. Though he claimed the killings were a mistake, they took place shortly after the Battle of Little Bighorn, upsetting local lawmen.*

"His equal for sheer inborn savagery has never lived."

EMERSON HOUGH (1857–1923), JOURNALIST AND AUTHOR

Did you know?

■ Billy the Kid was once thought to have killed more than 20 men during his lifetime. That number is now believed to be four.

■ Many historians believe that the Kid's real name was Henry McCarty.

■ Though Billy the Kid was one of the Wild West's most dangerous outlaws, women reportedly found him quite attractive.

△ AFTER A LAST VISIT *with his girlfriend Paulita Maxwell, Billy the Kid was finally killed by Sheriff Pat Garrett, who had been Billy the Kid's friend back in Lincoln. So close had they been, in fact, that Garrett was nicknamed "Big Casino" and Billy the Kid was called by some "Little Casino."*

"WILD BILL" HICKOK

(1837–1876)

JAMES BUTLER "WILD BILL HICKOK," one of the Wild West's most legendary marksmen and lawmen, brought order to some of the frontier's rowdiest outposts while helping to create the myth of the West.

△ HICKOK WAS BEST KNOWN *for his marksmanship, though his dashing good looks and long hair also received comment. Legend has it he kept his hair long to tempt scalpers, but others believed it was vanity.*

THE FASTEST GUN

Born in Troy Grove, Illinois, Hickok as a young man aided his father in the escape of runaway slaves and was a vocal supporter of the abolition of slavery. He joined the Union army during the Civil War as a scout and a spy, escaping from Confederate captivity on several occasions. After the war, Hickok became a marshal in Hays City (1869) and Abilene, Kansas (1871), gaining a reputation as a tough but fair enforcer of the law. Though he was as quick to shoot a troublemaker as he was to protect citizens who needed his help, he also shot a few soldiers and once a deputy—explaining in part his frequent moves. After years of taming towns on the Western frontier, Wild Bill Hickok married Agnes Lake in Cheyenne, Wyoming, but later that year he was murdered—for no apparent reason— by a drunken stranger named Jack McCall during a card game in Deadwood, South Dakota.

△ AFTER GAINING FAME *as a lawman, Hickok joined his friend Buffalo Bill Cody's Wild West show for a time in 1873 and toured the East. He left after seven months and returned to Wyoming to prospect for gold.*

▽ HE MADE HIS FIRST MARK *in Nebraska, in 1861, when, as constable, he drew the McCanles Gang into town with the lure of liquor and women. When the gang showed up, Hickok ambushed them, killing three.*

Did you know?

■ When he was murdered, Wild Bill Hickok reportedly held a poker hand consisting of two aces and two eights—a hand known ever after as the "dead man's hand."

■ Hickok was said to have fought off a bear attack single-handedly, armed with nothing but a bowie knife.

■ Presidents George Bush and George W. Bush are descendents of Hickok's mother's family.

WILD BILL

J.B.HICKOCK

Killed by the Assassin
JACK McCALL
—in—
DEADWOOD.1876.

August 2nd 1876.
Pard We Will
meet Again
in the happy
hunting ground
to part no more.

GOOD BYE

COLORADO
CHARLIE.
C.H.UTTER

△ HICKOK WAS BURIED *at Mount Moriah Cemetery in Deadwood. Calamity Jane (Martha Jane Cannary) is buried next to him, though they were only acquaintances.*

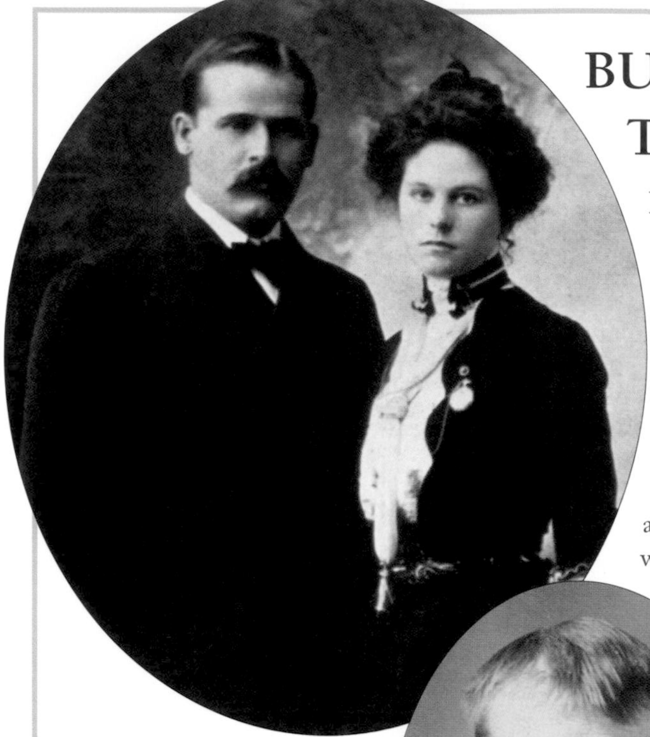

BUTCH CASSIDY (1866–1909)
THE SUNDANCE KID (1870–1909)

BUTCH CASSIDY AND THE SUNDANCE KID left a trail of crime that stretched from the Wild West to South America during their tenure as a train-robbing, bank-heisting outlaw team.

ROMANTIC OUTLAWS

Cassidy, born Robert Leroy Parker, had a knack for rustling cattle and handling a six-shooter, thanks to his mentor, Mike Cassidy, a cowboy who worked for Butch's father. The Sundance Kid, born Harry Longabaugh, had a reputation as a gunslinger with a deadly aim. Butch and Sundance met while members of a notorious group of criminals known as the Wild Bunch. Together, Butch Cassidy and the Sundance Kid pulled off some of the most daring robberies of their time. After robbing the Great Northern Flyer train in Montana in 1901, the Wild Bunch was tracked down by lawmen, and most of the gang members were killed or imprisoned.

The two escaped and headed to Argentina, where they resumed their criminal ways. They reportedly were killed in a 1909 shootout with soldiers near San Vicente, Bolivia, after stealing a mining-company payroll.

△ ETTA PLACE, *the Sundance Kid's girlfriend, was known for her abilities with a gun and a horse.*

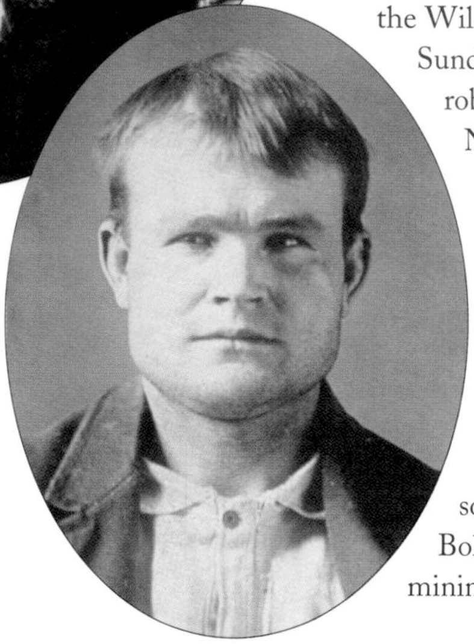

△ AFTER SERVING *18 months for horse stealing, Cassidy was pardoned by the Wyoming governor, on condition that he leave the state permanently.*

△ CASSIDY, RAISED *a Mormon, claimed to never have killed a man during all his years of bank holdups.*

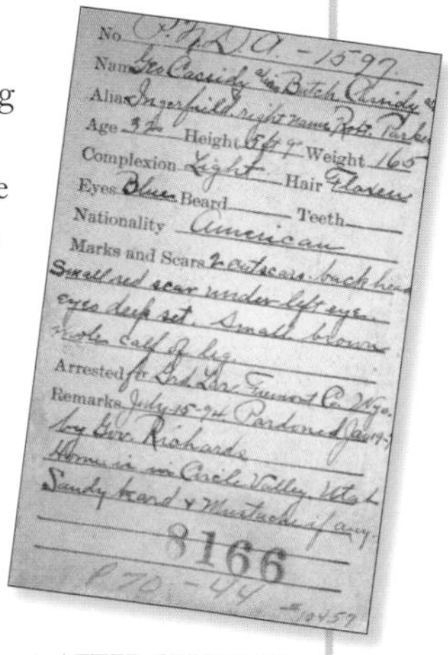

Did you know?

■ Robert Leroy Parker was known as "Butch" because of his occasional stints as a butcher and "Cassidy" from his mentor, Mike Cassidy.

■ The Sundance Kid got his name after serving a prison sentence in Sundance, Wyoming.

■ Cassidy's first train robbery—with outlaws Tom and Bill McCarty—ended in failure when the gang couldn't figure out how to open the train's safe.

Bill Carver
Kid Curry
The Sundance Kid
Ben Kilpatrick
Butch Cassidy

▷ THE WILD BUNCH, *photographed together in Fort Worth, Texas, in 1901.*

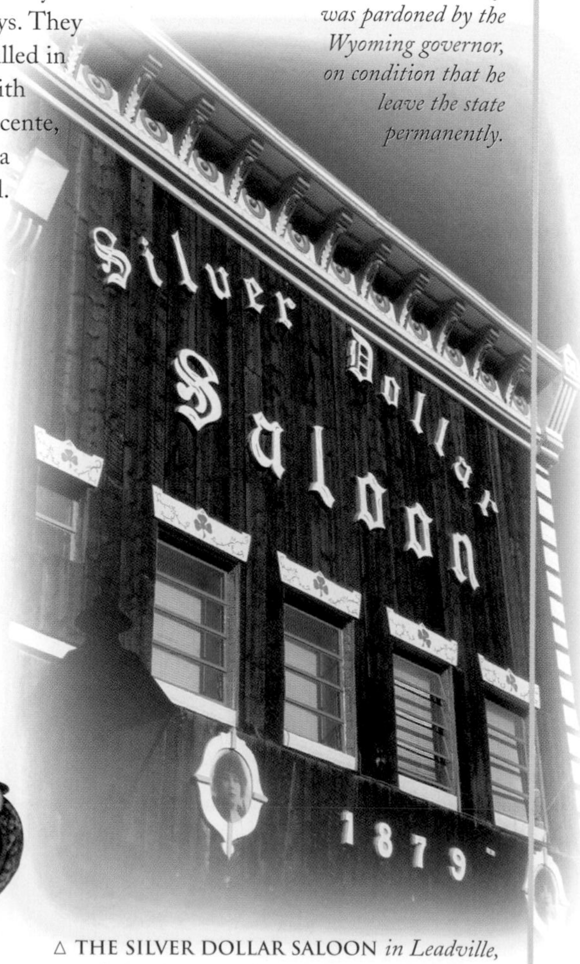

△ THE SILVER DOLLAR SALOON *in Leadville, Colorado, was a favorite haunt of both Butch Cassidy and Doc Holliday of O.K. Corral fame.*

WYATT EARP
(1848-1929)

WYATT EARP, A CAREER LAWMAN, was known for his skilled gunfighting and tough attitude toward criminals, and especially for his legendary shootout at the O.K. Corral.

GUN-FIGHTING MARSHAL

Earp was born in Monmouth, Illinois, the third of five boys. When he was 16, his family moved west to avoid the Civil War and its politics and young Wyatt found himself with many opportunities to live up to his pioneer ancestors. By the time he was 21, he had been a stage coach driver, wagon master on a wagon train, and a scout for the US Cavalry. In 1876 he became chief deputy marshal of Dodge City, Kansas, where he met his future sidekick, John Henry "Doc" Holliday, a former dentist whose skill with a gun was matched by his taste for liquor. Earp headed to Tombstone, Arizona Territory, in 1879, where he was quickly joined by three of his brothers and Doc Holliday. His brother Virgil Earp soon became town marshal, and the other Earps took on the role of occasional lawmen. Hostility between the Earps and a local gang of cattle rustlers and robbers called the Cowboys culminated in the famous shootout at the O.K. Corral on October 26, 1881. In a bloody skirmish, three of the four Cowboys were killed; Wyatt Earp was the only man to walk away unharmed. Resentment toward the Earp brothers ran high in Tombstone afterward, and Wyatt left town after two of his brothers were murdered by unknown assailants. He eventually settled in Los Angeles, where he lived until his death at the age of 80.

△ AFTER HIS ADVENTURES IN TOMBSTONE, *Earp and his second wife, Josie, tried their hand at gold prospecting. Later he served as a consultant to early movie studios as they began to make Westerns. Earp became friends with actors such as William S. Hart, and influenced the young John Wayne.*

△ DURING A TRIP *back east to Illinois in 1868, Earp fell in love with and married Urilla Sutherland. He planned to remain in Illinois with her, but when she died of typhoid in 1869, Earp headed back out west permanently.*

> "Fast is fine, but accuracy is everything."
>
> WYATT EARP

Did you know?

- While living in Los Angeles, Earp worked as a miner, policeman, and real-estate speculator.

- A lifelong lawman, Earp was also an inveterate gambler.

- As a referee in a San Francisco boxing match in 1896, Earp reportedly took off his jacket in the ring, exposing his pistol, and was fined $50 for carrying a concealed weapon.

△ THE GUNFIGHT AT THE O.K. CORRAL *lasted less than a minute, and didn't actually take place at the corral, but approximately 90 yards down a nearby alley.*

THE RENAISSANCE

THE RENAISSANCE, THE EUROPEAN TRANSITIONAL MOVEMENT between medieval to modern times, began in the 14th century until 1527, when Rome was sacked by Holy Roman Emperor Charles V's troops.

"Renaissance" is French for "rebirth, and indeed, the period saw rapid growth of commerce, the discovery of new continents, and a multitude of technological advances. Perhaps the most lasting influence of the Renaissance upon the world springs from the period's great flowering of thought and art. Dante Alighieri produced the Renaissance's greatest and most enduring work of literature, *The Divine Comedy*. Nicolo Machiavelli's *The Prince* (based partly upon the exploits of the Borgia family) provided the world with a cornerstone of contemporary political theory. Michelangelo's sculptures and paintings influenced the course of art for centuries to come. But the Renaissance spirit found its embodiment in Leonardo da Vinci, a genius who made innumerable contributions to science and art.

△ AN ENGRAVING FROM A SERIES OF PRINTS *called* Nova Reperta (New Discoveries), *published in Antwerp in the 1580s; each print depicted aspects of Renaissance achievements and inventions.*

MICHELANGELO
(1475–1564)

ITALIAN SCULPTOR, painter, architect, and poet Michelangelo was among the greatest artists of the Italian Renaissance.

△ MICHELANGELO, *in a 1560 engraving. His father, a nobleman, was initally against his son becoming an artist.*

RENAISSANCE MAN

Born Michelangelo Buonarroti in Caprese, Michelangelo became an apprentice at age 13 to prominent Florentine painter Domenico Ghirlandajo. After only one year, Michelangelo left, claiming there was nothing more for him to learn. Soon he was taken under the wing of Florentine prince Lorenzo de Medici, and began to study sculpture. After Lorenzo died, the Medici family fell from power, and amid the political turmoil, Michelangelo left for Rome. He received his first major commission in Rome through a local banker—the large-scale *Bacchus*, followed two years later by the *Pieta*, now in St. Peter's Basilica. These achievements brought him grand-scale commissions from popes and other distinguished clients, but it was his colossal sculpture *David*, commisioned by a Florentine merchant guild in 1504, that established him as Italy's greatest sculptor. Called to Rome by Pope Julius II, Michelangelo began his commission to paint the ceiling of the Sistine Chapel, a massive space filled with hundreds of biblical figures. Later in his life, Michelangelo devoted himself to architecture and poetry until his death at 88.

△ DETAIL FROM THE SISTINE CHAPEL, The Creation of Adam. *It took Michelangelo four years (1508-1512) to paint the ceiling. Despite its enormity, Michelangelo did almost all of the work alone.*

The original David is now in the Galleria dell'Accademia and a replica was placed in the Palazzo Vecchio. Both sculptures are 13.5 feet high.

DANTE ALIGHIERI
(1265–1321)

ITALIAN POET DANTE ALIGHIERI wrote *La Divina Commedia* (*The Divine Comedy*), the great poetic composition of the Middle Ages and the first masterpiece to be written in the Italian language.

THE POET

Born to an aristocratic family, Dante was raised in luxury and provided with a good education. He began writing poetry in his youth, and his poems to Beatrice, the young woman he loved from afar, inspired his whole creative life. A deeply political man, Dante served the city-state of Florence as a politician and as a soldier.

△ DETAIL *from a 14th-century* Commedia.

He wrote *De monarchia* as a statement of his political philosophy. Fearing for the independence of Florence, he opposed the rule of Pope Boniface VIII and was exiled in 1302. *La Divina Commedia* was written during his exile. The poem tells of the poet's journey to God through Hell, Purgatory, and Heaven. Written in vernacular Italian instead of the customary Latin, it helped establish Italian as a literary language. Its imaginative style and powerful verse make it a seminal work of medieval literature and an enduring classic.

△ DANTE'S Divine Comedy *has inspired many artists, including English artist and poet William Blake. Seen here is a painting of the mythical Greek giant Antaeus (1824), one of his many illustrations for the poem.*

△ ORIGINALLY PLANNED *to adorn the facade of the Florence Cathedral; the David was instead put in front of the Palazzo Vecchio.*

Did you know?

■ Michelangelo was the first artist to have his biography published while he was still alive.

■ He worked on and off for more than 40 years on a tomb for Pope Julius II, claiming: "I find I have lost all my youth bound to this tomb."

△ A 19TH CENTURY PAINTING DEPICTING DANTE IN EXILE. *After Dante departed from Florence, he lived in Verona, Poppi, Lucca, and finally Ravenna, where he eventually died in 1321.*

Did you know?

■ During his exile, Dante was twice offered a pardon by the citizens of Florence, but he refused each time. Consequently, he and his children were sentenced to death as rebels should they ever return to the city.

■ Dante only saw Beatrice three times: the first when he was 9, then again when he was 18 and 25.

LUCREZIA BORGIA
(1480–1519)

BORN INTO THE INFAMOUS and influential Borgia family, Lucrezia Borgia was a central figure in the Italian Renaissance. Daughter of Cardinal Rodrigo Borgia (later Pope Alexander VI) and sister of the power-hungry Cesare, she became the pawn through which the Borgias amassed political power.

LUCREZIA BORGIA

THE TOOL OF POWER

When she was only 11 years of age, Lucrezia was married to her first husband, Giovanni Sforza, in an attempt to form an allegiance between the Borgias and Sforzas against the Aragonese dynasty of Naples. But when Lucrezia's father banded with Naples and Giovanni fled in fear of his life, the marriage was annulled. Lucrezia then married Alfonso, Duke of Bisceglie, in order to strengthen the Borgias' ties with Naples. However, Cesare formed an alliance against Naples and had a servant murder Alfonso. For her final marriage, in order to secure Cesare's position in Romagna in northern Italy, Lucrezia was wed to Alfonso d'Este, son of the Duke of Ferrara. Cesare, again for political expediency, wanted to annul her marriage, but this time, both her husband and his father refused; they had become fond of Lucrezia, and also did not want to return her dowry. After the death of her father (1503) and brother (1507), she became a patron of the arts, and in her final years turned to religion.

▷ AN 1870 FRENCH MAGAZINE COVER *depicts a caricature of actress Marie Laurent, who starred in the play* Lucrece Borgia, *Victor Hugo's dramatization of Lucrezia's life.*

△ PRE-RAPHAELITE *artist Dante Gabriel Rossetti painted* The Borgia Family (1863); *Lucrezia sits between Cesare on the left and her father on the right.*

Did you know?

■ The Borgia line produced two popes.

■ Sforza accused Lucrezia of sleeping with her father, Alexander. Her attendance at an orgy in Alexander's Vatican fueled this claim.

■ Between marriages she was seen with a young boy named Giovanni, rumored to be her son by either her brother Cesare or her father.

LEONARDO DA VINCI
(1452–1519)

ITALIAN PAINTER, sculptor, architect, musician, scientist, and inventor Leonardo da Vinci created some of the world's most famous works of art. He remains the epitome of Renaissance genius.

THE ORIGINAL RENAISSANCE MAN

Leonardo was born the illegitimate son of a Florentine official and a peasant woman. At age 15 he was apprenticed to Andrea del Verrocchio, a leading Florentine artist. After his apprenticeship, he stayed on as Verrocchio's assistant. Around 1481, da Vinci received his first major church commission, to paint *Adoration of the Magi*, now in the Uffizi Museum. He accepted the post of court artist for the Duke of Milan in 1482, where he stayed for 16 years, recording in notebooks his observations on a broad range of subjects including anatomy, painting, town planning, mechanics, and architecture. *The Last Supper* and *The Virgin of the Rocks* altarpiece were painted while he served in Milan. After the French overthrew the Duke in 1499, da Vinci returned to Florence in 1500 as a renowned artist. He came back to Milan in 1506 to pursue his interests in scientific affairs, specifically anatomy, until he left for Rome in 1513. In 1516, Da Vinci was made part of the court of French King Francis I, in the town of Amboise, France, staying there until his death.

Did you know?

■ Niccolò Machiavelli and da Vinci were friends.

■ His inventions include the bicycle, the diving suit, and the escalator.

■ He often wrote notes backward, as a form of code, requiring a mirror to read them.

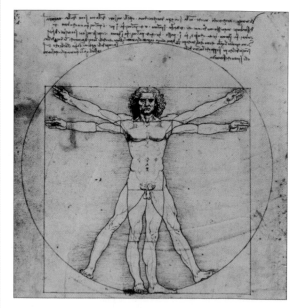

△ DA VINCI *drew* Vitruvian Man *in 1492; his anatomical studies were so precise that they are still accurate today.*

MACHIAVELLI
(1469–1527)

A DIPLOMAT AND POLITICIAN in Renaissance Florence, Niccolò Machiavelli's political works, in particular *The Prince*, established him as the father of modern political theory.

POLITICS AND FATE

Machiavelli was born at a time when Italy was divided into four rival city-states and, therefore, at the mercy of stronger governments in the rest of Europe. The young Machiavelli became a minor diplomat after the temporary fall of Florence's ruling family, the Medici, in 1494. Because he was involved in an unsuccessful attempt to organize a Florentine militia against the return of the Medici to power in 1512, Machiavelli was tortured and banished from any active role in political life. He used the opportunity, however, to read Roman history and to write political treatises, most notably *The Prince*. The main theme of this short work about monarchal rule and survival is man's capacity for determining his own destiny in opposition to the power of fate. This has been interpreted that one may resort to any means in order to establish and preserve total authority.

△ ONLY TWO OF MACHIAVELLI'S *works were published while he was alive: the satirical play* The Mandrake *(1524) and his treatise* On the Art of War *(1521).*

Did you know?

- While many believe the character of "the prince" was based upon the infamous Cesare Borgia, some scholars feel it is a satire.

- Machiavelli liked to shock his associates by appearing more shameless than he truly was, earning himself a reputation for deviousness.

- Pope Clement VIII condemned *The Prince* for its endorsement of rule by deceit and fear.

Other Italian Masters

RAPHAEL (1483–1520) His informal, animated style had great influence on future artists.

ANDREA DEL SARTO (1486–1531) The fresco artist known as the "Faultless Painter."

GIOTTO (1266–1337) First genius of Italian Renaissance, master of perspective and emotion.

△ THIS MASTERFUL SELF-PORTRAIT *was drawn by da Vinci in 1512, while living in Milan.*

▷ A FLORENTINE *merchant's wife was da Vinci's model for the* Mona Lisa *(1503).*

∧ MACHIAVELLI'S TOMB *is in the church of Santa Croce, in Florence—which he was banned from entering during the last years of his life (he lived just outside of the city).*

> "Since love and fear can hardly exist together, if we must choose between them, it is far safer to be feared than loved."
>
> NICCOLO MACHIAVELLI

WATCHING TWO PEOPLE CHAT WITH ONE ANOTHER DOES NOT, ON THE FACE OF IT, sound very entertaining, but since the inception of television, the talk show has proven itself one of the medium's most popular and enduring forms of programming.

The great talk-show hosts are a varied lot. Steve Allen helped create the modern late-night talk-show format as host of "The Tonight Show" in its first incarnation. Jack Paar followed Allen as host of "The Tonight Show," but made it his own with his quirky behavior and an odd assortment of guests. Johnny Carson sat behind "The Tonight Show" desk after Paar, and was a late-night TV institution for more than 30 years. Most recently, Oprah Winfrey has used her position as a pioneering daytime-TV talk-show host to build a media empire. And then there was Groucho Marx, whose vaudevillian roots made him a sardonic foil for his unwitting guests. For more than 50 years, Americans have invited such hosts into their homes and, through them, have met the world.

△ TALK SHOW HOSTS *make people comfortable, and no one did that quite as well as Johnny Carson in his stint on* The Tonight Show. *Rumor has it that occasionally a guest's mug held something stronger than coffee.*

OPRAH WINFREY
b. 1954

OPRAH WINFREY'S MEDIA SAVVY, empathetic personality, and business acumen have made her a one-woman multimedia powerhouse.

△ OPRAH'S *media empire ranges from print to TV to movies.*

QUEEN OF THE AIRWAVES
Born in Kosciusko, Mississippi, Winfrey endured an abusive childhood while living with her mother in Milwaukee. In her mid-teens she went to Nashville to live with her father, Vernon, a strict disciplinarian who emphasized the importance of education. In 1971 she enrolled at Tennessee State University and took a job as a reporter at Nashville radio station WVOL. The next year, she broke into television as the first African-American anchor at local CBS affiliate WTVF-TV.

After graduation, Winfrey worked as a reporter and co-anchor at Baltimore's WJZ-TV, and became the popular host of the chat program "People Are Talking." After eight years, Winfrey moved to Chicago to host "A.M. Chicago," a morning show losing the ratings battle to talk-show king Phil Donahue. Contrary to expectations, the show shot to number one in the ratings. In 1985 it became "The Oprah Winfrey Show" and quickly found success with a national audience. Winfrey renegotiated her contract and took ownership of the show, starting her own production company.

The show remains wildly successful. Winfrey's well-publicized struggle to stay fit has inspired millions to take on similar challenges, and the show's Book Club segment has revitalized interest in reading quality fiction.

Late Night Stars

DAVID LETTERMAN b. 1947 Sardonic host of "Late Night."

JAY LENO b. 1950 Stand-up comedian who took Johnny's chair on "The Tonight Show."

△ WHEN TALK SHOWS *in the 1990s turned to risqué topics, Winfrey, here with Vice-President Al Gore, eschewed sensationalism.*

JACK PAAR
b. 1918

JACK PAAR HAD NO SINGING, dancing, or acting talent, but he was blessed with "the gift of gab." That gift was enough to endear him to millions of American television viewers during his tenure as host of NBC's "The Tonight Show."

BULL IN HIS OWN CHINA SHOP

Paar was born in Canton, Ohio. He began a career in radio, and as a comedian in a US Army special services unit he entertained troops during World War II. After the war, Paar landed roles in a handful of early-1950s movies. In 1952 he made his first forays into television, hosting game shows and variety shows. He replaced Steve Allen to become the second host of NBC's "The Tonight Show" in 1957. His eccentric guest list, including such varied personalities as Nobel Peace Prize-winner Albert Schweitzer and actor Peter Ustinov, complemented Paar's eccentric personality. Paar was notorious for feuding with prominent reporters such as Walter Winchell, as well as with NBC executives. He once walked off "The Tonight Show" just minutes into the program when NBC censored a joke about a "water closet." He left the show in 1962 and hosted a weekly variety show until 1965, when he bought and managed a television station in Poland Spring, Maine. In 1975 he briefly hosted a show as part of the ABC Wide World of Entertainment, his last hosting job to date.

△ **PAAR WITH TWO ADMIRERS** *in front of a Channel 4 sign. After walking off the set of "The Tonight Show" at the beginning of a live show, he returned five weeks later.*

Did you know?

■ Paar dropped out of high school in the 10th grade to take a job as a radio announcer and DJ.

■ In 1961 he broadcast live from the newly erected Berlin Wall.

■ The first US prime-time footage of the Beatles was aired in 1964 on *The Jack Paar Show.*

> "My life seems like one long obstacle course with me as the chief obstacle."
>
> JACK PAAR

△ **OPRAH RECEIVED** *a special honor at the 1999 National Book Awards for her ongoing contribution to reading and the publishing industry.*

Did you know?

■ She is one of just three women to have owned their own film studios. The others were Lucille Ball and Mary Pickford.

■ Winfrey earned an Academy Award nomination for her performance as Sofia in Steven Spielberg's 1985 adaptation of the novel, *The Color Purple.*

■ Winfrey has been romantically linked to PR executive Stedman Graham since 1992.

▷ **PAAR IN A SKETCH** *with a few of his regulars on "The Tonight Show." Not as adept at sketch comedy, he more often relied on his monologues, and discoveries, such as Bill Cosby and Bob Newhart, for laughs.*

Jack Paar

Tonight Show *announcer* Jack Haskell

Orchestra leader Jose Melis

Actress Edie Adams

JOHNNY CARSON
b. 1925

FOR MORE THAN 30 YEARS, millions of Americans tuned in each night to Johnny Carson's late-night television talk show, "The Tonight Show." Carson's sophisticated and sometimes risqué humor and affable Midwestern charm endeared him to both viewers and celebrity guests, helping to make "The Tonight Show" one of NBC's highest-rated programs for three decades.

△ **CARNAC THE MAGNIFICENT** *was probably the most popular of the characters Carson performed on the show.*

Did you know?

■ An estimated 50 million viewers tuned in to Johnny Carson's final appearance as host of "The Tonight Show."

■ On a December 19, 1973, show, Carson joked that a toilet-paper shortage was taking place. Millions around the country took him seriously.

HEEEERE'S JOHNNY!

John William Carson was born in Corning, Iowa. He graduated from the University of Nebraska in 1949 and moved to Hollywood in the early 1950s. His low-budget TV show, "Carson's Cellar," attracted the attention of celebrities such as Groucho Marx and Red Skelton, and in 1954 Carson began working for "The Red Skelton Show" as a writer and performer, which in 1958 led to a job in New York City hosting "Who Do You Trust?," a successful daytime game show. Carson frequently filled in as guest host of Jack Paar's "The Tonight Show" from 1958 until 1962, when he became the show's full-time host. The show moved location to Los Angeles in 1972. Carson continued to sit behind the desk on the set of "The Tonight Show" until his graceful exit on May 22, 1992.

△ **ALTHOUGH LONGTIME** *sidekick Ed McMahon opened the show for decades, Groucho Marx introduced Johnny on his first program in 1962.*

GROUCHO MARX
(1895–1977)

GROUCHO MARX, one of the 20th century's greatest comic minds, influenced many of today's leading comedians.

WHY A DUCK?

Julius Henry Marx, born in New York City, was the third of five performing boys of Minnie Schoenberg—who came from a long line of entertainers—and Sam "Frenchie" Marx. The brothers' 1914 vaudeville act, "Home Again," drew crowds and critical acclaim in the United States and England and served as a springboard for their 1924 Broadway debut in *I'll Say She Is*. Broadway productions of *Cocoanuts* (1925) and *Animal Crackers* (1928) quickly followed, and were eventually made into motion pictures. The Marx Brothers' unique mix of physical and verbal comedy—led by Groucho's quick-witted, thinly veiled barbs and comedic asides—translated well to the silver screen, winning the brothers box office success and critical acclaim. A string of Marx Brothers films followed, highlighted by *Animal Crackers* (1930), *Duck Soup* (1933), *A Night at the Opera* (1935), and *A Day at the Races* (1937). The Marx Brothers disbanded in 1949, and in 1950 Groucho began hosting the television version of "You Bet Your Life," a quiz show he had hosted on radio since 1947. The show focused less on prizes and questions than on the wisecracks aimed at contestants and ran for 11 years. After its cancellation, Groucho continued performing and making movies until the early 1970s.

Did you know?

■ Groucho's mustache was usually painted on.

■ Writer William Peter Blatty appeared on "You Bet Your Life" and used his winnings to continue his work on *The Exorcist*.

■ Marx had a long correspondence with famed poet T. S. Eliot.

◁ **GROUCHO MARX** *in 1952. He was the first Marx brother to enter show business, as a boy soprano.*

▽ THE MARX BROTHERS *were, from left, Harpo, Groucho, Chico, and Zeppo—featured on a poster for the 1933 film,* Duck Soup.

STEVE ALLEN
(1921–2000)

LIFELONG TELEVISION entertainer Steve Allen was best known as the first host of "The Tonight Show." He also was an accomplished musician, composer, author, and actor, with many books, musical compositions, and films to his credit.

"STEVERINO"

Steve Allen was born in New York City to parents in vaudeville. After the death of his father, Allen and his mother moved to Chicago. In 1947 he began hosting a radio talk show for the Los Angeles CBS affiliate and made frequent television appearances.

△ ALLEN COMPOSED *more than 5,000 pieces of music, including film scores and songs for the Broadway musical* Sophie.

Those appearances helped Allen make a name for himself in the burgeoning television industry, and in 1953 he created "The Tonight Show" for a local New York television station. The show's format—a new fusion of talk show and variety show—was an unqualified success and NBC took it national in 1954. Allen's clever monologues, quirky supporting characters, and wide variety of guests helped create the pattern for contemporary late-night talk shows. Allen in 1956 left "The Tonight Show," but continued hosting television shows, writing books, and acting until his death.

Did you know?

■ On "The Tonight Show" Allen delivered his monologues sitting in front of a piano and would often punctuate his comments with riffs on the instrument.

■ Allen wrote more than 50 books, including volumes of poetry, humor, social criticism, and biblical analysis.

"Quote me as saying I was misquoted."

GROUCHO MARX

▷ *Marianne Gaba was Groucho's cohostess on "You Bet Your Life" in 1958.*

△ BANDLEADER SKITCH HENDERSON *and Allen's wife Jayne Meadows join him at Sardi's Restaurant in 1958 to celebrate their place on the wall.*

COMMUNIST REVOLUTIONARIES

THE POLITICAL AND ECONOMIC PHILOSOPHY that became known as communism claims that a society should share its property and work load communally, with all benefits distributed according to need.

COMMUNIST POLITICAL BUTTON, C. 1935

Once these conditions were met by the state, a utopic society could emerge, and the need for the state would "wither away." Ironically, this philosophy, conceived by Karl Marx and Friedrich Engels in the mid-19th century, led to the establishment of some of the most repressive governments in history. The world's first communist state, the Soviet Union, emerged in 1917 when V.I. Lenin's Bolshevik Party seized power in Russia. The Red Army, led by Leon Trotsky, quashed anti-Bolshevik forces in the ensuing civil war. Communism spread to China; after 1949, Mao Zedong adapted it to his country's needs and to his own ambition. In Cuba, Fidel Castro and Che Guevara established a dictatorship in 1959 that survived the Cold War.

△ THIS 1995 MOSCOW RALLY *marking the 78th anniversary of the Bolshevik Revolution demonstrates the continuing appeal of communism for many people, even after the end of the Cold War in the late 1980s.*

V. I. LENIN
(1870–1924)

LENIN WAS THE LEADER of the Bolshevik Party, the leader of the first Soviet state, and among the most influential statesmen of the 20th century.

THE FATHER OF THE SOVIET UNION

Born Vladimir Ilyich Ulyanov, Lenin was drawn into revolutionary activity early in life: His brother Aleksandr was executed in 1887 for plotting to assassinate Tsar Alexander III. In the autumn of that year Lenin entered Kazan University to study law, but was expelled in the winter for demonstrating. He moved to his mother's home in Kokushkino, studied Marx, and completed his law degree at Saint Petersburg University in 1892. He practiced law only briefly, devoting himself to revolutionary activities. Lenin was exiled to Siberia from 1895 to 1900, and then moved to London to begin working on the revolutionary newspaper *Iskra* ("The Spark"). He attended the meeting of the Russian Social Democratic Labor Party in 1903 (held in Brussels and London), where the party split into two factions: the Bolsheviks, led by Lenin, and the Mensheviks, led by Georgi Plekhanov. During the early years of World War I Lenin lived in Switzerland, but when the Russian Revolution broke out in 1917, he made his way back to Russia, aided by the Germans —they allowed Lenin to cross their borders in a sealed railway car, hoping he would help ruin the Russian war effort. After a failed uprising, he fled to Finland, but quickly returned to bring the Bolsheviks to power, creating the world's first communist state. Lenin soon became dictator. He negotiated an armistice with Germany, abolished private land ownership, nationalized banks, and replaced all religion with official atheism while his police force suppressed opposition. After a 1918 assassination attempt and a 1922 stroke, his health declined until his death in 1924.

△ A LENIN MURAL *in St. Petersburg. The former royal capital was renamed Leningrad in 1924 in Lenin's honor, and reverted in 1991.*

▷ A WELL-KNOWN SOVIET-ERA PAINTING, *Valentin Serov's* Lenin Proclaiming Soviet Power *(c. 1940s) originally depicted Stalin standing next to Lenin. In 1957, one year after Nikita Khrushchev's "thaw" of Stalinist policies, Serov painted a group of workers and soldiers over Stalin's image.*

Did you know?

- For many years in Paris, Lenin's mistress Inessa Armand lived next door to him and his wife Nadezhda Krupskaya.

- Despite their comfortable upbringing, five of the Ulyanov children became revolutionaries.

- After his death, Lenin's body was embalmed and placed in a mausoleum.

△ STATUE OF LENIN *in Red Square, Moscow.*

▽ A PROLIFIC WRITER. *Lenin's collected works fill 45 volumes; his writings were highly respected by his followers and widely translated. Below are Russian, French, and German editions of several different treatises.*

"So long as the state exists, there is no freedom. When there is freedom, there will be no state."

LENIN

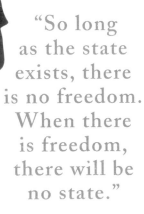

◁ LENIN, *1922. Although he suffered a stroke in 1922, that year Lenin succeeded in the total elimination of all opposition within the Communist party.*

Joseph Stalin

Vladimir Lenin

Mikhail I. Kalinin

△ AT THE EIGHTH MEETING *of the Bolshevik Communist Party, held in Moscow in March 1919, Stalin sat at Lenin's right hand, though Lenin would later turn against him.*

MAO ZEDONG
(1893–1976)

MAO ZEDONG, an important Marxist theorist, became one of the founders of the People's Republic of China and the chairman of China's Communist Party.

CHAIRMAN MAO

Mao Zedong was born to a prosperous Hunan peasant family. After the overthrow of the Manchu Dynasty, he rose through the ranks of the Communist party and in the early 1930s set up a communist government in Jiangxi to rival the nationalist, or Guomindang, authorities. Driven out by the Guomindang in 1934, Mao led the 6,000-mile Long March to Yan'an to reestablish communist power. With the Japanese invasion of 1937 (the Second Sino-Japanese War, 1937–45), the Chinese united and Mao's popularity grew. Civil war broke out at the war's end and in 1949 the Communists drove out the Guomindang. As party chairman, in 1950 Mao led China into the Korean War and instituted massive agrarian reforms as part of the Great Leap Forward, an economic plan that failed, resulting in mass starvation. His belief in the need for constant revolution spawned the Cultural Revolution from 1966 to 1969, which brutally destroyed any remnants of pre-communist China. During this time, while working with the Gang of Four, a group of politicians that included his wife, Jiang Qing, Mao eliminated his enemies. In the 1970s he worked to establish ties with the US—an action that, ironically, helped lay the ground for China's turn to free markets.

△ A POEM *by Mao. Despite the anti-intellectual stance of the Cultural Revolution, Mao was himself a poet.*

△ MAO ZEDONG *in his trademark uniform (undated photo). By 1958, he had forced almost the entire population of China into work communes.*

> "Political power grows out of the barrel of a gun."
>
> MAO ZEDONG

△ MAO SPEAKS AT A RALLY, *c. 1930. In 1931 he was elected chairman of the new Soviet Republic of China, in Jiangxi province.*

▷ CHINESE CHILDREN (*c. 1968*) *hold copies of Mao's* Little Red Book, *a collection of his sayings that solidified his personality cult, especially among students.*

Did you know?

■ Mao's childhood heroes included George Washington and Napoleon Bonaparte.

■ Mao's body is preserved in a building at Tiananmen Square, in Beijing.

■ At least 20 million Chinese starved to death during Mao's Great Leap Forward economic reform.

FIDEL CASTRO

b. 1926

DICTATOR OF CUBA for more than 40 years, Fidel Castro has ruled one of the few surviving bastions of communism in the post-Cold War world.

THE GUERRILLA PRINCE

The son of a plantation owner, Castro was a gifted athlete and received a doctorate in law from the University of Havana. He was running for a seat in parliament when General Fulgencio Batista staged a coup. Cuban courts threw out Castro's petitions against Batista, at which point he organized a rebel force. Imprisoned and exiled, Castro returned to Cuba in 1956 with a small band of revolutionaries to wage a guerrilla campaign that in 1959 finally overthrew Batista. Though not originally a communist, Castro transformed Cuba into a totalitarian socialist state. He nationalized private commerce and industry and instituted sweeping land reforms. He created a one-party government, and made education and health care free to all Cubans.

His nationalization of U.S.-owned businesses, the 1961 declaration of his Marxist-Leninist philosophies, and strong ties to Russia all led to hostile relations with the United States, which culminated in the failed invasion of Cuba at the Bay of Pigs, followed by the Cuban Missile Crisis. Cuba's political isolation and economic policies have led to widespread poverty, but Castro remains the country's central political figure.

△ A 1974 CUBAN STAMP *depicts Soviet leader Leonid Brezhnev and Fidel Castro joining hands. The Soviet Union was Cuba's main trading partner and sustained the Cuban economy through the 1970s, but since the fall of Soviet communism, Cuba has suffered.*

Communist Theorists

KARL MARX
(1818–1883) German creator of Marxism.

FRIEDRICH ENGELS
(1820–1895) Co-author of *The Communist Manifesto*

GEORG HEGEL
(1770–1831) Philosopher; Marx adapted his theory of history and dialectic.

Lt. Universo Sanchez, Castro's adjutant

Fidel Castro (his brother Raoul is in the center foreground

George Sotus, aide-de-camp

△ CASTRO SWINGS *the bat to open the Cuban baseball season in a 1960s game. In his late teens, he was a minor league pitching prospect for the Pittsburgh Pirates, but they decided his fastball was not good enough. Castro left organized baseball and went on to law school in Havana.*

◁ CASTRO AND THE COMMANDERS *of his revolutionary force pose at a secret base in the Cuban mountains, July 1957.*

Did you know?

■ Only 12 rebels remained with Castro after his second coup attempt, but by 1959 the guerilla force had grown to 800 men.

■ Castro speaks fluent English, but refuses to do so in public.

■ Castro's daughter, Alina Fernandez Revuelta, defected to the US in 1993.

CHE GUEVARA
(1928–1967)

ONE OF FIDEL CASTRO'S TOP LIEUTENANTS and closest friends, lifelong revolutionary Che Guevara embodies for many the idealism and romance of revolution.

REVOLUTIONARY DOCTOR

Born Ernesto Guevara to a politically active middle-class family in Rosario, Argentina, Che became a voracious reader of Marx and Engels. After studying to become a doctor, he traveled extensively across Latin America, ending up in Mexico City in 1954. There he met Fidel Castro. The two men formed a lasting friendship and in 1956 left for Cuba to overthrow dictator Fulgencio Batista. Guevara had joined Castro's army as a doctor, but his heroics as a guerrilla warrior soon made him a commandante. After the revolution, he became president of the Cuban National Bank, moving Cuban trade away from the US to the USSR. He acted as minister of industry from 1961 to 1965, helping to guide Cuba's transition to communism. Guevara eventually left Cuba to support revolutions in Africa and Latin America. He was captured in Bolivia and executed by the Bolivian army.

Did you know?

■ There is some debate as to how the nickname "Che" originated. Some attribute it to an Italian word meaning buddy or chum.

■ Che's severe asthma played a major role in his decision to study medicine in Argentina.

■ Che's remains weren't returned to Cuba until 1997.

△ CHE (LEFT) AND CASTRO (CENTER) *with a third comrade, in the 1950s, meet in their Sierra Maestra stronghold. Che served as Castro's doctor during the revolution, but he also trained as a guerrilla fighter and became Castro's chief lieutenant soon after the rebel invasion of Cuba in 1956.*

Other Red Guerillas

ROSA LUXEMBURG (1870–1919) co-founder of German Communist party, murdered in 1919 uprising.

NIKOLAI BUKHARIN (1888–1938) *Pravda* editor, politburo member, executed by Stalin .

△ STILL A REVERED *figure in Cuba, Che's image decorates the outside of the Ministry of Defense building in Havana.*

△ A BILLBOARD *in Havana. In the late 1960s Che broke with the Soviets and eventually Castro himself, becoming an advocate of worldwide violent revolution.*

▷ A PHOTOGRAPH OF CHE *in China, November 1960, paying a state visit to China as head of the Cuban government economic delegation. The two countries signed the first Agreement on Economic and Technical Cooperation.*

LEON TROTSKY

(1879–1940)

MARXIST THEORIST LEON TROTSKY was one of the leaders of the October Revolution—the 1917 Bolshevik coup that brought defeat to the czarist Russian government—and commissar of foreign affairs and war under Lenin.

FATHER OF THE RED ARMY

Born Lev Davidovich Bronstein, Trotstky began studying Marxism in 1896, and in 1898 was arrested and exiled to Siberia for revolutionary activity. He escaped to London on a forged passport, and there met Lenin. Trotsky returned to Russia in 1917 after Tsar Nicholas II was overthrown, and helped Lenin bring the Bolsheviks—a faction of the Russian Social Democratic Labor Party—to power in the October Revolution. He led the Red Army to victory in the brutal civil war that followed the revolution. After Lenin's 1924 death, Trotsky, though favored by Lenin to succeed him, lost the ensuing power struggle when Stalin was named general secretary of the Communist party. Exiled once more, Trotsky devoted himself to writing and to anti-Stalin agitation. In 1937, Stalin had Trotsky sentenced to death for treason by a Soviet court. He was assassinated with an ice pick wielded by a Stalinist agent in Mexico City on August 20, 1940.

Did you know?

- Trotsky took his name from the head jailer at the Odessa prison where he was held.

- Lenin and Trotsky worked together on the newspaper *Iskra* ("The Spark").

◁ HAMMER AND SICKLE, *symbol on Soviet flag, created in 1918; symbolizes peasants (sickle) uniting with workers (hammer). The red field denotes blood spilled by workers in the fight for freedom.*

△ TROTSKY ON A HUNTING TRIP *in the Caucasus, March 1924. A hunting enthusiastic, he claimed in his autobiography that "the attraction in hunting is that it acts on the mind as a poultice does on a sore."*

◁ TROTSKY WAS RESPONSIBLE *for growing the Red Army from 800,000 soldiers to nearly 3 million during the Russian Civil War.*

"The end might justify the means as long as there is something that justifies the end."

LEON TROTSKY

△ TROTSKY TOOK REFUGE *in Mexico in 1936, where he and his wife (far left) stayed with the painter Frida Kahlo (second from left), wife of muralist Diego Rivera.*

TYCOONS & MOGULS

THE INCREDIBLE ADVANCES IN INDUSTRY, BUSINESS, AND TECHNOLOGY over the last two centuries have produced mountains of wealth for an enterprising few.

From John D. Rockefeller's Standard Oil to Bill Gates's Microsoft Corporation, these tycoons and moguls faced competition with ingenuity and a dash of ruthlessness, reinvented industries through innovation, and, in many cases, built modern-day empires from the ground up.

Pursuing the American dream paid off for each of these moguls and tycoons. Millions of other people also were affected by their actions, which have helped to transform entire industries. Some observers and historians deplore the results, which include great concentrations of wealth and economic power in the hands of a very few. Others applaud the great capitalists for their charitable giving and for the economic growth they fuel. Such contradictions are what make these moguls and tycoons so fascinating.

△ THE NEW YORK STOCK EXCHANGE, *hub of global capitalism, began with a 1792 agreement signed by New York stock brokers—under a buttonwood tree—to form an investment community with five stocks.*

SAM WALTON
(1918–1992)

SAM WALTON FOUNDED and built the largest retail-sales chain in the United States, revolutionizing the retail business in the process.

HIGH VOLUME, LOW PRICES

Born in Kingfish, Oklahoma, Walton graduated from the University of Missouri in 1940 with a degree in economics. He began his retail career as a management trainee at a J.C. Penney department store, and later managed a group of retail franchise stores with his brother. In 1962 he opened the first "Wal-Mart" discount store in Arkansas. Wal-Mart became a national chain of stores in small towns and rural areas, offering low prices supported by high-volume purchases. His stores were so successful that many local merchants were forced to close their doors because of the competition.

Walton's leadership and celebrated hands-on management style made Wal-Mart the nation's largest retailer by the early 1990s, with more than 1,700 stores nationwide. Walton served as Wal-Mart's president and CEO until 1988. He died of cancer in 1992.

Other Retail Giants

FRANK WOOLWORTH (1852–1919) Inventor of the five-and-dime.

AARON WARD (1843–1913) Creator of catalog shopping.

MARSHALL FIELD (1834–1906) High-end retail pioneer and philanthropist.

△ WALTON, *at a 1986 conference. By 1991 he was the richest man in America.*

△ A WAL-MART IN RHODE ISLAND, 1997. *The first store opened in 1962, in Bentonville, Arkansas, the same year as the first K-Mart.*

JOHN D. ROCKEFELLER
(1839–1937)

JOHN D. ROCKEFELLER, founder of the Standard Oil Company, was an enormously wealthy industrialist and philanthropist in America.

THE WORLD'S OILMAN

Rockefeller was born in Richford, New York, to a farm family that also traded commodities such as salt and lumber. The family moved in 1853 to Cleveland, Ohio, where Rockefeller began his career as a bookkeeper at a salary of $3.50 per week. After a few years, he and business partner Maurice B. Clark formed an extremely successful wholesale grocery business. In 1864, Rockefeller married Laura Celestia Spellman, daughter of a prosperous businessman. Together they had four children, in whom they instilled a sense of industry and public responsibility.

In 1865 Rockefeller left the wholesale grocery business to enter the oil industry. The oil business at that time was characterized by numerous small operators, cutthroat competition, overproduction, and alternating periods of boom and bust. Rockefeller's emphasis on efficiency soon had his oil refinery, Standard Oil, producing twice as much as any of the other nearly 30 refineries in Cleveland. In 1872, Rockefeller offered to buy out all the other Cleveland oil companies, and over the next few years Standard Oil became a regional monopoly. He then moved Standard Oil's corporate headquarters to New York City; by 1884 the company was responsible for 80 to 90 percent of the oil produced in the United States.

The federal government repeatedly prosecuted Standard Oil for violating antitrust laws, which forbid businesses from monopolizing a market or restraining free trade. The company broke apart into several smaller companies in 1911. Rockefeller had by this time made an enormous fortune. His interests turned to philanthropy. He donated generous sums to the University of Chicago and in 1901 founded the Rockefeller Institute for Medical Research (now Rockefeller University), and the Rockefeller Foundation (1913).

△ **WALTON** *began computerizing Wal-Mart operations as early as 1966.*

> "High expectations are the key to everything."
>
> SAM WALTON

Did you know?

■ As a child during the depression, Walton helped with family finances by delivering newspapers and milking cows.

■ Walton was awarded the Presidential Medal of Freedom in March 1992 by President George Bush, Sr., who referred to him as "an American original who…epitomizes the American dream."

■ During World War II, Walton served as a US Army intelligence officer.

◁ **ROCKEFELLER** *gave away more than half a billion dollars in his lifetime.*

△ **LOCATED ON THE SHORES** *of the Great Lakes and near the oil fields of Pennsylvania, Cleveland was prime for development as an oil center in the late 1860s when Rockefeller began his corporation.*

Did you know?

■ Apart from a three-month college-level bookkeeping course, John D. Rockefeller had no formal education beyond high school.

■ He avoided being drafted in the Civil War by paying a substitute to fight in his place.

■ For years, he taught Sunday school and served on church boards.

BILL GATES
b. 1955

WILLIAM (BILL) HENRY GATES III—computer programmer, entrepreneur, and multibillionaire—co-founded Microsoft Corporation, the world's largest software company, with Paul Allen.

△ AS A PUBLIC FIGURE, BILL GATES *uses his position to urge the adoption of computer technology.*

WINDOWS TO THE FUTURE

Born in Seattle, Washington, Gates demonstrated an affinity for computers at an early age. He dropped out of Harvard University in his junior year to start Microsoft Corporation with his hometown friend Paul G. Allen. In 1981 Gates licensed a personal computer operating system, MS-DOS, to International Business Machines (IBM), then the world's largest computer supplier. With the introduction the same year of the IBM PC, IBM, as well as the many IBM-compatible computer manufacturers, became dependent on Microsoft for software. In 1995, Gates changed his company's focus from software to the Internet, achieving great success with Microsoft's popular Explorer web browser. Microsoft also licensed its flagship product, the Windows operating system, at lower rates to clients who installed its browser. That strategy intensified concerns about Microsoft's power in the marketplace. The US District Court in November 1999 issued a preliminary decision that Microsoft was a monopoly and should be broken up, but a federal appeals court in July 2001 overturned the lower court's order.

△ BILL GATES IN 1984, *the early days of Microsoft; the company's aggressive marketing has paid off.*

Did you know?

■ The Gates family calls him "Trey" in reference to the III after his name.

■ Gates wrote his first computer program at 13.

■ Gates's charitable donations were minimal until his 1994 marriage to Melinda French, a marketing executive at Microsoft. The Bill and Melinda Gates Foundation has since made several billion dollars' worth of donations, primarily to advance literacy.

WILLIAM RANDOLPH HEARST
(1863–1951)

AMERICAN PUBLISHER and media baron William Randolph Hearst built the nation's largest newspaper chain and pioneered sensationalistic tabloid journalism.

CITIZEN HEARST

Born in San Francisco, California, Hearst was the only son of the gold-mine owner and US senator George Hearst. The younger Hearst began his career in 1887 by taking control of a struggling San Francisco newspaper that his father had bought for political reasons. The *San Francisco Examiner* showed a profit within two years thanks to Hearst's unique approach, a combination of investigative reporting and sensationalist writing. In 1895 he used similar tactics to turn around the unsuccessful *New York Morning Journal.* He then moved on to acquire or found a series of other newspapers, in Chicago, Boston, and many other cities. Hearst also built magazines such as *Harper's Bazaar, Cosmopolitan, Good Housekeeping*, and *Town and Country* into profitable operations. Hearst's empire, at its peak, included 20 major newspapers, along with magazines, radio stations, and news and motion picture syndicates.

HEARST FOR MAYOR

MUNICIPAL LEAGUE NOMINATION
MARK YOUR BALLOT IN THE CIRCLE UNDER THE SCALES

△ HEARST LOST HIS BIDS FOR MAYOR *of New York City (1905) and for Governer of New York (1909) after two terms in the House of Representatives.*

△ HEARST BEGAN *plans on his palatial 171-room home, San Simeon, in 1919; it remained unfinished at his death in 1947.*

◁ HEARST, *in the 1930s—Orson Welles' classic 1939 film* Citizen Kane *is based on Hearst's life.*

"In suggesting gifts: money is appropriate, and one size fits all."

WILLIAM R. HEARST

Did you know?

■ During his years at Harvard University, Hearst worked on the staff of the *Harvard Lampoon*.

■ Hearst based his papers' sensational style on the papers of his mentor and later rival Joseph Pulitzer.

DONALD TRUMP
b. 1946

DONALD JOHN TRUMP IS AN AMERICAN real estate developer and business tycoon known for his shrewd deal-making, elaborate financing schemes, flamboyant personal style, and high-risk ventures.

△ TRUMP HAS PURSUED *publicity almost as hard as business. He became a fixture in New York society in the 1980s.*

THE ART OF THE DEAL

Trump was born the son of a real estate developer who specialized in middle-income housing in the New York City boroughs of Brooklyn, Staten Island, and Queens. After Donald graduated from the Wharton School of Finance at the University of Pennsylvania in 1968, he joined his father's company, the Trump Organization. Trump invested the company's funds to purchase several ailing hotel properties in Manhattan, and he then rebuilt them into successful hotels, relying in part upon generous financial concessions from local government. Trump's empire soon included high-rises and condominiums, more than 25,000 rental and co-op apartment units, and several opulent hotel-casinos in Atlantic City. His reputation grew with the publication of his best-selling book, *The Art of the Deal* (1987). The real estate downturn at the end of the 1980s was almost his undoing: Trump missed payments to banks and bondholders, but he managed to avoid bankruptcy by arranging a series of last-ditch loans. His fortunes rebounded with the strong economy of the 1990s.

Did you know?

■ Trump's parents sent him to the New York Military Academy as a child in the hope that he would benefit from the discipline.

■ Trump briefly considered running for the presidency in 2000 on the Reform Party ticket.

■ Trump is the producer of the annual Miss Universe Pageant.

"Deals are my art form."

DONALD TRUMP

△ THE TRUMP TAJ MAJAL in *Atlantic City is one of the largest casinos in the world.*

THE FIGHT FOR JUSTICE

In the Post-World War II era, issues of justice and human rights have risen to the forefront of global affairs.

The work of organizations such as the United Nations, along with the increasing hunger for freedom, democracy, and equality throughout the world, has fueled demand for political and economic justice and a greater attention to human rights. Progress in these areas would have been impossible without the struggles of men and women who endured great hardship, fought for many years, and sometimes even gave their lives in the ongoing fight for global justice. Using nonviolent protest, both Mohandas Gandhi and Kwame Nkrumah opposed British rule in their countries (India and Ghana, respectively) and eventually won freedom for their nations. Corazon Aquino restored democracy to the Philippines and became its first female president. Susan B. Anthony fought for equal rights for women in the United States, and Nelson Mandela suffered for decades in a South African prison for his opposition to apartheid. Their courage, and the courage they inspire in others, continues to change the world.

△ THE SPREAD OF THE INTERNET *has made it more difficult for governments to keep out the outside world and to control dissent.*

NELSON MANDELA
b. 1918

NELSON MANDELA was perhaps the most important political figure in the struggle against South African apartheid.

△ MANDELA *was elected president of South Africa on April 27, 1994.*

APARTHEID'S END

Mandela was born to a Xhosa chief in Transkei, but renounced his claim to the chieftainship to study law. He earned his law degree from the University of South Africa in 1942, and two years later joined the African National Congress (ANC), a black-liberation group resisting the apartheid policies of South Africa's National party. He was elected president of the ANC Youth League in 1951. At this time, Mandela was a strong advocate of nonviolent protest; in 1952 he was arrested for his role in leading the nonviolent resistance movement, receiving a suspended prison sentence. The Sharpeville shootings in 1960—56 black protesters were killed and more than 200 wounded—convinced Mandela that nonviolence was inadequate, and he led the paramilitary *Umkhonto weSizwe* ("Spear of the Nation") in a campaign of sabotage against the white government. He was jailed in 1962, charged with treason, and in 1964 sentenced to life imprisonment. Mandela remained in prison for 27 years and became a symbol of the anti-apartheid struggle. The threat of civil war combined with international boycotts and diplomatic pressure against South Africa led President F. W. de Klerk to release Mandela in 1990. He was elected president of the ANC and with de Klerk worked to end apartheid and establish a racially integrated democracy. They shared the Nobel Peace Prize in 1993 and in 1994 Mandela was elected president in South Africa's first open election.

△ RESIDENTS OF SOWETO, *a notorious South African shantytown, anxiously awaited Mandela's release in 1990.*

MOHANDAS GANDHI
(1869–1948)

LEADER OF THE INDIAN nationalist movement against British rule, Mohandas (later Mahatma, meaning "Great Soul") Gandhi brought his nation to independence with nonviolent protest.

INDIA'S "LITTLE FATHER"

Born in Porbandar, India, and raised in a strict Hindu household, Gandhi was a mediocre law student in London and an inept lawyer in India. He took a clerical position in a firm in South Africa in 1893. His activism began there, and he fought for Indian equality in South Africa for 20 years, returning to India in 1914 with the goal of liberating India from British rule. Starting in World War I, he refashioned the Indian National Congress and began a policy of Indian noncooperation with British colonial authority. The turning point of the struggle came in 1930 with Gandhi's Salt March—a 24-day hike to the sea protesting the British salt tax. He was arrested but continued to lead nonviolent campaigns of noncooperation, and in 1946 the British surrendered their claims to India. A Hindu fundamentalist assassinated Gandhi on January 30, 1948.

"We must become the change we want to see."

GANDHI

△ YOUNG GANDHI *developed his concept of* satyagraha *or "truth force"—the power of passive resistance—in South Africa. Its first use was in 1906, to protest an ordinance in Transvaal against Indian immigrants.*

△ AS PRESIDENT *of South Africa, Mandela had to contend with corruption, high unemployment and a lack of housing, as well as resentment lingering from the apartheid era. Mandela stressed reconciliation as much as justice in his term in office.*

GANDHI IN INDIA, 1940

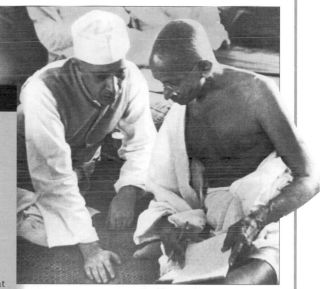

△ AT THE ALL INDIA CONGRESS OF 1942, *Gandhi worked with Pandit J. Nehru, who would later become the first prime minister of India, to pass a resolution demanding that England end its presence in the subcontinent.*

CORAZÓN AQUINO
b. 1933

PHILIPPINE PRESIDENT CORAZÓN AQUINO, the country's first woman president, helped overthrow the dictatorship of Ferdinand Marcos and restored democracy to the Philippines.

△ **AQUINO** *often wore yellow during the uprising, investing the color with political meaning.*

PEOPLE POWER

Born to a wealthy, politically powerful family, Aquino graduated from the College of Mount St. Vincent in New York in 1954. In 1955 she married Benigno Simeon Aquino, Jr., a young politician who would later become Philippine President Ferdinand Marcos's chief opponent. In 1972, Benigno was arrested by Marcos for exposing his plan to declare martial law. Benigno was jailed for eight years, and after his release, the Aquinos were exiled to the US. Upon Benigno's return to the Philippines in 1983, he was assassinated by a military guard at the Manila airport. When the assassins were acquitted, Corazón Aquino declared her candidacy for president. Both sides claimed victory in the 1986 election, but Aquino accused Marcos of ballot rigging, and embarked on a nonviolent "people power" campaign, which eventually succeeded in overthrowing Marcos. During her six-year term, she displayed a steely calm, restoring the bicameral congress and breaking up business monopolies held by Marcos's allies. After endorsing a former political rival to succeed her as president, Aquino has remained vocal in Philippine politics while working to advance democracy.

Did you know?

■ There were six coup attempts against Aquino while she was in office.

■ The last elected office Aquino held before president of the Phillipines was president of her sixth-grade class.

■ She was *Time*'s Woman of the Year in 1986.

△ **WHILE AQUINO PLAYED** *a major role in the downfall of Ferdinand Marcos, she once again spoke out against a Philippine leader in 2001 when she advocated the removal of President Joseph Estrada—to the dismay of his supporters (shown here).*

KWAME NKRUMAH
(1909–1972)

GHANAIAN STATESMAN Kwame Nkrumah fought against white domination of Africa and was a major proponent of the Pan-African movement.

Pan-African Leaders

PATRICE LUMUMBA (1925–1961) Congolese premier and national hero.

JOMO KENYATTA (1889–1978) Kenyan president, president of Pan-African Federation.

THE GHANDI OF AFRICA

The son of a goldsmith, Nkrumah was a brilliant student, and went to study in the United States and London. While in London, he held several posts in African nationalist organizations. He returned to the Gold Coast in 1947 to serve as general secretary of the United Gold Coast Convention party, but in 1949 he formed his own political party, the Convention People's Party, and began a program of nonviolent protests and boycotts against British rule. Imprisoned by the British in 1950, he was released when his party swept the general election in 1951. He became prime minister in 1952 and began to work on a new constitution for the nation. Under his leadership, the Gold Coast gained independence in 1957, becoming the Republic of Ghana in 1960. Nkrumah also played a major role in the creation of the Organization of African Unity in 1963. In office, though, he became increasingly authoritarian and in 1964 he declared himself president for life. Opposition parties were outlawed. Nkruman was overthrown in a coup while visiting Beijing in 1966, and though he called for the nation to fight against the new leadership, most Ghanaians ignored his call. He died six years later in Bucharest.

◁ NKRUMAH *considered becoming a Jesuit priest before deciding to study at Lincoln University and the University of Pennsylvania.*

"Go to the people, live among them, learn from them, love them, plan with them, start with what they know, build on what they know."

KWAME NKRUMAH

◁ AS WELL AS A POLITICAL *leader, Nkrumah brought a sense of style to his office, as seen here at a feast in Accra accompanied by his Egyptian wife, Fathia, in 1963.*

SUSAN B. ANTHONY
(1820–1906)

△ THE SUSAN B. ANTHONY COIN, *introduced in 1979, was the first coin in US history that depicted a woman.*

AMERICAN SOCIAL REFORMER Susan Brownell Anthony fought for temperance and against slavery before helping to launch and sustain the women's suffrage movement.

THE SUFFRAGETTE
Born to Quaker parents, Anthony's first job in the New York school system ended after she complained of the inequality of men's and women's wages. She founded the first women's temperance (anti-alcohol) association, and at a meeting in 1851 met Elizabeth Cady Stanton, who would be a lifelong friend and compatriot in the movement for women's rights, including suffrage—the right to vote.

Anthony worked tirelessly, campaigning door to door, and forming, with Stanton, the National Woman Suffrage Association in 1869. Anthony voted illegally in 1872 and was arrested and tried for civil disobedience; she lost her case, but refused to pay the $100 fine. She served as president of the National American Woman Suffrage Association from 1892 to 1900, and continued to struggle for women's rights until her death. She gave her most famous speech one month before she died—her last public words were "Failure is impossible."

△ THIS 19TH-CENTURY POLITICAL CARTOON *of Susan B. Anthony was titled "The Woman Who Dared."*

◁ ANTHONY *at her desk, 1898. The 19th Amendment, granting the vote to all US women over 21, was not passed until 1920.*

FOUNDING FATHERS

AS THE REVOLUTIONARY WAR ENDED, THE INTELLECTUAL AND POLITICAL FRAMEWORK of the United States took form in the minds of a few remarkable thinkers. Their ideas, revolutionary for the time, became America's guiding principles.

Benjamin Franklin, a man of prodigious talents, secured funding for the American cause in the Revolutionary War and negotiated the peace with Britain. George Washington, commander of the American forces, was elected president, staying at the new country's helm for eight years. Washington's vice president, John Adams, one of the drafters of the Declaration of Independence, succeeded him, and Thomas Jefferson, having lost to Adams by a mere three electoral votes in the second presidential election, followed. As president, Jefferson helped define the role of the federal government and approved the Louisiana Purchase. James Madison, the fourth president, secured individual liberties through his support for adding a Bill of Rights to the Constitution.

△ THE DECLARATION OF INDEPENDENCE *begins with the now-famous words: "We the people."*

△ THE DECLARATION OF INDEPENDENCE. *signed on July 4, 1776, was in many ways the culmination of the Enlightenment, an 18th century philosophical movement that favored rationalism over traditional ideas.*

THOMAS JEFFERSON
(1743–1826)

THOMAS JEFFERSON, the third American president, helped define American democracy as principal author of the Declaration of Independence and as a leading advocate of state and individual rights.

WHO SHALL BE FREE?

A complex, contradictory, and amazingly accomplished man, Jefferson grew up in a family of wealthy Virginia slaveholders, and studied at the College of William & Mary before becoming a lawyer. At the Second Continental Congress in Philadelphia in 1775, Jefferson wrote the first draft of the Declaration of Independence. Virginia's governor during the Revolutionary War, he was a delegate to the Continental Congress in 1782 and was minister to France for five years before becoming secretary of state under Washington.

As the Federalists advocated a strong central government, Jefferson argued for the rights of states and individuals and became the leader of the country's first opposition party, the Democratic Republicans. He served as vice president to John Adams, and was elected president in 1800. As president, he paid France $15 million for the Louisiana Purchase, tripling the nation's size. He was ambivalent about slavery; though he was a slaveowner, he felt it violated the principles of the Declaration of Independence. Yet he supported slavery in the Western territories, worrying all the while that the nation's growing divisions over the issue could lead to civil war. After a second term, he retired to Monticello to continue studying subjects ranging from architecture to philosophy. He died on July 4, 1826.

△ JEFFERSON NOT ONLY *founded the University of Virginia in 1819; he designed its buildings and created its curriculum.*

GEORGE WASHINGTON
(1732–1799)

A MILITARY LEADER AS WELL as a political one, George Washington led the Continental Army to victory in the Revolutionary War, then took over the reins of government as the nation's first president.

THE FATHER OF HIS COUNTRY

Washington grew up on his family's Virginia plantation, Mount Vernon, and worked as a surveyor before joining the Virginia militia in 1753. He fought bravely in the French and Indian War, taking command of Virginia's forces in 1755. After the fighting ended, he entered the Virginia legislature in 1758, and the following year married Martha Custis, a wealthy widow. With the Revolutionary War underway, the Second Continental Congress appointed Washington commander in chief of the Continental army in June 1775. He led the bold crossing of the Delaware to defeat enemy forces at Trenton on Christmas night of 1776, and held the army together from the terrible winter encampment at Valley Forge (1777–78) until the final victory at Yorktown (1781). Washington was elected president in 1789 on the strength of his military record and personal reputation. He served two terms, remaining relatively aloof from political clashes between Federalists and those who supported a more decentralized government. He retired in 1796 to Mount Vernon, but took over again as commander in chief of the army in 1798, when war against France seemed imminent. Washington died at Mount Vernon in 1799.

△ ACCORDING TO A POPULAR LEGEND, *Washington and several members of Congress asked a seamstress, Betsy Ross, to create the first American flag.*

Did you know?

■ "The father of his country" lost his own father when he was 11 years old.

■ Washington inherited his estate at Mount Vernon from his brother Lawrence, who had taken him in as a boy.

△ **WHILE JEFFERSON** *called slavery "an abominable crime," by 1796 he owned nearly 170 slaves, and he sold about 100 during his lifetime to settle his considerable debts. He freed only seven slaves; the rest were auctioned after his death.*

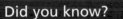

Did you know?

■ In January 2000 the Thomas Jefferson Memorial Foundation accepted the conclusion (supported by DNA testing) that Jefferson had between one and six children with his slave Sally Hemmings.

■ Thomas Jefferson reportedly wrote 1,200 letters in a single year after his retirement from the presidency.

▷ **CROSSING THE DELAWARE RIVER** *in late 1776 allowed the Continental army to take Trenton, New Jersey, providing the young nation with a much-needed victory after Washington had abandoned New York City to the British.*

◁ **GEORGE WASHINGTON,** *in one of a several famous portraits by Gilbert Stewart. This one was painted in 1796.*

"First in peace, first in war, first in the hearts of his countrymen."

HENRY LEE'S DESCRIPTION OF WASHINGTON

JAMES MADISON
(1751-1836)

JAMES MADISON, fourth president of the United States, was an important voice in early debates that shaped the federal government's role in the young democracy.

THE FEDERALIST

A native of Port Conway, Virginia, Madison attended the College of New Jersey (later Princeton) and as a young man held various positions in Virginia's government. He then served three years (1780 to 1783) as a state delegate to the Congress under the Articles of Confederation, where he was a powerful advocate for a stronger national government. Those views influenced his work at the Constitutional Convention of 1787, where he helped engineer important compromises. He also was instrumental in adding the Bill of Rights to the final document. Madison's views on the federal government's role changed over time, and he later became affiliated with the Democrats, including Thomas Jefferson, who strongly supported state and individual rights against federal incursions. Madison served in the US House of Representatives and was President Jefferson's secretary of state before serving as president himself, from 1809 to 1817. He was Jefferson's successor as rector of the University of Virginia and died in Montpelier, Virginia.

△ JAMES MADISON, *portrayed on an 18th-century clay pitcher.*

Did you know?

■ Madison abhorred slavery. When his valet ran away and was captured, Madison set him free and hired the man for wages instead of punishing him.

■ Author Washington Irving described Madison as "a withered little Apple-John" (a line from Shakespeare's *Henry IV*).

Other Framers

ALEXANDER HAMILTON (1755–1804) Proponent of centralized governmental powers and a strong national economy.

JOHN JAY (1745–1829) Chief author of the Constitution.

▷ MADISON'S ROLE *at the 1787 Constitutional Convention earned him the name "Father of the Constitution."*

BENJAMIN FRANKLIN
(1706-1790)

BENJAMIN FRANKLIN PLAYED A CRUCIAL ROLE in shaping politics and diplomacy in the early days of the American republic, but is also remembered for his scientific inventions and discoveries, and his homespun philosophy.

△ ONE OF FRANKLIN'S *early business successes was the printing of Pennsylvania's state currency.*

POOR RICHARD

Franklin was 10 years old when he went to work in his father's chandlery. He later worked in a brother's printing house, and by 1730, when he was 24, owned a successful printing business that included the *Pennsylvania Gazette*. Franklin first gained fame as publisher of the annual *Poor Richard's Almanack*, which consisted of pithy sayings in support of virtues such as hard work and frugality. In 1736 he became a clerk in the Pennsylvania Assembly, and later served as joint deputy postmaster for the colonies (1753 to 1774). Meanwhile, he retired from business in 1748 to pursue his scientific interests, including experiments with electricity that brought him international renown. Franklin in 1776 went to France to represent the nascent American republic, winning crucial financial aid for the American Revolution. He negotiated a peace treaty with Britain in 1783, and returned to the United States in time to help calm competing factions at the 1787 Constitutional Convention.

Did you know?

■ Ben Franklin was the 15th child in his family.

■ Franklin's many inventions included the fuel-efficient Franklin stove, the lightning rod, bifocals, and a device for lifting books from high shelves.

■ In 1731, Franklin helped establish the first lending library in the United States.

▷ FRANKLIN'S FAMOUS KITE *experiment in 1752 proved that lightning is an electrical discharge.*

▽ BENJAMIN FRANKLIN NATIONAL MEMORIAL, *Philadelphia, Pennsylvania (1934–1937), created by sculptor Earl Fraser.*

"We must indeed all hang together, or, most assuredly, we shall all hang separately."

FRANKLIN AT THE SIGNING OF
THE DECLARATION OF INDEPENDENCE

JOHN ADAMS
(1735–1826)

A PROPONENT OF A STRONG FEDERAL GOVERNMENT, prickly John Adams was the second president of the United States.

PATRIOT THINKER

Adams was born in Braintree (now Quincy), Massachusetts. He graduated from Harvard in 1755, began practicing law, and married Abigail Adams in 1764. In 1765 Adams argued successfully against the Stamp Act, a law passed by the British to tax the American colonists' documents. Five years later, however, he defended the British soldiers involved in the Boston Massacre, earning not-guilty verdicts for all but two of the nine soldiers. He served as a Massachusetts delegate to the First and Second Continental Congresses, where he headed the committee to draft the Declaration of Independence. He was elected vice president under George Washington in 1789 and 1792, and in a divided cabinet sided with Alexander Hamilton's Federalists against Thomas Jefferson's Democrat-Republicans. He ran for president against Jefferson in 1796, winning by only three electoral votes. Adams's presidency was difficult. The Alien and Sedition Acts, designed to squelch dissent against the government, caused a popular backlash and galvanized his opposition. Meanwhile, the United States became involved in an undeclared naval war with France. Adams's refusal to declare war angered Hamilton and Federalists, and the dissension among the party contributed to Adams's defeat to Jefferson in the 1800 election. Adams rarely left his Quincy farm during the ensuing 26 years. He wrote prolifically and maintained a long correspondence with Thomas Jefferson. He died on July 4, 1826—just a few hours after Jefferson's death.

△ ADAMS RETIRED *from politics in 1770, but was drawn back in three years later as the American Revolution took form.*

△ JOHN QUINCY ADAMS COPPER CENT, *from the 1824 presidential election. In the 1800s, politicians used coins for free advertising.*

Did you know?

■ John Adams's last words were "Thomas Jefferson survives!" However, Jefferson had died several hours earlier.

■ Detractors called him "His Rotundity," referring to his girth.

■ Adams's son John Quincy Adams was elected as the 6th US president in 1824.

GIANTS OF JAZZ

JAZZ MAY BE AMERICA'S MOST IMPORTANT NATIVE ART FORM, BORN OF the experimentation and freedom at the heart of its continued vitality.

The music of Louis Armstrong and Duke Ellington may sound familiar today, but Satchmo's style and technique in the late 1920s and the Duke's swingin' Cotton Club compositions were revelations in their time. Following in the path of Armstrong and Ellington came a new generation of jazz artists who pushed the form further, including the elegant vocalist Ella Fitzgerald, the spiritual saxophonist John Coltrane, and the hip, cerebral trumpeter Miles Davis.

Today, a new generation of superb musicians brings to jazz precise technique and a keen understanding of history and style that recalls the work of past masters. It's only a matter of time before a performer as creative and determined as the Duke or Trane emerges from the jazz underground and transforms the sound yet again.

△ LOCATED ON BROADWAY *and 52nd Street in midtown Manhattan, the original Birdland was one of jazz music's main stages. It was named after legendary composer and saxophonist Charlie Parker, known as "Bird."*

LOUIS ARMSTRONG
(1901–1971)

NO MUSICIAN HAD MORE INFLUENCE on the evolution of jazz than trumpet virtuoso, singer, and bandleader Louis "Satchmo" Armstrong.

"SATCHMO"
Born at the turn of the 20th century in New Orleans, Armstrong came of age in the roaring juke joints of the city's red-light district, having learned to play cornet while at a home for juvenile delinquents. After playing in a band on a Mississippi riverboat, and at the urging of bandleader Joseph "King" Oliver, in 1922 he moved to Chicago. There, Armstrong recorded his sessions with the Hot Fives (and later the Hot Sevens). His revolutionary use of rhythm and improvisation made the recordings a blueprint for jazz as it is now known.

With his profound sense of style and technique, Armstrong emerged as an artistic genius and a commercial celebrity as well. By the mid-1930s, he had begun recording albums that focused on his signature vocal style and appealed to a wider audience. He toured the United States and Europe with a 15-piece big band, made frequent radio and film appearances, and became one of the world's most popular entertainers. By the early 1950s, though, Armstrong had fallen from favor with emerging "hard-bop" players of the day, who in some cases considered him a sellout. In 1954, he switched record labels from Decca to Columbia and the albums he made there brought him back into the public eye. A renewed interest in traditional New Orleans jazz in the 1960s further boosted him, and he soon found himself a goodwill ambassador, dispatched around the world by the US State Department. Still able to occasionally achieve the brilliance of the Hot Five recordings, he remained a beloved entertainer until his death in 1971.

Key Horn Pioneers

DIZZY GILLESPIE (1917–1993) Be-bop star with the bent horn.

WYNTON MARSALIS b. 1961 Technical master leading the return to traditional forms.

BIX BEIDERBECKE (1903–1931) Jazz pioneer on the cornet.

△ ARMSTRONG WITH HIS TRUMPET, *c. 1935. He bought his first a cornet at seven, with money borrowed from his employers, a family of Jewish immigrants.*

▷ **ARMSTRONG** *not only invented new ways to play the trumpet, he also created scat singing, the improvised use of nonsense syllables by a singer to replicate the sound of an instrument.*

"All we can do is be glad we live in the same century as Louis Armstrong"

WYNTON MARSALIS

Did you know?

■ Armstrong's 1964 vocal rendition of "Hello Dolly!" knocked the Beatles from the top of the Billboard charts.

■ Armstrong was inducted into the Rock and Roll Hall of Fame in 1990.

■ An archive and research facility at Queens College in New York is dedicated to studying Armstrong's considerable impact on American culture.

Armstrong could play up to 30 high Cs in a row.

▽ ONE OF SATCHMO'S EARLY RECORDS WITH COLUMBIA. *For creating a new idiom of artistic expression, many consider Armstrong an equal to Pablo Picasso and James Joyce.*

HOT JAZZ CLASSICS
KING LOUIS
COLUMBIA RECORDS
SET C-28

album 1 in a series of re-issues of the original records that made jazz history

∧ **BETWEEN 1944 AND 1946,** *Armstrong recorded with legendary jazz singer Billie Holiday. Although World War II kept him from touring as aggressively as he was accustomed, Armstrong instead appeared in numerous films and headlined a groundbreaking jazz concert at the Metropolitan Opera House.*

ELLA FITZGERALD
(1917–1996)

ELLA FITZGERALD'S ELEGANT interpretations and stunning vocal dexterity became the inspiration for almost every female jazz singer who came after her.

THE FIRST LADY OF SONG

Born in Newport News, Virginia, Fitzgerald came to New York with her mother after her father died. She wanted to be a dancer, and entered an amateur competition at Harlem's Apollo Theater in 1934. Her body froze on stage so she sung instead, and found her true gift. Soon after, she began singing with bandleader Chick Webb, quickly becoming the band's main attraction. After Webb died in 1939, Fitzgerald continued to front the ensemble until 1942. In 1955 she teamed with producer Norman Granz for a series of records, each devoted to the work of a single composer. Using her distinct vocal range, with its fresh, youthful quality, she created a series of jazz masterpieces, greatly widening her audience. Fitzgerald toured until the mid-1980s, interpreting works by artists such as Marvin Gaye and the Beatles. Complications stemming from diabetes finally stopped her from performing in 1993.

△ FITZGERALD'S PRECISE *diction and care with lyrics made her a favorite of composers, yet she never received any formal training.*

Other Jazz Divas

BILLIE HOLIDAY (1915–1959) Lady Day's emotional style matched her tempetuous life.

DINAH WASHINGTON (1924–1963) Mellow-voiced crossover star.

BESSIE SMITH (1894–1937) Her powerful, raw delivery made her the Empress of the Blues.

▷ FITZGERALD *won 13 Grammy awards—more than any other jazz musician or female artist.*

"I never knew how good our songs were until I heard Ella Fitzgerald sing them."

IRA GERSHWIN

Did you know?

■ Ella Fitzgerald sold over 40 million albums

■ It is rumored, but not confirmed, that as a child Fitzgerald ran way from her abusive stepfather after the death of her mother, and made money performing on the sidewalks of Harlem.

■ Fitzgerald sang across a three-octave range, more than many opera singers.

◁ A POSTER FOR A 1944 SHOW *at the RKO Albee in Cincinnati, advertising Fitzgerald and the hot 1940s black vocal group the Ink Spots.*

JOHN COLTRANE
(1926–1967)

JOHN COLTRANE WAS one of jazz music's most innovative and influential saxophonists.

"TRANE"

Born in Hamlet, North Carolina, Coltrane was raised in his preacher grandfather's house and played saxophone in public school and studied music briefly when he graduated from high school. After two years playing in a US Navy band during World War II, Coltrane started performing in the mid-1940s with bands led by such celebrated musicians as Dizzy Gillespie and Johnny Hodges. Coltrane first attracted critical notice while playing with Miles Davis's legendary quintet. There he developed a rapid, textured delivery described as "sheets of sound." He left the band in 1957. After overcoming drug and alcohol addiction, Coltrane began his solo career. His 1960 rendition of "My Favorite Things" was extremely popular and its success allowed Coltrane to explore, and eventually lead, the new movement of free improvisation emerging in the jazz community. As Coltrane became more engrossed in discovering the full potential of his artistry, he used varied instrumentation and modal systems of improvisation. Coltrane's impassioned style and deeply spiritual approach made him one of the most widely imitated musicians in jazz history. He died of stomach cancer at the age of 41.

◁ DEVOTED TO *his art, Coltrane was known for the amount of practice he put into any new idea before trying it out in public.*

△ ISSUED IN 1960, Giant Steps *was Coltrane's first major statement.*

Did you know?

■ The St. John Coltrane African Orthodox Church in San Francisco uses Coltrane's music and philosophy as sources for religious discovery.

■ The California folk-rock group The Byrds used Coltrane's modal style as a basis for their 1966 hit "Eight Miles High."

■ Jazz instrumentalist Alice MacLeod married Coltrane in 1965. She played piano on many of his later recordings.

◁ IT WAS WHILE *playing with Dizzy Gillespie (right) between 1949 and 1950 that Coltrane switched from playing mainly alto saxophone to tenor, the instrument he would use to make his mark.*

DUKE ELLINGTON

(1899–1974)

MANY MUSIC CRITICS AND HISTORIANS of jazz consider Duke Ellington—composer, bandleader, and pianist—the most important all-around talent in jazz history.

"THE DUKE"

Born Edward Ellington in Washington, D.C., he began playing piano around the age of eight. Though his first job was selling peanuts at Washington Senators' games, he soon moved into music, forming his first ensemble in 1918. By 1923 he was playing piano regularly with the five-piece Washingtonians. Ellington eventually assumed creative control of the group and expanded it to a ten-piece ensemble. The band landed a regular gig at the most coveted venue in jazz: Harlem's Cotton Club. During his reign there, Duke played everything from straight jazz to pop standards and dance tunes. The variety helped ensure the group's success and provided him with a new approach to composing. By the 1930s "Duke Ellington and His Orchestra" had become a sensation across the country. When Ellington left the Cotton Club in 1932, the group toured the US and Europe, and in 1943 performed the first of many concerts at New York's Carnegie Hall. After a discouraging creative slump from the mid-'40s into the 1950s, Ellington rebounded and began a more compositionally mature era in his career. He expanded his band to 18 members as he experimented with nuances in tone and musical color. Incorporating both jazz and classical elements, Ellington in his later career composed elaborate, politically charged work and movie soundtracks.

△ ALTHOUGH ELLINGTON *is best known for his more traditional work, he often collaborated with bop and free jazz stars such as drummer Max Roach (center) and legendary bassist and composer Charles Mingus (right).*

Did you know?

■ Jazz icons Willie "the Lion" Smith and Fats Waller were responsible for introducing Ellington to the New York music scene in the early '20s, and for convincing him to pursue a solo career.

■ He composed the soundtrack to the 1959 Otto Preminger thriller, *Anatomy of a Murder*, and was nominated for an Oscar for his soundtrack to Martin Ritt's 1961 film *Paris Blues*.

■ Ellington received an art scholarship to Pratt Institue in Brooklyn.

△ ELLINGTON PRODUCED OVER 100 RECORDINGS *in the 1950s, including the two seen here. Although big band music gave way to smaller ensembles in the postwar years, Ellington made a comeback in a memorable concert at the Newport Jazz Festival in 1956.*

◁ THE DUKE *got his nickname from a young schoolmate who noticed the future bandleader's classy mannerisms and style—even back then.*

"In the royalty of American music, no man swings more or stands higher than the Duke."

RICHARD NIXON

MILES DAVIS
(1926–1991)

TRUMPETER MILES DAVIS'S ability to create and reinvent musical styles made him one of modern jazz's genuine trailblazers.

THE COOL PRINCE OF DARKNESS

Davis was born in Alton, Illinois, and began playing in local bands as a teenager. He moved to New York in 1945, intending to study at the Juilliard School, but instead gigged with bop great Charlie "Bird" Parker from 1946 to 1948. After a few years with Bird, Davis went solo and soon created a new style known as "cool jazz." In 1958 he formed his famous quintet, which included saxophone giant John Coltrane. The band recorded a trio of subtle yet urgent albums, including the seminal *Kind of Blue*, that remain some of the finest works in jazz history. The 1960s and '70s were an especially creative time for Davis. Playing with pianist Herbie Hancock, he fused psychedelic rock with his own warmly lyrical jazz sensibilities to create a curious and influential hybrid. While some jazz fans did not like Davis's new turn, many did—his 1970 album *Bitches Brew* is the best-selling jazz album of all time. Despite drug and alcohol problems that plagued him throughout his life, he continued to record and experiment until his death.

▷ DAVIS IN THE STUDIO, c. 1950s. He achieved a remarkable spontaneity on Kind of Blue (1959): there was no rehearsal; players were only given its musical themes upon arrival at the recording studio.

"A sound is the most important thing a musician can have, because you can't do anything without a sound."

MILES DAVIS

Did you know?

■ Davis was married to actress Cicely Tyson, one of three marriages.

■ Davis recorded a hip-hop record in the early 1990s entitled *Doo-Bop* with rapper Easy Mo Bee.

■ He appeared as a street performer in the 1988 film starring Bill Murray, *Scrooged*.

△ DAVIS at a 1989 photo shoot. Although famed for his intensity and devotion to privacy, he collaborated with a wide range of performers, from Charlie Parker to Prince.

▷ SOME OF DAVIS'S MOST FAMOUS ALBUMS were arranged by noted jazz composer-arranger Gil Evans, including Sketches of Spain (1959).

BASIC PRINCIPLES

THE SIMPLEST QUESTIONS ARE OFTEN THE MOST DIFFICULT TO ANSWER. WHERE do we come from? What are we made of? What makes the heavens move?

Throughout history a select few people gifted with genius, commitment, and courage have attempted to solve humankind's most elusive puzzles. Even in the face of opposition and doubt, these thinkers have proposed, illuminated, or proved some of the basic principles of science, and changed the course of human history. Mathematician Isaac Newton's work in the laws of motion and gravity laid the groundwork for what would become modern physics. Heisenberg, much later, altered the course of physics by creating the field of quantum mechanics. Einstein's theories about time and space led to the development of the atomic bomb and revolutionized thinking about the nature of the universe. Galileo's discoveries with a crude telescope and Darwin's theories of evolution opposed religious authorities' views of the universe. In fact, the work of each of these men ignited debate about the very nature of humanity.

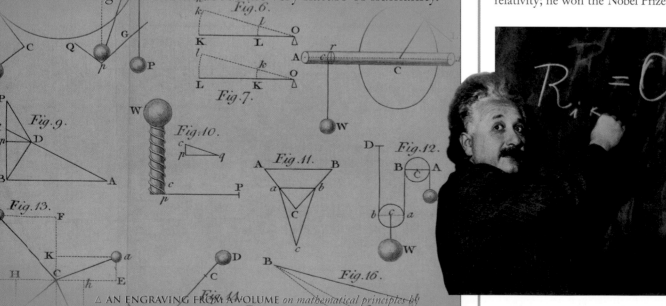

△ AN ENGRAVING FROM A VOLUME *on mathematical principles by Sir Isaac Newton. A master of chemistry, optics, astronomy, and philosophy, he is best remembered for his amazing achievements in mathematics.*

ALBERT EINSTEIN
(1879–1955)

ONE OF HISTORY'S most brilliant minds, physicist Albert Einstein fundamentally altered beliefs about the relationship between gravity, space, and time.

GENIUS

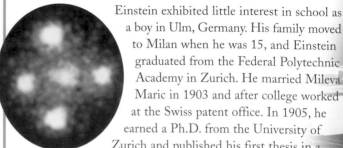

△ EINSTEIN *proved the existence of atoms, which was not yet fully accepted.*

Einstein exhibited little interest in school as a boy in Ulm, Germany. His family moved to Milan when he was 15, and Einstein graduated from the Federal Polytechnic Academy in Zurich. He married Mileva Maric in 1903 and after college worked at the Swiss patent office. In 1905, he earned a Ph.D. from the University of Zurich and published his first thesis in a German physics monthly. He published four more papers during this period, each with theses that ended up serving as foundations of modern physics. As his peers began to recognize the brilliance of his work, Einstein left the patent office and moved to Berlin in 1914 with his wife and two sons. His family vacationed in Switzerland without him that summer, but the outbreak of World War I prevented their return; the separation led to divorce. Meanwhile, he worked on. In 1916 he published his general theory of relativity, which stated that space and time were not independent entities, as was previously thought. Einstein also developed the mass-energy equivalence theory ($E=MC^2$), showing that mass could be converted into energy—a cornerstone in the development of nuclear energy. The Royal Society of London announced in 1919 that it had verified certain ideas postulated in his general theory of relativity; he won the Nobel Prize for physics two years later.

In 1928, he started to work on a "unified field theory," an attempt to describe the connected nature of all matter and energy. When Hitler became German chancellor in 1933, Einstein moved to the US. Though a pacifist, he reluctantly advised the atomic weapons program. The rest of his life was devoted to solving unified field theory, and world peace.

△ EINSTEIN LECTURING *in 1931. He worked at Princeton University, in New Jersey, from 1935 until his death in 1955.*

SIR ISAAC NEWTON
(1642-1727)

ENGLISH SCIENTIST AND MATHEMATICIAN Isaac Newton laid the foundation for modern physics.

UNIVERSAL GRAVITATION

A native of Woolsthorpe, Lincolnshire, Newton was orginally meant to follow in the footsteps of his father, a farmer, but his early talents earned him a place at Trinity College, Cambridge. In 1664, while Newton was studying for his master's degree, an outbreak of the plague caused the university to close. During the resultant 18-month stay back in Woolsthorpe, Newton formulated the basis for his theories on optics and gravitation. When the threat was over, he returned to Cambridge, where he was named professor of mathematics in 1669; he remained there for another 27 years. In 1687 Newton published his magnum opus, *Philosophiae Naturalis Principia Mathematica*, which became a milestone of modern science. Newton worked at the Royal Mint from 1696 until his death. Elected president of the Royal Society in 1703 and knighted in 1705 for his work, he was buried in Westminster Abbey upon his death in 1727.

△ **NEWTON'S INSIGHT** *into gravity was supposedly inspired by a falling apple; once considered legend, today the story is thought to be true.*

Did you know?

■ Newton wrote the groundbreaking *Principia* in only 18 months.

■ Newton became entangled in several academic quarrels, including a dispute with Gottfried Leibniz about which one of them had invented calculus.

■ Newton invented the reflecting telescope in 1668.

PHILOSOPHIÆ
NATURALIS
PRINCIPIA
MATHEMATICA.

Autore JS. NEWTON, Trin. Coll. Cantab. Soc. Matheseos Professore Lucasiano, & Societatis Regalis Sodali.

IMPRIMATUR
S. PEPYS, Reg. Soc. PRÆSES.
Julii 5. 1686.

LONDINI,
Jussu Societatis Regiae ac Typis Josephi Streater. Prostat apud plures Bibliopolas. Anno MDCLXXXVII.

△ **IN HIS 1686 TREATISE** Prinicipia Mathematica, *Newton outlined laws of motion and universal gravitation and applied them to falling bodies on earth as well as the motion of planets and comets.*

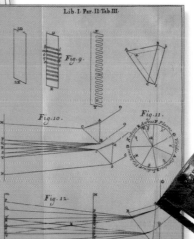

△ **NEWTON'S WORK IN OPTICS** *introduced the use of prisms to break down white light into colored rays.*

▷ **THE REFLECTING TELESCOPE,** *Newton's revolutionary invention. He donated this prototype to the Royal Society of London in 1671, where it remains today.*

△ **ALBERT EINSTEIN** *in his library, Berlin, c. 1930.*

Did you know?

■ Einstein was an accomplished violinist, though he played only for relaxation.

■ He championed Zionism, and traveled throughout the United States to raise money for Chaim Weizmann's Zionist fund.

■ Einstein gave all his Nobel Prize money to his ex-wife.

Key Energy Theorists

GABRIEL FAHRENHEIT (1686–1736) Responsible for mercury thermometer.

WILLIAM T. KELVIN (1824–1907) Invented temperature scale based on absolute zero.

ANDERS CELSIUS (1701–1744) Developed centigrade scale.

GALILEO
(1564–1642)

ITALIAN ASTRONOMER, PHYSICIST, PHILOSOPHER, and mathematician Galileo Galilei proved Copernicus's heliocentric (sun-centered) theory of the universe.

THE HERETIC

Born in Pisa, the son of a well-known musicologist, Galileo angered his colleagues at the University of Pisa in 1589 by developing theories on bodies in motion that contradicted the teachings of Aristotle and the Roman Catholic Church. In 1592 Galileo began lecturing on mathematics at the University of Padua, where he remained for 18 years. There, in 1609, after hearing of a Dutch magnifying device, he set about constructing his own telescope. With this instrument, Galileo discovered the mountains on the moon, the moons of Jupiter, the phases of Venus, the spots on the sun, and the fact that the Milky Way is composed of millions of stars. In 1632, he published *Dialogue Concerning the Two Chief World Systems*, supporting Copernicus's belief that the Earth revolves around the Sun, a stance that, unfortunately, had been condemned by the Catholic Church in 1616. For his beliefs, Galileo in 1663 was tried by the Inquisition in Rome, which made him reject his views and sentenced him to life in prison. Galileo spent the rest of his life under house arrest in various palaces and villas, but he continued working on treatises in physics and mathematics until his death.

Did you know?

■ Galileo's first telescope magnified objects only up to 20 times.

■ Pope John Paul II in 1979 asked that Galileo's conviction be annulled. But it was only in 1992 that the Catholic Church lifted its 1616 prohibition on the teaching of Copernican theory.

△ THESE EARLY TELESCOPES *were used by Galileo in his research. He published his discoveries in a 1610 volume entitled* Sidereus Nuncius (Message from the Stars).

△ ALSO KNOWN FOR *his work in mechanics, Galileo published this volume in 1605:* Operation of the geometric and military compass.

▷ DESPITE HIS PERSECUTION *by the Catholic Church and the results of his scientific work, Galileo remained a devout believer his entire life.*

CHARLES DARWIN
(1809–1882)

ENGLISH NATURALIST Charles Darwin formulated the idea of natural selection, which became the cornerstone of the theory of evolution.

THE DESCENT OF MAN

In 1831, the young Darwin eagerly accepted a post as naturalist on a naval mission to survey the southern coasts of South America on a small Royal Navy ship, the *Beagle*. During his five years on the *Beagle*, Darwin made detailed observations and collected numerous specimens which led him to doubt the view that all species were created simultaneously and never change. He returned to England in 1836 as a renowned scientist, but it wasn't until 1859 that he published *On the Origin of Species*, which outlined his theory that species evolve through random permutations which are "naturally selected" by their environment. While Darwin's theories slowly gained acceptance, his character was attacked by the clergy and scientists alike. He spent the rest of his life researching and writing.

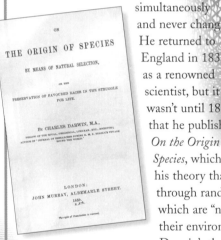

△ DARWIN *considered* The Origin of Species *as the outline of a larger work on natural selection that he never finished.*

△ THE DIVERSITY OF SPECIES *in the remote Galapagos Islands, including these tortoises, inspired Darwin's concept of natural selection.*

△ AN 1871 CARTOON *depicts Henry Bergh, founder of the ASPCA, scolding Darwin for offending a gorilla by claiming that man could be descended from apes. Darwin's ideas were not immediately accepted and were fodder for the press.*

▷ DARWIN *is believed to have died of Chagas' disease, contracted from parasites while he was in South America.*

Did you know?

■ Darwin suffered from seasickness on the *Beagle*, so he traveled overland from port to port whenever possible.

■ Darwin's grandfather, Erasmus Darwin, was a renowned botanist.

■ While Alfred Russell Wallace was the first to propose a theory of evolution, Darwin was the first to present concrete evidence of a mechanism driving it.

"I love fools' experiments. I am always making them."

CHARLES DARWIN

WERNER HEISENBERG
(1901–1976)

GERMAN PHYSICIST AND PHILOSOPHER Werner Heisenberg revolutionized quantum mechanics—the science of discrete energy states.

QUANTUM PIONEER

Born in Wurzburg, Germany, Heisenberg eanred a doctorate in physics at the University of Munich. He went to the Institute for Theoretical Physics in Copenhagen in 1924 to study under Niels Bohr. In 1925, Heisenberg arrived at a reinterpretation of the principles of basic mechanics and two years later formulated his famous "uncertainty principle," which explained the

△ HEISENBERG'S *radical ideas put him at odds with his peers, including Einstein, but his discoveries had a lasting impact on physics.*

behavior of electrons in mathematical terms and stated that at any given time it is impossible to know both the position and momentum of a particle. Originally formulated in connection with the electron, his thesis was soon applied to

Did you know?

■ Heisenberg taught himself calculus.

■ Heisenberg was an avid Boy Scout before entering college.

■ He was passionate about classical music, and saw a deep affinity between physics and music.

other particles as well. In 1932 he was awarded the Nobel Prize. He served as a professor at the University of Leipzig from 1927 to 1941, at which point he began working on Hitler's atomic bomb project. Later he made significant contributions to the study of peaceful uses for nuclear energy. His historic role as a self-proclaimed secret sabateur to the project was challenged in February 2002 when the family of Niels Bohr released accusatory letters Bohr wrote to Heisenberg (but never sent). One claimed that under Heisenberg, "everything was being done in Germany to develop atomic weapons."

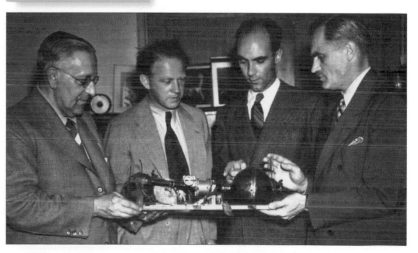

△ NOBEL LAURFATES *(left to right, Victor Hess, Heisenberg, Carl Anderson, and Arthur Compton) discuss a cosmic ray meter in June 1939, at the University of Chicago.*

AGE OF ELIZABETH I

Queen Elizabeth I reigned from 1558 to 1603, an era commonly known as the Elizabethan Age. Her reign marked a dramatic turning point for England. Elizabeth's cunning and political savvy unified and helped transform England from a small, troubled island nation into a major economic and military power.

Possessed of great wit and resolve, cruel when necessary but eager to be kind to those of whom she approved, Elizabeth, with all her opulence, brilliance, and fire, became the symbol of her nation's glittering new identity, and assumed goddesslike proportions in the national culture. During her reign, art and culture flourished in England, producing the unrivaled genius of William Shakespeare and Francis Bacon. Adventurers such as Sir Walter Raleigh looked beyond England's shores as the nation began the maritime expansion and global exploration that would produce the British colonial empire. The age is also remembered for court intrigues, and for courtiers such as the Earl of Essex, who felt both the warmth of Elizabeth's favor and the power of her wrath.

△ IN 1596, ENGLISH FORCES SURPRISED *the third Spanish Armada in the bay of Cadiz. Led by Raleigh and Essex, they destroyed King Philip II's navy and one of Spain's most prosperous cities.*

ELIZABETH I
(1533–1603)

ELIZABETH I REIGNED over England for 45 years, unifying the nation against foreign enemies. During her rule England became a world power in politics, commerce, and the arts.

THE VIRGIN QUEEN

Elizabeth I was the daughter of King Henry VIII and his second wife, Anne Boleyn. During the short reign of her half-brother, Edward VI, she was suspected of plotting to marry Baron Thomas Seymour, the Lord High Admiral, and make him king. Seymour was executed. Elizabeth survived, only to be imprisoned for unwittingly playing a part in a Protestant plot to overthrow her half-sister Mary I, the Catholic queen. In 1558 she succeeded her sister, inheriting a nation in financial and political turmoil. She appointed Sir William Cecil as her chief secretary; he would remain her closest advisor. In 1559 she reintroduced Protestantism with the Acts of Supremacy and Conformity. Stabilizing labor conditions and attempting to remedy the effects of widespread poverty, she took steps to enact currency reforms and improve English credit abroad. She also faced the dual threat of France and Spain, which were militarily stronger than England. She ended Mary I's war against France in 1559. Relations with Spain deteriorated, culminating in the defeat of the first Spanish Armada in 1588, as it tried to invade England. That victory marked the zenith of Elizabeth's reign. An indecisive war with Spain leading to a prolonged economic crisis dominated the last years of her reign, until her death in 1603.

QUEEN ELIZABETH'S BOOTS

△ WHILE ELIZABETH HAD MANY SUITORS, *including Raleigh, she decided that any marriage would be politically disadvantageous. Her choice earned her the nickname "The Virgin Queen."*

SIR FRANCIS BACON
(1561–1626)

THE VERSATILE MIND OF SIR FRANCIS BACON made him successful in many disciplines, including politics and the law as well as science. Today he is best known for championing logical reasoning and empirical observation.

THE INDUCTIVE METHOD

Sir Francis Bacon was born to the Lord Keeper of the Seal of Elizabeth I and received his education at Trinity College, Cambridge University. Elected to the House of Commons in 1584, Bacon offered proposals for the unification of England and Scotland, and the quelling of Roman Catholic unrest, for which he was knighted in 1603. He became attorney general, lord keeper, lord chancellor, Baron de Verulam, and Viscount de St. Albans. However, his enduring fame rests on his philosophical and scientific inquiries, especially the inductive method of modern science: drawing conclusions from a set of facts. He ended his career in disgrace in 1621 after accepting a bribe while acting as a judge. Dismissed from court, he continued his writings, which include *The Novum Organum* and *The New Atlantis*. In 1626 he died from bronchitis, which he contracted while experimenting with the preservative qualities of snow

△ PUBLISHED IN 1694, Opera Omnia *is the first compilation, or complete works, of Francis Bacon.*

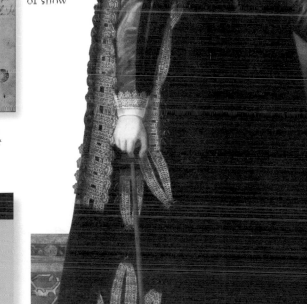

"Chiefly the mould of a man's fortune is in his own hands."

SIR FRANCIS BACON

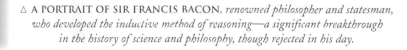

△ A PORTRAIT OF SIR FRANCIS BACON, *renowned philosopher and statesman, who developed the inductive method of reasoning—a significant breakthrough in the history of science and philosophy, though rejected in his day.*

Did you know?

- Some have argued that Bacon was the true author of Shakespeare's works.
- Though he married at 48, contemporary accounts indicate that Bacon was a homosexual.
- There is evidence that he edited the King James version of the Bible.

△ ELIZABETH HAD HER *first lesson in court treachery very young, when her father, Henry VIII, ordered her mother beheaded to pave the way for his third marriage.*

Did you know?

- In 1570 Pope Pius V excommunicated Queen Elizabeth for heresy.
- After the publication of a pamphlet decrying her proposed marriage to a Catholic duke in 1579, Elizabeth had the author and publisher arrested and their right hands chopped off.
- Elizabeth knew seven languages and enjoyed playing practical jokes.

Bacon's Circle

JAMES I (1566–1625) Elizabeth's successor and Bacon's greatest patron.

WILLIAM CECIL (1520–1598) Elizabeth's secretary of state, Bacon's enemy.

SIR EDWARD COKE (1552–1634) Bacon's rival, both politically and romantically.

EARL OF ESSEX
(1567–1601)

THE 2ND EARL OF ESSEX was an English soldier and courtier named Robert Devereux who had the ability to court the queen's favor or invoke her wrath.

△ ELIZABETH I *with Robert Devereux, in a 19th century cartoon that spoofed their tempestuous relationship.*

THE QUEEN'S FAVORITE
Robert Devereux became the 2nd Earl upon the death of his father in 1576, when he came under Lord Bughley's guardianship. He became a favorite of Queen Elizabeth I after distinguishing himself while fighting in the Netherlands in 1586. From that time forward, Essex walked a fine line, inspiring both her love and her anger. He violated her wishes twice, first by taking part in English operations against Lisbon (1589), and then by marrying the widow of poet Sir Philip Sidney (1590). In 1594, however, Essex uncovered a plot against the queen's life; in 1596 he became a national hero as a leader of the force that sacked Cadiz, Spain. In the end, Elizabeth decided that Essex was ungovernable, and he fell from her favor for good. He deserted his post in Ireland, and was deprived of his offices in 1600. A year later, he led some 300 followers in a doomed revolt against the queen. He was found guilty of treason and executed.

Did you know?

- Essex turned his back on the queen during a dispute; she responded by slapping his face and boxing his ears.
- Elizabeth herself signed Essex's death warrant.
- Poet John Donne was among those on Essex's expedition against the Spanish at Cadiz.

◁ MUCH OF ESSEX'S WEALTH *came from taking the taxes levied on imported sweet wines, a right sold to him by the queen. After his poor showing in Ireland, Elizabeth restored these profits to the crown, thereby driving Essex into poverty and opposition to her.*

WILLIAM SHAKESPEARE
(1564–1616)

THE WORKS OF WILLIAM SHAKESPEARE—perhaps the greatest playwright of all time—show a deep understanding of the human experience that continues to appeal to contemporary readers and audiences worldwide.

THE BARD OF AVON
Shakespeare was born in Stratford-on-Avon to John Shakespeare, a glove maker, and Mary Arden, the daughter of a landowner. Educated only through grammar school, Shakespeare married Anne Hathaway, eight years his elder, in 1582. After working in various trades and dissatisfied with his marriage, he moved to London around 1591 to join the Lord Chamberlain's Men, an acting troupe that became the King's Men in 1594. With the support of patrons, he stayed with the company as playwright and actor for nearly 20 years, writing more than 150 poems and 30 plays, including *Romeo and Juliet*, *Hamlet*, *Othello*, and *Macbeth*. Wealthy from his writing as well as shrewd investments, he retired in 1613 to Stratford, where he lived out his life in comfort.

△ A "FIRST FOLIO" *of his plays, published in 1623 and sold then for a pound, has sold for as much as $6,166,000 at auction.*

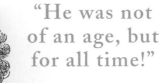

> "He was not of an age, but for all time!"
>
> BEN JONSON

◁ A PORTRAIT OF SHAKESPEARE BY HIS DESK. *Investing his profits from the theater in real estate allowed him to retire in comfort.*

Did you know?

■ Shakespeare coined (among many others) the phrases "fair play," "foregone conclusion," "disgraceful conduct," and "catch cold."
■ One of Shakespeare's twins was named Hamnet.
■ Legend has it that Shakespeare died after a drinking bout with writer Ben Johnson.

◁ THE GLOBE THEATER, *built in 1599 by the King's Men; until 1608 it was the only theater in which Shakespeare staged his plays. The Globe burned down in 1613.*

SIR WALTER RALEIGH
(1552–1618)

ENGLISH SOLDIER, explorer, and writer Walter Raleigh, a favorite of Queen Elizabeth, was one of the most colorful characters of the Elizabethan Age.

ELIZABETH'S EXPLORER

Raleigh fought in the Wars of Religion in France as a young man, received an education at Oxford University, and fought against Irish rebels in 1580. His criticism of English policy in Ireland brought him to the queen's attention, and by 1582 he had become her favorite courtier. The queen bestowed upon Raleigh estates, influence, knighthood, and the position of captain of the Queen's guard. In 1592 she discovered his marriage to a maid in her court, and the two were imprisoned. Released later that year, he led an expedition to the Americas in 1595. In 1603 Elizabeth died and James I became king. Raleigh led a second mission to the Americas in 1616 in search of the legendary El Dorado, "City of Gold." In violation of orders, he attacked a Spanish town, and was executed upon his return.

Did you know?

■ Spenser's *The Faerie Queene* was written partially under Raleigh's patronage.

■ Some scholars have read Shakespeare's *Love's Labour's Lost* as a satire on Raleigh.

■ While on the block, Raleigh joked with his executioner and gave the signal to proceed with his own beheading.

▽ RALEIGH WAS WIDELY *disliked during Elizabeth's reign for the great fortune he amassed.*

△ A MAP OF RALEIGH'S HOLDINGS IN VIRGINIA *c. 1600. Raleigh named the colony after his Queen; he never visited it, content to sponsor expeditions in hopes of profit.*

GANGSTERS

THE MEN WHO ORCHESTRATED THE RISE OF ORGANIZED CRIME IN THE UNITED STATES during the 20th century combined business skills, brutal tactics, and crowd-pleasing panache—traits which made them compelling figures in a national drama.

At the beginning of the last century, various organizations controlled criminal activity in New York, Chicago, and other cities. Prohibition, which took effect in 1920, was a boon to gangsters like Al Capone, who expanded their operations to supply the demand for bootleg liquor. The Mafia as we know it began in the late 1920s, after a series of gang battles that came to be known as the Castellammarese War. In the aftermath, Lucky Luciano, Meyer Lansky, and Joseph Bonanno forged a commission made up of the heads of the leading crime organizations to regulate disputes. The Mafia's strength waned toward the end of the 20th century, as competition from other criminal organizations, infighting, and law enforcement took their tolls. The man whom many consider the last major Mafia figure, John Gotti, was convicted of murder and sentenced to life in prison in 1992, where he remains, close to death.

△ DURING THE 1920S AND '30S. *organized crime and its bloody turf wars turned major cities such as New York and Chicago into battle zones, wtih innocent bystanders slaughtered as mobsters invoked codes of honor.*

LUCKY LUCIANO
(1897–1962)

LUCKY LUCIANO CREATED the modern structure of organized crime in the United States.

ORGANIZER OF CRIME

Born Salvatore Lucania in Sicily, the future gangster came with his family to New York City at age nine. He met future partner Meyer Lansky when Luciano tried unsuccessfully to shake him down. During the early 1920s, Luciano and Lansky worked with Arnold Rothstein to supply booze to New York speakeasies. Later in the decade, there was a bloody power struggle between Giuseppe "Joe the Boss" Masseria and Salvatore Maranzano of the Sicilian Castellammarese crime family. Luciano ended the war by executing Masseria and soon afterward had Maranzano killed as well. Now leader of the most powerful organized-crime family in the United States, he established a system by which two dozen family bosses controlled various criminal operations, with the focus always on the bottom line. In 1936, Luciano was convicted of compulsory prostitution and sentenced to 30 to 50 years in prison. In return for helping US intelligence during World War II he was released from prison to exile in Sicily, though he soon reappeared in Cuba. US authorities claimed that he was planning a massive drug-smuggling operation, and had him deported again. He died of a heart attack in 1962.

△ LUCIANO *spent most of his later years in Naples, accompanied by his dog (above).*

Mafia Assassinations

ALBERT ANASTASIO (1903–1957) Murder Inc. hitman, iced at barbershop.

DION O'BANION (unknown–1924) Mobster John Torrio's Irish rival; shot in his own florist shop.

Body-guard · Lucky Luciano · Slim Aarons · Bodyguard

△ THE ITALIAN GOVERNMENT *laid down strict rules for Luciano while in exile; Aarons was one of few journalists allowed to see him.*

AL CAPONE
(1899–1947)

AL CAPONE BECAME AMERICA'S MOST FAMOUS gangster during Prohibition, and his high-profile image elevated the gangster to the status of a public figure.

SCARFACE

Capone was born in Brooklyn, New York, to an Italian immigrant family. Expelled from school at age 14, he joined a gang run by mobster Johnny Torrio. Torrio recommended the 18-year-old Capone to gangster Frankie Yale, who hired Capone to tend bar. At 19, Capone married Mae Coughlin, moved to Baltimore, and began working as a bookkeeper for a legitimate construction firm, but after his father's death in 1920, Capone again took up with Torrio, who had moved and now ran speakeasies, brothels, and gambling houses in Chicago. Soon after the reunion, Torrio was shot and decided to leave crime. He turned himself in and gave control of his empire to Capone, who quickly became a celebrity, making widely noted appearances at charity functions, the opera, and sporting events, as as well as providing a soup kitchen for Chicago's poor. Capone ran into trouble in 1926, when his men accidentally killed a prosecutor, forcing him into hiding for three months. He finally gave himself up, but the case was thrown out for insufficient evidence. Capone then moved to Miami, ordering a hit on Frankie Yale for stealing from their bootlegging business, and devising the infamous St. Valentine's Day Massacre in an unsuccessful attempt to kill rival mobster Bugsy Moran. Federal officials became determined to bring Capone down. By 1930, Treasury agent Eliot Ness had shut many of Capone's breweries, and Capone was named the FBI's first "Public Enemy No. 1." He pled guilty to tax evasion in 1931 and was sentenced to 11 years in prison. Released in 1939, Capone spent his last years in Miami, dying in 1947 of a stroke.

△ CAPONE TRIED *to plea-bargain a shorter sentence for his tax evasion crimes, but the court refused and forced him to stand trial in 1931.*

△ THE FINGERPRINTS OF AL CAPONE, *taken by Philadelphia police.*

△ AL CAPONE'S *hideout in Couderay, Wisconsin had the trappings of a hunting lodge.*

> "You can get a lot more done with a kind word and a gun than you can with a kind word alone."
>
> AL CAPONE

∧ LUCIANO NEGOTIATED *with dictator Fulgencio Batista to turn Cuba into a Mafia playground. Leaving Italy was against the terms of his sentence. Here he is shown returning to Sicily in 1947, after being arrested in Cuba.*

Did you know?

■ Luciano helped intelligence agents find the German spies responsible for the dockside sinking of the ocean liner *Normandie*.

■ Some say "Lucky" Luciano got his nickname by surviving a knife attack which left him with a droop in his right eye, others say it was for his luck at picking horses.

Did you know?

■ While working at Yale's Harvard Inn, Capone got involved in a fight over a woman and received three knife slashes on his face. The resulting disfigurement earned him the nickname "Scarface."

■ Capone was a patron of many of the top jazz artists of his day.

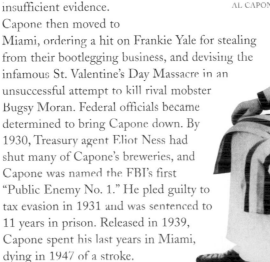

◁ AFTER EIGHT YEARS *in prison, five spent at Alcatraz, Capone was released for good behavior and because the ravages of syphilis had rendered him largely incompetent.*

MEYER LANSKY
(1902–1983)

MEYER LANSKY, THE MOST SUCCESSFUL JEWISH GANGSTER of the 20th century, was the brains behind the first nationwide Mafia syndicate.

MOB MASTERMIND

Born Maier Suchowljanksy in Grodno, Russia, Lansky moved with his family to New York City in 1911. Lansky met future mobsters Bugsy Siegel and Lucky Luciano when the three were boys, and as a teenager, he joined with Siegel to run a gambling/car-theft ring.

In 1920, Lansky and Luciano began running illegal liquor with Arnold Rothstein, then the undisputed leader of the New York underworld. Soon afterward the Castellammarese War broke out between rival Italian mobs run by Joe Masseria and Salvatore Maranzano. Lansky, being Jewish, did not get involved in the war, but Luciano did. After both Masseria and Maranzano were murdered, Luciano and Lansky proposed the crime syndicate that evolved into New York's five Mafia families. Luciano took over Masseria's family, later to become the Genovese family, and Lansky stayed on as his right-hand man.

After Prohibition, Lansky focused primarily on gambling, setting up illegal casinos in New Orleans, Arkansas, Kentucky, and Florida to go along with legal operations in Cuba, Las Vegas, London, and the Caribbean. He helped finance much of the building of Las Vegas and was in charge of bookkeeping and money laundering. When he died in Miami, he was worth an estimated $300 million.

△ LANSKY SAID *that he turned to a life of crime as a young boy after losing a nickel in a craps game on New York's Lower East Side.*

Did you know?

■ The US House Committee on Assassinations in 1979 voiced suspicions that Lansky was involved with the assassination of Lee Harvey Oswald.

■ Lansky never spent a day of his life in prison.

■ He once claimed that the Mafia was "bigger than US Steel."

△ THE HOTEL RIVIERIA IN HAVANA, *a large casino and hotel complex, was built by Meyer Lansky in 1957. It is seen here only days before the fall of Fulgencio Batista in January, 1959. The hotel was forced to close by the Castro government.*

JOHN GOTTI
b. 1940

JOHN GOTTI LED NEW YORK CITY'S GAMBINO CRIME FAMILY from 1985 until 1992. His lavish lifestyle, charisma, and thuggish behavior helped define the romantic public image of the Mafia.

THE DAPPER DON

Gotti was born into a family of 13 in the South Bronx. He started running errands for local mobsters at an early age, and quit school at 16 to pursue a life of crime. He married Victoria DiGiornio in 1962, and in 1966 the couple moved to the middle-class Ozone Park neighborhood in Queens. Gotti was convicted of hijacking goods in 1968 and served three years in prison. He committed his first murder in 1971, but lawyer Roy Cohn helped him strike a deal that reduced his prison sentence to two years. Upon release, Gotti worked his way up through the Gambino family by maneuvering his crew into gambling and drug-dealing. Dissatisfied with Gambino boss Paul Castellano, Gotti helped arrange his 1985 shooting outside Sparks Steakhouse in Manhattan—after which Gotti replaced him as head of the Gambinos. Gotti faced trial in 1986 for racketeering and in 1989 for assault. Acquitted both times, he earned the nickname "The Teflon Don." The FBI, however, was determined to convict Gotti, and spent almost $75 million on surveillance and other activities. Tapes of Gotti and his associates led to his 1992 conviction for Castellano's murder. Though sentenced to life in prison without parole, he is reportedly near death from throat cancer.

Mob Busters

RUDY GIULIANI b. 1944 New York mayor, made his name as D.A., crusading against the mob.

J. EDGAR HOOVER (1895–1972) Ruthless FBI chief, took on the mob.

ELIOT NESS (1903–1957) Detective of *The Untouchables* fame.

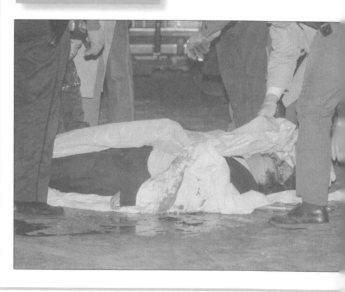

"This is gonna be a Cosa
Nostra till I die."

JOHN GOTTI, OVERHEARD BY FBI SURVEILLANCE

◁ PAUL CASTELLANO'S
driver, Thomas Bilotti,
was also murdered by
Gotti's hit men outside
Sparks Steakhouse in the
same rub out on
December 16, 1985,
that killed Castellano.
Here police cover up the
driver's bloody body.

Did you know?

■ When Gotti was 14, he
and some friends tried to
steal a portable cement
mixer; it fell on his toes.
He has walked with a
limp ever since.

■ Gotti studied
Machiavelli's *The Prince*,
and could quote long
sections from memory.

■ Cosa Nostra means
"Our Thing."

JOSEPH BONANNO
b. 1905

JOSEPH BONANNO HEADED THE
COUNTRY'S most powerful Mafia
family during the Mob's heyday,
and exerted a strong influence
on popular notions of
Mafia chieftains.

THE GODFATHER

Bonanno grew up in Sicily, and as
a very young man was involved in
organized crime there. He was exiled to
Cuba in 1925, along with other Mafiosi,
and made his way to Brooklyn, New York,
where he worked his way up through the local
mob. The Castellammarese War broke out in
1928 between two rival Mafia gangs, and both
leaders—Salvatore Maranzano and Joe Masseria
—were killed. Bonanno, just 26 years old, was
elected to lead Maranzano's former operation,
and he helped form a commission of the heads
of New York's organized crime families.

Bonanno was spectacularly successful during
the next 30 years. His criminal network
corrupted legitimate businesses and expanded
the family's influence in casinos in Las Vegas
and Cuba and drug-running operations in
Canada, among other ventures. His success
earned him the nicknames "Boss of Bosses"
and "The Godfather."

In 1962, Bonanno, following a series of
deaths among his allies, concocted a plot to
consolidate power by killing other Mafia
bosses. The other New York crime families
learned of his plan and forced him to retire
from crime and leave the country. Later,
suffering from poor health, he was allowed
to move with his family to Arizona,
where he remains.

△ WHILE BONANNO
always stressed the role of
honor and tradition in his
family's criminal dealings, the
Bonanno family was likely
involved in opening the
international drug trade to
the Mafia and headed the
famous "Pizza Connection"
drug ring during the 1980s.

Did you know?

■ Joe Bonanno invented
the "double coffin,"
which allowed mobsters
to dispose of a dead body
by stashing it in a secret
lower compartment built
into a coffin.

■ As a teenager, Bonanno
fought against
Mussolini's Fascists, who
were trying to seize
power in Sicily.

THE JOSEPH BONANNO FAMILY

◁ JOSEPH
BONANNO'S
FAMILY CHART, *used
as an aid in the Senate
investigating trial of
October 1963.*

CREATORS OF TELEVISION

Television now reaches into nearly every corner of the globe, a presence many accept without question, like running water and the rising sun.

But just fifty years ago, television was still a wobbly young medium trying to find its legs. Thanks to expensive TV sets and a dearth of good shows, television could have been just another fad if not for the five performers in this section, who helped make television a fact of life. The legendary programming created by these five set the blueprint for what we still watch today. From Lucille Ball and Jackie Gleason came the situation comedies, still the most popular kind of programming; Sid Caesar and *Your Show of Shows* (whose writers included Woody Allen, Neil Simon, and Mel Brooks) gave us sketch comedy; and it's hard to imagine *"Saturday Night Live"* or *"Monty Python"* without the innovations of Ernie Kovacs. And Milton Berle? He showed us how good men could look in dresses.

△ AT NBC'S STUDIO 8-G, *in New York's Rockefeller Center, crews broadcast four shows at a time, as television began to emerge as the prime medium of the second half of the twentieth century.*

MILTON BERLE
(1908–2002)

Milton Berle's slapstick comedy helped to sell millions of television sets in the medium's early days, earning Berle the nickname "Mr. Television."

UNCLE MILTIE

Berle, born Mendel Berlinger in New York City, was a natural entertainer. He worked as a child on the vaudeville stage, modeled Buster Brown shoes, and appeared in more than 50 silent films before becoming a comedian. He successfully worked the nightclub circuit during the 1940s, but was unsuccessful in several attempts at a career in radio comedy. It was as the host of an NBC variety series called "Texaco Star Theater" that Berle became a household name in 1948. Television was still new at the time, and hadn't yet been adopted by the masses, but Berle's wacky visual humor, consisting of elaborate costumes and bodily contortions, changed all that: The buzz on Berle prompted millions of Americans to purchase TVs and tune in. The show aired until 1956. Berle's TV popularity subsequently diminished, but he continued to attract work as an actor, emcee, and headlining nightclub comedian in Las Vegas and elsewhere. He and fellow comedians George Jessel, Bing Crosby, Bob Hope, and Jimmy Durante started the Friar's Club of California, the famous social club for comedians and show-business personalities. In 1984 he was one of the first inductees into the Television Academy Hall of Fame. Berle worked well into his eighties, receiving an Emmy nomination at age 87 for a guest turn on "Beverly Hills 90210."

"I feel like a 20-year-old, but there's never one around"

MILTON BERLE

▷ BERLE WAS FINALLY *knocked off the air in the late sixties by "The Man From U.N.C.L.E.," which ran against his variety show "The Milton Berle Show."*

MILTON BERLE

▷ BERLE'S SHOWS WERE *only a few steps away from the old vaudeville tradition. A variety of regular acts appeared along with guests, and each show opened with Milton Berle in another outrageous outfit, and often times women's clothing.*

△ ALTHOUGH THE NAME *of Berle's second television show was "The Milton Berle Show" (1954–1956), he alternated with Martha Raye, Bob Hope, and Steve Allen as the host.*

Key TV Producers

NORMAN LEAR b. 1922 "All in the Family," "The Jeffersons," and "Maude."

GARRY MARSHALL b.1934 "The Odd Couple," "Happy Days," "Mork & Mindy."

JAMES BURROWS b. 1940 "Taxi," "Cheers," and "Friends."

Did you know?

■ Berle was sometimes accused of lifting jokes from other comics—a practice that earned him the nickname "The Thief of Badgags."

■ Berle appeared in the first-ever feature-length comedy, *Tillie's Punctured Romance* (1914), which starred Charlie Chaplin.

■ In 1977 Berle launched a magazine called *Milton*. Its motto: "We drink. We smoke. We gamble."

▷ BERLE HAD FOUR *children, including Vickie, seen here, whom he adopted in the early 1950s with his third wife, Ruth Cosgrove.*

LUCILLE BALL

(1911–1989)

LUCILLE DESIREE BALL, famed as TV's Lucy, helped to define television during a career that took her from bit-part movie actress to America's favorite comedienne and TV-production heavyweight. Her landmark show "I Love Lucy" established the half-hour situation-comedy format, as well as the method of shooting in front of a live studio audience.

HERE'S LUCY

Born in Celeron, New York, Ball had little success in her early attempts to break into theater. However, she landed a role in the 1934 movie *Roman Scandals*, which kicked off a highly successful film career. From 1947 to 1951 she played the wife of a staid banker on a popular radio show, and CBS approached her about taking the show to television. She agreed, on the condition that her real-life husband Desi Arnaz would star with her. "I Love Lucy" was an instant hit from its premiere on October 15, 1951: Ball's unique physical comedy and zany misadventures glued viewers to their sets. It was the number-one-rated show during four of its six seasons, and never dropped below number three. "I Love Lucy's" success allowed the couple's production company, Desilu, to buy RKO Pictures, making Desilu a major player in a highly competitive field.

△ BALL'S MOVIE *career included more than 60 films, including the 1938 film* Room Service *with the Marx Brothers. She continued to work in movies into the 1980s. She died in 1989 at age 77.*

▷ LUCY *with Desi Arnaz in a 1950s episode of "I Love Lucy." The couple divorced in 1960, and Ball bought Arnaz's share of Desilu, making her the sole owner of the world's largest production company.*

COMPANY LOGO

Other funny ladies

DORIS DAY b. 1924 Born Doris von Kappelhoff, coy queen of '50s and '60s comedy romance genre.

SHIRLEY MACLAINE b.1934 Vulnerable beauty of classic comedy films, including Billy Wilder's *The Apartment* (1960).

JOAN SIMS (1930–2001) Star of over two dozen British *Carry On* films.

▷ LUCILLE BALL *was one of Bob Hope's regular leading ladies. This scene is from* The Facts of Life *(1960). Shooting this scene, Ball fell and hit her head on the side of a boat. She was hospitalized and kept under observation for 24 hours.*

"I'm not funny. What I am is brave."

LUCILLE BALL

Did you know?

■ Ball went to drama class with Bette Davis. Bette had rave reviews from her teachers; Lucy was sent home.

■ Lucy's studio contract stipulated that she always had to remain twenty pounds overweight.

■ The episode in which she gave birth to Ricky Jr. was broadcast the night Lucy gave birth to her real son, Desiderio.

JACKIE GLEASON
1916–1987

COMEDIAN JACKIE GLEASON earned a permanent place in television history playing the lovable loudmouth Ralph Kramden in "The Honeymooners."

THE GREAT ONE

Gleason, born Herbert John Gleason in Brooklyn, worked as a comedian in local nightclubs and appeared in several Broadway shows before being discovered by Jack Warner in the 1940s. He was signed to a movie contract in Hollywood, but his movies bombed, and he soon moved back to New York. He did television work, including a starring role in "The Life of Riley" in 1949. His career finally took off, though, in 1950, when he hosted a television show called "Cavalcade of Stars." In 1952 he hosted "The Jackie Gleason Show" for CBS, in which he appeared as a number of comic characters—including a bus driver named Ralph Kramden. The Kramden skits were enormously popular, and eventually became the basis for the half-hour situation comedy "The Honeymooners." The show ran for only one season, but its 20.5 hours have remained some of television's most beloved thanks to their almost constant presence in syndication. Gleason during the 1960s hosted television variety shows and appeared in such notable films as *The Hustler* (1961) and *Requiem for a Heavyweight* (1962). His later career never reached its early heights, although he reunited with his old cast for a series of Honeymooners specials in the late 1970s and continued to appear in occasional films.

Did you know?

■ Gleason wrote the song "You're My Greatest Love," the theme from "The Honeymooners."

■ Gleason won a Tony Award in 1959 for his performance in the musical *Take Me Along*.

■ He was nominated for an Oscar for his work as pool champ Minnesota Fats in *The Hustler*.

△ AS A COMPOSER AND arranger, Gleason released romantic music records during the 1950s. Two, *Music for Lovers Only* (1953) and *Music to Make You Misty* (1955), earned gold records. He made twenty albums in all, though he could not read music.

▽ GLEASON CELEBRATED HIS 40TH BIRTHDAY *with some of television's most beautiful stars: from left, Polly Bergen, Jayne Meadows, Joyce Randolph, Audrey Meadows, and Jayne Mansfield.*

△ BEHIND GLEASON'S *lead, Audrey Meadows as his wife, Art Carney as his friend, and Joyce Randolph as Norton's wife, Trixie, became the prototypical TV foursome in "The Honeymooners."*

"One of these days, Alice. Pow! Right in the kisser!"

RALPH KRAMDEN TO HIS LONG-SUFFERING WIFE

ERNIE KOVACS
(1919–1962)

COMEDIAN ERNIE KOVACS created a distinct brand of surreal sketch comedy that has influenced contemporary talk-show hosts—including David Letterman—and comedy troupes such as The Kids in the Hall.

THE FIRST MAN TO MASSAGE THE MEDIUM

Kovacs, born in Trenton, New Jersey, worked in radio and as a newspaper columnist before landing a job as host of a cooking show in Philadelphia. His comedic approach led him to several successful local shows, such as "Ernie in Kovacsland." Kovacs moved to New York City in 1952, hosting popular shows on CBS—"Time for Ernie," "The Ernie Kovacs Show," and "Kovacs Unlimited"—that often incorporated music with ad-libbed skits, brief conceptual bits, and recurring characters, such as the poet Percy Dovetonsils. One of his most famous skits, the Nairobi Trio, involved the cast—in hats, trench coats, and gorilla masks—hitting each other with mallets while playing lounge music. In 1957, his "The Silent Show" garnered Kovacs the cover of *Life* and a movie contract with Columbia Pictures. He moved to Los Angeles and appeared in films such as *Bell, Book and Candle* (1958). He died when his car crashed into a utility pole as he was driving home from Billy Wilder's house.

△ **DURING A STRETCH IN 1955**, *Kovacs created 20.5 hours of original comedy every week for radio and television.*

Did you know?

■ Kovacs's ex-wife once kidnapped his two daughters. Kovacs recovered them after a two-year search.

■ Kovacs died in a Corvair , the car Ralph Nader later called "unsafe at any speed."

■ He regularly gambled with high rollers like Frank Sinatra and Dean Martin.

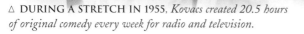

> "Television is often called a medium because it's so rarely well done."
>
> ERNIE KOVACS

△ **KOVACS'S SECOND WIFE, EDIE ADAMS**, *was Miss U.S. Television when she met him in 1951 as a dancer on his show "Ernie in Kovacsland."*

▷ **KOVACS PIONEERED** *the use of the blackout—a short, visual gag—on television, from its roots as a vaudeville comedy form.*

SID CAESAR

b. 1922

SID CAESAR'S EVERYMAN APPEAL made him one of television's first major stars. In 1987 he was awarded the Lifetime Achievement Award in Comedy.

YOUR SHOW OF SHOWS

Born in New York to a family of Jewish immigrants, Caesar began his show business career while a teenager, playing saxophone and clarinet for the Shep Fields band. He joined the Coast Guard during World War II, making his stage debut at a service show, *Tars and Spars* (1945). He appeared in the 1946 film version of the show, and went on to star in NBC's "Your Show of Shows" (1950 to 1954), a comedy variety series that is regarded as a high point of early television.

Caesar's career declined after "Your Show of Shows," in part due to alcoholism, which he did not conquer until the late 1970s. He starred in the Broadway musical *Little Me* (1962–63), and occasionally appeared in films in the 1970s and '80s. His signature act involved a gag called "doubletalk," a multilingual pseudo-patter that seemed to include smatterings of French, Italian, German, and Spanish.

△ CAESAR'S CO-STAR *on "Your Show of Shows" was Imogene Coca, whose training in music and ballet put her in good stead for the physical comedy required by the show. Coca had been a full-time vaudeville performer by the time she was 13.*

△ INSPIRED BY HIS HERO *Charlie Chaplin, Caesar loved clowning and, especially, pantomime.*

NBC

MAX LIEBMAN
PRESENTS
SID CAESAR
AND
IMOGENE COCA
IN

Your Show of Shows

CENTER THEATRE
AVENUE OF THE AMERICAS
NEW YORK

9-12-5

◁ PRODUCER MAX *Liebman adapted the format he had used for years as a director of theatrical revues in Florida and the Catskills to create "Your Show of Shows."*

Did you know?

■ Mel Brooks, Woody Allen, Neil Simon, and Larry Gelbart all learned to write comedy while working with Caesar.

■ His strength—and temper—were infamous. He was known to punch through walls, and once punched a horse.

■ Caesar studied saxophone at the Juilliard School in New York before taking up acting.

THE GREAT EXPLORERS

WHILE MOST OF US ARE HAPPY TO LIVE OUR LIVES WHERE WE ARE, THERE ARE PEOPLE who cannot rest without seeing what lies beyond the next hill.

Whether driven by a taste for adventure or by greed, scientific interest or simple curiosity, the great explorers of the past braved long and difficult voyages as they looked through the limits of the familiar world and into the unknown. Marco Polo's adventures in China in the 14th century provided the first descriptions of the East for Europeans and inspired generations of later explorers, including Vasco Da Gama, whose voyage to India opened up trade between Europe and the Subcontinent. Columbus's voyages to the Americas launched a new era of colonization and discovery for Europe, and Magellan's first circumnavigation of the globe provided the world with proof that the Earth was round. James Cook's expeditions charted much of the Pacific and set the standard for later scientific expeditions. Facing starvation, mutiny, disease, shipwreck, hostile natives, and countless other dangers, these five men broadened Europe's knowledge of the world and cleared the path for all who came after them.

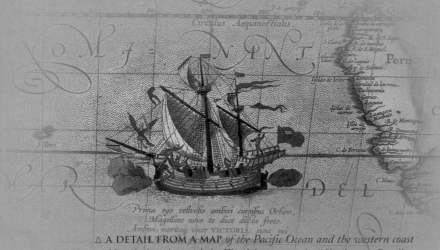

Prima ego velivolis ambivi cursibus Orbem, Magellane novo te duce ducta freto. Ambivi, meritóq vocor VICTORIA: sunt mi
△ A DETAIL FROM A MAP *of the Pacific Ocean and the western coast of South America made by Flemish cartographer Abrahamus Orteliu in the 16th century.*

VASCO DA GAMA
(ca. 1460–1524)

PORTUGUESE EXPLORER VASCO DA GAMA was the first European to successfully navigate to India by sea. His voyages to Asia helped Portugal reap riches from the spice trade and establish itself as a world power.

THE BRIDGE TO INDIA
The son of a nobleman, Vasco da Gama sailed from Lisbon with four vessels on July 8, 1497. He crossed the Cape of Good Hope and reached Calicut (Calcutta), India, on May 20, 1498, after a deep-sea voyage revolutionary for his time. The Hindu ruler Zamorin refused to make a treaty with him, but da Gama returned to Portugal a hero nevertheless. Made Admiral of the Indies by King Emmanuel I, he began another, successful, voyage in 1502 to avenge the killing of Portuguese explorers in Calicut and destroy the Muslim traders who had opposed his entry into the market during his first journey. In 1524 he returned to India as viceroy, but died shortly after his arrival.

TELESCOPE

▷ DA GAMA *in traditional dress, holding the head to a suit of armor and a stick.*

△ DA GAMA PRESENTS A LETTER *from the King of Portugal to the court of Calicut in 1498. While the Portuguese were at first accorded welcome, the Hindu ruler did not open his territory to trade and instead forced da Gama to leave the contents of his ships as a tax.*

CHRISTOPHER COLUMBUS
(1451–1506)

THOUGH EXPLORERS since the Vikings had journeyed to the continents dubbed by Europeans the "New World," the four journeys of Italian navigator Christoforo Columbo initiated European colonization and exploitation of the Americas.

JOURNEY TO THE NEW WORLD

Columbus began his career as a seaman in the Portuguese merchant marines. After a shipwreck in 1476, he made his way to Lisbon and joined his brother Bartholomew in the chart-making trade. He also worked as a sugar buyer and entrepreneur, and between 1478 and 1479 sailed to Iceland, Ireland, and Madeira. Columbus believed that by sailing westward across the Atlantic he could reach the riches of Asia quickly and easily. In 1484 he asked Portugal's king, John II, to fund such a voyage. Refused, he left for Spain in 1485 to seek the aid of King Ferdinand and Queen Isabella. Though again turned down, he remained in Spain and in 1492 Ferdinand and Isabella finally granted his request. He set off with three ships, the Nina, Pinta, and Santa Maria, on August 3, 1492, reaching what some think to be Watling Island (now San Salvador) in the Bahamas on October 12. Believing he had landed in India, Columbus called the natives he met "Indians." Upon his return to Spain in 1493, he convinced Ferdinand and Isabella to fund another expedition in search of gold. He returned to the New World three more times between 1493 and 1503, establishing colonies and earning the title "Admiral of the Ocean Sea."

Did you know?

■ One of Columbus's motivations was to make enough money to be able to take Jerusalem back from the Muslims.

■ In 1500 Ferdinand sent an inspector to Hispaniola; he found total anarchy and Columbus was sent back to Spain in chains. He was released, but lost governorship of the colony.

▽ A 1608 DUTCH MAP *retracing Columbus's journey. Despite all evidence to the contrary, Columbus maintained a lifelong belief that he had reached Asia on his first journey.*

Did you know?

■ Da Gama's father, Estevao, was chosen by King Manuel I to lead the initial expedition to India, but he died before the voyage could take place, and Vasco went instead.

■ On his second voyage to India, da Gama captured an Arab ship containing between 200 and 400 passengers. He burned the ship and killed all the passengers to intimidate Portugal's enemies in the region.

"Along this track of pathless ocean it is my intention to steer."

CHRISTOPHER COLUMBUS

◁ COLUMBUS, IN A 1519 PORTRAIT. *Although the US celebrates a national holiday in his honor every October, there is ongoing controversy over his legacy. It is acknowledged that Columbus believed that he was on a divine mission, yet in the past decade, there has been a refocus on the colonizers' often brutal treatment of the Native American peoples.*

MARCO POLO
(ca. 1254–1324)

ITALIAN TRAVELER AND MERCHANT Marco Polo's accounts of his overland journey to China were the West's chief source of information about Asia during the Renaissance—inspiring later generations of explorers.

THE SILK ROAD

Polo was probably born in what is now Croatia. His father, Niccolo, and his uncle Maffeo had befriended the Mongol ruler of China, Kublai Khan, on a previous trading journey from Venice to China. In 1271 Marco joined his father and uncle on a second journey. Upon arriving in Cambuluc (now Beijing) in 1275, the Polos were accepted into the Khan's court. Marco became a close friend of Kublai Khan, and was employed by him on expeditions throughout Southeast Asia and India. The Polos eventually left China in 1292 as escorts to a Mongol princess, thus ending a 16- to 17-year sojourn in Asia. Upon returning to Venice in 1295, Polo joined forces fighting the Genoese and was captured. In prison for a year, he dictated his account of his travels to a fellow prisoner, Rusticiano of Pisa; it was published as *Il Milione*, or *The Million Lies*—and many thought they were lies. He was released from prison in 1299, becoming a politician and advocate for those of common birth. He lived in Venice until his death; his last words were "I have only told the half of what I saw."

△ A 1310 ENGRAVING *of Marco Polo, a legend in his own time.*

Did you know?

■ Some scholars believe that while in China, Polo ruled the city of Yangzhou for a time.

■ Among the wonders Polo observed in China were eyeglasses, coal, and paper currency.

■ Polo's name doesn't appear in any Chinese documents, leading some to believe that he never made it to China.

△ AFTER A JOURNEY OF 5,600 MILES *and three and a half years, young Marco Polo arrived in Kublai Khan's court in 1275, then situated in what is now Beijing, a moment depicted in this miniature from Mandeville's* Book of Marvels *(early 14th century).*

JAMES COOK
(1728–1779)

BRITISH NAVIGATOR James Cook probably did more to fill in the map of the world than any other explorer in history.

TO THE ENDS OF THE EARTH

Cook was apprenticed to a Quaker shipowner by age 18, but eventually joined the navy and was promoted to ship's master at age 29. Cook commanded a captured ship for the Royal Navy during the Seven Years War (1756–63), and in 1768 he took command of the first scientific expedition to the Pacific. On his ship *Endeavor*, Cook discovered and charted New Zealand and the Great Barrier Reef of Australia. After his return he was chosen to circumnavigate and explore Antarctica. On this voyage he charted present-day Tonga, Easter Island, New Caledonia, the South Sandwich Islands, and South Georgia, and disproved the existence of Terra Australis, a fabled southern continent. His voyages helped guide generations of explorers, and provided the first accurate map of the Pacific. Cook died in a skirmish with islanders during a winter layover in Hawaii.

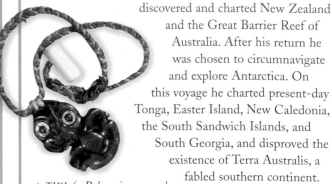

△ TIKI *(a Polynesian carved image of a god) owned by Cook.*

Did you know?

■ Cook fought scurvy (a deadly disease caused by vitamin deficiency) by feeding his crew a diet that included watercress, sauerkraut, and orange extract.

■ Cook named the Hawaiian Islands the Sandwich Islands after the Earl of Sandwich.

> COOK WAS KILLED *in 1779 by Hawaiian islanders in a fight over a theft.*

◁ CAPTAIN JAMES COOK, *depicted in a c. 1830 engraving.*

Other Explorers

JOHN CABOT (1450–1498) First Englishman to reach North America.

IBN BATTUTA (1304–1368) Traveled to all Muslim lands of his time.

LEIF ERICKSON (c. 1000) Viking mariner, landed on North America.

"I had ambition not only to go farther than any man had ever been before, but as far as it was possible for a man to go."

JAMES COOK

FERDINAND MAGELLAN
(c. 1480–1521)

PORTUGUESE NAVIGATOR AND EXPLORER Ferdinand Magellan discovered the Strait of Magellan, providing a westward route to the Pacific Ocean. His ships crossed the Pacific and eventually completed the first circumnavigation of the globe.

THE FIRST EXPEDITION AROUND THE GLOBE

Magellan was born to an aristocratic family. He served in the Portuguese fleet in India from 1505 to 1512 and in Morocco from 1513 to 1514. Magellan was accused of financial misconduct in Morocco and lost favor with Portugal's King Manuel I.

Magellan went to Spain in 1517, where he took the name Fernando de Magallanes. Spain's King Charles I approved of Magellan's plan to reach the spice-rich islands of Asia by a western route, and on September 20, 1519, Magellan set sail from Sanlúcar de Barrameda, Spain, with 5 vessels and some 265 men. He discovered the Strait of Magellan at the tip of South America on October 21, and sailed through it into the Pacific. Magellan was killed by natives in the Philippines, but his remaining ship did reach Asia, and from there returned to Spain.

△ MAGELLAN SAILED *in search of the Spice Islands, hoping to claim them for Spain.*

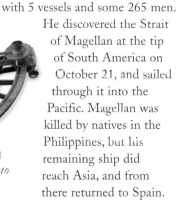

△ MAGELLAN *used a sextant to navigate the uncharted seas.*

Did you know?

■ Magellan gave the Pacific Ocean its name because it was so calm.

■ Magellan quelled a mutiny by executing one ship's captain and marooning another off the coast of Brazil.

■ Food ran so low that the men ate the leather off the ship's rigging.

◁ A MAP OF THE STRAITS OF MAGELLAN *from a 1606 Dutch engraving. Magellan originally named the passage the "Strait of All Saints." When he sighted the Pacific Ocean at the western end, he reportedly wept with joy.*

THE GREATEST SPORTSMEN

THE GREATEST SPORTSMEN OF THE 20TH CENTURY BECAME SOME OF ITS BIGGEST celebrities, and their influence wasn't limited to the playing field.

Instead, they became international symbols, affecting everything from popular trends to political movements. The end of the 19th century saw the development of national athletic leagues and the birth of the modern Olympic Games. Shortly afterward the new technology of film and radio allowed people to follow the stars created by organized sports—men such as Jim Thorpe, who won both the pentathlon and the decathlon at the 1912 Olympics, and Babe Ruth, baseball's signature player, who was as famous for his gargantuan appetites as for his feats on the diamond. Later in the century, the mold was broken and a different kind of sports star emerged. Muhammed Ali enchanted and polarized Americans with his brash and charming personality and his controversial politics. Pelé, meanwhile, helped make soccer the world's most popular game. The corporate world of the 1980s and '90s found its man in Michael Jordan, whose basketball accomplishments and promotional savvy made him a cultural icon.

△ INTEREST IN SPECTATOR SPORTS *started to grow during the Industrial Revolution, which caused increases in urban populations and leisure time. Today, organized sports are a multimillion dollar industry.*

MUHAMMAD ALI
b. 1942

MUHAMMAD ALI WAS AMONG the most successful boxers of all time, but it was his powerful personality and controversial politics that made him one of the world's most recognizable figures.

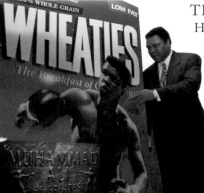

THE GREATEST
He was born Cassius Marcellus Clay in Louisville, Kentucky, and learned to box from local policeman and part-time trainer Joe Martin. Martin eventually steered Clay to Fred Stoner, who guided him through a highly successful amateur career: Cassius Clay won 100 of 108 amateur fights, capped by winning a gold medal at age 18 at the 1960 Olympics in Rome. At the Olympics, Clay began to develop the witty, boastful persona that came to define his public image. He turned pro upon returning home, and at age 22 knocked out the heavily favored Sonny Liston for the heavyweight title, then won their rematch a year later.

△ THOUGH HALTING *in speech, Ali—once the world's most famous man—is again making public appearances.*

Clay became an increasingly vocal critic of racism in the United States. After the first Liston fight he announced that he had changed his name to Muhammad Ali and joined the Nation of Islam. These steps, along with his refusal to serve in the Vietnam War, tarnished Ali's reputation among some Americans. He was sentenced in 1967 to five years in prison for draft evasion and stripped of his boxing title. He was released on appeal, however, and three years later his sentence was overturned.

Ali returned to the ring in 1970 and in 1971 suffered his first professional defeat, at the hands of heavyweight champion Joe Frazier. He avenged that loss by beating Frazier in 1974, earning the right to fight then-champion George Foreman in Zaire, in the bout that became known as "The Rumble in the Jungle." Ali knocked out the heavily favored Foreman to regain the title, and a year later defended it by again beating Frazier, this time in "The Thrilla in Manila." He lost the title to Leon Spinks in 1978, but later defeated Spinks to earn the championship for a third time.

Ali retired from boxing in 1981. Since his retirement, he has been diagnosed with Parkinson's Disease, a neurological disorder that may have been exacerbated by trauma to the head during his years of boxing.

▷ ALI RELIED ON AGILE FOOTWORK *and speedy hands, rather than a knockout punch, to wear out opponents such as Karl Mildenberger, whom he beat on September 10, 1966, in Frankfurt, Germany.*

> "I'm fast, I'm handsome, I'm pretty, and can't possibly be beat!"
>
> MUHAMMAD ALI

BABE RUTH
(1895–1948)

BABE RUTH WAS THE FIRST modern sports superstar and the most dominant force in early 20th-century baseball.

THE SULTAN OF SWAT

Born George Herman Ruth in Baltimore, Maryland, Ruth lived in poverty above his family's saloon until age seven, when his parents sent him to St. Mary's Industrial School for Boys, a reformatory and orphanage where he learned how to play baseball. By age 19, Ruth joined the major-league Boston Red Sox, where he pitched and played outfield. He led Boston to the 1918 World Series title, and in 1919 his 29 home runs broke the single-season record. The Red Sox in 1919 sold Ruth's contract to the New York Yankees for the then-unprecedented price of $100,000. He soon became baseball's top player, leading the American League in home runs from 1919 to 1924 and 1926 to 1931, and making the Yankees the league's most powerful team. With his heroics at the plate, his generosity, and his larger-than-life appetites, he became one of America's most beloved people. In 1923, the Yankees built a new stadium, often called "The House That Ruth Built," to accommodate the crowds he attracted, and he gave fans even more reason to come in 1927, when he hit 60 home runs, a record that stood until broken by Roger Maris in 1961. He finished his career with the Boston Braves and retired in 1935 with 714 homers, a total unsurpassed until Hank Aaron hit his 715th in 1974.

△ THE "LIVELY" BALL, *seen here, was introduced in the 1920 season. It was bouncier than the old "dead" ball, enabling Ruth to hit 54 homers.*

△ RUTH WAS CROWNED *the fictitious "King of Swat" by Yankees Manager Miller Huggins who placed this foot-high silver crown on his slugger's head on October 13, 1921.*

Lou Gehrig—The Iron Horse—Yankee first baseman

Ruth batted in front of Gehrig in the Yankee lineup

Home Run Kings

HANK AARON b. 1934 Career leader in home runs—hit 755 homers from 1954–1976.

MARK MCGWIRE b. 1963 Broke Maris's record with 70 home runs in 1998 season.

BARRY BONDS b. 1964 The champ, hit 73 runs in 2001.

◁ THE 1927 YANKEES *are believed by many to have been the greatest baseball team ever assembled. Led by Ruth's 60 home runs and Gehrig's 175 runs batted in, they won 110 games in the regular season and then swept the Pittsburgh Pirates in four games for the World Series title.*

JIM THORPE
(1887–1953)

JIM THORPE IS considered by many to have been the greatest athlete of the 20th century; he excelled in numerous sports.

THORPE'S FOOTBALL SHOE

BRIGHT PATH

Thorpe, a Native American, was born in a one-room cabin in Oklahoma, then still known as Indian Territory. He attended the Carlisle Indian Industrial School in Pennsylvania from 1903 to 1912, where, in his last two years, he earned All-America football honors. Thorpe in 1912 won Olympic gold medals in both the pentathlon and decathlon, but Olympic officials rescinded his medals after ruling that he had violated the Olympics' amateur eligibility requirements by participating in semi-professional baseball in 1909.

Thorpe played major-league baseball from 1913 to 1919, but he had trouble hitting the curveball so he concentrated on football. He dominated the early years of professional football, leading the Canton Bulldogs to the unofficial world title in 1916, 1917, and 1919. He became the first president of the American Professional Football Association, the precursor to the National Football League (NFL), while he was still playing, and helped found the NFL in 1922. Thorpe retired from professional football in 1926, though he made one final appearance for the Chicago Cardinals in 1928. He spent much of the rest of his life traveling around the country eking out a meager living through public speaking and low-paying menial jobs. By now drinking to excess, Thorpe died in Lomita, California, after suffering his third heart attack.

△ THORPE PLAYED *four positions on the gridiron during his football career: halfback on offense, defender, punter, and place kicker.*

Did you know?

■ Thorpe's Native American name, *Wa-Tho-Huk*, translates into "Bright Path."

■ Thorpe once won a national ballroom dancing championship.

■ In 2001, ABC's "Wide World of Sports" named him Athlete of the Century.

▷ THORPE MET WITH NATIVE AMERICANS *from a nearby reservation during training camp in St. Petersburg, Florida, in 1926.*

MICHAEL JORDAN
b. 1963

MICHAEL JORDAN MAY WELL be the greatest basketball player of all time, and was largely responsible for the sport's rise in popularity across the globe.

Did you know?

■ As a freshman, Jordan was cut from his high-school basketball team.

■ During his short baseball career, Jordan only hit .204 with the minor-league Birmingham Barons.

■ Jordan was named most valuable player in each of his six NBA championship series with the Chicago Bulls.

AIR JORDAN

Jordan was born in Brooklyn and in 1981 was recruited by legendary coach Dean Smith to attend the University of North Carolina. In his freshman year, Jordan hit a last-second shot that won the 1982 NCAA championship game over Georgetown.

Drafted by the Chicago Bulls in 1984, Jordan won NBA rookie-of-the-year honors that season. With the arrival of coach Phil Jackson, he led the Bulls to three straight NBA championships beginning in 1992. During that time he became the most recognizable athlete in the world, and revolutionized basketball by helping catapult the NBA (and Nike shoes, which he promoted) to international prominence. He surprised his fans by retiring in 1994 to pursue a short-lived career in minor-league baseball, but in 1995 he returned to the Bulls and led them to three more NBA championships. Jordan retired again in 1999 to take over the helm of the Washington Wizards. In 2001 he came out of retirement, divesting his stake in the Wizards to sign a two-year contract to join the team.

△ ALTHOUGH JORDAN RETIRED *briefly from the Chicago Bulls in 1995 to try his hand at baseball with a Chicago White Sox farm team, he did not retire from endorsing products, as seen in this ad.*

"He was the best player ever involved in a team sport of any kind."

BASKETBALL COACH BOBBY KNIGHT

PELÉ

b. 1940

Perhaps the greatest soccer player ever, Pelé helped make it the world's most popular sport.

BLACK PEARL

Born Edson Arantes do Nascimento in Três Coraçoes, Brazil, Pelé dropped out of school at age nine to pursue his dream of becoming a professional soccer player. He played with a local minor-league club as a teenager, catching the eye of Brazilian soccer great Waldemar de Brito, who in 1956 recruited him for the Santos Football Club. Pelé went on to play with Santos for 18 years, winning nine Brazilian championships.

It was Pelé's playing in the 1958 World Cup that brought him to international prominence: The 17-year-old scored two dramatic goals and led Brazil to a 5-2 victory over Sweden. He cemented his legend by leading Brazil to two more World Cup victories, in 1962 and 1970, the latter with a memorable header that also happened to be Brazil's 100th goal in World Cup play. His masterful playing, photogenic smile, and seemingly boundless energy made him one of the world's biggest sports superstars.

Pelé retired in 1974, but came out of retirement a year later to play for the New York Cosmos of the North American Soccer League. He retired again in 1978, finishing his 1,362-game career with 1,280 goals—a record second only to fellow Brazilian Arthur Friedenreich.

△ BRAZIL HONORED *Pelé with a postage stamp in 1969 when he scored his 1,000th goal. He was declared a national treasure.*

Did you know?

■ Nigeria and Biafra once called a cease-fire in their war so everyone could watch Pelé play in an exhibition match.

■ His father, Joao Ramos, was also a professional soccer player, best known for his heading abilities.

■ Pelé composed the score to the 1977 film about his life, *Pelé.*

△ SEEN HERE IN *his performance against Sweden in the 1958 World Cup final, Pelé displays the speed and ball-handling skills that made him nearly impossible to defend against. He is the only man to win three World Cups.*

THE GREATEST SPORTSWOMEN

THE EMERGENCE OF PROFESSIONAL WOMEN'S SOCCER AND BASKETBALL, the ascendancy of the Williams sisters in tennis—these and countless other successes in women's sports almost make us forget the struggles of those who came before them.

Not only did the pioneers of women's sports perform great athletic feats—they also challenged conventional thinking about women's place in society. Sonja Henie's artistry and drive led to ten consecutive world figure-skating championships and a long and profitable career. Babe Didrikson, a superb natural athlete, proved the range of women's abilities by moving easily from sport to sport, while tennis star Billie Jean King used her success to promote equality. Teenaged Romanian gymnast Nadia Comaneci scored the first perfect 10s in Olympic history, and on the track, Jackie Joyner-Kersee shattered records and raised the bar for all athletes, female and male.

△ A GOLD *medal from the 1932 Los Angeles Olympics.*

△ SOPHIE KURYS *of the Racine Belles slides into third during a game against the South Bend Blue Sox in June, 1947. Women's professional baseball was popular in the American Midwest during World War II.*

BILLIE JEAN KING
b. 1943

KNOWN FOR HER AGGRESSIVE STYLE of play, tennis legend Billie Jean King won 39 major titles, including 20 Wimbledon championships, and helped bring women to the forefront of sports, both competitively and financially.

QUEEN OF THE COURT

Born Billie Jean Moffitt to a working-class family in Long Beach, California, King excelled at sports from an early age, winning her first tennis championship at age 14. She played her first Wimbledon tournament in 1961, losing in the women's singles but winning the doubles title with partner Karen Hantze. In 1966 she won her first Wimbledon singles title, and the next year won that championship again, as well as the US Open singles. Billie Jean married attorney Larry King in 1968 and turned professional that same year. Three years later, rolling up title after title, King became the first woman athlete to earn more than $100,000 in a year. Her greatest season in tennis was 1972, when she won the Wimbledon women's singles and doubles, US Open singles, and French Open titles; *Sports Illustrated* named her "Sportswoman of the Year."

King began to criticize the fact that women players received considerably less prize money than their male peers, a view that dovetailed with the women's liberation movement of the 1970s, and culminated in the famous 1973 "Battle of the Sexes" match, pitting King against men's champion Bobby Riggs, then 55. King easily beat Riggs, a win seen as a victory for the women's movement. Intensifying her struggle for equality in tennis, King then co-founded the Women's Tennis Association in 1973, and also helped form World Team Tennis, a coed tennis league which she would become commissioner of in 1984, after she retired from the professional circuit. King continues to work for equality in athletics.

△ BILLIE JEAN KING *shares a lighthearted moment in New York with Bobby Riggs, two months before their 1973 "Battle of the Sexes".*

Net Women

VENUS WILLIAMS b.1980 Reigning queen of the current tennis scene.

MARTINA NAVRATILOVA b. 1956 The greatest modern women's player.

CHRIS EVERT b. 1954 Brought cool sex appeal to the court.

◁ **KING BEAT BOBBY RIGGS** 6–4, 6–3, 6–3 with her speed and her ability to volley almost at will against her older competitor.

"Be bold. If you're going to make an error, make a doozy, and don't be afraid to hit the ball."

BILLIE JEAN KING

△ **KING HOISTS** her award for winning the 1966 women's title at Wimbledon. All told, she would win six singles titles there, ten doubles, and four mixed doubles championships.

△ **AUSTRALIAN** Evonne Goolagong (center) and Englishwoman Virginia Wade (top) provided some of Billie Jean King's toughest competition during the late 1960s and early 1970s.

Lisa Raymond

Lindsay Davenport

Billie Jean King

Monica Seles

Jennifer Capriati

▷ **KING CAPTAINED** the all-star United States Federation Cup tennis team to victory on November 25, 2000. During her active career, King helped the United States team take seven titles by winning 51 out of 55 matches.

Did you know?

■ At the "Battle of the Sexes" match, King was carried to the court by four muscular men dressed as ancient slaves, à la Cleopatra. Riggs was brought in on a rickshaw pulled by sexy models dubbed "Bobby's Bosom Buddies."

■ King's bisexuality was revealed to the public in 1981, when she was sued for palimony by former female lover and secretary Marilyn Barnett.

■ King's brother Randy Moffitt was a pitcher for the San Diego Padres.

BABE DIDRIKSON
(1914–1956)

AMERICAN ATHLETE MILDRED ELLA "BABE" DIDRIKSON was one of the greatest and most versatile athletes of the 20th century, male or female.

THE ALL-AROUND ATHLETE

Already an athletic sensation as a young woman, Didrikson was recruited at age 15 by the Golden Cyclones, a Dallas basketball team that won national championships the next three years.

Didrickson turned her attention to track, and at the 1931 National Women's American Athletic Union Track Meet, she placed first in five out of the eight events in which she entered, winning the team title single-handedly. At the 1932 Olympic Games in Los Angeles, she won gold medals in the javelin throw and the 80-meter hurdles, setting new world records in both events.

Didrikson next began to train as a golfer. She won the US Women's Amateur tournament in 1946 and 17 tournaments during the following year, and became the first American to win the British Ladies' Amateur Championship. She turned professional in 1948, and won the US Women's Open in 1948, 1950, and 1954, the last by a record twelve shots even as she was suffering from cancer. She passed away two years later.

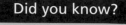

Did you know?

■ Didrikson was nicknamed "Babe," after Babe Ruth, during a childhood baseball game in which she hit 5 home runs.

■ In 1938 Didrikson married professional wrestler George Zaharias, also known as "The Crying Greek from Cripple Creek."

■ Didrikson pitched an inning for the St. Louis Cardinals in an exhibition game.

△ ON HER WAY *to Los Angeles for the 1932 Olympics, Didrikson did exercises in the aisles and ran back and forth the length of the train to keep in shape, much to the amusement of her competitors.*

△ DIDRIKSON WITH CLARK GABLE *(center) after her amazing performance at the 1932 Los Angeles Olympics.*

"My main idea of competition always has been to go out there and cut loose with everything I've got."

BABE DIDRIKSON

▷ WHEN ASKED *how she hit the golf ball so far, Didrikson told her questioner, "You've got to loosen your girdle and really let the ball have it!" Didrikson won 35 LPGA titles in her golfing career.*

JACKIE JOYNER-KERSEE

b. 1962

ONE OF THE GREATEST FEMALE ATHLETES of all time, track-and-field star Jackie Joyner-Kersee won six Olympic medals and was the first athlete to score more than 7,000 points in the heptathlon, a seven-part track and field competition.

△ HER RECORD OF 7,291 *points in the heptathlon, set at the Seoul Olympics, still stands. She owns the top six performances in the history of the event. Joyner won the heptathlon again in the 1992 Olympics in Barcelona, Spain.*

THE INSPIRATION

Born in the slums of East St. Louis, Illinois, Joyner excelled at basketball and track, and often practiced the long jump on sand her friends spread out for her in front of her home. She received a basketball scholarship to UCLA, but soon switched her focus to track. She began training with assistant track coach Bob Kersee, whom she later married. While still in college, Joyner in 1984 won the silver medal in the Olympic heptathlon, despite a pulled hamstring. Her reputation as a heptathlete, however, was forged at the 1986 Goodwill Games, where she scored a world-record 7,148 points in the event. She went on to win gold medals at the 1998 and 1992 Olympic Games, and took home the bronze medal in the event at the 1996 games. Joyner-Kersee retired from competition in 1998, worked as a motivational speaker, and briefly played professional basketball for the Richmond Rage. She came out of retirement for a short time in 2000, however, to make an unsuccessful attempt at joining the US Olympic long jump team. She is currently involved in a variety of business enterprises, including sponsorship of a NASCAR team.

◁ JOYNER'S FIRST MEDAL *was a heptathlon silver at the 1984 Los Angeles Olympics. She had needed to finish second in the 800 by .33, but she finished 2.6 seconds behind. Her brother Al won gold in the triple jump.*

Did you know?

■ Joyner-Kersee decided to compete in multiple events after seeing a 1975 television movie about multi-sport phenomenon Babe Didrikson.

■ Joyner-Kersee wrote an autobiography in 1997 called *A Kind of Grace: The Autobiography of the World's Greatest Female Athlete*.

Joyner supports a youth foundation for girls' sports

Britton stars in ABC's "Spin City"

△ JOYNER'S HEPTATHLON JUMP *at a competition in Indianapolis, Indiana, in July 1988. Two months later, she would set the Olympic record in the long jump at Seoul, with a leap of 24 feet three inches.*

∧ SINCE RETIRING, *Joyner has made the rounds of Hollywood as a celebrity. Here she attends a function with actress Connie Britton.*

NADIA COMANECI

b. 1961

ROMANIAN GYMNAST Nadia Comaneci at age 14 became the first woman to score a perfect 10 in an Olympic gymnastics event. Her performance at the 1976 Olympics in Montreal redefined her sport—and audiences' expectations of women athletes.

PERFECTION

Comaneci was discovered at the age of six by gymnastics coach Bela Karolyi (later to become the Romanian national coach). She won the Romanian National Junior Championships, and as a senior won the European Championship in 1975 and the American Cup in 1976.

Comaneci thrilled the world at the 1976 Olympics in Montreal by receiving seven perfect scores and winning three gold medals, for the uneven bars, balance beam, and individual all-around, together with a bronze medal for floor exercise and a silver medal as part of the second-place Romanian national team. She later won two gold and two silver medals at the 1980 Olympic Games in Moscow. She retired from competition in 1984 and worked as a coach for the Romanian team before defecting to the United States via Hungary in 1989. After appearing in a series of provocative underwear advertisements, she married American gymnast Bart Conner in 1996 and moved to Norman, Oklahoma. Comaneci currently does television commentary and writes for gymnastic publications.

Did you know?

■ The scoreboards at the 1976 Olympics were not designed to display a 10, and Comaneci's score read as "1.0".

■ Comaneci weighed only 86 pounds at the time of the 1976 Olympics.

■ In 1976 she owned more than 200 dolls, and traveled with an Eskimo doll for good luck.

△ NADIA RECEIVED A WORLD SPORTS AWARD OF THE CENTURY *in 1999 after being elected Athlete of the Century during a gala in Vienna, Austria. Here she acknowledges the applause.*

"Hard work has made it easy. That is my secret. That is why I win."

NADIA COMANECI

△ NADIA LIVED *in Dej, Romania, in the Carpathian Mountains, with her parents, Alexandrina and Gheorghe, an auto mechanic.*

◁ AFTER COACHING *the Romanian national team through two Olympiads, Bela Karolyi defected to the United States in 1981. Since then, he has led the nation's gymnastic program to its first World Championships.*

△ NADIA USED *the theme from the soap opera "The Young and the Restless" for her floor exercises.*

SONJA HENIE
(1912–1969)

NORWEGIAN-AMERICAN FIGURE SKATER Sonja Henie found success first as a world-champion figure skater, then went on to even greater fame as a Hollywood star.

Did you know?

■ Henie amassed an important collection of 20th-century art.

■ World champion at the age of 14, Henie was the youngest-ever world figure-skating champion until Tara Lipinski won in 1998; the latter was two months younger.

■ She had romances with fellow stars Tyrone Power and Clark Gable.

ICE PRINCESS

Henie began skating at the age of six and by the age of ten had won the first of six straight Norwegian national figure-skating championships. Trained in ballet, Henie used music and dance to add elements of performance to figure skating, which until then was primarily a technical event. She won the world amateur championship for women for 10 consecutive years, beginning in 1927. Henie also won gold medals in three consecutive Winter Olympic Games—1928, 1932, and 1936. By now Henie was world famous, and rather than modestly hide her skills, she turned professional after her third Olympics, and her ice carnival attracted millions of spectators during the next 15 years. She also was one of Hollywood's leading box-office attractions from 1937 to 1945, and starred in movies such as *One in a Million* (1936) and *Thin Ice* (1937). Between her ice shows and her film career, her stock in the New York Yankees and Madison Square Garden, Henie's earnings dwarfed those of contemporaries such as Babe Ruth and Joe Louis. She died of leukemia in 1969.

△ **BEFORE HENIE,** *figure skating was considered a sport for the wealthy, but she popularlized it and gave it a new, sexy edge. Her teacher had been a student of the Russian ballerina Anna Pavlova.*

> "All my life I've wanted to skate, and all my life I have skated."

SONJA HENIE

▽ **HENIE'S FILMS** *made an estimated $76 million dollars at the box office, putting her beyond stars such as Shirley Temple as a draw.*

Olympic Women

PEGGY FLEMING b. 1948 The epitome of grace on ice.

MIA HAMM b. 1972 Gutsy leader of US women's soccer team.

MARION JONES b. 1975 First woman to win five medals in a single Olympiad.

◁ **WHILE HENIE'S MOVES** *were comparatively subtle, she added an athleticism to figure skating which skaters such as Dick Button, seen here, would ultimately take to another level.*

THE FRENCH REVOLUTION

FRANCE HAD FALLEN UPON HARD TIMES UNDER THE RULE OF LOUIS XVI and Marie Antoinette during the late 18th century.

Short on food because of failing harvests and plunged into debt by its support of the American colonists during the Revolutionary War, France placed a heavy tax burden on its people—while the aristocrats continued to spend to excess. The revolution began in 1789, when a crowd of Parisians stormed the Bastille prison. Various political parties, including the Girondists, the Montagnards (led by Marat), and the Jacobins, vied for power. The Jacobins, led by Robespierre and Danton, eventually won out and initiated the bloody purge that became known as the Reign of Terror. This period saw the arrest and execution of numerous aristocrats—including the king and queen—and others declared "enemies of the revolution." Political and social upheaval swept France for a decade, inspiring revolutionary movements in other European nations. The revolt eventually led to a powerful conservative backlash, which set the stage for a military dictatorship under Napoleon Bonaparte.

△ RUMORS THAT LOUIS XVI *was about to dissolve the National Assembly and his firing of Jacques Necker, a popular advisor, drove a Parisian mob to storm the Bastille on July 14, 1789.*

MARIE ANTOINETTE
(1755–1793)

MARIE ANTOINETTE was the unpopular and carelessly extravagant queen of France at the time of the French Revolution.

△ MARIE ANTOINETTE'S *beheading. Reportedly she accidentally stepped on her executioner's foot.*

A HATED MONARCH

The daughter of Maria Theresa and Holy Roman Emperor Francis I of Austria, Marie Antoinette married Louis XVI of France in 1770 at the age of 14. She was reputed to be frivolous, reports of her extramarital affairs abounded, and her expenditures contributed to the huge debt incurred by France during the 1770s and 1780s. When the French Revolution broke out, Marie Antoinette proved herself to be stronger and more decisive than her husband. After a crowd stormed the Bastille on July 14, 1789, the queen failed to persuade Louis to take refuge with his army at Metz. She did convince him to resist the attempts of the revolutionary National Assembly to end feudalism and restrict royal powers. Marie Antoinette's role in these negotiations helped make her a target of agitators. In October 1789, the revolutionaries imprisoned the king and queen in their palace in Paris. Marie Antoinette opened secret negotiations, first with the Comte de Mirabeau, a prominent member of the National Assembly, and then with Antoine Barnave, leader of the constitutional monarchist faction, in an effort to restore the power of the monarchy. Both maneuvers failed, and after France declared war on Austria in April 1792, her secret efforts to undermine the revolutionary cause further enraged the French. That year, in no small part out of hatred for the queen, the monarchy was outlawed. Antoinette spent her remaining days in prison and was brought before a tribunal on October 14, 1793. She was guillotined two days later.

◁ IN AN EFFORT *to improve her wild reputation, the queen posed for portraits with her children.*

LOUIS XVI
(1754–1793)

LOUIS XVI WAS KING OF FRANCE during the eruption of the French Revolution, and died at the hands of revolutionaries.

THE LAST KING OF FRANCE

Born in Versailles in 1754, Louis XVI ascended the throne in 1774 following the reign of his grandfather, Louis XV. (His father, Louis XV's only son, died in 1765.) The young Louis XVI was ill-prepared to be King of France, and was a weak and inefficient ruler reputed to be more involved with his hobbies—hunting and making and mending locks—than with the governance of his country. He failed to support reform ministers who tried to prop up the tottering finances of the monarchy. In 1789 when the revolution erupted, Louis XVI allied himself with outraged aristocrats instead of the middle class. He was arrested in 1792 and found guilty of treason by the revolutionary tribunal. Louis XVI was guillotined in Paris on January 21, 1793.

△ AT FIRST LOUIS XVI *outwardly supported aspects of the revolution, but schemed behind the scenes to undercut its efforts.*

Did you know?

■ Though Marie Antoinette was widely blamed, Louis XVI was unable to father children initially, the first seven years of their marriage.

■ After the French Revolution broke out, Louis was stripped of his royal title and referred to by his last name: "Citizen Capet."

△ MARIE ANTOINETTE *posed in the latest fashion for this 1783 portrait. Historians doubt that she actually said "Let them eat cake!" in response to news that the French people were without bread.*

▷ THE REVOLUTIONARY CONVENTION *found Louis XVI guilty by a unanimous vote, then voted 361 to 288 to sentence him to death.*

"I die innocent of all the crimes of which I have been charged."

LOUIS XVI

Did you know?

■ Marie Antoinette tried to escape in 1791 with the help of her reputed lover Axel Fersen, but they were caught at Varennes.

■ During her reign, rumors spread that the queen had an affair with a cardinal in exchange for a diamond necklace.

■ At the time of her marriage to Louis XVI, she spoke no French.

◁ EVEN THOUGH FRANCE *was nearly impoverished, Louis XVI granted financial aid to the rebellious American colonies in their war against Great Britain.*

Ends of the Line

TSAR NICHOLAS II (1868–1917) The last emperor of Russia.

XUAN-TONG (1906–1967) a.k.a. Henry P'u-yi, last of the Manchu rulers of China.

UMBERTO II (1904–1983) The last king of Italy's House of Savoy.

GEORGES JACQUES DANTON
(1759–1794)

GEORGES JACQUES DANTON was a leading orator and key politician of the French Revolution.

A VOICE OF MODERATION

Born in Arcis-sur-Aube, Danton, a lawyer in Paris, was a member of the radical political group "Club de Cordeliers" (which met in the former Cordeliers Monastery). Elected to the revolutionary National Convention in 1792, he tried to resolve conflicts between revolutionary factions. In April 1793 Danton became the de facto leader of the Committee on Public Safety, created by the National Convention as the governing body of France. He became increasingly moderate, though, eventually challenging the dictatorial tactics of the revolutionary government—especially the radical Jacobins, a faction led by Robespierre. Robespierre would not tolerate any challenges to his growing authority, and had Danton and his closest followers arrested for conspiracy. They were all guillotined on April 5, 1794.

△ AT 6' 4", *Danton towered over most people of his day.*

◁ A POSTER *from the 1939 film biography of Danton.*

Did you know?

■ Although Danton voted to kill Louis XVI at his trial, another revolutionary, Comte de Lamath, later wrote that Danton had hoped to spare the king, before realizing it was politically impossible.

■ Some historians defend Danton as a great patriot, while others view him as a corrupt demagogue.

"Let me be led to death, I shall go to sleep in glory."

DANTON, AT HIS TRIAL

▷ A 1794 CARTOON *by French artist Villain depicts Danton's execution. When first warned that he might be arrested, Danton responded, "They will not dare."*

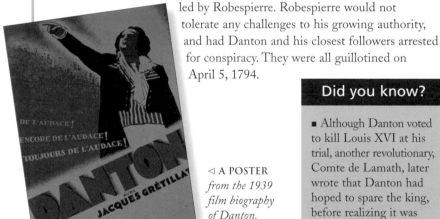

ROBESPIERRE
(1758–1794)

ROBESPIERRE, a leading political figure during the French Revolution, is closely associated with the Reign of Terror.

A MURDEROUS DANDY

Born in Arras, Maximilien Francois Marie Isidore de Robespierre was a lawyer and advocate for the poor. At age 30 he was elected representative from Arras to the States General. After the revolution broke out, he presided over the Jacobins, a radical political club that espoused republican ideas, universal suffrage, and separation of church and state. As the revolution progressed, Robespierre worked on the National Assembly and the Committee for Public Safety, attempting to keep the revolutionary factions united and ruthlessly eliminating thousands of "enemies of the revolution"—including Georges Jacques Danton—in what became known as the "Reign of Terror." Robespierre became an unpopular dictator and the revolution's governing Convention finally sent him to the guillotine on July 28, 1974.

Other Key Players

EMANUEL SIEYES (1748–1836) Author of the Declaration of the Rights of Man.

MARQUIS DE LAFAYETTE (1757–1834) Veteran of the American Revolution, he was torn between the king and the people.

▽ ARREST OF ROBESPIERRE *by Jean Joseph Tassaert depicts the events of July 27, 1794.*

△ KNOWN AS A
*fastidious dresser,
Robespierre sported
the powdered hair
and fashionable
clothing of the Old
Regime even during
the revolution.*

JEAN-PAUL MARAT
(1743–1793)

JEAN-PAUL MARAT, A FRENCH POLITICIAN, physician, and writer, led the Montagnard faction during the French Revolution.

THE RADICAL VANGUARD

Born in Boudry, Switzerland, Marat was a well-known physician in London in the 1770s. In 1777 he returned to France and became the physician of Louis XVI's brother and a number of other aristocrats. Increasingly disillusioned with the monarchic government, Marat resigned from his position as a court physician.

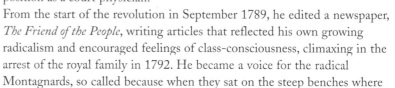

△ MARAT'S RADICAL NEWSPAPER *was one of the most widely read of its time.*

From the start of the revolution in September 1789, he edited a newspaper, *The Friend of the People*, writing articles that reflected his own growing radicalism and encouraged feelings of class-consciousness, climaxing in the arrest of the royal family in 1792. He became a voice for the radical Montagnards, so called because when they sat on the steep benches where the Assembly met, they looked like a mountain. Marat had vast popular support. In April of 1793, he was arraigned before a revolutionary tribunal by the Girondists, a moderate faction of the National Convention. His acquittal was the triumph of the Montagnards and the beginning of the decline of the Girondists. On July 13, 1793, Marat was killed when young Girondist supporter Charlotte Corday stabbed him to death in his bath.

Did you know?

■ At the revolution's onset, Marat published a pamphlet voicing his belief that the monarchy could solve France's problems.

■ He took frequent medicinal baths to relieve a painful skin condition, and was murdered while soaking in the bathtub.

■ Marat's dramatic murder made him a martyr.

Did you know?

■ In one of Robespierre's early memoirs, he praised Louis XVI and commended France on its ability to change its political system without bloodshed.

■ Robespierre advocated a state religion called "the cult of the Supreme Being."

■ While Robespierre ruled the revolutionary government, executions rose from 21 in the month of September 1793, to 688 in June of 1794.

△ MARAT *depicted in an 18th-century miniature. His work in chemistry and physics gained him the respect of Franklin, Volta, and Goethe.*

◁ MARAT'S NAME *was given to 21 French towns, but Jacques-Louis David's painting* The Death of Marat *is the most famous tribute of all.*

SHOWMEN

PEOPLE LOVE TO BE ENTERTAINED. WE ALL WANT TO BE THRILLED, AMUSED, FRIGHTENED—anything to distract us from the grind of home and work. Throughout history, geniuses have arisen to sweep us away to the special places they've created in their imaginations.

Before movies came along, ingenious hucksters like P. T. Barnum tapped into our desires with the straight-ahead glitz of the Big Top and the prurient sideshow right alongside it. In the age of vaudeville, Florenz Ziegfeld's Follies provided escapism packaged in splendor. The emergence of movies brought tremendous new possibilities that great minds—including Walt Disney's—seized upon. From one rubbery little whistling mouse was born an empire of entertainment—not just movies, but entire invented worlds for us to lose ourselves in. With the advent of advanced technologies, a new notion of the showman has emerged: one who can make computer images seem more real than real life. And all we ask is that it not be real—that it be entertainment.

△ WHILE THE CONCEPT *of the chorus line can trace its lineage back to Greek drama, it's hard to imagine that Sophocles ever imagined anything quite like this one from the 1920s.*

△ TOM THUMB, *actually born Charles Stratton, was received by Queen Victoria and Abraham Lincoln.*

P. T. BARNUM
(1810–1891)

P. T. (PHINEAS TAYLOR) BARNUM'S FAME rests largely on half-truths, outright deceit, and good old-fashioned grifting, but he remains one of America's truly groundbreaking entertainers.

AMERICAN HUMBUG

Barnum's major break as a purveyor of the preposterous came just after a stint as a New York City shopkeeper in 1835, when he met a woman, Joice Heth, who claimed to be the 161-year-old nurse of President George Washington. Unconcerned about the validity of this claim, Barnum began displaying the woman for a small fee. Heth's historical yarns were an instant hit throughout the country, and became even more successful when Barnum himself, under an assumed name, began accusing the woman of fraud in local papers. The ensuing controversy only increased Barnum's business. Such creative hucksterism became the hallmark of Barnum's success. With his knack for inventing outrageous spectacles the public found irresistible, Barnum assumed control of the American Museum in New York City in 1841. He used the museum to exhibit such human oddities as Annie Jones, the bearded lady; Siamese twins Chang and Eng; and "General" Tom Thumb, a 25-inch-tall five-year-old from Connecticut billed as an 11-year-old from England. Barnum's relentless promotion always ensured an audience. His most lasting legitimate contribution to popular entertainment was his 1881 joint venture with rival James Bailey: the Barnum and Bailey Circus. He died in New York City at the age of 81.

Did you know?

■ Barnum enhanced his reputation by bringing Swedish opera star Jenny Lind to the United States in 1850.

■ Barnum never actually uttered the famous phrase "There's a sucker born every minute." It was said by a competitor of his, a banker named David Hannum.

"More persons are humbugged by believing nothing than by believing too much."

P .T. BARNUM

△ PROGRAM COVER *for P. T. Barnum & Adam Forepaugh's Circus in 1887. Barnum's two greatest legacies are the Ringling Bros., Barnum and Bailey Circus and his reputation as a promoter.*

△ BARNUM WAS ELECTED *mayor of Bridgeport, Connecticut, in 1875.*

WALT DISNEY

(1901–1966)

WALT DISNEY'S VISIONARY APPROACH to animation, television, and film has had a greater impact on American popular culture than the work of almost any other artist of the last century.

THE MAGIC KINGDOM

Born in Chicago, Disney studied drawing and design at an advertising firm in Kansas City. He moved to Hollywood in 1923, where he started a production company with his brother Roy. His first effort of note was the now-legendary *Steamboat Willie*, a short film that featured an early incarnation of his most famous creation, Mickey Mouse. The stable of Disney characters grew to include such animated icons as Donald Duck, Goofy, and Minnie Mouse, and in 1937 the company produced *Snow White and the Seven Dwarfs*, the world's first feature-length cartoon. By the mid-1950s, the Disney entertainment empire had grown into a multimedia operation featuring live-action films, documentaries, and eventually, hit TV programs. The Disneyland theme park opened in 1955, and soon after Disney began plans for a new park, Walt Disney World, in central Florida.

He died in 1966, six years before Disney World opened. After his death, his entertainment kingdom grew into what is today the monolithic Disney Corporation, which includes numerous theme parks, TV networks, film production companies, and publishing imprints.

Epic Imaginations

GEORGE LUCAS
b. 1944 Brains behind the *Star Wars* empire.

CECIL B. DEMILLE
(1881–1959) Prolific director of epics like *The Ten Commandments*.

JAMES CAMERON
b. 1954 Produced and directed *Titanic*.

△ WALT DISNEY HIMSELF *provided the voice for Mickey Mouse until 1946 and the film* Mickey and the Beanstalk. *At that point soundman Jim Macdonald took over the job.*

Did you know?

■ Disney World's EPCOT Center was conceived as a research facility for the study and creation of futuristic cities to be owned and run by Disney.

■ Walt Disney gave the names of rumored Hollywood communists in his 1947 testimony to the House Un-American Activities Committee.

◁ THE DISNEY CORPORATION *owns eleven theme parks in the US, France, Japan, and Hong Kong.*

FLORENZ ZIEGFELD, JR.
(1867–1932)

FLORENZ ZIEGFELD FILLED A DISTINCT VOID in early 20th-century American entertainment with his extravagant stage revue, the Ziegfeld Follies. Marked by magnificent sets and flashy costume designs, Ziegfeld's shows cornered the market for popular live entertainment in their time.

△ THE IDEA of opulent showgirls came from Parisian revues.

GIRLS, GIRLS, GIRLS

Florenz was born in Chicago and worked for several years in and around show business with his father before creating the Follies in 1907. The Follies presented a lavish array of comedians, singers, and glamorous "Ziegfeld girls." By 1911 the extravaganza, which was then officially billed as the Ziegfeld Follies, became known nationwide for its first-rate entertainment—including such comedians as W. C. Fields, Ed Wynn, Will Rogers, and Fanny Brice. Ziegfeld went on to produce a number of notable Broadway shows, such as *The Three Musketeers* and *Showboat*, many of which ran at his own Ziegfeld Theater in New York City. He died in 1932 while living with his second wife, Billie Burke, best known as Glinda the Witch of the North in *The Wizard of Oz*.

Did you know?

■ Ziegfeld's first success was a strongman, The Great Sandow.

■ The Follies were reprised in 1945, starring comedian Milton Berle.

■ Ziegfeld produced two variations on the Follies, the Ziegfeld Nine o'clock Revue and the Ziegfeld Midnight Frolic.

◁ COVER OF SHEET MUSIC *for the song "Hold Me," from the Ziegfeld Follies of 1920.*

▷ ZIEGFIELD, A LADIES' MAN, *was said to date many of his showgirls despite marrying his star Anna Held and later Billie Burke.*

STEVEN SPIELBERG
b. 1946

STEVEN SPIELBERG'S DEDICATION to cinema as spectacle, through the use of cutting-edge special effects and imaginative storytelling, has made him the highest-grossing director in movie-industry history.

△ ONE OF SPIELBERG'S *favorite visual images is of light coming at the viewer .*

SCREEN MAGIC

Born in Cincinnati, Ohio, Spielberg and his family moved frequently. He became intrigued by movies at an early age. A short film he produced as a college student brought led to his directing Joan Crawford in an episode of the TV movie *Night Gallery*. After several more made-for-TV films and his first big-screen film, *The Sugarland Express*, triumph came with the 1975 thriller *Jaws*. Spielberg went on to produce *Close Encounters of the Third Kind*, the Indiana Jones trilogy, and *E.T.* These films attracted huge audiences and set new standards for box-office returns, helping give rise to modern Hollywood's single-minded pursuit of blockbuster hits. In the 1990s, Spielberg garnered both critical and popular success for making more socially relevant films, including *The Color Purple, Schindler's List,* and *Saving Private Ryan.* In 1994 he partnered with record mogul David Geffen and producer Jeffrey Katzenberg to launch DreamWorks SKG, an entertainment mega-conglomerate.

> "The most expensive habit in the world is celluloid, not heroin, and I need a fix every few years."
>
> STEVEN SPIELBERG

△ SPIELBERG WON *two Golden Globe awards for* Saving Private Ryan *with its shockingly realistic depiction of the Allied landing on D-Day, June 6, 1944.*

◁ SPIELBERG EARNED *millions of dollars from* E.T. *and made Drew Barrymore a star. The movie was also unique in presenting an alien as a benign force rather than a dangerous invader from another planet.*

Did you know?

■ Actress Debra Winger provided the voice for Spielberg's beloved character E.T.

■ At age 16, Spielberg made his first commercially successful film, *Firelight*. It cost $500 to make and earned $600.

■ Eight of Spielberg's films are among the 50 highest-grossing films of all time.

HARRY HOUDINI

(1874–1926)

HARRY HOUDINI WAS THE ULTIMATE escape artist of the 20th century. His feats of dexterity and illusion continue to influence countless performers today.

ESCAPE ARTIST

Houdini's family moved from Budapest, Hungary, to Wisconsin when he was four. The son of a rabbi, he left home at 12 to earn money for the struggling family. As a teenager he began working in show business with a simple magic show that would later develop into an act that included such feats as escaping from a straitjacket while suspended upside down, and emerging unscathed from a locked safe under water. By his late twenties, his "Challenge Escapes" had made him an international star. A steadfast anti-spiritualist, he strongly maintained that his acts were not the product of paranormal energy, but rather of his own creativity. On October 22, 1926, following a performance in Canada, Houdini was approached by a fan interested in testing the magician's claim that he could withstand harsh blows to the stomach. The fan then proceeded to deliver several punches to the unsuspecting Houdini's midsection. Houdini died of internal bleeding nine days later.

> "My brain is the key that sets me free."
>
> HARRY HOUDINI

△ HOUDINI MADE AN EFFORT *to expose hoaxes committed by supposed clairvoyants while alive. Yet, he left a secret code with his wife, Bess—"Rosabelle believe"—and instructions to try contacting him through a medium after he died. Legend has it that she succeeded, but it was never confirmed.*

Did you know?

■ Harry Houdini, born Ehrich Weiss, took his stage name from French illusionist Robert Houdin.

■ The verb "hou-di-nize," meaning "to release or extricate oneself from (confinement, bonds, or the like), as by wriggling out," was included in Funk & Wagnall's 1920 edition of its dictionary.

◁ AN INCREDIBLY STRONG *and flexible person, Houdini had to twist his body into contortions in order to escape from the cuffs and shackles locked around him.*

THE KENNEDYS

OFTEN CALLED "AMERICA'S ROYAL FAMILY," THE KENNEDYS WERE AT THE CENTER of American politics and culture for much of the 20th century, experiencing both triumph and tragedy squarely in the public eye.

Joseph P. Kennedy, Sr., amassed a fortune in various businesses and had great plans for his sons. After his oldest brother, Joe, Jr., was killed in World War II, John fulfilled his father's ambition by beating Richard Nixon in the 1960 election. Americans were enchanted with JFK and his wife Jacqueline—both were smart, attractive, young, and at the forefront of culture and fashion. President Kennedy's assassination in 1963 remains one of the nation's defining moments. John's brother Robert ran for the presidency in 1968, generating excitement that turned to despair when he, too, was felled by an assassin's bullet. When John Kennedy, Jr., died in a plane crash in 1999, it reinforced public fascination with this talented, often ill-fated, clan.

△ THE KENNEDY FAMILY *on November 9, 1960, from left, seated: Eunice, Rose, Joe, Jackie, and Ted. Standing: Ethel, Steve Smith, Jean, Jack, Bobby, Pat, Sargent Shriver, Joan, and Peter Lawford.*

JOHN F. KENNEDY
(1917–1963)

JOHN FITZGERALD KENNEDY, 35th president of the United States, brought the nation a sense of promise and an activist approach to government.

THE KING OF CAMELOT

Born in 1917 in Massachusetts, Kennedy graduated from Harvard University and joined the US Navy during World War II. When his older brother Joe, a pilot, was killed on a combat mission, the family's political ambitions focused on John. In 1946 he won a seat in Congress. A liberal on many domestic issues, he was also an early supporter of hard-line Cold War policies. In 1952 he was elected to the US Senate, and in 1953 he married Jacqueline Bouvier, whose socially prominent family and personal charm further enhanced the young senator's image. In 1960 he announced his presidential candidacy and narrowly defeated Republican candidate Richard Nixon. The handsome young president and his attractive, elegant wife seemed to breathe new life into the nation as the Kennedys made the White House into a cultural hub. A CIA plot to invade Cuba in 1961 proved disastrous, but Kennedy successfully managed the ensuing Cuban Missile Crisis. His greatest achievement in foreign affairs was the Nuclear Test-Ban treaty with Soviet premier Nikita Khrushchev. His desire to combat communism also led him to send military advisors and financial assistance to Vietnam, beginning the nation's ill-fated involvement there.

On November 22, 1963, Kennedy was assassinated in Dallas, Texas. The assassin, Lee Harvey Oswald, was shot two days later by Dallas nightclub owner Jack Ruby. Kennedy's assassination remains a source of controversy.

△ KENNEDY AS A NAVAL WAR HERO, 1944. *When his PT (patrol torpedo) boat was sunk in 1944, he led his crew to safety on a nearby island, towing an injured man three miles as he did so.*

◁ STUNNED BY *the assassination, 100 million people watched Kennedy's funeral on television, while 220 representatives from 102 nations attended in person.*

The Cabinet

ROBERT MCNAMARA b. 1916 Former president of Ford Motors, became Secretary of Defense.

DEAN RUSK (1909–1994) Philanthropist, Secretary of State.

◁ ALTHOUGH KENNEDY'S *youth buoyed the nation's attitude, it also worked against him in the early days of his presidency, especially in a July 1961 summit with Soviet premier Nikita Khrushchev. He felt the Soviet leader "savaged" him because of his inexperience.*

"My fellow Americans, ask not what your country can do for you: Ask what you can do for your country."

JOHN F. KENNEDY, INAUGURAL ADDRESS

△ **EASTER 1963.** *The Kennedy family in Palm Beach, Florida. Jackie was pregnant with a second son, Patrick, who died two days after birth.*

▷ KENNEDY'S ROCKING CHAIR, *which often gave him relief from lifelong pain caused by injury sustained while playing football at Harvard. His exploits on the PT-109 boat he captained during World War II also aggravated the injury.*

Did you know?

■ John F. Kennedy was the youngest man and the first Roman Catholic to be elected president of the United States. He also was the first 20th-century president born in the 20th century.

■ Kennedy received a Pulitzer Prize in 1957 for his book *Profiles in Courage.* Many contend that his aide Theodore Sorensen wrote most of the book.

△ **THE FIRST LADY** *made such an impression during an official visit to France that the nation loaned the* Mona Lisa *to her personally.*

JACQUELINE ONASSIS
(1929–1994)

JACQUELINE KENNEDY ONASSIS (born Jacqueline Lee Bouvier) was the wife of President John F. Kennedy and a popular and influential first lady.

JACKIE O

Born in New York City, Jacqueline graduated from George Washington University in 1951 and began her photojournalism career, working for the *Washington Times-Herald*. In 1953 she married John F. Kennedy, a popular Massachusetts congressman. After he was elected president in 1960, Jackie captured the hearts of the American people with her style and charm. She restored the White House to its original elegance so that it would better serve as a historical monument and social center for America's most talented citizens. President Kennedy was assassinated in November 1963. Jackie's grace and dignity in the aftermath endeared her to the American public. In 1968 after the assassination of Robert, she married Greek shipping magnate Aristotle Onassis the same year, and after his death worked as a book editor in New York City. She died in 1994 after a brief battle with lymphatic cancer.

△ **ARI ONASSIS** *had been a longtime friend of Lee Radziwill, Jackie's sister, and the Kennedys before he and Jackie married.*

▷ **DESIGNER OLEG CASSINI** *created this ivory satin gown for Jackie to wear at her husband's inauguration gala. Cassini became her advisor on a broad range of style issues in the early 1960s.*

Did you know?

- Jackie, a headstrong child, was initially a discipline problem at the fashionable Manhattan private school she attended as a young girl.

- The Hearst newspaper gossip column named Jackie debutante of the year in 1947.

- During her junior year of college, Jackie studied in Paris at the Sorbonne, polishing her French and developing her affinity for French culture and style.

△ **JACKIE AND JOHN** *married on September 12, 1953, at St. Mary's Church in Newport, RI, before 750 guests (1,300 came to the reception). Bobby was best man and Jackie's sister Lee was matron of honor.*

JOSEPH P. KENNEDY
(1888–1969)

JOSEPH PATRICK KENNEDY, AN AMERICAN BUSINESSMAN is best known for being the father of three political leaders, President John F. Kennedy, Senator and Attorney General Robert Kennedy and Massachusetts Senator Ted Kennedy.

△ KENNEDY *often had his lover Gloria Swanson to Hyannisport, the Kennedy family Cape Cod enclave.*

THE PATRIARCH

Born to an Irish Catholic family in Boston, Kennedy overcame the class prejudices of the era and attended Harvard University. Always financially astute, he was running a bank by the age of 25. In 1914, he married Rose Fitzgerald; the couple would eventually raise four sons and five daughters. Brilliant and driven, Joseph mastered the arts of stock trading and corporate finance, and became a millionaire by the age of 30 through investments in the movie business and alcohol distribution. In the 1920s he ran a movie studio, during which time he had an affair with actress Gloria Swanson. In return for his support in the 1932 presidential election, Franklin Roosevelt named Kennedy chairman of the US Securities and Exchange Commission and later the US Maritime Commission. In 1937 he was appointed US ambassador to Great Britain, but three years later he resigned, convinced that Britain would be taken over by Nazi Germany and that America's only hope lay in staying out of the coming conflict. After the loss of his first son during the war, Kennedy stepped back from public life and concentrated on grooming his three remaining sons for political office. He died at the age of 81, after suffering a debilitating stroke in 1961.

△ UPON RETURNING *from England on the eve of World War II, Kennedy said, "Democracy is finished in England. It may be here." Along with his anti-Semitism, desire to appease Hitler, and his womanizing, Kennedy was reputed to have ties to organized crime.*

Famous Spouses

PETER LAWFORD
(1923–1984) Pat Kennedy's husband, and Rat Packer.

ARNOLD SCHWARZENEGGER
b. 1947 Actor, married to Maria Shriver.

> "We don't want any losers around. In this family we want winners!"
>
> JOSEPH P. KENNEDY

Did you know?

■ The Kennedy children were encouraged to read *The New York Times* at an early age, and only national issues were discussed during dinner.

■ Joseph retired from stock trading at 41, amassing enough capital to build million-dollar trust funds for each of nine children.

■ He was the first Irish-American to serve as the US British ambassador.

Joseph Jr. — RFK — Rosemary — Jean — Joseph Sr. — Rose — Patricia — Eunice — JFK — Kathleen

△ JOSEPH SR. *and his wife, Rose, pose with eight of their children at the compound in Hyannisport, Massachusetts, in the 1920s.*

ROBERT F. KENNEDY
(1925–1968)

ROBERT FRANCIS KENNEDY WAS US ATTORNEY GENERAL and advisor during the administration of his brother John F. Kennedy, and was a contender for the Democratic presidential nomination in 1968.

RFK

Robert Kennedy attended Harvard University, interrupting his studies to serve in the US Navy during World War II and graduating in 1948. He received his law degree from the University of Virginia law school in 1951, and managed his brother John's 1952 campaign for the US Senate. After serving in several political positions, Robert ran John's 1960 presidential campaign, and in 1961 he was appointed attorney general by his brother. As attorney general, Robert cracked down on organized crime and sent 400 federal marshals to protect Martin Luther King, Jr., and other civil rights activists during the 1961 protests in Montgomery, Alabama. He resigned in 1964, after JFK's assassination, and a year later was elected US senator from New York. He announced his presidential candidacy in early 1968, but was assassinated in California on June 6 by a Palestinian immigrant, Sirhan Sirhan, who claimed to be retaliating for the defeat of the Arab coalition in the Six-Day War (1967) against Israel.

△ THE SEVENTH *Kennedy child, RFK was best known within the family for his sensitivity. Out of the eleven children he had with his wife, Ethel, two died and six of the remaining nine have pursued careers in political activism.*

Did you know?

■ Robert Kennedy served as assistant counsel on the Investigations Committee chaired by Senator Joseph McCarthy and, although he later developed a liberal reputation, he participated in red-baiting and anti-union tactics in the 1950s.

■ Jackie was always very close to Bobby. In her later years, the only Kennedy picture she had in her office was one of her late brother-in-law.

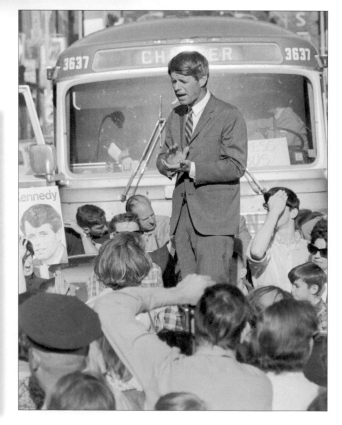

△ ROBERT KENNEDY *won the 1968 Democratic primaries in Indiana, Nebraska, South Dakota, and California before his assassination.*

"Some men see things as they are and say why. I dream things that never were and say why not."
ROBERT KENNEDY

◁ KENNEDY *heard about King's assassination while on the stump in Indiana. His ad-libbed speech on race relations is credited by many for keeping the peace in Indianapolis while many other cities burned.*

JOHN F. KENNEDY, JR.

(1960–1999)

THE SON OF FORMER US president John F. Kennedy, John F. Kennedy, Jr., pursued a career as a lawyer and, later, as a magazine publisher.

JOHN JOHN

Born in Washington, D.C., JFK, Jr. won America's heart—and the media spotlight—at the age of three when millions watched as he bravely saluted his assassinated father's casket during the solemn funeral procession. After graduating from Brown University and New York University law school (and steadfastly avoiding any political office) he worked as an assistant district attorney in New York City, going 6-0 as a prosecutor dealing with white collar crime, then resigned in 1993, unhappy with being a lawyer. Though many thought he would go into politics, he pursued journalism instead. In 1995, he launched a political magazine, *George*, which focused on the personalities of politics. A year later he married his girlfriend, Carolyn Bessette. The nation was riveted by another Kennedy tragedy when, on July 16, 1999, the single-engine private plane JFK, Jr. was piloting crashed into the waters off Martha's Vineyard, Massachusetts. His wife and her sister, Lauren Bessette, were killed with him.

△ REGULARLY *featuring sexy supermodels on its cover, George was for a time the best-selling political magazine in America. It was shut down in 2001, after John's death.*

△ WHILE JACKIE *tried hard to keep the children away from the limelight, JFK would sometimes invite photographers in when she was away from the White House, knowing that it helped his popularity to be seen with John John and Caroline.*

Did you know?

■ In 1997, in answer to a criticism that he was not exploiting his own popularity to benefit the magazine he published, JFK, Jr. appeared nude in the pages of *George*.

■ He was named the "sexiest man alive" by *People* magazine in 1988. He had a relationship with the actress Daryl Hannah, and was linked once with Madonna.

◁ CAROLYN BESSETTE *met John in 1994 and the two wed secretly in 1996 on Cumberland Island off the coast of Georgia. While Bessette came from an affluent New York family and once worked as a fashion publicist, she was uncomfortable with the constant attention focused on her and John.*

△ AFTER KENNEDY'S *untimely death, his apartment building in New York's Tribeca neighborhood became a shrine, covered with bouquets from mourners.*

LEADERS OF WORLD WAR I

AN ESTIMATED 8.5 MILLION SOLDIERS PERISHED IN WORLD WAR I, from August 1914 to November 1918. The deadly result of colonial ambition and twisted allegiances, it was the largest, most disastrous war the world had seen.

Triggered by the assassination of Archduke Ferdinand of Austria-Hungary in Sarajevo on June 28, 1914, Kaiser Wilhelm of Germany declared war on Russia and France. The conflict pitted the Central powers—Germany, Austria-Hungary, and Turkey—against the Allied forces of Great Britain, Russia, Italy, Japan, France, and, later, the United States. Fought mostly on European soil, World War I introduced trench warfare, tanks, and chemical weapons. In the Middle East, Englishman T. E. Lawrence ("Lawrence of Arabia") rallied Arabs to the Allied cause. After the Allied victory, US president Woodrow Wilson, British statesman David Lloyd George, French premiere Georges Clemenceau, and other diplomats constructed the Treaty of Versailles. Despite the peace it enforced, its draconian terms played a significant role in destabilizing Europe for generations.

△ THE BATTLEFIELDS *of World War I could barely be described by those who experienced them. Only after humans had stepped on the moon could we accurately compare the stretches of barren, deadly land.*

WOODROW WILSON
(1856–1924)

SCHOLAR AND STATESMAN Woodrow Wilson, 28th president of the United States, led the nation through World War I and drove the creation of the League of Nations.

THE INTERNATIONAL AMERICAN

△ 1912 WILSON *campaign poster. His platform promoted lower tariffs and higher personal income taxes.*

Wilson graduated from Princeton University in 1879 and studied law at the University of Virginia. He gave up law after two years to earn a Ph.D from Johns Hopkins University. After teaching at Bryn Mawr, Wesleyan, and Princeton, he became president of Princeton in 1902, where his activist tenure attracted publicity. A Democrat, he was elected governor of New Jersey in 1910. His progressive politics helped him win the presidency two years later. Wilson's administration helped establish the Federal Trade Commission and the Federal Reserve System. He won his second term in 1916 with a promise to keep the US out of World War I, but relations with Germany deteriorated in 1915 after a German submarine sank the British liner Lusitania, killing many Americans on board. In 1917 Germany renewed its submarine warfare, and on April 2 Wilson asked Congress to declare war. The money, supplies, and manpower provided by the United States turned the tide and Germany sued for peace on November 11, 1918. He attended the Paris Peace Conference and spent seven months working for a generous peace and the creation of the League of Nations, which he had proposed in his "Fourteen Points" speech earlier that year. The Treaty of Versailles fell short of his hopes. He suffered a stroke while seeking support for the League, and spent the remainder of his presidency virtually incapacitated.

△ WILSON'S WIFE *Ellen, second from left among their daughters, died in 1914. Two years later Wilson married Edith Bolling Galt.*

T. E. LAWRENCE
(1888–1935)

BRITISH SOLDIER, SCHOLAR, AND AUTHOR Thomas Edward Lawrence became a legend in his own time helping to lead the Arab revolt against the Turks during World War I.

LAWRENCE OF ARABIA

Lawrence became an expert in Arab affairs as a junior archaeologist in Carchemish on the Euphrates River from 1911 to 1914, and entered British intelligence after the start of the war. He joined Amir Faisal al Husayn's revolt against the Turks as political liaison officer and led a guerrilla campaign that harassed the Turks behind their lines. After a major victory at Aqaba, Lawrence's forces supported British General Allenby's campaign to capture Jerusalem.

In 1917 Lawrence was captured at Dar'a and tortured and sexually abused, leaving emotional scars that never healed. By 1918 Lawrence had been promoted to lieutenant colonel and was awarded the Distinguished Service Order but refused the medals, in support of Arab independence. Spiritually and physically exhausted, and uncomfortable with his fame, he returned to England and published an account of his adventures, *The Seven Pillars of Wisdom*. After the war, Lawrence joined the Royal Air Force under an assumed name. He died in a motorcycle accident.

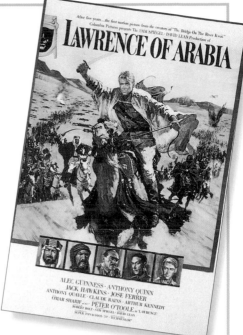

△ DAVID LEAN'S *1962 film based on his life won the Academy Award for Best Picture.*

"All men dream: but not equally."

T. E. LAWRENCE,
THE SEVEN PILLARS OF WISDOM

△ A NATIVE OF VIRGINIA,
Wilson was the first Southerner to become president since Andrew Johnson in 1865.

Did you know?

■ Wilson was the only professional academic to become president of the United States.

■ Although staunchly progressive in many ways, Wilson was unconcerned about the plight of African-Americans and supported segregation.

"Only a peace between equals can last."

WOODROW WILSON
JANUARY 22, 1917, ADDRESS TO THE US SENATE
ON ESSENTIAL TERMS OF PEACE IN EUROPE

△ BEFORE THE WAR *Lawrence worked for the British Museum on archaeological excavations along the Euphrates River.*

Did you know?

■ At a royal audience with King George V in October 1918, Lawrence politely refused the Distinguished Service Order and the Order of Bath awards.

■ In his quest for anonymity, Lawrence had his name officially changed to T. E. Shaw.

■ The 1962 film of his life, starring Peter O'Toole, won 7 Oscars.

▷ LAWRENCE *made his headquarters in 1918 in this fortress in Aqaba, a port city on the southern coast of what is now Jordan.*

HENRI-PHILIPPE PéTAIN
(1856–1951)

ETAT FRANCAIS
24 AVRIL 1943
1f20 POSTES +1f40

△ **PÉTAIN**, *depicted on a 1943 Vichy postage stamp.*

FRENCH GENERAL HENRI-PHILIPPE PÉTAIN became a national hero at the Battle of Verdun, but ended his life imprisoned for treason.

A HERO TURNED TRAITOR

As a colonel in charge of France's 2nd Army during World War I, Pétain was commanded to defend the fortress at Verdun against German attack. He reorganized the front's defenses and won one of the most devastating engagements of the war. Against Pétain's troops, the Germans lost an average of one man every 45 seconds during the first five weeks of the battle of Verdun. Pétain became a military hero and was named French commander in chief in 1917 and a marshal in 1918. When Germany invaded France in World War II, Pétain urged the government to sign an armistice with Germany, whose troops then moved in to occupy more than half of France. In 1940 French statesman Pierre Laval persuaded the National Assembly to name Pétain chief of state of the unoccupied part of France, which was "governed" from Vichy under German oversight. Pétain was convinced that France could only be saved by "an honorable collaboration." This proved to be Pétain's undoing, and at the war's end he was sentenced to death for treason. His sentence was commuted by Charles de Gaulle to life in prison, and he died in solitary confinement at age 95.

"They shall not pass."
HENRI-PHILIPPE PÉTAIN AT VERDUN

Did you know?

■ The French lost approximately 400,000 men at Verdun.

■ Pétain at first advanced slowly in the French army due to his resistance to the doctrine of the high command, which supported offense at all costs.

△ **PÉTAIN WITH HIS STAFF** *at their Paris headquarters, 1918. One of Pétain's prime motivations during the war was to improve the morale of his soldiers.*

KAISER WILHELM
(1859–1941)

FRIEDERICH WILHELM VIKTOR was *kaiser* (emperor) of Germany from 1888 to the end of World War I.

GERMAN OVER ALL

Born to Germany's Frederick III and Victoria, the youngest daughter of England's Queen Victoria, Wilhelm became kaiser at age 29. The young kaiser dreamed of building Germany into a major naval, colonial, and economic power. Determined to have his own way, he forced Chancellor Otto von Bismarck to resign in 1890, and took charge of domestic and foreign policy himself.

A series of inept political moves and his fear of being encircled by enemy states strained Germany's relations with Britain, France, and Russia—moves which helped lead to World War I. During the war, Wilhelm allowed his military advisers to dictate German policy. When he realized that Germany would lose the war, he abdicated the throne on November 9, 1918, and fled to the Netherlands, where he lived as a country gentleman until his death.

Wilhelm's Allies

FRANZ JOSEF (1830–1916) Hapsburg Emperor, Austro-Hungarian ruler.

CONRAD VON HÖTZENDORF (1852–1925) Chief-of-staff of Austro-Hungarian Army.

ENVER PASHA (1881–1922) Turk minister of war.

Kaiser Wilhelm

President Theodore Roosevelt

△ RUSSIAN POSTCARD *of Wilhelm marching to victory. He nicknamed the German soldiers "Huns," encouraging them to fight in the Chinese Boxer Rebellion like Attila's troops.*

▷ WILHELM II AS A CHILD, *wearing Highland dress. His parents, particularly his British mother, Princess Victoria, tried to provide him with a liberal education and a love of England.*

Did you know?

■ Kaiser Wilhelm enraged Britain by sending congratulations to Boer (Dutch South African) leader Paul Kruger following the defeat of a British raid into Boer territory in 1896.

■ Wilhelm was born with a withered arm. Some historians believe his insecurity over this handicap fueled his erratic behavior.

◁ THEODORE ROOSEVELT *with Wilhelm during a 1910 European tour. Roosevelt later advocated the US entering the war on the Allied side.*

DAVID LLOYD GEORGE
(1863–1945)

WELSH STATESMAN DAVID LLOYD GEORGE dominated Britain's politics during the later years of World War I; he was a primary architect of the Treaty of Versailles.

△ IN HIS MEMOIRS, *Lloyd George condemned the actions of much of the British military leadership and praised the bravery of common soldiers.*

THE WELSH WIZARD

Entering Parliament in 1890 as a Liberal, Lloyd George developed a huge following among Britain's working class over the years, supporting social welfare programs and opposing the war against the Boers in South Africa. In 1915 he served as minister of munitions. Following the death of Lord Kitchener, Lloyd George became minister for war and prime minister of England's coalition government. He formed a small war cabinet to facilitate the decision-making process, and enforced a convoy system to fight the submarine forces threatening to starve Britain.

At the 1919 Paris Peace Conference, Lloyd George tried to strike a balance between the harsh demands of Clemenceau and the non-punitive proposals of Wilson. His contribution was instrumental in shaping the Treaty of Versailles.

Lloyd George stepped down as prime minister in 1922 when his government lost the support of the Conservatives. He continued as leader of the Liberal party until 1931, though he never served in public office again. Lloyd George was made an earl two months before his death.

△ LLOYD GEORGE *(left) and Winston Churchill (right), London, 1908. Churchill served as Lloyd George's minister of munitions.*

> "You cannot cross a chasm in two small jumps."
>
> DAVID LLOYD GEORGE

Did you know?

■ Lloyd George played a leading role in establishing England's welfare state.

■ Nicknamed "the Welsh Wizard," he was often criticized as being unscrupulous and opportunistic.

■ He was a notorious womanizer.

MUSIC MAKERS OF THE '60s & '70s

THE 1960s AND 1970s WERE PERIODS OF DRAMATIC, PROFOUND CHANGES in American culture, politics, race and gender relations, and sexual mores.

Many young Americans voiced their dissatisfaction with their political leaders, with the war in Vietnam, with social injustice, and with the moral strictures erected by their parents. Nowhere were these issues given voice more vehemently than in their music. Musicians were influenced by the dynamic culture in which they performed, and they in turn influenced a generation that looked to rock 'n' roll not just for entertainment, but for artistic, social, and even political expression. In the process, they invented entirely new sounds in popular American music, and expanded rock 'n' roll into a true art form. Bob Dylan fused poetry with music, while David Bowie added theatrics and sexual ambiguity to the mix. Jimi Hendrix became the first guitar god, inspiring countless musicians who followed. Janis Joplin offered a potent blend of blues and acid rock. And Aretha Franklin addressed civil rights and female equality with her rousing version of "Respect."

△ PERHAPS MORE *than any other single event, the three-day music and art festival at Woodstock in 1969 came to symbolize the counterculture movement of the 1960s—over 450,000 people attended.*

ARETHA FRANKLIN
b. 1942

THE UNDISPUTED QUEEN OF SOUL, Aretha Franklin has more gold records than any other woman in recording history. Her sizzling, powerful blend of gospel, R&B, blues, and rock took America by storm in 1966 with her first hit single: "I Never Loved a Man (the Way I Loved You)."

LADY SOUL
The road to success was not easy for the Detroit preacher's daughter, who recorded her first gospel album at age 14 and gave birth to her first son, out of wedlock, at 15. In 1960, she went to New York to pursue her singing career and signed a six-year deal with Columbia, who totally misunderstood her genius and produced a series of watered-down pop albums.

When her contract expired in 1966, she signed with Atlantic and immediately returned to her R&B roots, bringing America to its knees with her amazing voice and red-hot soul. A string of smash hits followed, including "Chain of Fools" in 1968—the year in which she sang at Martin Luther King, Jr's funeral. She won a Grammy every year between 1969 and 1975. And in 1987, she became the first woman to be inducted into the Rock and Roll Hall of Fame.

◁ IN THE SEVENTIES, *Franklin released a series of critically acclaimed albums, including* Young, Gifted and Black. *Her success earned her the sobriquet "Lady Soul."*

△ HERE, FRANKLIN *is photographed with her 1969 hit album produced by Atlantic's Jerry Wexler. She remained with Atlantic until 1980, when she signed a new deal with Arista.*

BOB DYLAN
b. 1941

ARGUABLY THE MOST INFLUENTIAL SINGER-SONGWRITER of his time, Bob Dylan was named one of the 100 most important Americans of the 20th century by *Life* magazine.

THE VOICE OF A GENERATION

Born Robert Allen Zimmerman, Dylan changed his name when he started playing folk music in Minneapolis student hangouts in 1959, at 18. He dropped out of college in 1960 to pursue his music. Dylan's first gig was as opener for bluesman John Lee Hooker at New York's Gerde's Folk City in 1961. He was an immediate sensation, and the biting social commentary of the solo acoustic albums he recorded over the next four years defined the attitude of his generation. This early folk phase culminated in 1964 with his album *The Times They Are A-Changin'*, which was associated with the civil-rights movement and anti-war protest. In 1965, however, Dylan was booed off the stage by folk purists when he appeared at the Newport Folk Festival with an electric guitar. He responded with a landmark rock album, *Highway 61 Revisited*, and a six-minute smash hit single, "Like a Rolling Stone"—the longest single ever recorded. Subsequently, Dylan's musical repertoire expanded to include rock, country & western, blues, and even gospel in his 1979 *Slow Train Coming*. Since then he has continued to tour and record, including the critically acclaimed *Oh Mercy* in 1989. In 1997 he performed for Pope John Paul II.

△ DYLAN SANG *at the August 1963 March on Washington, D.C., which featured King's "I Have a Dream" speech.*

Did you know?

■ Dylan refused to sing on *The Ed Sullivan Show* because he couldn't sing "Talking John Birch Society Blues."

■ Dylan's son Jakob leads the Grammy-winning band The Wallflowers.

Other Key Players

JOAN BAEZ b. 1941
Female voice of civil-rights movement and once Dylan's girlfriend.

JONI MITCHELL b. 1943
Influential songwriter and leading folksinger.

PHIL OCHS 1940–1976
First political folkie, and first to go electric.

△ THE ELEGANT DIVA *of soul in 1967. "Respect," her smash hit of that year, was interpreted not only as a cry from the heart of black America but also as a protest from women everywhere. Just a decade later, in 1977, she sang "God Bless America" at Jimmy Carter's presidential inauguration.*

Did you know?

■ Franklin curtailed her touring in the late '70s after a bad flight left her afraid to fly.

■ In 1999, President Clinton awarded Franklin a prestigious National Medal of the Arts.

"People can learn everything about me through my songs, if they know where to look"

BOB DYLAN

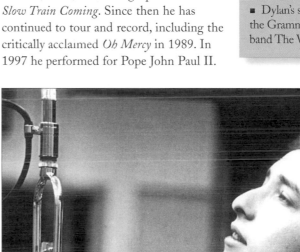

▷ DYLAN'S *favorite harmonica is the Hohner Marine Band. Many harmonica purists bemoan Dylan's rough style on the instrument.*

△ DYLAN'S EARLY TRADEMARK *was the distinctive harmonica rack. One of his harmonicas (with rack) was auctioned at Christie's in 1995 for nearly $10,000.*

JIMI HENDRIX
(1942–1970)

THOUGH HE COULD NEITHER read nor write music, Jimi Hendrix was probably the most innovative player ever to pick up an electric guitar. Hendrix coaxed sounds out of his instrument that no one had imagined possible before.

Did you know?

- The Kronos Quartet, a classical ensemble, recorded an album of Hendrix covers.
- Hendrix was dropped from a US tour with The Monkees in 1967.
- Eddie Murphy paid $7,150 at auction for one of Hendrix's vests.

THE HENDRIX EXPERIENCE

A self-taught virtuoso, Hendrix got his first electric guitar when he was 16, and left his native Seattle at 20 to play backup for Little Richard and other stars. In 1966, he formed Jimmy James and the Blue Flames, playing coffeehouses in Greenwich Village until Chas Chandler, bassist with the British rock band The Animals, talked him into changing his name and going to London. In England, Hendrix joined the psychedelic scene and recorded his first hits, "Hey Joe" and "Purple Haze," in 1967.

The US debut of The Jimi Hendrix Experience at the 1967 Monterey Pop Festival made him a superstar overnight, and his radical 7:30 A.M. version of "The Star Spangled Banner" at Woodstock is legendary. His three albums, *Are You Experienced?*; *Axis: Bold as Love*; and *Electric Ladyland*, were recorded in just a year and a half (1967–68). In 1970, he died of a drug overdose.

△ A FENDER STRATOCASTER *guitar, the signature instrument that Hendrix used in his performances and recordings.*

Hendrix played his guitar upside-down

"I hear sounds and if I don't get them together, nobody else will."

JIMI HENDRIX

Great Guitar Hands

ERIC CLAPTON b. 1945 Premier white bluesman since the 1960s.

JIMMY PAGE b. 1944 Rock idol and collaborator with lead singer Robert Plant in Led Zeppelin.

ROBERT JOHNSON (1911–1938) Delta blues master whose style helped form the genre.

△ A LEFT-HANDED *guitarist, Hendrix played a right-handed guitar upside down. He often played guitar with his teeth.*

▷ THIS PSYCHEDELIC *poster dates from 1969, just a year before Hendrix died from an overdose of barbiturates.*

15.1.69 EXPERIENCE

DAVID BOWIE
b. 1947

BRITISH ROCKER David Bowie was one of the most influential artists of the 1970s. His constantly changing look and sound helped spawn glam-rock, new wave, and ambient music —sometimes years before the trends took hold.

CHAMELEON OF POP

The self-proclaimed "Chameleon of Pop," David Bowie's first identity change came in 1965, when he dropped his birth name, David Jones, to avoid being confused with the Monkees star. He became a cult hero in England when he released the haunting "Space Oddity" in 1969, the same year in which Neil Armstrong walked on the moon. In 1972, he signed with RCA and released *Hunky Dory*, inspired by Andy Warhol and the underground art scene in New York. Within a span of just four years (1972–76), Bowie became the sci-fi alien messiah Ziggy Stardust; sold out Carnegie Hall on his first US tour; produced Lou Reed's *Transformer* and Mott the Hoople's *All the Young Dudes;* released *Diamond Dogs* and *Young Americans;* and starred in the successful science-fiction movie *The Man Who Fell to Earth*. In 1976, he relocated to Berlin to record a series of darker albums, including the acclaimed *Low* with Brian Eno, which was an innovative mixture of rock and ambient music. In 1980, Bowie radically changed his image yet again, releasing the album *Scary Monsters* and the early MTV hit single "Ashes to Ashes," harking back to his first hit "Space Oddity."

△ ZIGGY STARDUST

△ BING CROSBY *and Bowie sang "The Little Drummer Boy" on Crosby's Merrie Olde Christmas in September 1977. The odd couple's duet was released as a single and was a big Christmas hit.*

JANIS JOPLIN
(1943–1970)

ONE OF THE FIRST FEMALE rock superstars, blues diva Janis Joplin embodied the uninhibited spirit of her day.

WILD CHILD

A recluse as a teenager, an overweight beatnik-style artist in an oil-refinery town, she ran away from her home in Port Arthur, Texas, at 17. However, she established herself as America's hottest white blues-mama in 1966, aged just 23. In 1967, Joplin's stunning version of "Ball and Chain" at the Monterey Pop Festival netted a major-label record contract for her band, Big Brother and the Holding Company. Their subsequent album *Cheap Thrills* shot to the top of the charts and went gold. Joplin soon overshadowed the rest of the band, and by the end of 1968, she had gone solo. Following a historic performance at Woodstock, her solo album, *Kozmic Blues,* went gold. She died of an overdose in 1970, while she was working on *Pearl,* an album bearing her nickname.

△ FUELED BY *heroin, amphetamines, and the bourbon she drank straight from the bottle during gigs, Joplin's unrestrained sexual style and raw, gutsy sound mesmerized her audiences.*

◁ A STAINED-GLASS *window in San Antonio's Hard Rock Cafe pays tribute to Joplin. She died from a heroin overdose in Hollywood's Landmark Hotel on October 4, 1970.*

△ AFTER TAKING *time out to focus on other artistic goals, Bowie returned to his music in 1983 with his most commercially successful album* Let's Dance, *which contained four hit singles, including* "Modern Love."

Did you know?

■ Bowie contemplated becoming a Buddhist monk before pursuing a career in music.

■ Bowie married supermodel Iman in 1992.

Peter Albin
Janis Joplin
Dave Getz
James Gurley
Sam Andrew

△ BIG BROTHER AND THE HOLDING COMPANY *gave Joplin her first real break when she joined them in mid-1966, on the advice of the rock promoter Chet Helms.*

Did you know?

■ The 1979 Bette Midler film *The Rose* is loosely based on Joplin's life.

■ Joplin made TV appearances with Ed Sullivan, Dick Cavett, and Tom Jones.

■ The hit single "Me and Bobby McGee" from the posthumous album *Pearl* was written by her former lover Kris Kristofferson.

LEADERS OF THE CIVIL WAR

THE AMERICAN CIVIL WAR WAS THE BLOODIEST CONFLICT IN THE NATION'S HISTORY, taking more lives in its four years—more than 800,000—than most other American wars combined.

Decades of tension and debate between northern and southern states—mostly but not exclusively about slavery—led the southern states to secede from the Union in opposition to Republican Abraham Lincoln's election as president in 1860. The war began with a Confederate attack on Fort Sumter in the harbor at Charleston, South Carolina, in April 1861. Despite its enemy's larger population and stronger economy, the Confederate forces achieved many initial victories, but the Confederate surrender at Appomattox, Virginia, in April 1865 was largely the result of superior numbers and a naval blockade

△ CONFEDERATE FLAG

△ UNION FLAG

that cut the Confederacy off from outside help. Among the leaders of the Civil War were some of the greatest and most controversial figures in American history, including two presidents, two brilliant military commanders, and a woman devoted to freeing the slaves.

△ DEPARTING FROM THE *orderly European tactics that evolved in the 18th century, generals on both sides of the Civil War reverted to a more encompassing, and more brutal, way of fighting.*

ABRAHAM LINCOLN
(1809–1865)

RAISED ON THE FRONTIERS of Kentucky and Indiana, Abraham Lincoln was a self-taught lawyer practicing in central Illinois when he was elected to Congress in 1846. Often described as America's greatest president, Lincoln put an end to slavery and saved the Union from splitting in two.

"HONEST ABE"

Lincoln earned the nickname "Honest Abe" due to his strict morality and his commonsense approach to politics. In 1858, he ran against Stephen Douglas for the US Senate, and the two held a series of debates that crystallized the conflict over slavery. Although he ultimately lost the contest, Lincoln won the presidential nomination of the Republican party in 1860.

As a vocal opponent of the expansion of slavery, Lincoln's election drove the southern states to secede from the Union, and the Confederate attack on Fort Sumter in April 1861 ignited the war. The incompetence of the Union military high command between 1861 and 1864 forced Lincoln to take an active role in the war, and it was largely as a wartime stratagem that he declared the southern slaves free in 1862. Despite victories at Gettysburg and Vicksburg in July 1863, the Union's inability to achieve a decisive victory raised the possibility in 1864 of Lincoln's ouster from the White House that November. However, once General Grant was given command of the Union Army in April 1864 and began his relentless drive to Richmond, victory for the Union was assured and Lincoln was reelected. With the surrender of Robert E. Lee in April 1865, Lincoln prepared to rule a nation once again whole. But just a few days later, the President was assassinated at Ford's Theater, Washington, D.C.

△ THE GETTYSBURG ADDRESS *was delivered in November 1863 at the battlefield where 48,000 Union and Confederate troops had fallen in July of that year. The speech drove home Lincoln's firm belief that the US was not just a political union, but a nation.*

△ THIS PRINT *shows Lincoln with the fomer slave Sojouner Truth. In a speech delivered in 1854, Lincoln declared, "The monstrous injustice of slavery…enables the enemies of free institutions…to taunt us as hypocrites."*

▷ MORE THAN SIX FEET TALL, *Lincoln's striking appearance made him the butt of many jokes. This* Harper's Weekly *cartoon bore the caption: "Long Abraham Lincoln a Little Longer," referring to his reelection.*

Pose was highly characteristic among gentlemen of his day.

Headline refers to Lincoln's reelection for another 4-year term as president

▷ FOLLOWING VICTORY *at the Battle of Antietam in September 1862, Lincoln made an impromptu visit to inspect the troops. He is flanked, left to right, by detective Allan Pinkerton, the Union Army's intelligence chief, and General John A. McClernand.*

▽ AN ACTOR, *John Wilkes Booth, shot the president at Ford's Theater, Washington, on April 14, 1865. The contents of the president's pockets that night are shown below.*

Eyeglasses

Penknife

Wallet

Seal

"My poor friends, you are free—free as air….Liberty is your birthright"

ABRAHAM LINCOLN TO FREED SLAVES AT THE CAPTURE OF RICHMOND, 1865

George Washington

Thomas Jefferson

Abraham Lincoln

Theodore Roosevelt

Did you know?

■ Lincoln served as a military captain in the Blackhawk War of the 1830s.

■ In 1848, Lincoln turned down the opportunity to be the first governor of Oregon.

■ Lincoln was unusually tall for his day. His familiar stove-pipe hat accentuated his height.

△ THE MOUNT RUSHMORE NATIONAL MEMORIAL *stands as a remarkable tribute to America's greatest presidents. The monument was sculpted between 1927 and 1941. Each head is about 60 ft (18 m) high.*

△ DESCRIBED AS COLD AND HAUGHTY *by detractors of the day, Davis lacked Lincoln's sense of humor and deft political hand.*

JEFFERSON DAVIS
(1808–1889)

JEFFERSON DAVIS SERVED AS PRESIDENT of the Confederate States of America during the Civil War.

REBEL PRESIDENT

Born in Fairview, Kentucky, Davis graduated from West Point in 1828. Mississippi voters elected him to the US House of Representatives in 1845, but he resigned in 1846 to serve in the Mexican War, where he distinguished himself by leading troops to victory at the Battle of Buena Vista. Davis returned to public service after the war, first as a US senator from Mississippi (1847–51) and then as US secretary of war (1853–57). He returned to the Senate in 1857, but resigned in 1861 when Mississippi seceded from the Union. Soon afterward he was chosen to head the Confederacy.

Davis had a rocky tenure beyond even the challenges of war. A lack of coordination between the Confederate states, poor choices of subordinates, and Davis's own low tolerance for disagreement handicapped his government. At the end of the war he fled the Confederate capital of Richmond, Virginia, rather than surrender to Union forces, but they caught him on May 10, 1865. Davis spent the next two years in prison and was released without trial.

Did you know?

■ In 1835 Davis married the daughter of US President Zachary Taylor; her death three months later sent him into a deep depression.

■ His selection as president of the Confederacy came as a surprise: Davis had expected to be given command of the Confederate armies.

"He did not know the arts of the politician and would not practice them if understood."

VARINA DAVIS, HIS WIFE

△ TO "SEE THE ELEPHANT" *was military slang for experiencing battle for the first time.*

△ THE FIRST WHITE HOUSE *of the Confederacy was this building in Montgomery, Alabama. In summer, 1861, Davis moved his family to Richmond, Virginia, along with the government.*

ROBERT E. LEE
(1807–1870)

CONFEDERATE GENERAL ROBERT E. LEE'S bold and sometimes brilliant military strategy and powerful leadership qualities made him a legendary figure, particularly in the South.

△ DEVOTED TO HIS *home state of Virginia, Lee followed it into the Confederacy though Lincoln offered him command of the Union army.*

Did you know?

■ In 1831 Lee married Mary Custis, great-granddaughter of George Washington.

■ His father, "Light-Horse Harry" (Henry) Lee, served with distinction under George Washington in the Revolutionary War.

■ In 1859, soldiers under Lee ended John Brown's insurrection at Harper's Ferry, West Virginia.

THE LAST CAVALIER

Born in northern Virginia, Lee in 1829 graduated second in his class from the United States Military Academy, where he earned the nickname "Marble Statue" for graduating with no demerits—an astounding achievement. After serving with distinction in the Mexican War, Lee took an engineering post at Baltimore's Fort Carroll and later was appointed superintendent of the Military Academy at West Point. Lee joined the Confederate army at the outset of the Civil War, and was made a full general and military advisor to Confederate president Jefferson Davis in 1862. Lee led his troops to many key victories, including Chancellorsville (May 1863), but also suffered notable defeats, including Gettysburg (July 1863).

Outnumbered and undersupplied, Lee ultimately surrendered at Appomattox, Virginia, to General Ulysses S. Grant on April 9, 1865. The full Confederate surrender came a month later. After the war, Lee supported the reunification of the South and the North. In September 1865, he became president of Washington College in Lexington, Virginia (now Washington and Lee University), a post he held until his death.

▽ TRAVELLER, LEE'S FABLED *gray horse, was high-spirited and even a bit nervous, once pulling him down a hill during the Second Battle of Bull Run, injuring Lee.*

△ THIS CAISSON (ARTILLERY AMMUNITION VEHICLE) *was used by Lee's Army of Northern Virginia. Like Napoleon, Lee had been an expert artilleryman early in his military career.*

"It is well that war is so terrible, or we should get too fond of it."
ROBERT E. LEE

BATTLE SWORD
AND SHEATH

ULYSSES S. GRANT
(1822–1885)

ONCE A BRIGHT WEST POINT graduate who served admirably in the Mexican War, Ulysses Simpson Grant had survived a string of business failures, and was reduced to working in his father's leather goods store in Galena, Illinois, when Fort Sumter was fired upon.

TOTAL WAR

An Ohioan, he led the 21st Illinois regiment into Missouri in the summer of 1861. After a few months he was named a brigadier general. Following victories at Forts Henry and Donelson in 1862, a tactical error by Grant allowed the Condeferates to surprise him at Shiloh. The high casualty count stirred controversy around his methods that never stopped. On July 4, 1863, Grant took Vicksburg, Miss., after a long siege. Elevated to command of the Western Department, Grant defeated the Rebels at Chattanooga in November 1863. Lincoln then promoted him to Lieutenant General. In April 1864, he led the Army of the Potomac south. For all its horrors, Grant's campaign and his unmerciful approach to warfare brought the army to the outskirts of Richmond until Lee surrendered to Grant in April 1865, effectively ending the Civil War. Following Lincoln's assassination and the presidency of Andrew Johnson, Grant served two terms as president (1869–1877), though his administration was wracked with corruption. He ran unsuccessfully for a third term in 1880 and by 1884 was bankrupt. Dying of throat cancer, Grant wrote his memoirs over his last year to provide income for his family.

Did you know?

■ Some scholars think that Mark Twain ghostwrote much of Grant's autobiography.

■ For a time in the 1850s, Grant oversaw slaves of his father-in-law in Missouri.

△ A STUDIO PORTRAIT OF GRANT *from the 1860s, by Matthew Brady. In 1866 Congress made Grant the first four-star general in United States history.*

Grant's Generals

WILLIAM T. SHERMAN (1820–1891) Led the March to the Sea through Georgia.

PHILIP SHERIDAN (1831–1888) Aggressive cavalry leader, he stopped Lee at Appomattox.

GEORGE MEADE (1815–1872) Victor at Gettysburg, but pushed aside for Grant for his later inaction.

△ GRANT *is depicted on a US fifty-dollar bill. During his two-term presidency, the dollar moved toward stabilization, and the war debt was funded on a sound basis.*

▷ PRIOR TO THEIR *meeting for the Surrender at Appomattox, Grant and Lee had met during the Mexican-American War, when Grant was only a lieutenant.*

HARRIET TUBMAN
(1820–1913)

BORN INTO SLAVERY IN MARYLAND, Harriet Tubman became one of American slavery's most celebrated and successful adversaries.

▷ BORN ARAMINTA ROSS. *Tubman made her first escape in 1849 to avoid being sold. Later, she led hundreds of slaves to safety. In all her journeys, she was never caught and "never lost a single passenger" on the Underground Railrod.*

FIFTY DOLLARS REWARD.

Ran away from Mount Welby, Prince George's County, Maryland, on Monday, the 2d inst., a negro man calling himself Joe Bond, about 25 years of age, about 5 feet 6 inchesin height, stout built, copper complexion; the only mark recollected is a peculiar speck in one of his eyes. Had on when he went away a frock tweed coat, dark brown, and cap near the same color. I will give twenty-five dollars if taken in Prince George's County, Md., or in Alexandria County, Virginia; and fifty dollars if taken elsewhere and returned to me, or secured so that I get him again.
T. R. EDEL
Piscataway, Prince George's, December 5 1850.

△ **THE FUGITIVE** *Slave Law of 1850 required all Americans, North and South, to aid in the return of escaped slaves into captivity.*

"MOSES"

Tubman escaped from bondage in 1849 to Pennsylvania, conducted a series of rescues that brought her entire family to freedom, and then began working to free other slaves. Her efforts, along with those of abolitionists Susan B. Anthony, William Still, and others, led to the creation of the Underground Railroad—a network of safe houses used to transport fugitive slaves northward, usually to freedom in Canada. Tubman herself guided roughly 300 slaves during the 1850s and 1860s, earning her the nickname "Moses." Tubman expanded her role in the struggle against slavery during the Civil War. She acted as a scout for the Union army and led 750 southern slaves to freedom during a single campaign. Tubman also worked as a nurse. A lifelong reformer, she later in life devoted herself to furthering the causes of women, children, and the elderly.

◁ **A PORTRAIT OF TUBMAN**, *c. 1870. She became well-known to Southern authorities in the 1850s—a $40,000 reward was posted for her capture. Unable to read, she was nearly caught once when she fell asleep under a wanted poster of herself.*

Did you know?

■ When a slave had second thoughts about escaping, Tubman would pull a gun and say, "You'll be free or die."

■ She was struck in the head with an iron weight while attempting to save another slave from punishment. For the rest of her life she suffered periodic blackouts.

△ THIS HOUSE *in southern Illinois was a stop on the Underground Railroad. During its existence, approximately 3,000 "conductors" helped some 100,000 slaves escape from bondage into the North and Canada. Houses such as these were called stations and often held secret rooms where fugitive slaves could rest and hide during the day before resuming their journeys.*

HEALERS

SINCE TIME BEGAN, PEOPLE HAVE STRUGGLED TO FREE THEMSELVES FROM THE PAIN and suffering of illness or injury. From prehistoric man's first crude efforts after a losing encounter with prey, to the shamans and aboriginal herbalists, to the genetic alteration therapies of the 21st century, prolonged life and health has been one of man's great cumulative achievements.

Indeed, modern medicine developed out of the work of previous generations of healers. In the fifth century B.C., Greek physician Hippocrates began to separate medicine from superstition, while Florence Nightingale in the early 19th century ignored the class distinctions of her society to establish the nursing profession. Clara Barton left teaching to nurse the wounded on the front lines of the American Civil War and later founded the American Red Cross. Jonas Salk discovered the polio vaccine in the 1950s, freeing generations from fear of this dreaded disease. Fifty years later, David Ho made breakthroughs that allow AIDS victims to live longer. Just as they have built upon the work of those who came before them, the efforts of these pioneers will be the foundation for tomorrow's healers.

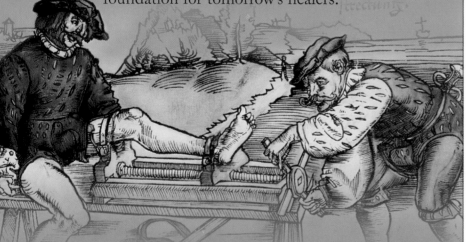

△ SETTING A BROKEN KNEE *on an extension table, 1526 woodcut. Early European medicinal techniques often seem closer to butchery than to healing. Less intrusive methods of therapy had long been used in Asia.*

FLORENCE NIGHTINGALE
(1820-1910)

ENGLISH NURSE FLORENCE NIGHTINGALE pioneered the nursing profession, hospital reform and the objective study of social phenomena.

△ THIS LAMP *was carried by Nightingale on her nightly hospital rounds, and inspired her sobriquet.*

THE LADY WITH THE LAMP

Born in 1820 in Italy, to wealthy English parents, Nightingale was educated largely by her father. At a time when women of her class were relegated to social and domestic duties and despite her family's protests, she enrolled in nursing school in Germany. In 1853 she was appointed superintendent of the Institution for the Care of Sick Gentlewomen in London. A year later, the Crimean War broke out. Nightingale volunteered to work as a nurse for the British and French armies in Turkey. Her friend Sidney Herbert, the British secretary of war, asked her to take charge of nursing at the military hospital in Scutari, Turkey. Nightingale and her party of 38 women nurses found the rat-infested facilities dismally inadequate. The battle of Inkerman, fought the day she arrived, only made matters worse, and the hospital was soon overcrowded with wounded. Nightingale endured hostile officials and insubordinate nurses, many of whom were sent home to England for drunkenness or poor conduct. By year'e end she had made significant improvements in the hospital, imposing strict sanitary and nursing standards which greatly reduced the number of deaths from wounds or illnesses. Returning to England in 1856, Nightingale suffered a breakdown, after which she worked to improve public health conditions, filing reports to the government until her death.

△ SOME BELIEVE THAT NIGHTINGALE *suffered from posttraumatic stress disorder after her devastating experience in Turkey.*

HIPPOCRATES

(c. 460 B.C.–c. 377 B.C.)

HIPPOCRATES OF ANCIENT GREECE was the first physician to conceive of the body as a whole living organism rather than viewing each part in isolation.

THE FATHER OF MEDICINE

Did you know?

■ The Hippocratic Oath, which still governs the ethical conduct of doctors today, may not have been written by Hippocrates, but it clearly represents his ideals and principles.

■ Hippocrates supposedly discovered aspirin by chewing on the bark of a white willow tree.

Though facts about his life are scarce, Hippocrates was probably born around 460 BC on the island of Kos. He is said to have traveled widely in Greece and Asia Minor (modern-day Turkey) before resettling on Kos to teach and practice medicine. He helped to free medicine from superstition through his use of unbiased clinical observations. His writings were among the first to promote the idea of preventative medicine through better sanitation and eating habits (he advised the Greeks to boil water before drinking it to avoid disease), and he also put forth the then-revolutionary notion that diseases may have environmental rather than divine causes. The Hippocratic Corpus, compiled at the time of the Emperor Hadrian (A.D. 117–138) is the first known Western medical text.

△ AN EARLY ISLAMIC *painting of Hippocrates, who was considered to be a medical authority by Islamic scholars.*

▷ SOME HISTORIANS *believe that as few as six of the 70 works often attributed to Hippocrates were actually written by him.*

△ THE HIPPOCRATIC OATH, *printed on a 1940s document. The oath requires doctors to do no harm to their patients, to give no medicine that will harm them, and to keep all patient information confidential.*

Doctors of Letters

AVERRHOES (1126–1198) Moorish thinker and physician.

ANTON CHEKHOV (1860–1904) Russian playwright and doctor.

WILLIAM CARLOS WILLIAMS (1883–1963) American poet and family doctor.

△ NIGHTINGALE *remained a recluse for the 53 years after her return from Crimea.*

Did you know?

■ When Florence Nightingale returned to England a public heroine after her work in Turkey, she shunned every kind of public reception.

■ A pioneering woman in a field largely reserved for men, Nightingale nevertheless had little sympathy for the growing feminist movement, and expressed doubts as to whether women should be allowed to be doctors.

DAVID HO
b. 1952

DAVID HO'S CONTRIBUTION to AIDS research may be the most significant of any individual's to date; his work has influenced the understanding, investigation, and treatment of HIV/AIDS worldwide.

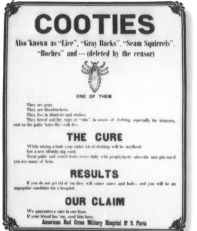

DEFEATING AIDS
Born Da-i Ho in Taichung, Taiwan, Ho moved to California when he was 12 to reunite with his father, who had come to the US nine years earlier. After attending Harvard Medical School, he began his research on the AIDS virus at Boston's Massachusetts General Hospital. Dr. Ho's research in

△ FOR HIS *groundbreaking accomplishments in AIDS treatment,* Time *magazine named Dr. Ho its 1996 Man of the Year.*

the late 1980s proved that, contrary to previous thinking, once the AIDS virus (HIV) enters the body it reproduces itself in massive quantities almost immediately. Previously, it was believed that after an initial infection, the HIV virus lay dormant for years before ravaging a patient's immune system. Thus, drugs were withheld until a patient developed visible symptoms of full-blown AIDS, usually three to eight years after infection. Ho's research heralded a significant reversal in long-held precepts of AIDS research and treatment, introducing the early use of a "cocktail" of drugs to retard the advance of the virus upon the detection of HIV in the patient.

▷ PHYSICS, *not medicine, was Ho's first choice of profession, but he changed his mind as an undergrad at Caltech.*

Did you know?

■ In 1990 Ho became the director of the Aaron Diamond AIDS Research Center.

■ Ho has authored or co-authored over 250 publications.

■ Until he was 12 he was known by his Chinese name, Da-i, which means "Great One." When the family arrived in the US, his father, a devout Christian, picked "David" out of the Bible.

CLARA BARTON
(1821–1912)

CLARISSA (CLARA) HARLOWE BARTON served fearlessly on Civil War battlefields and founded the American Red Cross.

△ A RED CROSS POSTER *with information on lice, prime irritants and disease carriers that Barton fought in the Civil War.*

"THE ANGEL OF THE BATTLEFIELD"
Born in 1821 in Massachusetts, Barton began her career in teaching, but soon turned to nursing. When the Civil War broke out in 1861, Barton quickly got involved, tracking soldiers' lost baggage and securing medicine and supplies for the Union Army. She traveled as far south as Charleston, South Carolina, with the army, moving through the battle lines to nurse the wounded and distribute supplies. Her level of involvement in war relief was unheard-of for a woman at the time. In 1865, a project she conceived to locate missing soldiers received an endorsement from President Lincoln. She organized an American chapter of the international relief organization the Red Cross in 1881. Through the rest of her life, Barton continued to dedicate herself to social service, gaining international repute for her efforts to provide relief measures during natural disasters both in the United States and abroad. Her last active work was to assist victims of the 1900 flood in Galveston, Texas. She retired in 1904 and died in 1912.

Did you know?

■ When Clara was 11, her brother David fell from a barn roof and injured himself. Clara nursed him through a two-year convalescence.

■ From 1866 to 1869, Clara raised funds for her missing soldiers project by giving lectures in the New England area and as far west as Wisconsin and Michigan.

▷ THROUGH HER *friendships with Susan B. Anthony and Frederick Douglass, Barton became an advocate of women's suffrage and African-American civil rights.*

"I may be compelled to face danger but never fear it."

CLARA BARTON

△ THE HEADQUARTERS OF THE AMERICAN RED CROSS, *located in Washington, D.C., one block from the White House.*

JONAS SALK
(1914–1995)

JONAS SALK, an American immunologist and researcher, was best known for developing the first vaccine against polio.

SHOT IN THE ARM

Born in New York City, Salk received his M.D. in 1939 from New York University where he performed studies with another doctor, Thomas Francis, Jr., on inactive virus vaccines. Salk in 1947 became head of the virus research laboratory at the University of Pittsburgh, and began his research on polio, a crippling and universally feared disease which left thousands of children in wheelchairs. Salk's research progressed more quickly than his rivals. He first demonstrated that the inactive polio virus could induce antibody formation in monkeys. Next, Salk tested his vaccine on children, first choosing children who had already had the disease, and then subjects who had never had it. The tests were successful, and in 1954 Francis conducted a mass field test of the vaccine, which showed that it safely reduced the incidence of polio. The polio vaccine was released for use in the United States in 1955. Salk continued to conduct immunology research, and was awarded the Presidential Medal of Freedom in 1977.

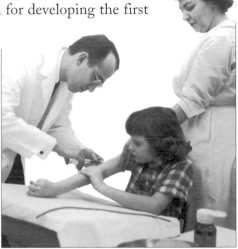

∧ SALK REFUSED TO PATENT *the vaccine because he wanted it to be widely available and had no desire for personal profit.*

Did you know?

■ John Enders was the first to cultivate polio in a test tube. He, not Salk, received a Nobel Prize for polio research.

■ Salk originally intended to study law at New York University.

■ Salk became unpopular among many scientists by holding a press conference to announce the success of his vaccine rather than publish the results in journals.

▷ PRESIDENT EISENHOWER AWARDS SALK *the first Congressional Medal for Civilian Service, April 1955.*

MODERN BRITISH ROYALS

THE BRITISH ROYAL FAMILY IS ONE OF THE RICHEST FAMILIES IN THE WORLD, enoying celebrity status across the globe. The royal family has protected the monarchy's special place in British society, while adapting to modern times.

The Queen Mother continues to enjoy great popularity. Her daughter, Queen Elizabeth II, has modified her role, heeding criticism of the family's privileged position, opening royal residences to the public, and quietly enduring the controversies around her children. Prince Charles struggled with the constraints of marriage and his royal position, and has devoted himself to charitable causes. His late wife, Diana, more than other royal, brought the Windsors into the contemporary world. Duchess of York Sarah Ferguson suffered from the press's needling and brought scandal to the royal family before divorcing her husband, Prince Andrew.

△ KING EDWARD III *founded the Order of the Garter in 1348; it includes only the inner circle of royalty.*

△ THE ROYAL FAMILY *at the turn of the century. The imperial gleam may be dimmed, but they enter the new century proud and still assured of a vital role in both the workings and the spirit of their nation.*

PRINCESS DIANA
(1961–1997)

DIANA FRANCES SPENCER WAS THE WIFE of Charles, Prince of Wales, heir to the British throne, and mother of Prince William, the future royal heir.

Other Princesses

HRH THE PRINCESS MARGARET 1930–2002 Younger sister of Queen Elizabeth.

THE PRINCESS ROYAL b. 1950 Daughter of the Queen and Duke of Edinburgh; formerly known as Princess Anne.

THE PEOPLE'S PRINCESS

The youngest daughter of Edward John Spencer, Viscount Althorp, and his first wife, Frances Ruth Burke Roche, Diana was born in Norfolk, England, and raised in a mansion next to the royal family's Sandringham estate. When her father became Earl of Spencer in 1975, she became Lady Diana Spencer. After attending a Swiss finishing school, Diana returned to England to teach kindergarten in London. She rekindled her childhood friendship with the royal family in 1980 and became especially close to Prince Charles, whom she married in 1981. The press called the ceremony, broadcast worldwide from St. Paul's Cathedral, "the wedding of the century." The couple had two sons, Prince William (b. 1982) and Prince Harry (b. 1984). Diana's popularity as princess was unprecedented. Her beauty, charm, and position made her one of the most photographed women in the world and allowed her to further the many charitable causes she was involved in, including the arts, children's education, AIDS, the homeless, and third world health care. Unfortunately, the marriage was not happy. Diana and Charles both carried on amorous relationships outside of their marriage and she suffered psychological problems. They continued to jointly raise their children before divorcing in 1996. She received a substantial settlement and continued her charitable work until her death in a car accident in Paris in 1997, with companion Dodi Fayed.

△ THE ROYAL WEDDING *on July 29, 1981, was watched by a global TV audience of 750 million. Diana said she was overwhelmed by the attention.*

△ DIANA, AGE 9 OR 10 *during a summer holiday in Itchenor, West Sussex.*

▽ DIANA'S DEATH *sparked a global outpouring of grief. Flowers carpeted the streets surrounding Buckingham Palace, Kensington Palace, and St. James Palace.*

◁ DIANA *at Christie's New York auction house in June 1997. Her dresses were sold at auction, with the proceeds from the sale going to AIDS and cancer charities. The same year she also became actively involved in campaigning for a ban on the manufacture and use of land mines.*

"Her overall effect on charity is probably more significant than any other person's in the 20th century."

STEPHEN LEE, DIRECTOR OF BRITAIN'S INSTITUTE OF CHARITY FUNDRAISING MANAGERS

Did you know?

■ As a child, Diana was given an award for being the student most helpful to her teachers and peers.

■ In a 1995 interview she admitted to affairs, driving the queen to request Diana and Charles to divorce.

△ THE PRINCESS *herself was suspected to have collaborated with Andrew Morton on his 1992 biography. The book portrays Charles in a poor light, and describes her suicide attempts and her battle with depression.*

△ TWO OF DIANA'S *few happy moments as a royal were the births of her sons William and Harry. That both were boys came as a great relief to her—it meant there would be no further pressure to present her husband and the nation with an heir.*

△ **WHILE QUEEN ELIZABETH** *was heralded at first as a monarch for the modern age, by the radical 1960s her position as a royal made her a symbol of arch-conservatism.*

"I simply ache from smiling."

QUEEN ELIZABETH II

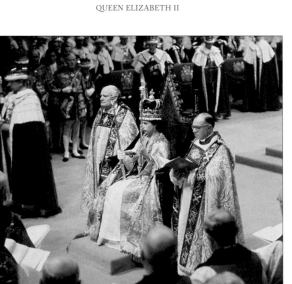

△ **ELIZABETH'S CORONATION** *on June 2, 1953 was the first such ceremony to be televised.*

ELIZABETH II
b. 1926

ELIZABETH ALEXANDRA MARY WINDSOR (Elizabeth II) is the United Kingdom's queen, a symbol of Britain to the world for the last 49 years .

DUTIFUL QUEEN

Elizabeth was the first child born to the Duke and Duchess of York, and spent most of her childhood at Windsor Castle outside of London. The Duke of York was not heir to the throne, but when his brother Edward VIII abdicated in order to marry a divorced woman, Elizabeth's father became King George VI in 1936, making Elizabeth next in line for the throne. In 1947 she married Lieutenant Philip Mountbatten and the couple had their first child, Charles, a year later.

King George VI's health had declined by the summer of 1951, and Elizabeth began to represent him at state events. When he died in early 1952, Elizabeth immediately took over his duties. Her coronation ceremony took place in 1953.

The queen has worked hard to adapt the monarchy to the modern world. She traveled widely in the early years of her reign and was the first reigning British monarch to visit Australia, New Zealand, South Africa, and the Persian Gulf countries. She has also maintained the dignity of her office despite family scandals. In 1970 she allowed some of the royal family's domestic life to be televised, and condoned the formal dissolution of her sister's marriage in 1978. She accepted her sons' divorces with dignity, although she was known to be chilly toward Princess Diana. Despite her position, the queen has made great efforts to appear a "normal" Briton. She also has made significant concessions to critics of the monarchy, agreeing to pay income tax, giving up the royal yacht, and limiting the number of royals receiving public funds. She has remained a popular queen and one of the world's wealthiest women. Prince Charles stands to become king when her reign ends.

Did you know?

■ An avid horsewoman, the Queen attends races and keeps racehorses.

■ Her nickname is Lilibet, from "Tillabet," the name she called herself as a child.

■ The Queen officially celebrates her birthday on June 11 (her natural birthday is April 21).

Princess Anne, born in 1950

▷ **ELIZABETH I** *and family c. 1952. She and Prince Philip met in 1939. She was just 13 and he was an 18-year-old, soon to become a cadet in the Royal Navy.*

PRINCE CHARLES

b. 1948

CHARLES PHILIP ARTHUR GEORGE, Prince of Wales, eldest child of Queen Elizabeth II and Prince Philip, is heir-apparent to the British throne.

A PRINCE AMID SCANDAL

Prince Charles was born in London. In a break with royal tradition, his parents sent the shy and not especially studious child first to a local day school and next to a Scottish boarding school, Gordonstoun, known for its spartan living, strict discipline, and dedication to social responsibility. Though he was next in line to the throne of England, Charles often found himself the mark of bullies there and discovered an outlet in art and dramatics. He then studied at Trinity College, Cambridge, before attending the Royal Air Force College, where he learned to fly jet aircraft. With great pressure on him to wed and continue the royal line, Charles married Lady Diana Spencer in 1981. Diana's beauty, style, and public works brought her adoration and even eclipsed her husband's position. The couple had two children, but the marriage, intensely scrutinized by the tabloid press, was troubled, and Charles resumed a relationship with Camilla Parker-Bowles, with whom he'd been in love since college. The prince and princess separated in 1992 and divorced in 1996, with the public largely blaming him. When Diana died in a tragic accident in 1997, Charles struggled against popular opinion to become a more devoted father and to appear more prepared to assume the throne when his mother leaves it.

△ QUEEN ELIZABETH *and Prince Philip were so often away from home during Prince Charles's youth that he once reportedly did not recognize his mother upon her return.*

△ CHARLES WAS 32, DIANA 20, *when they married in 1981 in a storybook wedding with all the royal trimmings. Less than a year later, their first son, William, was born.*

△ LONDON TABLOIDS *in June 2000 urged Charles to marry longtime companion Camilla Parker-Bowles, even though the Archbishop of Canterbury has said that doing so would create a crisis for the Church of England.*

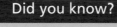
Did you know?

- Prince Charles is the permanent president of more than 200 organizations and the temporary president of another 100 or so.

- Prince Charles was the first heir to the British throne ever to earn a bachelor's degree (in 1970, at Trinity College, Cambridge).

- Charles's interest in architecture led him to found the Prince of Wales Institute of Architecture.

△ PRINCE CHARLES, *in his 50s, must wait until his mother dies or abdicates before he can rise to the throne. British royals can change their name upon taking the throne; Charles has said he will be King George VII.*

THE QUEEN MOTHER
(1900-2002)

ELIZABETH ANGELA MARGUERITE, beloved by the British people, was the queen consort of King George VI of the United Kingdom of Great Britain and Ireland and the mother of the present Queen Elizabeth.

THE NATION'S GRANDMOTHER

Elizabeth was born the daughter of an earl. She was a young debutante at the end of World War I when she met Albert, Duke of York, second son of King George V. At the time, Prince Albert was a shy young man with a stammer. When they married, Elizabeth had no reason to believe he would become king. But Albert's brother, King Edward VIII, unexpectedly abdicated in 1936 to marry American divorcée Wallis Simpson and Albert ascended the throne as King George VI, Elizabeth becoming queen consort. During her husband's reign, the royal couple emphasized devotion to home and family and they involved their daughters, the future Queen Elizabeth and the future Countess of Snowdon, in public functions. The queen quickly became known for her ability to connect with the people, and her refusal to leave Buckingham Palace during the German bombing of London in World War II made her a symbol to Britons of a brave fighting spirit. After George VI died of lung cancer in 1952, Elizabeth became queen mother when her daughter ascended the throne. In her later years she remained active in public duties in the UK and overseas.

△ **THE QUEEN MOTHER** *drew approximately $900,000 from the English treasury—with an additional overage of nearly $6,000,000—to fund her many cars and homes.*

△ **ALTHOUGH CHARLES** *had married Diana with the queen mother's approval, by the end of the marriage, she and Diana were said to have disliked each other.*

▽ **GEORGE VI** *and Elizabeth in 1949. When he died in 1952 she was left not only a widow, but stripped of her position as queen. She went into a period of deep mourning that lasted more than a year.*

Did you know?

■ Lady Elizabeth Bowes-Lyon received two marriage proposals from the future king of England before accepting him on his third try.

■ She had a renowned passion for horses and horse racing.

■ The wedding of Elizabeth and Prince Albert was England's first royal marriage based solely on love.

△ **QUEEN ELIZABETH** *accompanied King George VI as they stepped through the wreckage of a corner of Buckingham Palace, hit by a German bomb during the London Blitz on September 10, 1940.*

SARAH FERGUSON
b. 1959

SARAH FERGUSON, known to the public as "Fergie," married Prince Andrew and was the Duchess of York from 1986 to 1996.

△ ALTHOUGH THEY WERE *divorced in 1996, Ferguson moved back in with Prince Andrew at Sunninghill Park with their daughters Beatrice (left) and Eugenie (right) because of her debts.*

"FERGIE"

Sarah Ferguson came from a wealthy family and grew up in Ascot, England, where she distinguished herself in horseback riding, winning awards at horse shows. At school she was known for her ability in sports and her sense of humor. After graduating from Queen's Secretarial College she worked first at a public relations firm in London. Stints at an art gallery and a publishing company followed. She renewed her childhood friendship with Prince Andrew at a party at the royal Ascot horse race, and married him in Westminster Abbey on July 23, 1986. The couple had two daughters, Beatrice (b. 1988) and Eugenie (b. 1990).

Sarah was initially popular with the public, and was often seen with her sister-in-law, Princess Diana. Alternately praised by the press for her warmth and unpretentiousness, or criticized for her weight gain, her spending, and her lack of style, she grew increasingly unhappy with her marriage. She and Prince Andrew drifted apart amid public scandal involving her relationship with an American businessman. The royal couple divorced in 1996. Sarah, deeply in debt, returned to work, writing successful books (including books for children, self-help books, an autobiography, and several books on dieting) and endorsing products.

△ FERGUSON *wrote a series of children's books about Budgie the Helicopter, based on her experiences learning to fly.*

Did you know?

■ During Ferguson's marriage to Prince Andrew, the couple saw each other an average of 42 days a year, due to the prince's commitments to the navy.

■ When she gained weight in the late 1980s, the British tabloids unkindly dubbed her the "Duchess of Pork."

△ RATHER THAN LASH *out at anyone else for her many troubles while a member of the royal family, Ferguson assumed responsibility for her own actions in her autobiography.*

△ AT THEIR WEDDING, *Queen Elizabeth named Prince Andrew and Sarah Ferguson the Duke and Duchess of York.*

DESPOTIC RULERS

HISTORY PROVES THAT POWER CAN CORRUPT. FROM ANCIENT TIMES TO TODAY, men (and occasionally women) have become intoxicated by power.

While some monarchs are relatively benign, like the childishly demented King Ludwig II of Bavaria, many have tended towards violence and treachery. A ruler like Pol Pot—aka Saloth Sar—firmly believed that as leader of the Cambodian Khmer Rouge, his decisions were just, even if they led to torture and murder on a huge scale. Ugandan dictator Idi Amin used brutality to advance murky policies, while Russian Tsar Ivan the Terrible managed to put in place some positive reforms at the same time that he created a secret police force that roamed the nation on black horses, executing anyone that dared speak out against the tsar. Sadly, rulers like Serbia's Slobadan Milosevic continue to prove that power in the wrong hands can be an enormously destructive force.

△ **THOUGH KAISER WILHELM II** *is best remembered as the leader of Germany during World War I, he was regarded by some as an unhinged monarch who made a plaything out of his own nation.*

IDI AMIN
b. 1925

IDI AMIN OF UGANDA was one of the most ruthless and cruel dictators of the 20th century, ruling Uganda from 1971 to 1979,

DADA
A career soldier, Amin worked his way up the military ladder of the newly independent African nation of Uganda during the 1950s and '60s. He became commander of the Ugandan military in 1966 at the request of Prime Minister Milton Obote, but in 1971 Amin ousted Obote by military coup and quickly established himself as the country's new leader. A staunch nationalist and fanatical Muslim, Amin went on a reign of terror, banishing Jews and Asians, slaughtering thousands of minority tribespeople, and inflicting torture and mutilation upon innocent civilians. Amin also drove the nation's economy into ruin by handing over financial and business matters to his inept and corrupt political supporters. In the 1970s Amin aligned himself with Muslim terrorist groups and gave support to anti-Israel causes, making him a threat outside of Central Africa. In 1978 he invaded neighboring Tanzania, which counterattacked and defeated Ugandan forces. Amin fled to the Middle East, eventually settling in Saudi Arabia. The Saudi government banished him to Mecca in 1998 for trying to smuggle arms to contacts in Uganda. Uganda has yet to recover from his reign, but Amin remains in Saudi Arabia, from which he receives a pension.

Did you know?

■ Between 300,000 and 500,000 Ugandans were killed by Amin's forces.

■ In 1976, he facilitated the Palestinian hijacking of a plane carrying Israelis. Israeli soldiers liberated the plane in the famous Raid on Entebbe.

△ **AMIN HAD NO** *problem using mercenaries in his army. Here he watches as former officers of the British Army take the oath of allegiance prior to joining the Ugandan armed forces.*

IVAN THE TERRIBLE
(1530–1584)

THE FIRST TSAR OF ALL RUSSIA, Ivan the Terrible laid waste to his own nation. His violent reign left deep political and social scars on his country.

ORPHAN TURNED KILLER

The grandson of Ivan the Great, Ivan the Terrible became tsar in 1547, and proved to be a ruthless ruler. His goal was to conquer all remaining independent regions and create a larger, more centralized Russia. His initial efforts were successful, but his methods disrupted the economy and culture. He seized private lands and redistributed them among his supporters and created a police force dressed all in black, astride black horses, that existed more to crush dissent than to keep the peace. As Ivan's unpopularity grew and his wife died, his behavior became more erratic. He blinded the architect of St. Basil's Cathedral and killed his own son in a fit of rage. When Ivan the Terrible died, he left the country in disarray, and Russia would not emerge from the chaos until the reign of Peter the Great more than a century later.

> △ AN ORPHAN *by the time he was eight years old, young Ivan was left to fend for himself among the murderous aristocracy that seized control of the court. Surrounded by their terror, he tortured small animals as a boy, yet still managed to develop a taste for literature and music.*

> "Ivan the Terrible was right. You cannot rule Russia without a secret police."

JOSEPH STALIN

△ IVAN ALTERNATED *between periods of rage and repentance. In a 1851 rage, he ordered executions and in an angry fit, killed his son.*

▷ ST. BASIL'S CATHEDRAL *in Moscow's Red Square was commissioned by Ivan the Terrible to commemorate the conquest of the Tatar city of Kazan. It was built between 1555 and 1561.*

Did you know?

■ Ivan created the Oprichniki, the first official secret Russian police force.

■ Russian filmmaker Sergei Eisenstein directed the two-part epic *Ivan Groznyj* (1945 and 1958), considered one of the finest films of the Soviet era.

■ His nickname— "Grozny"—really translates as "awesome."

△ AN IMPOSING *figure, Amin first made himself noticed within the Ugandan Army as its heavyweight boxing champion for nine years. Living in comfortable exile, he still likes tennis, boxing, and soccer.*

> "In any country there must be people who have to die. They are the sacrifices any nation has to make to achieve law and order."

IDI AMIN

KING LUDWIG II
(1845–1886)

MAD KING LUDWIG II OF BAVARIA abandoned most of his responsibilities as leader in favor of a reclusive, fantasy-driven lifestyle. A danger less to the Bavarian people than to himself, he remains something of a historical anomaly.

THE DREAM KING

Ludwig assumed control of the throne in 1864 at the age of 18. Fascinated with opera composer Richard Wagner since he was 13, Ludwig ordered Wagner brought to him and the two began an unusually tight bond, with the young king enthralled and influenced by the 51-year-old composer. Bored by politics, Ludwig proved completely inept as a military leader during the Seven Weeks War between Bavaria's allies Austria and Prussia. After Prussia's victory in the Franco-Prussian war in 1871, Ludwig surrendered control of Bavaria to the newly united Germany and sank into an isolated life in elaborate castles he built in the mountains of Bavaria. Ludwig now ordered lavish productions of plays and operas, which he watched alone. Although his castles helped define modern notions of "fairy-tale castles" and formed his lasting contribution to German culture, they also drained Bavaria's treasury and forced a coup, which declared him insane in 1886. Later that year he was found drowned along with his doctor. No one knows the circumstances of their deaths.

△ SOME RESEARCHERS *surmise from his autopsy that Ludwig's insanity may have stemmed from syphilis contracted during sexual liaisons in the early 1870s.*

Did you know?

■ Legend has it that Ludwig requested that a doctor declare him unfit to be married in order to avoid marrying his fiancée, Sophie.

■ Ludwig's family had a history of instability; he had an aunt who believed that she had swallowed a glass grand piano.

△ NEUSCHWANSTEIN CASTLE *was only half-completed when Ludwig II died in 1886. Intended to epitomize Wagner's vision, its plans included an underground grotto and a throne room with a mosaic floor made of more than two million tiles.*

POL POT
(1928–1998)

Pol Pot's brutal rule as leader of the Communist Khmer Rouge guerrillas in Cambodia was one of the deadliest regimes in history. Almost two million Cambodians—about a third of the population— died during his reign.

SOWER OF THE KILLING FIELDS

Born Saloth Sar in Cambodia in 1928, then a French colony, Pol Pot in 1949 went to study in Paris, where he quickly became involved in the Communist Party and the anti-French resistance movement led by Ho Chi Minh. He returned to Cambodia in 1954 and attained a position as a schoolteacher, all the while working for the Cambodian revolutionary cause. He became leader of the Khmer Rouge (Red Cambodian) Party, and in 1976 Pol Pot seized power when Cambodia's government collapsed. Declaring "Year Zero," he forced millions of Cambodians to work in appalling conditions as part of the country's new agrarian economy, torturing and executing dissenters. Ousted in 1979 by Vietnamese forces, Pol Pot continued to influence guerrilla resistance in Cambodia for nearly two more decades, until he gave himself up to his own Khmer Rouge in 1997. Forced into house arrest, he died of natural causes the following year.

Leaders to Fear

SADDAM HUSSEIN b.1937 Iraqi leader gassed and starved his people.

JEAN-BEDEL BOKASSA (1921–1996) Cannibal despot of Central African Empire.

MANUEL NORIEGA b. 1934 Military leader of Panama, drug trafficker.

△ A MAN CLEANING A SKULL, 1996, *near a mass grave at a death camp run by the Khmer Rouge in the 1970s. During Pol Pot's regime, cities were evacuated and residents herded into countryside "re-education camps" where they were worked to death or slaughtered.*

△ **THOUGH RESPONSIBLE** *for the deaths of millions of Cambodians, Pol Pot was known for his soft voice, unprepossessing manner, and ability to quote French poetry. During his reign he was called "Brother Number One."*

> "I want you to know that everything I did, I did for my country."

POL POT

Did you know?

■ The Khmer Rouge's decision to overthrow Pol Pot was prompted by his order to execute his own wife and children.

■ Under Pol Pot, money was abolished in Cambodia, as were schools, newspapers, private property, and religion.

■ Only five of the more than 20,000 people who entered the Khmer Rouge's infamous Tuol Sleng prison are said to have survived.

△ **DOCTORS, TEACHERS,** *those who could speak a foreign language, or people who simply wore eyeglasses, were murdered by Pol Pot's regime.*

SLOBODAN MILOSEVIC
b. 1941

Did you know?

■ Both of Milosevic's parents committed suicide. His father shot himself in 1962; his mother hanged herself in 1973.

■ In addition to indictments for war crimes and human rights violations, Milosevic has been accused of embezzling Yugoslav public funds.

SLOBODAN MILOSEVIC, REFERRED TO by many as "Europe's last dictator," waged a campaign of ethnic terrorism in Yugoslavia that has been compared to the reign of Adolf Hitler.

SERBIAN STRONGMAN

Born in Serbia, one of the Yugoslav republics, Milosevic became active in the Communist party in the early 1960s, and by 1984 was appointed head of the Belgrade arm of the party. Capitalizing on the growing discontent of Serbs in the largely Muslim province of Kosovo, Milosevic gained control of Serbia's Communist Party in 1987. In 1989 he was elected president of Yugoslavia. He used a zealous pro-Serb platform and manipulative control of the media to maintain power as he annihilated thousands of Muslim Albanians in the province of Kosovo and forced thousands more into refugee camps outside the area in the interests of creating "Greater Serbia." NATO's attempts to topple Milosevic failed, but he was defeated in the general elections of 2000. He was arrested in April 2001, and sent to an international prison to await trial for war crimes and human rights violations.

△ **MILOSEVIC** *came to prominence in 1987, when he told Serb protesters, "No one shall ever beat you again!"*

> "Balkan graveyards are filled with President Milosevic's broken promises."

FORMER US PRESIDENT
BILL CLINTON

△ **AIRSTRIKES BY NATO** *forces destroyed Milosevic's home in the upscale Dedrize neighborhood in April 1999. Milosevic and his family were not home at the time and the bombing campaign was not enough to force him out of office.*

THE GREAT ARCHITECTS

ARCHITECTS DESIGN THE SPACES IN WHICH WE LIVE, WORK, PLAY, AND WORSHIP. Their designs must balance form and function with aestheticism.

An architect's buildings often communicate a vision for a society; in turn, famous structures such as the Egyptian pyramids, Roman monuments, Gothic cathedrals, or modern skyscrapers are symbols of a particular society's ingenuity, values, and beliefs. Palladio's work reinterpreted classical Roman structures and exemplified the Renaissance rediscovery of humanism. Gaudí's structures hearkened back to Catalan values during a time when those values were suppressed. Frank Lloyd Wright drew inspiration from the prairies of America's Midwest and created homes that incorporated, and harmonized with, nature. Modernist Mies van der Rohe used a cool, European intellect to marry art with technology in a style that helped create the blueprint for office buildings worldwide. As the 20th century came to an end, Frank Gehry rejected bland architectural styles and combined inexpensive materials with computer-aided design to create unexpected buildings for an unpredictable time.

△ A TRUE MARRIAGE OF HEART AND MIND, *architecture more than any other art form requires close attention to human needs.*

FRANK LLOYD WRIGHT
(1867–1959)

FRANK LLOYD WRIGHT united geometry with a unique, organic vision of building using bold plain forms and open areas.

△ STAINED GLASS *window from Robie House, 1909. Wright designed nearly every aspect of his buildings.*

AMERICAN ARCHITECT

Born in Richland Center, Wisconsin, Wright studied engineering at the University of Wisconsin because architecture courses were not available. In 1887 he moved to Chicago, where he soon became chief assistant to Louis Sullivan. When his mentor discovered in 1893 that Wright was moonlighting for his clients, Wright left to open his own practice. By his early 30s, Wright was acknowledged to be the best of the Prairie School architects; largely from the Midwest, the Prairie architects eschewed elaborate detailing in favor of bold, plain forms and roomy open living areas. Wright designed about 50 houses during his Prairie period, from 1900 to 1910, and throughout his career, his work bore the Prairie influence, with its organic detailing, earthy colors, rich textural effects, and concern with harmony between the building, its inhabitants, and its environment. Toward the end of this period, Wright became estranged from his wife, Catherine Tobin, whom he had married in 1889. She did not grant him a divorce until 1922. Wright carried on relationships with other women, creating controversy and making it difficult for him to land commissions, though his Imperial Hotel in Tokyo was built during this time. The Crash of 1929 further reduced demand for his services, and Wright began lecturing at Princeton and in Chicago and New York City. He reemerged as a leading architect in the late 1930s, moved to Arizona, and established a studio-workshop called Taliesen West, with branches in Wisconsin and Arizona. His later years saw some of his most famous work, including New York's Guggenheim Museum.

△ WRIGHT *in 1938, the year he moved to Arizona and designed Taliesen West.*

ANTONIO GAUDÍ
(1852–1926)

ANTONIO GAUDÍ I CORNET, a Catalan architect, developed a distinctive style characterized by freedom of form and rich color and texture.

ARCHITECT OF THE SPIRIT

Born in the Catalan region of Spain, the son of a coppersmith, Gaudí showed an early interest in architecture, and began studies in the subject in Barcelona in 1869. He was an important participant in the Catalan Renaixensa, a revival of traditional arts and crafts which called for a return to the regional Catalan way of life, long suppressed by the Castilian-dominated government of Spain. Gaudí displayed his version of Art Nouveau in a series of fanciful buildings, most notably his apartment buildings. In 1883, he was commissioned to design the Sagrada Familia (Church of the Holy Family), which became the religious symbol of the Renaixensa. While working on it, he became increasingly pious, and after 1910, he abandoned virtually all other work and even lived on the site. He died at age 75, when a tram hit him on his way to Mass.

△ THE CASA MILA *apartments (also known as the Quarry), were meant by Gaudí to resemble a wave.*

◁ GAUDÍ'S *detailing often drew from natural forms, such as these arches at the Sagrada Familia (Church of the Holy Family).*

▽ FOR BARCELONA'S CASA CALVET (CALVET HOUSE), *completed in 1904, Gaudí also designed the furniture, such as this oak armchair.*

Did you know?

- Gaudí remained a bachelor his whole life, and was believed by many to be celibate.

- Gaudí came from a family of metal-workers and was the first Gaudí in four generations to work outside this field.

- In addition to being a well-known architect, Gaudí was an accomplished sculptor.

▷ GAUDÍ SPENT *much of his time with his patron Eusebi Guell (left) and his friend Bishop Torras i Bages (right).*

△ THE GUGGENHEIM *Museum in New York City, with its organic, sculptural façade, was a response to the severity of modernism.*

> "A great architect is not made by way of a brain nearly so much as he is made by way of a cultivated, enriched heart."

FRANK LLOYD WRIGHT

Did you know?

- Wright created nearly a third of his projects during the last decade of his 70-year career.

- Wright attributed his love of architecture to a set of blocks his mother gave him as a child.

- Wright's own home was repossessed in 1927.

ANDREA PALLADIO
(1508–1580)

BY REINTERPRETING CLASSICAL structures, Andrea Palladio became one of the greatest and most influential architects of Renaissance Italy.

△ THE BENEDICTINE MONASTERY *and Church of San Giorgio Maggiore (1565–1580) is sited on the basin of St. Marks in Venice.*

PROPORTION AND SYMMETRY

Andrea Di Pietro Della Gondola was born in Padua, the son of a miller. He worked as an assistant in a Vicenza masons and stonecutters guild until he met amateur architect Giangiorgio Trissino, who became his mentor and renamed him Andrea Palladio, after Pallas Athene, the Greek goddess of wisdom. Palladio's early work consisted of palaces and villas for the aristocracy, including the much-copied Villa Rotonda near Vicenza. His style was a reinterpretation of classical Roman architecture. In the 1560s, he began to design religious buildings and created the plans for many of the churches in Venice. In 1570 he published a theoretical work, *The Four Books of Architecture,* which greatly influenced his successors. In the same year, he was appointed architectural advisor to the Venetian Republic, a job he continued until his death ten years later.

▽ PALLADIO *considered his buildings the most brilliant since ancient times, and devoted the second of his four books entirely to them.*

Did you know?

■ Palladio's 1554 book *The Antiquities of Rome* remained the standard guidebook to Rome for 200 years.

■ The enduring fame of *The Four Books of Architecture* comes from the influence it had on the work of 17th-century English architects such as Inigo Jones.

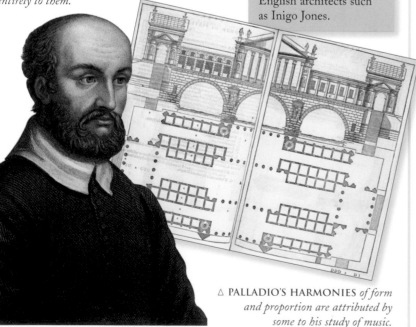

△ PALLADIO'S HARMONIES *of form and proportion are attributed by some to his study of music.*

FRANK O. GEHRY
b. 1929

CANADIAN-BORN ARCHITECT and designer Frank Owen Gehry has gained international renown for his work, which combines a diverse range of styles and materials in surprising ways.

Did you know?

■ Gehry was born Frank Goldberg. His family changed their last name when they emigrated to the United States.

■ Bilbao's Guggenheim, an abstract titanium structure, echoes the shape of a ship.

■ Gehry received the Pritzker Prize, considered the Nobel Prize of architecture, in 1989.

ARCHITECTURAL INNOVATOR

Born in Toronto, Gehry emigrated to Los Angeles with his family in 1947. He studied architecture at USC and city planning at Harvard University. After working for several architecture firms, he established his own company, Frank O. Gehry & Associates, in 1962. Like many of his contemporaries, Gehry broke away from standardized modernism and designed urban structures reminiscent of older architectural forms. With their inexpensive materials, many of his structures have a distinctive, unfinished look. Gehry has designed many high-profile buildings both public and private in the United States and abroad, including EuroDisneyland in Paris and the Guggenheim Museum in Bilbao, Spain.

▽ SCALE MODEL *of Guggenheim Museum complex, proposed for Lower Manhattan by Gehry in 2000. The project is estimated to cost $678 million.*

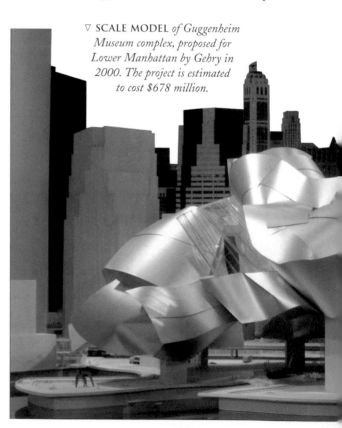

LUDWIG MIES VAN DER ROHE

(1886-1969)

THE ELEGANT, SIMPLE forms of German-born architect Ludwig Mies van der Rohe characterized modern architecture's "International Style."

Did you know?

■ During World War I Mies van der Rohe served as an enlisted engineer in the German army, building bridges and roads in the Balkans.

■ He added his mother's surname, van der Rohe, to "Mies" after he had established himself as an architect.

LESS IS MORE

Ludwig Mies was born the son of a master mason and at age 19 became an apprentice of furniture designer Bruno Paul. His first commission, a suburban house, was so impressive that it won him a job in Berlin with Peter Behrens, Germany's most progressive architect. Committed to art's role in society, he joined the Deutscher Werkbund, an association of artists who were "marrying art with technology," and then served as director of the Bauhaus school of design from 1930 to 1933. With Hitler in power in Germany, Mies moved in 1938 to the United States. As the corporation emerged as the leading institutional force in postwar America, Mies's austere style set the tone for its architecture. His work is best exemplified by the Seagram Building in New York and the Federal Center in Chicago.

△ UNCOMPROMISING *in his tenets, Mies locked horns with Walter Gropius, Wright, and Philip Johnson.*

▽ SEEMINGLY *plain, the Seagram Building in New York derives its beauty from its crisp lines and simplicity.*

△ GEHRY, *seen here in a recent photo, designed two lines of corrugated-cardboard furniture, Easy Edges and Experimental Edges.*

Great Architects

LOUIS SULLIVAN (1856–1924) "Form follows function."

PHILIP JOHNSON b. 1906 The first American to work in the International Style.

LE CORBUSIER (1887–1965) French high modernist.

△ THE BARCELONA CHAIR *was created for the German Pavilion at the 1929 International Exposition.*

> "It is better to be good than to be original."

LUDWIG MIES VAN DER ROHE

POLAR EXPLORERS

IN THE 19TH AND EARLY 20TH CENTURIES, WHEN SPACE TRAVEL WAS A DISTANT DREAM, the Earth's polar regions were the frontiers of great exploration and adventure.

The North Pole eluded conquest until 1909, when American Robert Peary, his assistant Matthew Henson, and five Inuits dogsledded across frozen seas to reach it. Explorers then turned their attention to the colder and more remote South Pole. Briton Robert F. Scott and Norwegian Roald Amundsen raced to be the first to reach the bottom of the world. Amundsen succeeded on December 14, 1911; Scott reached the Pole 34 days later, but all the members of his party died during the return journey. Ernest Shackleton led an expedition in 1915 that has in recent years become the most celebrated of Antarctic adventures: He aborted his mission to cross the continent after ice destroyed his ship, then led 28 men to safety despite enormous dangers. During the 1920s and '30s Richard E. Byrd used aeronautics to explore the polar regions.

△ SHACKLETON'S HUT *from the* Nimrod *expedition still sits on Cape Royds in Antarctica's McMurdo Sound, while Mt. Erebus, named after a place of great darkness in Hades, looms off in the distance.*

SIR ERNEST SHACKLETON
(1874–1922)

THOUGH NONE OF HIS polar expeditions achieved their goals, Ernest Shackleton has become the most admired explorer of his age by bringing all the men of his ill-fated *Endurance* expedition to safety.

△ THIS BISCUIT *from Shackleton's* Nimrod *expedition was auctioned for $11,383 in 1999.*

THE BOSS

Ernest Shackleton was born in County Kildare, Ireland. In 1884 his family moved to the London suburbs. Despite his father's wish that young Ernest study medicine, 16-year-old Shackleton became a merchant sailor, and by the time he was 24, he held a master's certificate. Illness forced him out of Scott's 1901 Antarctic expedition, and his 1908 *Nimrod* expedition came to within 97 miles of the pole. After Amundsen reached the South Pole in 1911, Shackleton decided to lead the first trans-Antarctic journey. Pack ice in the Weddell Sea trapped his ship, the *Endurance*, in January 1915 and finally crushed it in October. The crew drifted on an ice floe until April 1916, when they sailed to uninhabited Elephant Island in small boats. Leaving one party behind, Shackleton and five companions sailed 800 miles through massive seas and severe hunger and thirst to South Georgia Island. Next they had to traverse rugged mountains and glaciers until they finally reached the island's whaling station on May 16. After three rescue attempts, Shackleton at last reached Elephant Island on August 30, 1917, and brought all his men home safely. In 1919, despite heart problems, Shackleton joined British forces in Russia. The next year he led his last polar journey, but his health, further damaged by heavy drinking, failed him in South Georgia Island, where he died on January 5, 1922.

Sir Ernest Shackleton   *Robert E. Peary*   *Roald Amundsen*

△ THOUGH DISAPPOINTED *that he did not reach either pole, Shackleton admired the work of his rivals, Peary and Amundsen.*

▷ SHACKLETON'S SHIP, *the* Endurance, *1915. The ship was trapped in ice for 281 days. The men on board nicknamed their quarters the "Ritz." To entertain themselves, they played soccer and hockey, though killer whales in search of food would sometimes smash through the ice and temperatures dipped to minus 23° Fahrenheit.*

△ SHACKLETON *(right) and Frank Wild, first mate, 1916, in front of their tent on the ice floe that the* Endurance *crew drifted on for 165 days.*

Other Ice Explorers

FRIDTJOF NANSEN (1861–1930) Early polar explorer and diplomat.

DOUGLAS MAWSON (1882–1958) Made solo Antarctic journey.

JOHN FRANKLIN (1786–1847) Led fatal Arctic expedition.

"We had reached the naked soul of man."

ERNEST SHACKLETON

△ THE HUT AT CAPE ROYDS *was built in 13 days by the 1907–09 Shackleton party and was home to 15 men for a year. During the six-month Antarctic winter, they could only leave the building for brief periods.*

Did you know?

■ Shackleton felt his dismissal from Scott's 1901 party was unjust, and the incident sparked a bitter rivalry between the two that would last until Scott's death.

■ Shackleton sent a support party to the other side of Antarctica to lay supplies for the *Endurance.* That team didn't realize that he had been shipwrecked, and lost three of its members while sledging supplies.

▷ THE FARTHEST *south Shackleton would ever get was January 7, 1909, when the* Nimrod *party came within 97 nautical miles (roughly 111.5 land miles) of the pole.*

ROALD AMUNDSEN
(1872–1928)

NORWEGIAN EXPLORER Roald Amundsen was the first person to reach the South Pole and the magnetic North Pole; he also led the first expedition to navigate the Northwest Passage between the Atlantic and Pacific oceans.

THE LAST OF THE VIKINGS

The son of a ship owner, Amundsen grew up in Oslo, and was greatly affected by the story of John Franklin's polar journey in the 19th century—their ship trapped in ice, the survivors resorted to cannibalism and died of starvation and exposure. After his father's death, Amundsen studied medicine for two years as his mother wished. When she died, he left school to follow his dreams. In 1903 he embarked on the first journey through the Northwest Passage, in the ship *Gjøa*. His party began at the northern end of Baffin Island in the Canadian Arctic and made their way until they found harbor on King William Island, northwest of Hudson Bay. There they spent two years gathering data on the magnetic North Pole. Once Peary reached the North Pole in 1909, Amundsen set aim for the South Pole. With a team of expert skiers and dog teams, he reached it on December 14, 1911, beating English explorer Robert F. Scott by 34 days.

After a failed attempt in 1925, Amundsen flew across the North Pole in a dirigible with Umberto Nobile in 1926. In 1928 Amundsen tried to rescue Nobile, whose plane had crashed on a second expedition. Amundsen and his plane disappeared; Nobile was later rescued.

△ AMUNDSEN'S SHIP the Maud. *From 1918 to 1923 he took her through the Northeast Passage between Europe, Siberia, and the Arctic by allowing the ship to drift with the ice.*

△ WHILE AMUNDSEN *may have lacked Scott's romantic spirit, he planned every aspect of his expedition to maximize his chances for success and survival.*

Did you know?

■ When the *Gjøa* became trapped in ice after traveling through the Northwest Passage, Amundsen covered the nearly 500 miles to Eagle City, Alaska, by dogsled.

■ Amundsen's original goal was to reach the North Pole, but when Peary discovered it in 1909, he switched the destination of his ship, the *Fram,* without telling anyone, to surprise Scott.

▷ THE AMUNDSEN-SCOTT *South Polar Station was started in 1957, International Geophysical Year, and stands about 350 meters from the actual Geographical South Pole. Its dome is 165 feet high.*

ROBERT F. SCOTT
(1868–1912)

Robert Falcon Scott was the leading figure in one of the greatest tragedies of modern exploration. His party's return trip from the South Pole was one of the most arduous in recorded history; no one survived.

ENGLAND'S TRAGIC EXPLORER

Born into a naval family that made a fortune in the brewing business, Scott was raised in sheltered comfort. Though shy, sensitive and small for his age, he became a cadet in the Royal Navy when he was 13, as dictated by his father. Beginning in 1900 Scott made two fateful trips to Antarctica. Driven by an ambition as much his wife's as his own, he became determined to be the first man to reach the South Pole. In 1910, both Scott and Norwegian explorer Roald Amundsen set out for the pole. Ill-prepared for their journey, and hampered by Scott's failings as a leader, his team lost the race, and on January 17, 1912, arrived second at the South Pole. Low on food and fuel, having lost two of their party, Scott and his remaining men endured enormous suffering on the return journey—halted by a blizzard just 11 miles from a supply depot. Their remains and journals were found the following spring. Scott attained enormous posthumous celebrity in England, becoming the personification of the stiff-upper-lip British explorer.

△ **KATHLEEN SCOTT** *gave birth to their only son, Peter, just days after Scott announced plans for his fatal expedition.*

"Had we lived, I should have had a tale to tell of the hardihood, endurance, and courage of my companions which would have stirred the heart of every Englishman."

FROM ROBERT F. SCOTT'S FINAL JOURNAL ENTRY

△ **A STATUE OF SCOTT**, *sculpted by his widow, stands in Christchurch, New Zealand, which served as a base for many Antarctic expeditions. After Scott's death, Kathleen Scott was made a lady and his famous journal was edited to eliminate any evidence of Scott's bungling.*

Did you know?

- Most historians believe that Scott would have made it back from the South Pole if he had used his dogs for food, as Amundsen did.

- At the end of his life Scott described himself as having "always an inclination to be idle."

- Scott was a close friend of J. M. Barrie, author of *Peter Pan*, and even named his son after Barrie's fictional creation.

▷ **SCOTT'S PARTY** *at the South Pole, 1912. Despite their exhaustion, snow-blindness, and hunger, Scott insisted the men haul geological samples back with them, showing little sympathy for their physical or psychological difficulties. The last words in Scott's diary were "For God's sake look after our people."*

Laurence Oates

Robert F. Scott

Edgar Evans

Edward Wilson

H. R. Bowers

ROBERT E. PEARY

(1856–1920)

ROBERT PEARY IS WIDELY, but not definitely, credited with being the first person to reach the North Pole.

FIRST TO THE NORTH POLE?

Peary was born in Pennsylvania. In 1859, after the death of his father, his family moved to Maine. In 1881 he joined the US Navy Civil Engineers Corps, and three years later began his career in exploration as chief assistant on a surveying expedition to Nicaragua. Soon he became obsessed with the idea of reaching the North Pole. Between 1886 and 1897 he led five expeditions to Greenland and Arctic Canada in preparation. In 1906 he sledged to within 175 miles of the pole and, in 1909, finally succeeded in reaching it, or at least he claimed to have. Leading a party that consisted of himself, his African-American assistant Matthew Henson, and the Inuits Ootah, Egingwah, Seegloo, and Ooqueah, Peary had to fight against moving ice floes that may have caused him to miscalculate his position. When Peary returned to the United States he discovered that a one-time expedition mate of his—Frederick A. Cook—claimed to have discovered the pole a year earlier. Cook's claims were later discredited, but Peary did not have any verifiable proof that he had reached the North Pole either, and both men's reputations suffered. Though Peary traveled the world during his last years to great acclaim, the truth about his accomplishments still remains clouded.

△ ROBERT PEARY AND DR. FREDERICK COOK *on magazine cover, c. 1905. The ambitious Cook was president of the Explorer's Club, but Peary did not consider him a real rival.*

Did you know?

■ Peary's 1909 expedition employed 24 men, 19 sledges, and 133 dogs.

■ Peary brought back six live Inuits from one of his expeditions, and gave them to his chief sponsor, the American Museum of Natural History in New York, for display (all died but one boy).

■ During their Arctic tours in the 1890s, Peary and Henson fathered children by Eskimo women.

△ THOUGH PEARY WAS *a rear admiral and received 22 honorary medals from various countries, and 3 honorary doctorates, he had to testify before Congress about his claim that he reached the North Pole.*

> "Nothing easier. One step beyond the pole, you see, and the north wind becomes a south one."

PEARY, ON HOW HE REACHED THE NORTH POLE

◁ PEARY AND HIS TEAM *pose for a photograph upon reaching the North Pole, April 1909. Peary had the men display five flags: from left, Ooqueah and the Navy League flag; Ootah holds the DKE fraternity flag; Henson with the Polar flag; Egingwah holds the DAR Peace flag; and Seegloo has the Red Cross flag.*

△ LAUNCHED ON *March 23, 1905, the* Roosevelt *took Peary on two expeditions, first leaving New York City on July 16, 1905.*

RICHARD E. BYRD
(1888–1957)

RICHARD BYRD was the first man to fly over both the North and South poles, and contributed enormously to scientific and geographical knowledge about those regions.

△ BYRD WAS THE FIRST *American Antarctic explorer since the 1840s expedition of Charles Wilkes, and Byrd became a national hero during the Roaring Twenties.*

ALONE AT THE POLE

Byrd was born to a prominent Virginia family. He showed an early inclination for exotic travel, voyaging alone at age 11 to the Philippines to visit a relative. He entered the US Naval Academy at the age of 20. He began flying during World War I, and developed pioneering methods of landing seaplanes at night and navigating while out of sight of land. Byrd made the first flight over the North Pole on May 9, 1926, with copilot Floyd Bennett. Both men received the Congressional Medal of Honor for the achievement. Taking leave from the Navy, he then set his sights on Antarctica, and his 1928–1930 expedition was the first to employ a host of modern mechanical inventions: snowmobiles, airplanes, and aerial cameras. During that expedition, Byrd became the first person to fly over the South Pole, but it was his 1934 expedition that gave him his enduring fame. That winter, he manned a small hut 120 miles from his main base for almost five months, and nearly died of carbon monoxide poisoning. His memoir, *Alone*, was a best-seller and helped create American interest in the Antarctic.

△ AN EARLY AVIATOR, *during World War I Byrd made long flights over water beyond sight of land. Until then, pilots navigated largely by visual landmarks, but Byrd's work gave aerial navigation a reliable and scientific basis.*

△ BYRD REMAINED *an American hero decades after his polar travels. Here he helps load relief supplies for the 1948–1949 Berlin Airlift.*

Did you know?

■ On June 29, 1927, Byrd completed the first transatlantic flight by multi-engine plane, arriving in France just 30 days after Charles Lindbergh.

■ The first flight over the South Pole took place on November 29, 1929, in the *Floyd Bennett*, during a flight that lasted almost 19 hours.

■ Some scholars now think Byrd might have missed the actual site of the North Pole during his 1926 flight.

△ IN PREPARATION *for International Geophysical Year in 1957, which established a full-time research presence in Antarctica, Admiral Byrd took a team back to the site of his base, Little America, which he built in 1929.*

FIVE MAJOR SAINTS

FEW PEOPLE SET OUT IN LIFE TO BECOME SAINTS. THE PATH IS NEVER EASY; IT DEMANDS SACRIFICE AND SUFFERING. And yet these five men and the many hundreds of others deemed by the Roman Catholic Church to have led exemplary lives stand out for their profound effects on the world.

St. Paul's writings are among the earliest Christian works. He was extremely influential in establishing Christianity as a new religion, rather than a sect of Judaism. St. Augustine's writings adapted classical thought to Christian teaching and laid the groundwork for medieval Christian thought. St. Francis founded the Franciscan order; based on emulating the charity and poverty of Christ, it became the largest order in Roman Catholicism, producing 98 saints and six popes. St. Thomas Aquinas united theology with philosophy, wedding reason and religion. St. Ignatius founded the Jesuits, who focus on educational, missionary, and charitable works.

△ THE COMMUNION OF SAINTS, *a doctrine traced back to the seventh century, unites the saints in heaven, the believers on earth, and the souls in purgatory, all under the power of Christ.*

ST. PAUL
(A.D. 10–c. 67)

ST. PAUL WAS A JEWISH RABBI who converted to Christianity and became its major apostle, ensuring its place as a great faith.

△ ST. PAUL *depicted in a Biblical illumination. His interpretation of Christ's message was based on a belief that the world was about to end.*

SPREADING THE WORD

Originally named Saul, Paul was born in Tarsus, Sicilia (now Turkey). Given a strict Jewish upbringing, he became an enthusiastic member of the Pharisees, a Jewish sect that promoted purity and fidelity to the Law of Moses. He is believed to have been trained as a rabbi, and saw the new church of Christ as a threat to Judaism. Paul joined the crusade against Jews who converted to Christianity, but by his own account, in A.D. 33 he received a vision of Jesus while traveling to Damascus. Taking the name Paul, he began to preach the Christian gospel. Unpopular with authorities in Damascus, Paul moved to Jerusalem and met the apostle Peter, then went on to Antioch to assist in conversions of both Jews and Gentiles. From there, he set off on three missions covering Asia Minor and the Hellenic world, spreading Christianity and securing a place for gentiles in the new church. He was arrested in Jerusalem and is believed to have been executed by Nero around A.D. 67 Paul's epistles (letters) to churches and individuals about doctrine and practice form a major part of the New Testament.

△ ON HIS THIRD MISSIONARY *journey, Paul spent two and a half years in Ephesus, during which time he wrote four epistles.*

△ MICHELANGELO'S *heroic marble sculpture of Paul (1501–1504) matches his importance within the Christian tradition.*

SAINT THOMAS AQUINAS
(c. 1225–1274)

PHILOSOPHER AND THEOLOGIAN Thomas Aquinas had a great influence on the church as the first major figure to present theology as a rationally derived science.

SCIENTIST OF CATHOLICISM

Born in Sicily to an aristocratic family, Aquinas was placed as a prospective monk in a nearby monastery at a young age. Later he attended the University of Naples, where, against his family's wishes, he decided to join the Dominicans, a new religious order. In 1245 he began theological studies at the University of Paris. He studied the works of Aristotle and later drew upon them to lecture publicly on theology as a science. His most famous work, the *Summa Theologica*, included five proofs of the existence of God. His lectures raised a storm of opposition among faithful who believed that reason had no place in religion. Three years after Aquinas's death, the masters at the University of Paris—who held the highest theological jurisdiction in the church—condemned a series of propositions that included 12 of his theses. Despite the controversy, Aquinas was canonized in 1323. His writings had a tremendous influence on the church and resulted in a new relationship between faith and philosophy that endured long after his death.

△ **14TH CENTURY** *copy of Aquinas's* Summa Theologica; *he chose to finish this work rather than become Archbishop of Naples.*

Did you know?

■ Aquinas's own family kidnapped him when he was on his way to the University of Paris. They kept him prisoner for a year in an effort to prevent him from being a Dominican monk.

■ On one occasion, Aquinas's brothers sent a woman to tempt him to break his monastic vow of chastity. Aquinas drove the temptress away.

△ **THIS ITALIAN RENAISSANCE ALTARPIECE** *(1476) by Carlo Crivelli depicts the Madonna and Child flanked by saints. Aquinas is in the upper right corner.*

△ **A DETAIL OF AQUINAS** *from Crivelli's altarpiece. Albertus Magnus, Aquinas's professor, found him to be brilliant despite his quiet nature:* "We call this man a dumb ox, but his bellowing in doctrine will one day resound throughout the world."

SAINT AUGUSTINE
(354–430)

SAINT AUGUSTINE IS KNOWN AS THE GREATEST of the early "fathers" of the Christian faith and a founder of Western theology.

THE DOCTOR OF HIPPO

Born in Tagaste in Roman-ruled North Africa to a Roman father and a Christian mother, Augustine was raised as a Christian. At school in Carthage, he gave up his religion and became involved in Manicheanism, which taught a separation between the soul and the body. He lived a dissolute life and fathered a son before moving to Italy to teach. In 386 he professed Christianity and the next year was baptized in Rome. Augustine became a relentless antagonist of competitive sects, including Manicheanism. He became bishop of Hippo in 396 and spent the rest of his life spreading Christianity throughout Africa. His books, *The City of God* and his *Autobiography*, assigned a place to Christianity among other philosophies in the late Roman world. He was named a Doctor of the church in the early Middle Ages— an honor given to certain ecclesiastical writers.

△ **AUGUSTINE** *offered a vision of a heavenly City of God as a moral model during a time of great turmoil and brutality.*

▷ **AUGUSTINE PREACHING** *to his disciples, 12th-century English Anglo-Saxon illumination. The most important Christian thinker after Paul, Augustine applied Platonic philosophy to Christian thought.*

Did you know?

■ Upon becoming a Christian, Augustine chose to be celibate.

■ Many medieval libraries held more works of Augustine than of any other writer.

■ When Augustine asks himself in his early *Soliloquies* what he desires to know, he replies: "Two things only, God and the soul."

"To many, total abstinence is easier than perfect moderation."

ST. AUGUSTINE

SAINT FRANCIS OF ASSISI
(1181–1226)

SAINT FRANCIS FOUNDED the Franciscan order of monks, which played an important role in the growth and character of Christianity during the centuries after his death.

GOD'S SIMPLEST SON

Francis was born to a wealthy merchant family in Assisi, Italy, and began his career as a soldier. A vision, however, convinced him to change his life and dedicate himself to religion, much to the distress of his father. Further visions followed, leading Francis to renounce worldly goods and family ties to embrace an apostolic life of poverty. He began to preach his "simple rule" of following in the footsteps of Jesus Christ. Around 1209, Innocent III sanctioned the Franciscan order. Francis was known as a lover of nature—he is said to have preached to birds—and a celebrant of poverty, a man who dedicated himself to helping those in need. His version of God as a loving, gentle creator has greatly influenced Christian thought. He was canonized by Gregory IX on July 15, 1228.

△ **A RELIQUARY** *from the 13th century that once held a piece of the saint's body.*

SAINT IGNATIUS
(1491–1556)

THEOLOGIAN SAINT IGNATIUS OF
LOYOLA founded the Jesuit order,
known for its educational focus.

SOLDIER FOR CHRIST
Born to a wealthy noble family in the
Basque region of Spain in 1491,
Ignatius became a knight in the service
of a family relative in 1517. While
recovering from a wound, he spent time
reading the lives of great saints, and soon
experienced a spiritual awakening. In
1522, he embraced a life of poverty and,
sustained by alms, went on a pilgrimage to
Jerusalem, which was followed by periods of
study in Spain and France. In 1534, he and a group
of his followers took the monastic vows of chastity,
poverty, and obedience; in 1540 the group moved
to Rome, where the Pope approved of their
"Society of Jesus." This order, commonly known as
the Jesuits, became
famous around the
world as educators
and missionaries during the centuries that
followed. In the summer of 1556, Ignatius
died of a fever in Rome. He was canonized
by Pope Gregory XV in 1622.

△ IGNATIUS *wrote*
The Spiritual Exercises, *a
book of mystical reflections
and prayers, in 1522.
They are still used by
clergy and laypeople today.*

Other Monks

ST. ANTHONY (250–350)
The first Christian monk.

ST. BENEDICT
(c. 480–c. 543) Founder of
the Benedictine order.

THOMAS MERTON
(1915–1968) Trappist
thinker and peace activist.

"Everything that one
turns in the direction
of God is prayer."

ST. IGNATIUS OF LOYOLA

Did you know?

■ When Francis's father
forbade him to become a
monk, Francis publicly
removed his clothes and
renounced all material
possessions in favor of
his "father in heaven."

■ In the summer of
1224, while praying to
God, Francis is said to
have received "stigmata,"
marks of crucifixion
similar to those borne by
Jesus Christ

△ FRANCIS OF ASSISI *took the
rough cloth of Umbrian peasants
for his clothing, as depicted here in
Raphael's 1505 portrait.*

◁ GIOTTO'S *frescoes, painted from
1297–1300 at the Church of San
Francesco at Assisi, Italy, portray
the life of Francis. Here the saint
levitates during an ecstatic vision.*

Did you know?

■ Initially Ignatius had
been opposed to placing
the Jesuits in colleges
as educators of youth,
but by the last years of
his life he had reversed
his position.

■ St. Ignatius postponed
his ordination as a priest
for almost 12 years, to
allow sufficient time for
his education.

◁ FRENCH ARTIST *Claude Vignon
painted* The Triumph of St. Ignatius
six years after Ignatius's canonization.

179

LEADERS OF WORLD WAR II

WORLD WAR II (1939-1945), THE BIGGEST, BLOODIEST WAR IN HISTORY, had its roots in cultural and territorial conflicts stretching back for centuries.

These hostilities reached an apex after World War I, when political instability and economic depression gave rise to radical fascism and aggressiveness in Germany, Italy, and Japan. In the 1930s, Germany fell under the thrall of the Nazi party and the fiery Adolf Hitler, whose plan to forcibly extend the borders of Germany went into motion with the invasion of Poland on September 1, 1939. Hitler's forces quickly conquered most of Western Europe, leaving only Winston Churchill, England's Prime Minister, to rally the British against Hitler in the West. After Joseph Stalin, the brutal Soviet dictator who was once Hitler's ally, swiftly aligned with Churchill in June 1941, when Hitler turned against him. US president Franklin D. Roosevelt overcame American isolationism after the Japanese attack on Pearl Harbor on December 7, 1941, and the lines were now drawn: the Allies—Great Britain, France, the Soviet Union, and the United States—pitched into five years of fighting on fronts around the globe against the Axis—Germany, Japan, and Italy, the last led by the mercurial and incompetent Benito Mussolini.

△ THE LEADERS OF THE ALLIES *met at Yalta, a resort in the Soviet Union's Crimean Peninsula, in February 1945 to decide the fate of Europe after Hitler's fall.*

ADOLF HITLER
(1889–1945)

ADOLF HITLER, NATIONAL SOCIALIST (NAZI) LEADER and dictator, created one of the most brutal and despotic regimes in history.

DER FÜHRER

Hitler was born in Braunau, Austria. His family moved to Germany in 1913. He served in World War I, and in postwar Munich joined an anti-Semitic nationalist group eventually known as the National Socialist German Workers (Nazi) party. A powerful speaker, he was named the party's chairman in 1921. In 1923 Hitler and the Nazis made a failed coup attempt on Bavarian officials, landing him in prison for nine months. There he wrote *Mein Kampf*, filled with his beliefs and hatred of Jews—views that gained popularity by the 1930s. Hitler was appointed chancellor, then named himself *Führer* (leader) in 1934. He passed laws establishing sanctioned persecution of the Jews.

△ THE SWASTIKA *was an ancient good luck symbol before the Nazis adopted it as their emblem.*

Hitler invaded Poland on September 1, 1939, prompting France and Britain to declare war. He began setting up concentration camps, in which six million Jews, along with millions of other victims, were systematically murdered in what is now known as the Holocaust. German forces overran much of Europe during 1940. When he failed to defeat Britain, Hitler invaded the Soviet Union in 1941. Despite initial victories, Soviet counterattacks and a severe winter stopped the advance. The Allies won crucial battles in Italy and North Africa in 1942, and the 1944 invasion of France further strained the German military, now facing massive Soviet attacks from the east. As Berlin fell, he committed suicide with his mistress, Eva Braun, on April 30, 1945.

△ EVA BRAUN, *Hitler's mistress, moved into his Munich apartment in 1935 and followed him to his retreat in Berchtesgaden a year later. The Nazis accepted her, though the German public knew nothing of her.*

▷ MASS RALLIES
highlighted by Hitler's inflammatory speeches helped unify the German-speaking nations under the bloody Nazi banner.

"The great masses of the people will more easily fall victim to a big lie than to a small one."

ADOLF HITLER

△ HITLER'S UNIFORM *and his personal effects, on display at the Central Russia Armed Forces Museum.*

▽ THIS POSTER'S GERMAN SLOGAN *translates as "The People, the Reich, the Führer." Preparing for world conquest, Hitler rearmed Germany and annexed Austria and Czechoslovakia, all supposedly to gain "Lebensraum"—room to live—for the German people.*

Ein Volk, ein Reich, ein Führer!

Heinrich Himmler   Rudolf Hess   Adolf Hitler

△ NAZI LEADERS *at a pre-war conference in Berlin, c. 1937. Himmler commanded the Gestapo or secret police. Hess, Hitler's personal attaché, had no political role in the Reich aside from loyally supporting his leader.*

△ **EVEN AS HITLER** *marched on Moscow, Stalin remained in the Kremlin to direct the war effort, largely by himself.*

JOSEPH STALIN
(1879–1953)

ONE OF THE SOVIET UNION'S most powerful and feared leaders, Joseph Stalin effectively controlled the Soviet government for nearly thirty years.

MAN OF STEEL

Though a bright student at a theological seminary, Stalin was expelled in 1899 for his revolutionary activities and became a supporter of Lenin. Arrested and exiled many times, by 1917 he had established his place in the Bolshevik Central Committee. In the years after Lenin's death in 1924, Stalin emerged as dictator. He forcefully imposed vast industrial and agricultural programs, creating a highly centralized and repressive regime that included purges of any who were not unquestioningly loyal to him. Millions of Soviet citizens were murdered or sent to brutal labor camps.

In 1938 he signed a Non-Aggression Pact with Hitler, but when Germany invaded the Soviet Union in 1941, Stalin joined the Allies, playing a leading role in defeating Hitler. His involvement in the postwar conferences at Teheran and Potsdam left much of Eastern and Central Europe under communist rule. After his death, Khrushchev denounced, and Gorbachev later officially condemned, Stalinism.

Did you know?

■ Stalin was born into poverty in the Caucasian town of Gori, Georgia, and was the only one of his parents' four children to survive infancy.

■ Stalin was born Iosif Vissarionovich Dzhugashvili.

■ The dying Lenin warned against Stalin and his growing power.

> "A single death is a tragedy, a million deaths is a statistic."
>
> JOSEPH STALIN

△ **A SOVIET POSTER/CARTOON** *showing the Allies attacking Nazi Germany, personified by Hitler as a defeated wolf.*

△ **STALIN, IN WHITE UNIFORM,** *looking on as Vyacheslav Molotov, USSR Commissar for Foreign Affairs, signed the Non-Aggression Pact with Hitler's Germany in August 1939. When Germany launched a surprise attack in 1941, Stalin had a two-week nervous breakdown, then reappeared to take charge.*

FRANKLIN D. ROOSEVELT
(1882–1945)

FRANKLIN DELANO ROOSEVELT, the 32nd president of the United States, led the nation through two great crises: the Great Depression and World War II.

FDR

The scion of two prominent New York families, Roosevelt attended Harvard and worked as a lawyer on Wall Street before winning a seat in the New York State Senate. He later served as assistant secretary of the Navy in the Wilson administration, and was the Democratic nominee for vice president in 1920. Roosevelt was elected governor of New York in 1928 and in 1932 was elected president. The New Deal, Roosevelt's program of sweeping financial and social reforms designed to cope with the Great Depression, helped define the Democratic party for the rest of the century. Meanwhile, he prepared unwilling Americans for a role in World War II. Elected to an unprecedented third term in 1940, he urged Congress to declare war on Japan after its attack on Pearl Harbor in December 1941.

Roosevelt and Winston Churchill became close friends and together planned the Allied strategy. At the February 1945 Yalta Conference, he convinced Britain and the Soviet Union to form the United Nations and agreed to give the Soviets control of portions of Asia and Eastern Europe. By then, Roosevelt was serving his fourth term, and in failing health. He died two months later, on April 12, 1945.

△ ROOSEVELT MADE GREAT *use of radio to communicate, reassure, and rally the American public with his "Fireside Chat" radio speeches.*

Did you know?

■ During the war, Roosevelt hosted a nightly cocktail hour during which politics could not be discussed.

■ His crippling polio first appeared in 1921, during a vacation to Campobello Island. He never had full use of his legs afterward

The Bomb and After

HARRY TRUMAN (1884–1972), US president, made decision to drop atomic bomb on Japan in 1945.

GEORGE MARSHALL (1880–1959) Army chief of staff, his plan rebuilt Europe.

▽ ROOSEVELT MARRIED *his distant cousin Eleanor in 1905. During the war, her role as the wheelchair-bound president's "eyes and ears" made her indispensable to his management of the White House.*

Winston Churchill   Franklin Roosevelt   Joseph Stalin

△ CHURCHILL, ROOSEVELT AND STALIN *at the Yalta Conference, February 4–11, 1945. Roosevelt's concessions to Stalin led to criticism at home and helped usher in the Cold War.*

BENITO MUSSOLINI

(1883–1945)

DICTATOR OF ITALY during World War II, Mussolini is largely remembered for his political posturing, egocentrism, and questionable leadership.

IL DUCE

Born into a middle-class family dedicated to socialism, young Mussolini was a brilliant but headstrong student. By age 18 he had joined the Socialist party and soon created his own version of socialism. In 1914 he left the party in favor of an Italian fascist movement he developed based on nationalism, militarism, and a strong state. Elected to lead the National Fascist party in 1921, he rose to power with the help of ruling groups threatened by Italy's post-World War I economic crisis. He suppressed civil liberties and ruthlessly repressed workers' movements. His attempts to build a "new Roman Empire" by invading Ethiopia and supporting Franco in the Spanish Civil War put him at odds with Britain and France, so he joined with Hitler's Germany and with Japan. Woefully unprepared to fight when war broke out in 1939, Italy entered only after Germany conquered France in 1940 and Hitler's conquest seemed certain. Italy was rapidly defeated on all military fronts. Hitler installed Mussolini in a puppet government in northern Italy in 1943, but partisans captured and executed him in 1945.

△ MUSSOLINI *drew on imagery from the Roman Empire to bolster Fascist Italy.*

△ WHILE MUSSOLINI IS IDENTIFIED *with fascism, in fact his political philosophy was a mix of ideas, with bits of Marx, Nietzsche, and Machiavelli all merged into what he essentially saw as a class struggle.*

> ## "Blood alone moves the wheels of history."
>
> BENITO MUSSOLINI

Did you know?

■ Mussolini edited several political papers, including the socialist *Avanti!* and the fascist *Popolo d'Italia.*

■ Benito Mussolini was named after Mexican revolutionary Benito Juarez.

■ His own fascist government ousted him during the war and the king named a new prime minister.

△ MUSSOLINI HAD BEEN *in power for ten years before Hitler brought fascism to Germany. It was from Mussolini that Hitler learned the importance of highlighting the trappings of power.*

△ MUSSOLINI MARCHING WITH HIS STAFF *(1931). Many Italians supported his annexation of Ethiopia, but were dismayed by his support of Franco in Spain, and his alliance with Hitler.*

SIR WINSTON CHURCHILL

(1874–1965)

DURING HIS STORIED 90-year life, Winston Churchill was an accomplished soldier, statesman, politician, artist, and writer.

THE GUARDIAN OF FREEDOM

The son of a British lord and a mother from a rich American family, Churchill became a cavalry officer in 1895, and proved himself as both a soldier and a war correspondent. His success led to a position in Parliament in 1901. Churchill further built his political reputation by serving in several government positions, including first lord of the admiralty, home secretary, and secretary for the colonies. During the decade leading up to World War II, Churchill openly criticized British leadership, arguing for a build-up of British military forces and lobbying unsuccessfully for an alliance of nations against Nazi Germany. He was reappointed first lord of admiralty when World War II broke out in 1939, and in 1940 became prime minister. A renowned orator, Churchill made stirring speeches that helped galvanize Britain and the rest of the world against the Axis powers. While Britain fought alone after the fall of France in 1940, Churchill found a key partner in US president Franklin Roosevelt, who sent crucial supplies and declared war on the Axis powers after Japan attacked Pearl Harbor in December 1941. Germany surrendered in May of 1945. Churchill lost his bid for reelection in July, and focused on the growing influence of the Soviet Union, delivering his famous "Iron Curtain" speech the next year. Remaining in Parliament until shortly before his death, Churchill held various positions, including another term as prime minister from 1951 to 1955.

Prime Ministers

NEVILLE CHAMBERLAIN (1869–1940) Appeased the Nazis, but also bought time to prepare for war.

CLEMENT ATLEE (1883–1967) Churchill's Labour successor.

△ **AMERICAN WORLD WAR II POSTER** *depicting Churchill as a British bulldog.*

△ **IN HIS FIRST SPEECH** *to Parliament as prime minister on May 13, 1940, Winston Churchill said, "I have nothing to offer but blood, toil, tears, and sweat."*

△ **BLENHEIM PALACE,** *Churchill's birthplace in Oxfordshire. He is buried nearby in the village of Bladon.*

◁ **CHURCHILL** *with Field Marshal Alan Brooke, on a warship crossing the English Channel to Normandy, June 12, 1944. When Churchhill was reappointed by Neville Chamberlain in September 1939 as first lord of the admiralty, the message sent to the British fleet was simple: "Winston is back."*

Did you know?

■ Churchill won the Nobel Prize for Literature in 1953 for his historical writing.

■ Britain's Royal Academy regularly exhibited his paintings, and held a one-man show of his work in 1958.

■ Churchill was knighted in 1953 and made an honorary American citizen in 1963.

MILITARY LEADERS OF WWII

THE STATISTICS OF WORLD WAR II WERE UNIMAGINABLE: in seven years over 60 million people died. The massive numbers of soldiers required military leaders to coordinate their efforts on an unprecedented level, resulting in some of the most historic engagements in military history.

War tore across Europe in 1939 as Hitler invaded Poland, causing Britain and France to declare war on Germany. From there the conflict spread—Stalin entered the war after the Nazis invaded the Soviet Union in June 1941; the US joined the Allied forces after Japan's attack on Pearl Harbor, led by Adm. Yamamoto Isoroku in December 1941. In 1942, US forces led by Gen. Dwight D. Eisenhower united with Gen. Bernard Montgomery's British forces and the Free French Forces of Charles de Gaulle to roust the Nazi's top general, Erwin Rommel, from North Africa—the Allies' first decisive victory. Two years later Allied forces joined under Eisenhower to invade Normandy on D-Day, June 6, 1944, the victory that turned the tide of the war.

△ THE SUPREME COMMAND ALLIED *Expeditionary Force met at invasion headquarters in London on January 31, 1944. D–Day, the invasion of Normandy, was still five months away.*

DWIGHT D. EISENHOWER
(1890–1969)

DWIGHT D. EISENHOWER led Allied forces to decisive victory in Europe in World War II, and later served as 34th president of the United States.

"I LIKE IKE"

Born to a poor family in the Midwest, Eisenhower was a superb athlete as a young man. He played football at the Military Academy at West Point. After graduation, he was stationed in San Antonio, Texas, where he met and married his life partner, Mamie Doud.

During World War I, Eisenhower served as a captain at a tank training center. In 1933, he became an aide to Army Chief of Staff George C. Marshall. When America entered World War II in December of 1941, Eisenhower was assigned to the Army's War Plans Division in Washington, D.C., where he led many successful campaigns, including the invasions of North Africa, Italy, and Normandy. In December 1944, he was named a five-star general.

At the war's conclusion, Eisenhower was revered as a hero. Democrats and Republicans alike approached him as a potential presidential candidate, but he initially rejected their requests, opting for a post as president of Columbia University in 1949. Eisenhower then became supreme commander of NATO in 1950. In 1952, with President Harry Truman not running for another term, he decided that the Republican Party came closest to his values and he accepted the Republican nomination for president. He easily won the election over Adlai E. Stevenson, and his party captured both houses of Congress by a narrow margin. In his two terms as president, he relied on consensus and avoided controversial moves, often sidestepping controversial issues related to racial and economic equality. Eisenhower died in 1969.

△ COMMEMORATIVE 1941 POSTER. *The day of the attack on Pearl Harbor, Ike was on the General Staff in Washington, D.C.*

△ A STAR FOOTBALL PLAYER *at West Point until a knee injury ended his sports career, Eisenhower was well liked as a cadet.*

ERWIN ROMMEL
(1891–1944)

CALLED THE "PEOPLE'S MARSHAL" by his countrymen, Field Marshal Erwin Rommel was one of Hitler's most successful generals and one of Germany's most popular military leaders.

THE DESERT FOX

A native of Heidenheim and son of a teacher, Rommel joined the German infantry in 1910 and in World War I fought as a lieutenant in France, Romania, and Italy. He rejected advancement through the regular channels, choosing to remain in the infantry after the war ended.

In February 1940, he was named commander of the 7th Panzer division. One year later, he was appointed the commander of German troops (the Afrika Korps) in North Africa. Famed for leading his army from the front rather than the rear, as most generals did, for a time Rommel enjoyed an unbroken string of successes, and earned the nickname the "Desert Fox" for his surprise attacks. Promoted to field marshal by Hitler, he was defeated by superior British forces at the battle of El Alamein. With North Africa lost, he was recalled to Europe in 1943 to oversee the defense of the Atlantic coast.

◁ AFTER THE ALLIED *invasion in June 1944 and the resulting push across France, Rommel knew that Germany would lose the war and discussed surrendering with other officers. Implicated in a plot to overthrow Hitler, Rommel took his life on October 14, 1944.*

Did you know?

■ When his role in the plot against Hitler's life was revealed, Rommel was offered the option of taking poison instead of going to trial. He was given a full military burial.

■ As commander of the Afrika Korps, Rommel gained popularity in the Arab world as a liberator from British rule.

△ ONE OF *Eisenhower's most difficult tasks in World War II was keeping the high-strung, brilliant military leaders working in harmony.*

Did you know?

■ Ike's decision to go to West Point led his pacifist mother to tears.

■ 156,000 troops landed in Normandy on D-Day, and invading forces eventually reached one million.

■ Eisenhower sent 1,000 federal troops to Little Rock, Arkansas, in 1956, to desegregate Little Rock Central High School.

▷ ROMMEL IN BENGASI, LIBYA, *with Italian officers, 1942. Italian losses to the British in North Africa led Hitler to send Rommel to Libya, where he laid siege to the port city of Tobruk from April to December 1941. Repulsed by the British, he returned with the Afrika Korps in June 1942 and finally took the city. Five months later Britain recaptured it.*

Other key players

GEORGE PATTON (1885–1945) Brash genius of US armored forces.

OMAR BRADLEY (1893–1981) Commander of the entire US forces in Europe.

KARL DÖNITZ (1891–1980) Nazi submarine genius; Hitler's successor.

"What else matters but beating him?"

WINSTON CHURCHILL, CAIRO, 1942

187

CHARLES DE GAULLE
(1890–1970)

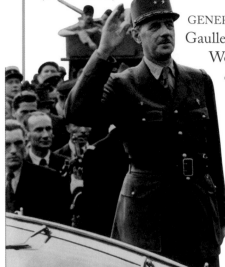

GENERAL AND STATESMAN Charles de Gaulle led the Free French Forces in World War II and was first president of France's Fifth Republic.

PILLAR OF FRANCE

The son of a philosophy teacher, de Gaulle grew up in Lille and served with distinction in World War I. After the war, de Gaulle warned against the danger of German aggression, pleading with France to develop a mechanized army, to no avail. At the outbreak of World War II, he was promoted to brigadier general and named under-secretary of state for defense and war. He opposed the Franco-German armistice, and fled from occupied France to London in June 1940 to establish the Free French Forces. A French military court sentenced him to death in absentia. Entering Paris with liberation forces on August 25, 1944, his leadership was officially recognized for the first time by the Allies. In 1945 he was elected provisional president of France but resigned, irritated by the coalition government. After the collapse of the Fourth Republic, he was inaugurated as President of the Fifth Republic in 1959. Under his hand, the new constitution created a more centralized government, which he led until 1969.

△ DEGAULLE *salutes crowd after liberating Paris on August 25, 1944. He rode into the city with the Allies in command of 500,000 soldiers, but did not make himself dictator.*

Did you know?

■ A soldier in World War I, de Gaulle was wounded three times, and was a POW for three years, during which he made five escape attempts.

■ De Gaulle was named *Time* magazine's Man of the Year in 1958.

△ GENERAL DE GAULLE *shakes hands with Lt. Gen. Alexander M. Patch, Comm. General US 7th Army, at a ceremony held in Saverne, France, February 11, 1945*

YAMAMOTO ISOROKU
(1884–1943)

ADMIRAL YAMAMOTO ISOROKU was Japan's greatest naval strategist and the architect of the Japanese bombing of Pearl Harbor.

SURPRISE ATTACK

Yamamoto graduated from the Japanese Naval Academy in 1904 and served in the Russo-Japanese war. He returned to his studies, graduating from Harvard University in 1921, and then served in the Japanese consulate in Washington, D.C., for several years. Rising up the ranks of the Japanese Navy in the 1930s, he developed expertise in aviation. Though tensions with the United States increased, Yamamoto opposed a war that he believed Japan could not win. He decided that Japan's only chance at victory lay in crippling the US Navy in a sneak attack. On December 7, 1941, Japan launched a massive air strike against the US Navy in Pearl Harbor, Hawaii, which smashed the US Pacific Fleet and drew the US into World War II. He was defeated by US Pacific forces at Midway in 1942. A campaign in the Solomon Islands also met with failure. He died in 1943, when US forces shot down the plane in which he was traveling.

△ AFTER PEARL HARBOR, *Yamamoto said he feared that Japan had awakened a sleeping giant—the United States*

Yamamoto Isoroku

Admiral Osumi, Secretary of the Navy

△ YAMAMOTO WAS MADE *an admiral in 1938 and became commander in chief of the Combined Fleet that year. Having studied in the United States, Yamamoto knew more about America and its military strength than many of Japan's older leaders.*

◁ YAMAMOTO *looking at charts. The attack on Pearl Harbor was based on the British attack at Taranto, Italy, in 1940.*

BERNARD MONTGOMERY

(1887–1976)

BERNARD LAW MONTGOMERY led the Allied forces at Normandy and was known as the best British field commander since the Duke of Wellington.

MONTY

Montgomery distinguished himself in World War I and gained a reputation as an efficient and outspoken leader. Winston Churchill in 1942 appointed him commander of the British 8th Army in North Africa, pitting him against the famed "Desert Fox," Erwin Rommel. Montgomery defeated Rommel at the Battle of El Alamein in November 1942.

Montgomery's overly cautious strategies drew fire from fellow Allied commanders, most of whom disliked him for his haughty attitude. He had many personal differences with Supreme Commander of Allied Expeditionary Forces Dwight Eisenhower, but served under him as field commander of all ground forces of the Normandy Invasion, which began on June 6, 1944. Montgomery was promoted to field marshal and led the British and Canadian 21st Army group across northern France, Belgium, the Netherlands, and Germany, finally accepting the surrender of the German northern armies on May 4, 1945.

After the war he was made a knight and a viscount, and served as chief of England's Imperial General Staff and deputy supreme commander of NATO forces in Europe.

△ **THOUGH AN EXCELLENT** *athlete, Montgomery as a child refused to participate in sports unless he was the captain. As unlikeable an attitude as that could be, it was self-confidence and drive that allowed Montgomery to lead effectively.*

"The fate of the empire depends upon this battle. Everyone will do his duty to the utmost."

Did you know?

■ Yamamoto lost two fingers on his left hand in battle during the Russo-Japanese war.

■ An avid gambler, he taught his aides to play poker, to help their strategic thinking.

■ Adopted as a child, Yamamoto's original family name was Takano.

Did you know?

■ His experience at the catastrophic Battle of the Somme influenced his cautious strategies.

■ In 1941 Montgomery was wounded through the lung. From then on he forbade smoking in his presence.

■ Montgomery wrote several books, including *Forward to Victory* and *A History of Warfare.*

▷ THE ATTACK on *Pearl Harbor involved 353 airplanes launched from three aircraft carriers.*

▷ MONTGOMERY *with US officers in Belgium in the autumn of 1944. As the Allies drove east, Montgomery endangered the offensive with a loss at Arnhem, his worst defeat of the entire war.*

SEX SYMBOLS

FROM THE VOLUPTUOUS FERTILITY GODDESSES OF PREHISTORIC CULTURES to the supermodels of today, every age has had its sex symbols: women and men who define the sexual climate of an era.

While tastes change, and what allured one age may be inexplicable to the next—the wiggle in a starlet's walk, the amorous glance of a dapperly dressed Romeo —sex symbols always embody the underlying morals and standards of their time. Marilyn Monroe, for example, symbolized the superficial innocence of the 1950s as much as she did the blond bombshell. Evelyn Nesbit projected both the virtues of virginal naïveté and the gilded underbelly of 1900s New York. In the 1920s, Rudolph Valentino, and in the 1980s, Madonna, each set new boundaries of sexual exoticism during decades known for decadent excess. While there's no predicting who will turn on future ages, it's certain that someone will.

△ THE MALE BODY *is as subject to trends as the female form, with tastes oscillating between muscular and lithe ideals.*

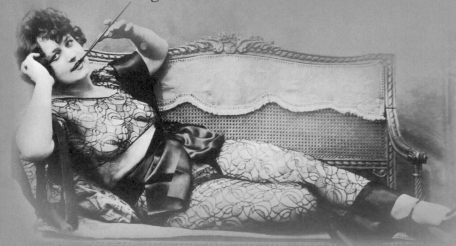

△ NAUGHTY "FRENCH" POSTCARDS, *such as this one from the 1900s, provided erotic images before the existence of the vast number of media outlets offering views of sex symbols in recent times.*

MARILYN MONROE
(1926–1962)

ONE OF THE 20TH CENTURY'S most famous female icons, Marilyn Monroe came to personify Americans' collective notions of sex, glamour, and Hollywood misfortune.

A TRAGIC BEAUTY

Born Norma Jeane Mortenson in Los Angeles to Gladys Baker, Marilyn was later baptized as Baker—she never knew her father. Because of her mother's mental instability, Marilyn lived with her only briefly, and was raised primarily by her mother's friend, Grace McKee, and in foster homes and an orphanage. Marilyn married merchant marine James Dougherty at age 16 and went to work in an aircraft plant. She divorced her husband in 1946 and began modeling to earn extra income. After several years of modeling—which produced, among other photos, Marilyn's famous nude shot for Champion's "Golden Dreams" calendar—she moved to Hollywood to become an actress and changed her name to Marilyn Monroe. Following a string of bit parts in forgettable films, Monroe gained notice for her appearances in *The Asphalt Jungle* and *All About Eve*, both in 1950. Studios homed in on Monroe's abundant sex appeal, and her career as a movie star was launched. Although some critics dismiss her as an actress, others praise her acute comedic ability in classics like *Gentlemen Prefer Blondes* (1953), *The Seven Year Itch* (1955), and *Some Like It Hot* (1959). Monroe was briefly married to baseball star Joe DiMaggio in 1954, and from 1956 to 1961 she was married to playwright Arthur Miller. The final years of her life were a tumultuous period of substance abuse, mental and emotional problems, and high-profile love affairs. Drug addiction and depression took a toll on her professional career, and in 1962 she was found dead in her Brentwood, California home of an apparent overdose.

△ MONROE ENTERTAINED *American troops in Korea in 1954. Afterward, she said it was the first day in her life she felt no fear.*

▷ STAMPS HAVE BEEN *issued in more than 125 different countries to honor Marilyn Monroe.*

△ MONROE HAD TO *be sewn into this dress, which she wore the night she sang an erotic version of "Happy Birthday" to President John F. Kennedy, on May 19, 1962 at Madison Square Garden. They were allegedly having an affair.*

▷ THIS SCENE *from* The Seven Year Itch *(1955) has become an iconic vision of how Monroe blended innocence and eroticism. Her then-husband Joe DiMaggio watched the shoot and was infuriated—it contributed to their divorce soon after.*

Did you know?

■ Monroe studied acting with Lee Strasberg at the Actor's Studio in New York City.

■ She was the centerfold model in *Playboy's* debut issue, December 1953.

■ Arthur Miller wrote the script for Monroe's 1961 film *The Misfits.*

▷ NEWLYWEDS *Monroe and Arthur Miller departing from their Roxbury, Connecticut, home for a picnic in 1956. The couple would remain married for five years.*

CASANOVA
(1725–1798)

THE MAN AGAINST WHOM ALL MASTERS of seduction are measured, Giacomo Girolomo Casanova, was an important literary talent and occasional businessman and diplomat.

THE ULTIMATE SEDUCER

Born in Venice, Italy, of theater parents, Casanova was abandoned by his mother as an infant and lost his father at the age of eight. He allegedly had his first sexual encounter at the age of 11, and by his teens had begun a series of jobs that would include violinist, clergyman, soldier, and writer. He was imprisoned under the Doge's Palace in Venice 1755 for performing magic, but escaped a year later. Casanova spent the next 30 years wandering throughout Europe entertaining men and women alike with tales of intrigue and adventure and befriending the likes of Voltaire and Madame de Pompadour, while swindling many others out of money. He is rumored to have seduced 132 women during these journeys. In 1785 he became the librarian for the Count of Waldstein in Bohemia, and began work on his exhaustive multivolume autobiography, which features most of the tales of romantic liaisons that make him famous today. His autobiography was first published in its entirety in the 1960s.

△ A 19TH CENTURY ENGRAVING *entitled "Casanova's Memories." His amorous exploits are so well known that his name has become a synonym for "lover" or "playboy."*

Legendary Lovers

LORD BYRON (1788–1824) Wrote *Don Juan* and had many affairs.

KING EDWARD VII (1841–1910) Reputedly made love to 3 different women a week.

KING IBN-SAUD (1880–1953) Arabian ruler with over 400 wives.

△ PORTRAIT OF CASANOVA, 1767. *Later in life he became friendly with Mozart while in Prague and attended the 1787 debut of Don Giovanni, which he may have inspired.*

Did you know?

■ Casanova worked as a spy for the State Inquisitor's Office in Venice.

■ In addition to his autobiography, Casanova published *History of the Government of Venice*, the five-volume *Icosameron*, and an Italian translation of the *Iliad*.

■ While living in Paris, Casanova organized the first state-run lottery.

▷ IVAN MOZZHUKHIN *starred as Casanova in the 1928 silent film* Casanova. *Here the great lover seduces Catherine the Great (played by Suzanne Bianchetti).*

"The easiest way to overcome a woman's virtue is to assume it is not there in the first place."

CASANOVA

EVELYN NESBIT

(1884–1967)

EVELYN NESBIT—MODEL, DANCER, AND ACTRESS—became a literal *femme fatale* when she emerged as the motivating factor behind the murder of prominent architect Stanford White.

THE GIRL IN THE RED VELVET SWING

Born on Christmas Day in a small town near Pittsburgh, Pennsylvania, Evelyn turned to modeling as a source of income after her father's death. Her beatific good looks caught the attention of artist Charles Dana Gibson's, and she became a principal model for his "Gibson Girl," an idealized rendering of the American woman popular at the turn of the century. At age 16, Nesbit became involved with architect Stanford White while working as a model and chorus girl, but broke off the affair and in 1903 married eccentric Pittsburgh millionaire Henry Thaw. Thaw, in a fit of jealous rage, fatally shot White in 1906 in the rooftop restaurant at Madison Square Garden in New York City and was committed to an insane asylum. Nesbit went on to star in several films from 1914 to 1922, after which she left public life and died in a nursing home in 1966.

△ NEWSPAPER ARTICLES *in* The World, *New York Evening Edition, June 25, 1906, about the Stanford White murder. The trial of Henry Shaw, featuring Nesbit as a witness in defense of her husband, was called "The Trial of the Century."*

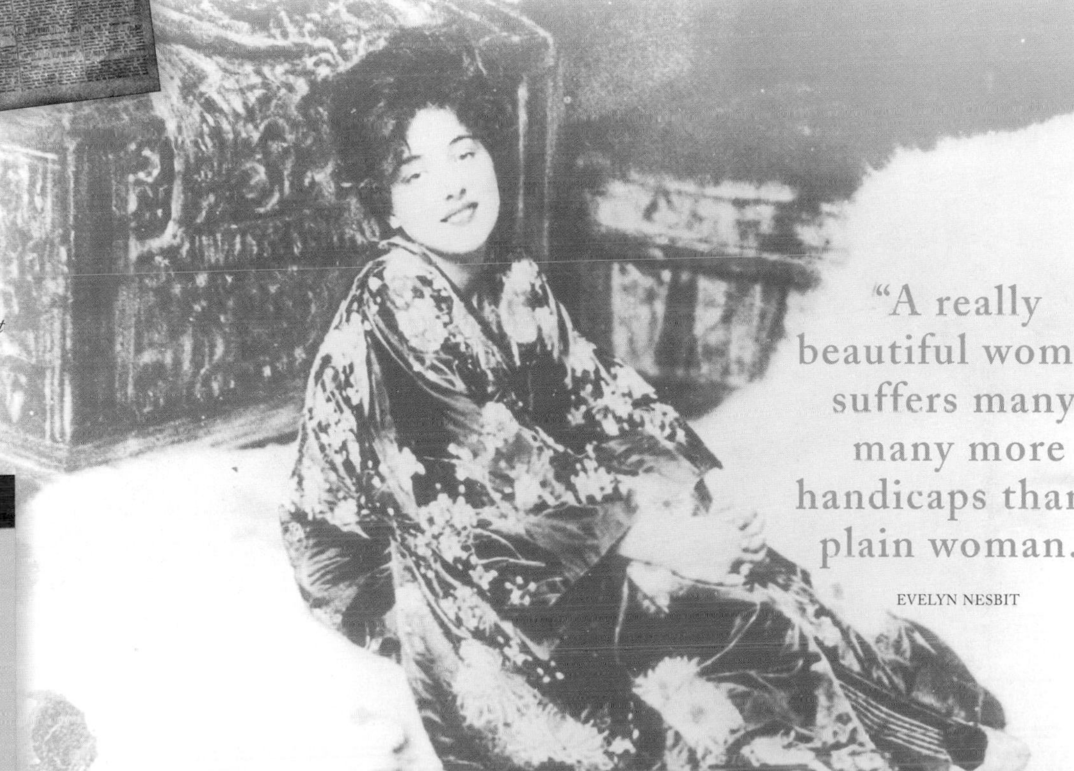

△ NESBIT WAS KNOWN *as the "Girl in the Red Velvet Swing" because one of Stanford White's favorite pastimes was to watch her rock back and forth while perched naked on a large swing he had had installed in his penthouse apartment.*

Did you know?

■ Nesbit, White, and Thaw are characters in E. L. Doctorow's historical novel *Ragtime*.

■ Joan Collins portrayed Nesbit in the 1955 film *The Girl in the Red Velvet Swing*.

■ Nesbit attended a girls' school run by the mother of Cecil B. DeMille.

△ STANFORD WHITE *paid portrait photographer Rudolph Eickemeyer to take this and 30 other photos of Nesbit from 1901 through 1902.*

"A really beautiful woman suffers many, many more handicaps than a plain woman."

EVELYN NESBIT

MADONNA
b. 1958

SINGER, DANCER, AND ACTRESS Madonna Louise Veronica Ciccone has become one of the most successful entertainers of her time by using sex to continually redefine her public image.

EXPRESS YOURSELF

Madonna's music—and films, videos, and books—have brought into the mainstream such previously taboo subjects as gay dance culture and sadomasochism. Born in Michigan, Madonna moved to New York City in the late 1970s, where she played drums in a band, acted in several underground films, and in 1983, released her debut album, *Madonna*, the first in a series of enormously successful dance-pop records. In 1985 she starred in her first feature-length film, *Desperately Seeking Susan*, which started the first of many fashion trends based upon Madonna's provocative and fluid personal style. She was married briefly to actor Sean Penn in the late 1980s, and married her second husband, director Guy Ritchie, in 2001. She has two children and continues to produce albums and perform in worldwide tours.

Did you know?

■ She is the founder and owner of Maverick Entertainment, which has released records by acts including Alanis Morissette and Prodigy.

■ Madonna has earned 23 gold records, more than any other female singer.

■ The 1990 video for Madonna's song "Justify My Love" was banned by MTV because of its sexually explicit imagery.

△ **MORE THAN ANY OTHER** *performer, Madonna used the emerging music video form in the early 1980s to make herself a household name. She has always pushed the boundaries of what is acceptable in entertainment.*

"Is sex dirty? Only when you don't take a bath."

MADONNA

△ **IN 2001**, *Madonna went so far in her sexual evangelism as to allow her name to be put on a brand of condoms.*

△ **WHAT WAS ONCE** *worn under fashion became fashion itself, as Madonna worked with top designers to bring underwear out. This corset by Jean-Paul Gaultier, above, was worn on Madonna's 1990 "Blonde Ambition" tour.*

◁ **MADONNA'S** *eclectic lingerie look of the 1980s influenced millions of "Madonna wannabes."*

RUDOLPH VALENTINO

(1895–1926)

ITALIAN ACTOR RUDOLPH VALENTINO was the original playboy of Hollywood's silent era.

THE SHEIK

Born in Castellaneta, Italy, Valentino moved to the United States in 1913 and entered show business as a dancer. By 1919, however, he had quit dancing to focus on a film career. Valentino landed his feature debut in Metro Pictures' *The Four Horsemen of the Apocalypse* (1921), which made him an instant celebrity and Hollywood's preeminent heartthrob. He went on to play the lead in such early Paramount landmarks as *The Eagle*, *The Sheik*, *Cobra*, and *Blood and Sand*. Despite a reportedly torrid marriage to Natacha Rambova, his relationships with other women (including a 1922 arrest for bigamy) were often the subject of Hollywood scandal. The publicity surrounding them helped enhance Rudolph's amatory image in the eyes of his female fans. Valentino died in 1926 of a stomach ulcer, leaving millions of devoted followers behind.

△ VALENTINO AND AGNES AYRES *in* The Sheik *(1921), a huge hit—especially with women, who found Valentino's combination of masculinity and tenderness irresistible. Men generally thought he was effeminate.*

> "A man should control his life. Mine is controlling me."
>
> RUDOLPH VALENTINO

◁ A FRENCH POSTER *for Valentino's last film,* The Son of the Sheik, *1926. Valentino made the exotic "Sheik" character into an archetypal male sex symbol in the 1920s.*

◁ VALENTINO *in a romantic pose. In addition to acting, he also published* Day Dreams, *a popular book of poetry, in 1923.*

HARLEM RENAISSANCE

AROUND THE TIME OF WORLD WAR I, HUNDREDS OF THOUSANDS OF AFRICAN-AMERICANS fled oppressive conditions in the South for work in northern cities, where an unprecedented exploration of black identity took place.

Nowhere was this movement more dynamic than in New York City's Harlem neighborhood, home to the greatest African-American artists and intellectuals of the era. Painter Aaron Douglas incorporated traditional African forms into a modernist aesthetic. Among many other poets, Langston Hughes stands out for his depiction of the everyday experience of black Americans while writers such as Zora Neale Hurston recast the folkways of blacks into literature. Scholar-activists like James Weldon Johnson and W.E.B. DuBois sought to empower African-Americans politically and fought racism on a global scale. The movement ended with the Depression, but its work continues to influence culture today.

△ DURING THE HARLEM RENAISSANCE, *white New Yorkers traveled uptown to nightspots such as the Cotton Club to hear jazz music and experience the "exotic" world of African-Americans.*

LANGSTON HUGHES
(1902–1967)

AMERICAN POET AND WRITER James Langston Hughes was the unofficial poet laureate of the Harlem Renaissance.

"I, TOO, SING AMERICA"

Born in Missouri, Hughes was raised mostly by his grandmother after his parents divorced. He had already distinguished himself as a writer by the time he graduated from high school in Cleveland, Ohio, in 1920. After a year of traveling in Mexico, Hughes began studies at Columbia University in New York City, just south of Harlem, and discovered that neighborhood's thriving rebirth of African-American culture. Hughes dropped out of Columbia after one year and did odd jobs in New York before signing on as a steward on a merchant ship sailing between New York and Africa. After a short stint in Paris and Montmartre in the spring of 1924, he moved to Washington, D.C., but he continued to visit Harlem. Hughes's poetry was influenced by the jazz and blues he heard in the clubs of Harlem and Washington as well as by the reality of Africa he had seen as a seaman, and his first published work, *The Weary Blues* (1926), contained poems with a rhythm and mood informed by music and African culture. Around this time, Hughes slipped his poems onto the plate of white poet Vachel Lindsay in the dining room of the hotel in which he was working as a busboy. Publicity surrounding this incident described him as Lindsay's protégé, which helped Hughes land a scholarship to attend Lincoln University in Pennsylvania. After graduating from Lincoln in 1929, Hughes traveled widely in the Soviet Union, Haiti, and Japan. He wrote poems, essays, book reviews, song lyrics, plays, and short stories, and received a Guggenheim fellowship for his work in 1935. During his later years, Hughes held teaching positions at the Universities of Chicago and Atlanta. During his career Hughes produced more than 47 volumes, translated into more than a dozen languages. He died of lung cancer in 1967.

◁ HUGHES, *widely targeted by right-wing forces, was subpoenaed by Senator Joe McCarthy to testify before Congress in 1953 regarding the radical views he had espoused during the 1930s.*

△ HUGHES LEFT *a job as an assistant to Dr. Carter Woodson, editor of the* Journal of Negro History, *to work as a busboy at the Wardman Park Hotel, but ironically, it was this menial job—which brought him into contact with the noted American poet Vachel Lindsay—that brought him his break as a poet.*

Did you know?

■ Hughes's father discouraged him from pursuing writing and initially agreed to pay for his Columbia education only if he agreed to study engineering.

■ During the Spanish Civil War Hughes became a friend of Ernest Hemingway, with whom he attended numerous bullfights.

W.E.B. DUBOIS
(1868–1963)

WILLIAM EDWARD BURGHARDT (W.E.B.) DuBois brought a powerful intellect and a deeply critical voice to the problem of racial injustice in the West.

THE TALENTED TENTH

DuBois grew up in Great Barrington, Massachusetts, and began college at the age of 15. A dedicated scholar, he was one of the first African-Americans to receive a doctorate from Harvard University. DuBois began a sociological investigation of the condition of African-Americans, and became impatient with the slow pace of social progress. An outspoken critic of Booker T. Washington, the most popular black leader of the time, he argued that Washington's tactics for creating social change were too timid, and called for sweeping improvements. In 1905, he founded the Niagara Movement, a group which later became the National Association for the Advancement of Colored People (NAACP). DuBois also founded, and edited for 25 years, *The Crisis*, the organization's publication. One of the creators of the Pan-African movement, he became increasingly disenchanted with the United States in the 1940s and 1950s, drifting further to the left until he finally became a communist. In 1961, at the invitation of Kwame Nkrumah, he moved to Ghana, where he died at the age of 95.

Did you know?

■ The first meeting of the Niagara Movement was held in Canada because the Buffalo hotel in which it was to be held would not allow the African-American men to stay there.

■ When DuBois called for outlawing atomic weapons in 1959, the Justice Department ordered him to register under the Foreign Agents Registration Act. He refused and was indicted, but the charges were dropped.

△ ONE OF DUBOIS'S *most influential and controversial concepts was "The Talented Tenth"—the idea that the upper echelon of educated African-Americans bore a responsibility to help lift up the rest of their race with their work and example.*

"The problem of the 20th century is the problem of the color line."

W.E.B. DUBOIS

Other Trailblazers

WALTER WHITE (1893–1955) Took over the NAACP from Johnson.

ARTHUR SCHOMBURG (1874–1938) Puerto-Rican bibliophile and patron.

MADAME C.J. WALKER (1869–1919) Entrepreneur and philanthropist.

◁ DUBOIS, *an international spokesman for peace as well as a scholar, meets here with Pablo Picasso at the 1949 World Congress of Partisans of Peace.*

JAMES WELDON JOHNSON
(1871–1938)

DIPLOMAT, POET, NOVELIST, critic, activist, and composer, James Weldon Johnson was one of the leading figures in the creation and development of the African-American artistic community known as the Harlem Renaissance.

"LIFT EVERY VOICE"

Johnson was born in Jacksonville, Florida, and graduated from Atlanta University. He worked as a principal in a grammar school, founded a newspaper, *The Daily American*, and passed the bar exam. In 1900, he and his brother wrote "Lift Every Voice and Sing," which would become the NAACP's official anthem. He moved to New York and studied literature at Columbia University, where he met other African-American artists.

△ THE SON OF A *freeborn Virginian father and a Bahamian mother, Johnson was raised without a sense of limitations amid a society focused on segregating African-Americans.*

In 1906 President Roosevelt appointed Johnson to diplomatic positions in Venezuela and Nicaragua. Upon his return in 1914, he became involved with the NAACP and by 1920 was the chief executive of the organization. He published hundreds of stories and poems, and produced works such as *God's Trombones* (1927), a collection that celebrates the African-American experience in the rural South and elsewhere, and the novel *The Autobiography of an Ex-Colored Man*, based, in part, on Johnson's own life. After retiring from the organization in 1930, he devoted the rest of his life to writing. He died in a car accident in Maine at age 67. Over 2000 people attended his funeral in Harlem.

Did you know?

■ Johnson was almost lynched for speaking to a fair-skinned black female journalist in the South.

■ James and his brother John wrote more than 200 songs for the Broadway musical stage.

■ *The Autobiography of an Ex-Colored Man* was published anonymously in 1912, but did not attract attention until Johnson reissued it under his own name in 1927.

James Weldon Johnson

Walter Damrosch

Roland Hayes

◁ JOHNSON *with conductor Walter Damrosch, and tenor Roland Hayes, at an African-American achievement awards ceremony, 1925.*

ZORA NEALE HURSTON
(1891–1960)

ZORA NEALE HURSTON'S WORK as a writer, folklorist and anthropologist contributed significantly to an appreciation of the richness of African-American culture.

HER EYES WERE WATCHING GOD

Growing up in the all-black town of Eatonville, Florida, Zora left home early and worked at odd jobs before enrolling at Baltimore's Morgan Academy and, later, at Howard University. Around 1920, she began to write and publish stories based on African-American folklore, which led five years later to an anthropology scholarship under Franz Boas at Barnard College in New York City. After graduating in 1928, Hurston worked as a folklorist, collecting stories while traveling around the rural South. In the 1930s Hurston received several academic fellowships, including two Guggenheim fellowships, for her research on folk religion in Haiti and Jamaica. After being falsely accused of molesting a young boy in 1948, Huston largely withdrew from the literary scene and moved back to Florida and worked as a maid. Until suffering a stroke in 1959, she continued to write and teach while performing other menial jobs. Hurston's death in 1960 went mostly unnoticed in the literary world. She was rediscovered by a wider public in the late 1970s after writer Alice Walker wrote about Hurston and her work.

▽ HURSTON *worked as an editor on the Florida volume of the WPA American Guide series, and was a drama coach for a WPA theater project in Harlem in 1935.*

△ IN 1926, DURING HER SHORT *time in New York, Hurston began a quarterly called* Fire!! *with Langston Hughes, Aaron Douglas, and novelists Bruce Nugent and Wallace Thurman.*

∧ THURSTON'S
collection of African American folktales, Mules and Men *(1935) was informed by her fieldwork with musicologist Alan Lomax, recording Southern folk music.*

Did you know?

■ Hurston's father, John, was elected to three terms as mayor of Eatonville, Florida.

■ Hurston was for a time employed by white writer Fannie Hurst as her driver, and inspired, in part, the book *Imitation of Life*.

■ Hurston's last, unfinished book was a biography of biblical king Herod the Great.

AARON DOUGLAS
(1899–1979)

COMBINING TRADITIONAL AFRICAN art forms and elements of Cubism, illustrator and muralist Aaron Douglas captured the passion of the Harlem Renaissance.

THE FATHER OF BLACK AMERICAN ART

Douglas was born in Kansas and studied art at the University of Nebraska, graduating in 1922. In 1925 he left Kansas for New York City, where he met and studied under German-American artist Winold Reiss. Douglas's first commission—to illustrate Alain Locke's book *The New Negro* (1925)—led to illustration requests from other members of the Harlem Renaissance, including Langston Hughes and James Weldon Johnson.

Douglas received his most important commission in 1934, a series of murals entitled *Aspects of Negro Life*, which was commissioned by the Works Progress Administration (later the Work Projects Administration, or WPA) for the New York Public Library. In 1939, as the Harlem Renaissance dissipated, Aaron Douglas left New York City. He accepted a job at Fisk University in Tennessee, where he taught for 27 years.

△ DOUGLAS, *shown here in an undated photograph, was renowned for adapting forms usually associated with Art Deco and abstract art and infusing them with a sense of movement and color. His innovations were greatly inspired by Harlem's fertile 1920s jazz scene.*

Did you know?

■ Though known as a muralist and illustrator, Douglas also occasionally painted naturalistic portraits and landscapes.

■ Aaron Douglas was president of the Harlem Artists Guild in 1935, and worked to obtain recognition and support for African-American artists from the WPA.

> "I refuse to compromise and see blacks as anything less than a proud and majestic people."
>
> AARON DOUGLAS

△ ONE OF HIS MURAL SERIES, Aspects of Negro Life, From Slavery Through Reconstruction, *is still on view at Harlem's Schomburg Library on 135th Street.*

INVENTORS OF THE MODERN WORLD

IT USUALLY TAKES A TEAM OF DEDICATED MEN AND WOMEN to bring an invention to final fruition. But many inventions begin with one mind working well outside the boundaries of conventional thought to change the world, often in the most practical ways.

Inventors Thomas Edison and Nikola Tesla were visionaries whose work continues to affect our daily lives. Henry Ford did not invent the car, but his invention of the production line made the progress of modern industry possible. Alexander Graham Bell's creation of the telephone was motivated not out of some futuristic notion of a "talking box," but from knowledge he gained while looking for ways to help the hearing impaired. Guglielmo Marconi's early experiments made radio communication possible; his later work laid the foundation for the development of microwave transmission. All of these great thinkers transformed the 20th century, ushering in an astonishing age of technological progress that continues, unabated, into the 21st century.

△ WHILE EDISON *patented the carbon filament incandescent light bulb in the United States in 1879, Sir Joseph Wilson Swan patented something very similar in England that same year.*

THOMAS EDISON
(1847–1931)

THOMAS ALVA EDISON was the man behind more than a thousand inventions, and he remains a symbol of the inspired mind.

THE WIZARD OF MENLO PARK

Edison was born in Milan, Ohio. By the age of ten he had a chemistry lab set up in his family's basement, and as a youth, he worked as a salesman for a railroad company. He moved to Boston in 1868 and took a job with Western Union Telegraph Company. A year later, he patented his first invention of note, the stock ticker. Ideas then began to pour out of him. He made improvements on the telegraph, paving the way for Bell's telephone, and in 1877 patented the phonograph. Originally manually operated and responding to impressions on metal cylinders, this machine evolved into the modern-day record player. Working in his famous Menlo Park, New Jersey, laboratory in the late 1870s, with backing from investors such as banker J. P. Morgan, Edison started exploring the field of incandescence during the late 1870s. By 1879, in his new laboratory in West Orange, New Jersey, he had produced and patented the first fully functioning incandescent lamp. A decade later, Edison created the first electric power station, which proved to be the model by which offices and homes were powered the world over, although using Tesla's AC system. By the mid-1890s Edison had perfected an early version of the movie camera known as the kinetograph. His company made nearly 2,000 movies, and helped usher in the era of sound at the turn of the 20th century. Although he was nearing 70 by the start of World War I, Edison worked to develop and improve military technology as a consultant to the US Navy. He was working on new methods to manufacture rubber when he died at age 84 in West Orange following a series of ailments.

△ A VINTAGE EDISON *product label, featuring a portrait of Edison and some of his inventions.*

△ AN EARLY MODEL OF THE KINETOSCOPE, *patented by Edison in 1887. He conceived of the idea and is credited for the invention, but his employee William Dickson developed it.*

△ EDISON ON HIS 75TH BIRTHDAY, *February 11, 1922, with Mina Miller, his second wife and constant champion of his efforts.*

◁ **AS OF 1911,** *Edison, seen here in his lab, had largely stopped exploring new inventions and concentrated on fully exploiting his existing achievements. His various companies were consolidated into Thomas A. Edison, Inc., and by the 1920s he worked mostly from home.*

△ **EDISON'S VERTICAL KINETOSCOPE.** *The viewer would look into a peep-hole in the cabinet in order to see the image move. Inside the box, a continuous band of film was spooled above a lamp-lit lens and a revolving shutter.*

"Genius is 1 percent inspiration and 99 percent perspiration."

THOMAS EDISON

△ **THE FIRST PHONOGRAPHS** *were marketed as business tools for taking dictation, but this strategy failed. When Edison was able to regain control of his patent in 1896, he sold phonographs primarily for use at home, for amusement.*

More Inventors

PHILO FARNSWORTH (1906–1971) Farmboy who invented the electronic television system at age 14.

SAMUEL MORSE (1791–1872) Inventor of the electric telegraph.

GEORGE EASTMAN (1854–1932) Put cameras in everyone's hands.

△ **EDISON WITH HIS FIRST PHONOGRAPH,** *c. 1880s. Although Edison invented this precursor to the record player, he was nearly deaf from the age of 12, when he was lifted onto a train by his ears. He claimed that deafness let him concentrate better.*

Did you know?

■ The Edison Electric Light Company became the present-day General Electric Company (GE).

■ During his rivalry with Nikola Tesla, Edison publicly electrocuted an elephant with AC current in an attempt to prove it was too dangerous for common use.

■ A poor student, Edison had only three months of formal education.

NIKOLA TESLA
(1856–1943)

ECCENTRIC INVENTOR Nikola Tesla used an unorthodox approach to scientific discovery to develop some of the most important inventions of the 20th century.

THE MAD GENIUS

Tesla, the son of a clergyman, was born in what is now Croatia. He knew more about electronics than most of his instructors at the Polytechnic Institute he attended in Gratz. Tesla moved to the US in 1884. After a brief stint working for Thomas Edison, he started his own engineering firm. In 1887 he invented the electromagnetic induction motor, which introduced AC (alternating current) technology and created a rivalry with Edison, who sold DC (direct current) technology. He sold the patent a year later to George Westinghouse, who then hired him. It is Tesla's system that the world still uses. His most famous invention is the Tesla coil (1891), a device for producing a high-frequency high-voltage current. In 1899 he built a lab in Colorado Springs, containing the largest Tesla Coil ever built, capable of generating some 300,000 watts of power and producing lightning. He constantly developed new machinery and new concepts, often well before other scientists made them public—for example, many historians believe that Tesla developed radio technology prior to its patent in 1896. Other inventions include the loudspeaker, fluorescent lights, the rotary engine, and remote control. Regarded as something of a mad scientist in his later years, Tesla cut off formal communication with the scientific community and worked alone, making advancements in radar, television, and X rays while doing odd jobs. He died in his laboratory/bedroom in a New York City hotel.

Did you know?

- Tesla had a lifelong fear of germs.

- Tesla claimed to have built a weapon based on theories of particle acceleration. He called it the "Death Ray."

- Tesla was a close friend of the writer Samuel Clemens (Mark Twain).

△ A PORTRAIT OF TESLA, c. 1900, the year he made the discovery he regarded as his most important—terrestrial stationary waves—proving that the earth could be used as a conductor and would respond to certain electrical vibrations.

△ TO DEMONSTRATE *the safety of electricity, Tesla had an electrical current go through his body. His system was used to light Chicago's 1893 Columbian Exposition. This led to a contract in 1896 to install machinery to bring power to the city of Buffalo, New York.*

▽ THE INSIDE OF THE TESLA COIL, *which can produce high voltage and high frequency currents. It is still used in electronic devices such as TVs.*

△ TESLA, c. 1910. *His greatest setback occurred several years earlier, when J. P. Morgan withdrew financing for Tesla's wireless world broadcasting tower on Long Island.*

ALEXANDER GRAHAM BELL
(1847–1922)

ALEXANDER GRAHAM BELL invented the telephone, one of the most important technological advancements in the science of communication.

THE SCIENCE OF SOUND

Born in Scotland and mostly educated by his family, Bell spent only three years in formal schooling. His mother was nearly deaf and his father and grandfather had both studied speech and communication. Bell followed suit, working to teach deaf people to speak and experimenting with sound frequency and resonation. While working on a way to send multiple messages on a single telegraph line, he began in 1873 to develop instead a new machine—the telephone. In 1876 he was granted a patent for his new invention. Bell debuted the telephone at the Centennial Exhibition in Philadelphia a few months later, and in 1877 the first telephone was installed in a private home. The Bell Company was established in 1881 to further advance the science of the telephone. Despite facing nearly 600 patent lawsuits, the company led the way in developing a long-distance phone system that by the turn of the century had spread throughout much of the United States.

In his later career Bell founded *Science* magazine and was president of the National Geographic Society. He abandoned his work in telephone communication to concentrate on advancements in aviation, but continued to work with the deaf community until his death.

△ BELL'S FIRST TELEPHONE *transmitter (top) and receiver (bottom). Bell realized his success when he spilled some acid and called for his assistant, who heard Bell over one of the machines in his office.*

△ BELL OPENS *the first long-distance line, 1892. His claim to the patent to the telephone was tied up in court for 20 years. Only hours after Bell had filed his patent application, Elisha Gray filed his, having invented nearly the same machine. Bell was determined to be credited with the invention.*

Did you know?

■ Bell worked as a private tutor for Helen Keller.

■ Bell gave his first public demonstration of the telephone on the same day as the Battle of the Little Bighorn.

■ His first memory was of sitting in a wheat field, listening for the sound of growing wheat.

"Leave the beaten track occasionally and dive into the woods."

ALEXANDER GRAHAM BELL

△ BELL SPEAKS INTO THE CENTENNIAL TELEPHONE, *c. 1876. Bell's motivation for inventing the telephone was not general communication. His work in the 1870s focused instead on devices to make vocal communication possible for the deaf.*

▷ IN 1877, *Bell married Mabel Hubbard, a deaf-mute and former student of his while he was teaching visible speech at the Boston School for Deaf Mutes. Hubbard's father was the founder of the National Geographic Society.*

HENRY FORD

(1863–1947)

INDUSTRIALIST HENRY FORD made crucial advances in automotive technology and developed manufacturing techniques that transformed 20th-century industry.

THE CREATOR OF CAR CULTURE

Born in Dearborn, Michigan, to Irish immigrants, Ford had his first vision of what he wanted to do when he was 13: he saw a steam engine mounted on wheels, being driven along a road by its owner. Consumed by this idea of self-propulsion, he worked at a series of engineering jobs for, among others, Thomas Edison, until his first automobile, the quadracycle, debuted in 1896. By 1899 it had evolved into a sturdy automobile ready for mass production, and in 1903, with ten investors, Ford founded the Ford Motor Car Company. Five years later he introduced the Model T. While demand for cars was high, they were prohibitively expensive, so Ford pioneered manufacturing procedures, including the assembly line, which slashed prices and put the car in reach of buyers. Although a hero to industrialists and a respected philanthropist who created the Ford Foundation, Ford was violently anti-union and anti-Semitic. He bought the *Dearborn Independent* newspaper in 1918 as a platform for his attacks until he sold it in 1927. In his later years Ford became interested in the development of soybean products; he also set up vocational training schools and sponsored a weekly radio show. He died at home, at age 84.

△ TO BROADEN *the market for his cars, Henry Ford developed the system of selling cars through dealerships and fought for improved roads throughout the country.*

△ FORD CELEBRATED *the 50th anniversary of the first car on June 4, 1946, by taking out this replica of his quadracycle for a drive. The vehicle had two speeds and no reverse.*

△ THE STREAMLINED *1950 Mercury belied one of Ford's dictums: "A Ford will take you everywhere, except into society."*

Did you know?

■ Henry Ford is the only American mentioned in Hitler's *Mein Kampf*.

■ Ford introduced the time clock, the eight-hour workday, and a daily minimum wage of $5.

■ The first Model Ts were available only in the color black.

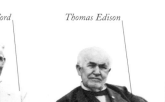

Henry Ford   Thomas Edison   Harvey Firestone

△ FORD AND EDISON *were close friends, and Ford bought the home next to Edison's in Florida so he and his wife could vacation with the Edisons. The two men also went on many camping trips with tire magnate Harvey Firestone.*

△ FORD LOST MANY *of his early investors because of his focus on auto racing, which he thought was crucial for publicity. In this 1902 letter, he describes to his brother-in-law how he plans to continue making money racing his cars even if the short sighted investors pull out.*

GUGLIELMO MARCONI
(1874–1937)

THROUGH HIS EXPERIMENTS in wireless telegraphy, Guglielmo Marconi developed the first effective system of radio communication.

WIRELESS COMMUNICATION

Born in Bologna, Italy, to a wealthy family, and educated largely at home, Marconi started experimenting with electromagnetics as a student at the Livorno Technical Institute. Incorporating the earlier findings of H. R. Hertz, he was able to develop a basic system of wireless telegraphy. In 1899, Marconi founded the London-based Marconi Telegraph Company. Although his original transmission traveled a mere mile and a half, on December 12, 1901, Marconi sent and received the first wireless message across the Atlantic, from Cornwall, England, to a military base in Newfoundland. He shared with Karl Braun the 1909 Nobel Prize in physics for his work with wireless communication. Marconi held several positions in the Italian Army and Navy during World War I, starting the war as a lieutenant in 1914 and finishing as a naval commander. He was sent on diplomatic missions to the United States and France. After the war, Marconi began experimenting with basic short wave radio technology; by 1926, his "beam system" was adopted by the British government as a design for international communication. Marconi continued to experiment with radio technology in his native Italy until his death from heart failure.

△ STARTING IN 1902, *Marconi worked on experiments that stretched the distance that wireless communication could travel, until he was finally able to establish transatlantic service from Glace Bay in Nova Scotia, Canada, to Clifden, Ireland.*

"Have I done the world good, or have I added a menace?"

GUGLIELMO MARCONI

△ MARCONI, HIS SECOND *wife, Countess Bezzi-Scali, and his daughter, photographed in February 1933. His daughter Elettra was named after his yacht.*

Did you know?

■ Marconi's wireless system was used by the crew of the *Titanic* to call for assistance.

■ Marconi was also involved in the development of radar.

■ In 1943 the US Supreme Court declared Marconi's radio patent invalid because work by other scientists, including Nikola Tesla, predated some of his findings.

▷ MARCONI USED *this spark gap machine in many of his wireless experiments in the 1920s. Marconi was instrumental in establishing the British Broadcasting Company.*

△ MARCONI ON HIS *beloved yacht,* Elettra, *from which he conducted experiments in the 1920s proving the efficacy of the beam system for long-distance communication. The next step would lead to microwave transmission.*

MAKERS OF THE WIRED WORLD

DIGITAL TECHNOLOGY HAS CHANGED CIVILIZATION IN A REMARKABLY short period of time. Computers manage huge volumes of information, while the Internet sends information across the world almost instantaneously. More than half of US households have personal computers.

Charles Babbage, a nineteenth-century British mathematician who first conceived of the computer, died believing his research had been futile. His insights came to the fore almost a century later when Alan Turing developed the first digital computer and wrote the first program for it. In the 1950s, the controversial American physicist William Shockley, integrated the use of transistors into electronic design. In 1976, Apple Computer founders Steve Jobs and Stephen Wozniak helped bring the personal computer home to the masses, while in 1991 Tim Berners-Lee created the World Wide Web.

△ A NOVELTY 20 YEARS AGO, *the computer is now a common feature not only at the office, but in the home as well.*

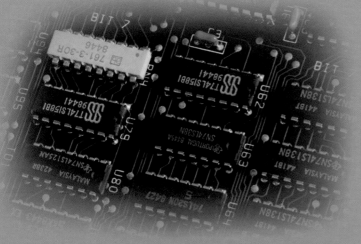

△ **A COMPUTER CIRCUIT BOARD** *with electronic components. For all the ups and downs of the "New Economy" created by technology, future electronics will only be smaller and more digital.*

TIM BERNERS-LEE
b. 1955

IN 1991, COMPUTER SCIENTIST Tim Berners-Lee created the architecture of the World Wide Web, the searchable system that links multimedia documents across the Internet.

THE ORIGINAL WEBMASTER
Born in London, Berners-Lee graduated from Queen's College, Oxford University, in 1976, with a degree in physics. He then spent several years developing networks for the telecommunications industry and writing software.

In June 1980, he began working for CERN, the European particle physics laboratory in Geneva, Switzerland. There he wrote "Enquire," a program that allowed storage and retrieval of information using random associations. This served as a prototype for the World Wide Web. From 1981 until 1984, Berners-Lee worked at Image Computer Systems Ltd., developing graphics and communications software and a computer language that could be read by different computer systems.

In 1989, Berners-Lee proposed the World Wide Web as a network to let people work collaboratively by sharing documents. He also constructed the first server (a computer that facilitates the sharing of files between other computers) and browser (a program that allows people to read and navigate between web pages) to support the network. The system made its debut at CERN in December 1991. By the end of the 1990s it contained more than a billion pages.

Berners-Lee in 1994 joined the Laboratory for Computer Science at the Massachusetts Institute of Technology. Since 1999, he has led the World Wide Web Consortium (W3), a group whose goal is to help the Web fulfill its potential as a communications medium.

△ **DESPITE THE** *commercial temptations of the 1990s Internet bubble, Berners-Lee has argued that the Internet must remain free.*

STEPHEN WOZNIAK b. 1950
STEVE JOBS b. 1955

STEPHEN G. WOZNIAK AND STEVE JOBS COFOUNDED Apple Computer, and played a crucial role in the development and commercial success of user-friendly personal computers.

THE COMPUTER REVOLUTION

In 1975, the two young men joined with friends to form a club around the Altair 8800, the first commercially available microcomputer. Wozniak, an intern at Hewlett-Packard in 1976, came up with a plan for his own microcomputer but HP was not interested. He decided to produce it himself and began operations in the garage of former high-school classmate Steve Jobs. They named their company "Apple," after the Beatles recording company or as a reference to Jobs's summer picking apples. Starting with a working circuit board, Wozniak produced the Apple II, the first microcomputer with popular appeal (a stand-alone machine in a custom-molded plastic case with a color display and superior information storage and retrieval), while Jobs secured financial support for the company. The new machine was an instant success. Apple's superior design and aggressive advertising established it as a key player in the increasingly competitive personal-computer market.

Wozniak took a leave of absence in 1981 to recuperate from a private plane crash. Jobs, who was named chairman of Apple in 1980, recruited former PepsiCo president John Sculley as president and CEO in 1983 (his tenure lasted until 1993). In 1984 Apple introduced the Macintosh computer with its graphical operating system. Although PCs with Microsoft's Windows operating system (itself influenced by the Mac) later captured most of the personal computer market, Apple continued to marry innovative hardware with software products. Jobs was ousted by Sculley in 1985 after a board-room power struggle, and left Apple to found NeXT Software and acquire Pixar Animation Studios, which produced the first fully computer-animated movie, *Toy Story*, in 1995. A year later Apple bought NeXT, and Jobs was invited back. He is now permanent CEO.

> ## "I want to put a ding in the universe."
> STEVE JOBS

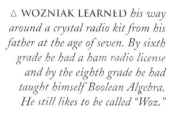

△ WOZNIAK LEARNED *his way around a crystal radio kit from his father at the age of seven. By sixth grade he had a ham radio license and by the eighth grade he had taught himself Boolean Algebra. He still likes to be called "Woz."*

△ IN 1999, TIME *magazine called Berners-Lee one of the 100 greatest minds of the century. He received a MacArthur Fellowship in 1998, and has been given many honorary degrees from institutions around the globe.*

Did you know?

■ Tim Berners-Lee built his first computer while in college, using spare parts and an old television set.

■ Berners-Lee's parents met while working on the Ferranti Mark I. Released in 1951, it was the first computer sold commercially.

■ Berners-Lee named the "Enquire" program after a Victorian-era encyclopedia he owned as a child— *Enquire Within Upon Anything.*

Did you know?

■ In the early years, Jobs sold his Volkswagen minibus and Wozniak his programmable calculator for working capital.

■ In 1971, while attending Berkeley, Wozniak teamed with Jobs to design "blue boxes"—devices that enabled users to illegally make free long-distance phone calls.

■ In 1990, Wozniak helped establish the Electronic Frontier Foundation, which counsels hackers who are criminally prosecuted.

◁ JOBS WAS *responsible for the user-friendly Macintosh interface. His first job was designing video games for Atari, the makers of Pong. He is shown here with the NeXT computer, which he developed after leaving Apple.*

ALAN TURING

(1912–1954)

BRITISH MATHEMATICIAN Alan Mathison Turing made major contributions to the fields of mathematics and biology, laying the foundations for both modern computer science and artificial intelligence.

△ TURING WAS *a world-class distance runner and a member of the Walton Athletic Club in Surrey, England. His best marathon time was 2 hours, 46 minutes.*

ENIGMATIC GENIUS

Turing was born in London and graduated in 1934 from King's College at the University of Cambridge, where he earned acclaim for his research in probability theory. A few years later, he published a seminal paper in which he conceived of a "Turing machine" that could read and respond to instructions encoded on a tape—a theory that eventually led to the digital computer. The paper brought him much attention and he left his job as an instructor at King's College to study mathematical logic at Princeton University in New Jersey. After receiving his Ph.D in 1938, he returned to England. Recruited by the British government, Turing spent the war years as a code-breaker, working tirelessly to crack German communication codes—an important factor in the Allied victory. When World War II ended, Turing went to work for the National Physical Laboratory (NPL) in London, developing the first complete program for a digital computer. Colleagues at NPL dismissed his engineering as too complex, and built a simpler, less sophisticated prototype instead. Pioneering the field of artificial intelligence, Turing theorized that a human brain acted much like a machine. Toward the end of his life, he worked on so-called "artificial life" or genetic modeling. Despite his brilliant work, Turing was persecuted for his homosexuality, and he committed suicide in 1954 by eating an apple laced with cyanide.

Did you know?

■ Turing in 1952 was convicted of homosexuality, then a crime in Britain, and sentenced to a year of hormone injections designed to dampen his sex drive. Judged a security risk, he lost his clearance to work on government computers.

■ He was a miserable student, particularly in the sciences.

◁ DURING WORLD WAR II TURING *used materials captured from a German U-Boat to break the Germans' code, which the Nazis sent via the Enigma machine (shown here).*

WILLIAM SHOCKLEY

(1910–1989)

WILLIAM BRADFORD SHOCKLEY shared the 1956 Nobel Prize for physics for the invention of the transistor, one of the great breakthroughs in technological history.

Did you know?

■ Even though he played a significant role in creating the $130 million semiconductor industry, Shockley considered genetics his most important work.

■ He once made his lab staff undergo polygraph tests to determine who was responsible for a minor injury to one of the office workers.

TAINTED GENIUS

Born in England, Shockley studied physics at Caltech, graduating in 1932. After earning his doctorate at Harvard, he worked at Bell Telephone Laboratories, where he experimented with semiconductors. He served during World War II as director of research for the Navy's Antisubmarine Warfare Operations Research Group and after the war returned to Bell as director of physics research. Shockley worked with John Bardeen and Walter H. Brattain using semiconductors to control and amplify electronic signals. The team developed the point-contact transistor in 1947 and a year later improved on it with the junction transistor. Shockley established the Shockley Semiconductor Laboratory in 1955 and became a professor at Stanford. During the 1960s, he began promoting his theory of "dysgenics," which claimed that people of African descent were intellectually inferior to Caucasians. Despite his substantial contribution to science, his reputation remains clouded by his inflammatory articles and speeches.

Dr. John Bardeen

Dr. William Shockley

Dr. Walter H. Brattain

△ SHOCKLEY SHARED THE 1956 NOBEL PRIZE *with Bardeem and Brattain, shown here at the Bell Laboratories in 1948.*

▽ **SHOCKLEY POSES IN HIS LAB** *on November 1, 1956, the day his Nobel Prize was announced. As well as replacing the vacuum tube in electronics, Shockley made a great contribution to the computer age by encouraging the industry's growth in the area that would become Silicon Valley.*

CHARLES BABBAGE
(1792–1871)

BRITISH MATHEMATICIAN and inventor Charles Babbage is regarded as the father of modern computers for his invention of machines that performed simple computations.

THE DIFFERENCE ENGINE

Born in London, Babbage attended Cambridge University. Around 1812 he developed the "Difference Engine"—a mechanical calculator that could perform limited computations of up to eight decimal figures. He founded the Analytical Society, which incorporated various discoveries made on the European continent into English mathematics. Babbage also founded the Royal Astronomical Society, and received government funding to design a calculator that would perform

△ **BABBAGE WROTE** *a consumer guide to life insurance, helped establish the first modern postal system in Britain, and developed mathematical codebreaking.*

computations of up to ten decimal figures. He was a fellow of the Royal Society of London and professor of mathematics at Cambridge University. Funding for Babbage's calculator project ran out before he could complete his research. He moved on to a related project, the development of an "Analytical Engine"—capable of performing any arithmetical operation based on user input, a memory unit that stored numbers, and other basic elements of the modern computer. Lack of funds again forced Babbage to give up his research in 1851, but his unpublished notes proved valuable to researchers who discovered them in 1937. Babbage also made important contributions to political and economic theory. His discussion of production theory is said to have influenced that of philosopher John Stuart Mill. He died a disappointed man, however, believing that his work had been fruitless.

Digital Pioneers

PAUL ALLEN b. 1954
Microsoft co-founder.

LARRY ELLISON b. 1943
Founder of software company Oracle.

STEVE CASE b. 1958
Took AOL from chat rooms to media powerhouse.

▽ **THE RAYTHEON** "8 TRANSISTOR" *portable radio, below, contained eight tiny transistors, each smaller than a dime. These transistors replaced ordinary vacuum tubes; they never burned out and were difficult to damage. They used so little power that four flashlight batteries ran the radio for a year.*

△ **THE ORIGINAL DIFFERENCE ENGINE—** *only this fragment of the machine was built. It is on display at the Science Museum, London.*

Did you know?

■ Charles Babbage hated street music, and was ridiculed for the letters of complaint he wrote to the London *Times*.

■ In 1991 London scientists carefully reconstructed the analytical engine from Babbage's notes.

■ A crater near the northern pole of the moon is named for him.

CHRISTIAN REFORMERS

FOR CENTURIES, THE ROMAN CATHOLIC CHURCH LOOMED IN THE MINDS OF WESTERN EUROPEAN CHRISTIANS as the institution that carried the word of God, its tenets and teachings presented as universally correct.

Some, however, sought to challenge the authority of the church and, in doing so, brought about changes both in Roman Catholicism and in Christianity as a whole. In 16th-century Europe, Martin Luther and John Calvin sparked the Reformation, which led to the rise of Protestantism. Joseph Smith's original, wholly American take on the story of Christ some three hundred years later served as a basis for the Church of Latter-day Saints, commonly known as the Mormons. Despite the new ideas of these three, though, some of the greatest reformers were conservatives: 15th-century Franciscan Girolamo Savonarola and Pope John Paul II in our time both worked to swing the pendulum of change toward tradition.

△ MARTIN LUTHER WRITES HIS THESES *on the church door in Wittenberg, in this 16th-century German woodcut. Luther's Protestantism rejected celibacy for the clergy, monasticism, and other traditional practices.*

JOHN PAUL II
b. 1920

POPE JOHN PAUL II'S REIGN in the Vatican has been marked by both a stringent moral conservatism and a progressive attitude toward understanding and unity between religions.

THE POLISH POPE

Born Karol Jozef Wojtyla in Wadowice, Poland, John Paul II lost both his mother and brother when he was very young. He entered a seminary in 1938 at the urging of his devout

father. After becoming a priest and earning a Ph.D in divinity, he served as a parish priest in Krakow, where he spoke out against Poland's communist leadership. Wojtyla was elected pope in 1978, following the sudden death of John Paul I. He quickly assumed an aggressive stance against any behavior he perceived as contradicting the moral dogmas of the church, including birth control, abortion, homosexuality, and premarital sex, earning the criticism of many progressive Catholics. Even after

△ ALI AGCA, *the would-be assassin of John Paul II, who visited Agca in 1983 and forgave him.*

a 1981 assassination attempt by Turkish radical Mehmet Ali Agca, John Paul II remained a very public pope. He has visited more countries than any other pope in history and has said Mass before audiences numbering in the millions. Intelligent and scholarly, John Paul II has embraced the changing demographics of Catholicism by appointing more people of color to positions of authority in the Vatican. He also has attempted to mend rifts between Catholicism and other religions. His landmark pilgrimage to the Holy Land in 2000 saw him ask for a renewed spiritual partnership between Christians and Jews, and an end to violence between Jews and Palestinians. Despite suffering from Parkinson's disease, he remains active in his role as an international religious leader.

△ VATICAN CITY'S *St. Peter's Square is the site of weekly audiences held by the Pope. Services are moved indoors during inclement weather.*

MARTIN LUTHER

(1483–1546)

MARTIN LUTHER OPENLY challenged the dominance of the Roman Catholic Church and provided the spark that ignited the Protestant Reformation.

THE FOUNDER OF PROTESTANTISM

Born to prosperous parents in Germany, Luther followed a fairly traditional academic path as a law student until he was struck by a spiritual revelation during a severe thunderstorm. Soon after the incident, in 1505, Luther joined an Augustinian monastery in Erfurt. In 1512, he earned his Ph.D in theology from the University of Wittenberg, and later assumed control of the department. His disgust with papal practices at the time yielded the famous 95 Theses, which, legend has it, he posted on the door of Wittenberg's town church. The document attacked the practice of granting indulgences—in which sins were forgiven in return for money—and argued that salvation was to be found through faith alone, not through good works. Despite criticism from the establishment church, Luther refused to retract his statements, and was excommunicated in 1521. Luther was the chief exponent of the Protestant Reformation, acting as an advisor to various noblemen who supported the new religious faith and translating the New Testament into German, which also contributed to the unity of the German-speaking peoples. In 1525 he married a former nun, and in 1534, his translation of the entire Bible, the Wittenberg Bible, was published. He died in his home town of Eisleben in 1546.

△ LUTHERIAN BIBLE, c. 1530. Luther claimed that while in hiding after his excommunication, he "drove away Satan with an inkwell" when the devil tried to tempt him from translating the Bible.

Did you know?

■ Martin Luther and wife Katharina von Bora had six children and a reputedly very happy marriage.

■ Like many Christians of his time, Luther could be violently anti-Semitic; among his writings is a book entitled *On the Jews and Their Lies*.

△ JOHN PAUL II *visited the United States for the first time in September 1979. While enjoying enormous media attention, he did not shrink from scolding Americans for not strictly adhering to the doctrines of the church.*

Did you know?

■ John Paul II is the first non-Italian pope in 450 years.

■ He is the author of many books, both fiction and nonfiction, including the play *The Jeweler's Shop* (1992).

■ John Paul II was once a proficient mountain climber and skier, and a practicing actor.

▷ A WOOD ENGRAVING *from Luther's Bible (1522), showing the opening of the pit of Hell. Luther's Bible was aimed at capturing the interest of the common man.*

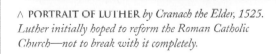

∧ PORTRAIT OF LUTHER *by Cranach the Elder, 1525. Luther initially hoped to reform the Roman Catholic Church—not to break with it completely.*

JOSEPH SMITH
(1805–1844)

As FOUNDER OF THE Church of Jesus Christ of Latter-day Saints (the Mormons), Joseph Smith developed a form of Christianity rooted in American history.

AMERICAN PROPHET

Born in Vermont, Smith settled in New York State with his family in 1816. In 1823 he had a vision in which an angel informed him that a lost gospel written on plates of gold lay hidden in the hills of western New York. Smith said that he translated the plates from an unknown dialect he called "reformed Egyptian." In 1830 he published them as the Book of Mormon, which maintains that a lost tribe of Israel—the Lamanites—migrated to the holy land of America to escape persecution, and that while in America, the tribe was visited by Christ before his ascension. Despite persecution from both lawmakers and ordinary citizens and an initial reluctance from his wife Emma to convert, by the mid-1840s Smith's church numbered almost 20,000 members. Smith claimed that polygamy—the practice of taking multiple wives—was divinely ordained in one of his visions. He introduced polygamy while living in the Mormon community of Nauvoo in Illinois by taking 33 wives. In 1844 Smith declared martial law in Nauvoo, and was thrown in jail on charges of treason. In June of that year he was murdered by a mob. The remaining Mormon congregation moved to Utah under the leadership of Smith's successor, Brigham Young.

△ JOSEPH SMITH, c. 1830. His triumphant theology directly connected the US with the Bible, hastening the spread of Mormonism in the 1840s.

Did you know?

■ Smith was an independent candidate in the presidential election of 1844.

■ Joseph Smith was a member of the mystical fraternity known as the Freemasons and integrated many Masonic rituals into early Mormon ceremonies.

▷ SMITH PREACHES TO NATIVE AMERICANS in a 19th-century illustration. Some believe that one of the reasons he introduced polygamy was so that whites would intermarry with Native Americans and make them "white, delightsome and just," as the Book of Mormon promised "the Lamanites" would become at the end of their days.

JOHN CALVIN
(1509-1564)

JOHN CALVIN, Martin Luther's successor as the preeminent Protestant theologian, made a powerful impact on the fundamental doctrines of Protestantism.

Protestant Thinkers

ULRICH ZWINGLI (1484–1531) Founder of Swiss reformation.

GUILLAUME FAREL (1489–1565) Calvin's consultant and confidant.

JOHN KNOX (1515-1572) Zealous Scottish leader and Protestant reformist.

THE PROTESTANT SCHOLASTIC

Born in France, Calvin was a law student at the University of Orleans when he first joined the cause of the Reformation. In 1536, he published the landmark text *Institutes of the Christian Religion*, an early attempt to standardize the theories of Protestantism. His religious teachings emphasized the sovereignty of the scriptures and divine predestination—a doctrine holding that God chooses a select few to enter Heaven regardless of their good works or their faith. Calvin lived in Geneva briefly, until anti-Protestant authorities in 1538 forced him to leave. In 1541 he was invited back again, and upon his return from Germany, where he had been living, he became an important spiritual and political leader. Calvin used Protestant principles to establish a religious government; and in 1555 he was given absolute supremacy as leader in Geneva. While instituting many positive policies, his government also punished "impiety" and dissent against his particularly spare vision of Christianity with execution. Under his rule, Geneva became the center of Protestantism, and sent out pastors to the rest of Europe, creating Presbyterianism in Scotland, the Puritan Movement in England, and the Reformed Church in the Netherlands.

△ AN ILLUSTRATION DEPICTING CALVIN'S RETURN to Geneva, September 13, 1541. After his return, the clergy of the city enjoyed absolute power.

△ CALVIN WAS KNOWN *for an intellectual, unemotional approach to faith that provided Protestantism's theological underpinnings, whereas Luther brought passion and populism to his religious cause.*

"On all hands there is abundance of ostentatious ceremonies, but sincerity of heart is rare."

JOHN CALVIN

Did you know?

■ Calvin allowed no art other than music, and even that could not involve instruments.

■ In the first five years of his rule in Geneva, 58 people were executed and 76 exiled for their religous beliefs.

■ No one knows where John Calvin is buried.

GIROLAMO SAVONAROLA
(1452–1498)

DOMINICAN MONK Girolamo Savonarola was an ardent reformer of the Roman Catholic Church and virtual dictator of Florence after the Medicis' fall.

THE BONFIRE OF THE VANITIES

Born in Ferrara, Italy, Savonarola joined the Dominican order in his early 20s. He moved to Florence in 1481 and soon became known for his impassioned sermons against the moral corruption of Florence during the reign of the Medicis. When Lorenzo de Medici died in 1491, the family was expelled from Florence and Savonarola became the city's political and spiritual leader, crusading for greater piety and religious devotion and criticizing the morals of Pope Alexander VI. When France invaded Italy in 1494, Savonarola supported the French and King Charles VIII in hopes that they would bring order to Florence. When the French departed, Savonarola was essentially given control of the city. His rule deteriorated into tyranny and in 1495 he defied a summons from the pope to defend his actions before him. The refusal caused the pope to ban Savonarola from preaching, yet the monk only increased his vocal opposition. In 1497 he was excommunicated for ignoring Alexander's orders. The following year pressure on Savonarola's rule increased: A dissenting priest offered to submit to the ordeal of fire; if he survived the flames, it would disprove Savonarola's doctrines. Challenged to do the same, Savonarola declined, though some of his followers agreed. The test never took place and the people of Florence turned against Savonarola. Taken captive, he was tried and condemned to death by hanging.

△ SAVANAROLA'S *objections to the frivolity and excess of Medici Florence led to a religious police force.*

Did you know?

■ Savonarola encouraged people to publicly burn clothing, jewelry, and mirrors at events called "bonfires of the vanities."

■ Savonarola was said to be able to predict the future and supposedly foretold the date of Pope Innocent VIII's death.

■ The painter Botticelli was deeply affected by Savonarola's teachings.

"Your sins make me a prophet."

GIROLAMO SAVONAROLA

◁ SAVONAROLA WAS FIRST HANGED, *then burned, for schism and heresy, in the Piazza Signoria on May 23, 1498, along with fellow friars Domenico da Pescia and Silvestro Maruffi.*

LEADERS OF THE VIETNAM ERA

FROM 1959 TO 1975, THE VIETNAM WAR HELPED SHAPE THE DESTINY OF SOUTHEAST ASIA, and divided American culture and politics between hawkish anticommunists and an antiwar movement that questioned the morality of the war and its chances for success.

After World War II, Vietnam remained a French colony until revolutionary leader Ho Chi Minh ejected the French in the mid-1950s and established communist North Vietnam. With backing from China and the Soviet Union, North Vietnam sought to unify with South Vietnam by force. In response to attacks on US military installations in Vietnam, Presidents Kennedy and Johnson eventually drew the United States deeply into the conflict, leading to heavy American casualties. Johnson's successor, Richard Nixon, with the counsel of Secretary of State Henry Kissinger, eventually negotiated the withdrawal of American troops.

△ THIS 1969 VIET CONG *propaganda poster reads: "Allegiance to Uncle Ho."*

△ THE MUDDLED AND ULTIMATELY *failed American involvement in Vietnam defined decades of foreign policy. Every military action by the United States since then has been judged against it.*

RICHARD NIXON
(1913–1994)

RICHARD MILHOUS NIXON, 37th president of the United States, played a defining role in postwar politics, but he was also to become one of the most vilified politicians in American history.

THE SHADOW PRESIDENT

Born in California, Nixon attended Whittier College and graduated in 1934 from Duke University law school. He returned to the town of Whittier to practice law, and married Thelma "Pat" Ryan in 1940. After serving in the US Navy during World War II, he was elected to Congress in 1946 as a Republican. His strong anticommunist stance made him popular, and in 1950 he won election to the Senate by insinuating that his opponent, a liberal Democrat, was a communist. When Eisenhower wavered in 1952 as to whether to name him his running mate, Nixon appealed on television for public support, securing his place on the ticket.

Nixon served two terms as vice president and narrowly lost the 1960 presidential election to John F. Kennedy. He rebounded in 1968 to defeat Democrat Hubert Humphrey for the presidency. Facing pressure to end US involvement in Vietnam, Nixon transferred combat roles to South Vietnamese troops. Yet he also secretly resumed the bombing of North Vietnam and expanded the air and ground war into neighboring Cambodia and Laos, causing widespread protests at home. A peace agreement negotiated in October 1972 was short-lived. December "Christmas bombings" of North Vietnam were followed by more negotiations, and a new agreement was finally reached in January 1973.

Nixon resigned from office in disgrace on August 9, 1974, after it was revealed that he had attempted to cover up the 1972 FBI break-in at the Democratic Party's headquarters in the Watergate building in Washington, D.C. He spent the rest of his life trying to rebuild his image and found a new role as an elder statesman on foreign policy and related matters.

△ NIXON'S *"five o'clock shadow" played poorly against Kennedy's clean-cut good looks in the first televised presidential debate in 1960.*

▷ A PROTEST
BUTTON *from an
antiwar march,
c. 1969–1972.*

◁ NIXON'S
*trademark double-
victory sign became
much parodied during
his presidency.*

△ NIXON, *seen here with
cheering supporters at his
Miami Beach headquarters in
1968, enjoyed the support of
what he called "the Silent
Majority" of Americans to back
his policies in Vietnam and at
home, in the face of protest.*

"I believe the second half of
the 20th century will be known
as the age of Nixon."

SENATOR BOB DOLE DURING A TELEVISED
ADDRESS SHORTLY AFTER NIXON'S DEATH

Did you know?

■ Nixon appeared on the
comedy show "Rowan
and Martin's Laugh-In"
in 1968. His line was
"Sock it to me."

■ Nixon's tendency to
brood earned him the
nickname "Gloomy Gus"
at Duke University
Law School.

■ Nixon's visit to China
in February 1972 and
his meetings with Mao
Zedong opened the doors
to Chinese-US relations,
which had completely
ended in 1949.

Nguyen Phu Duc   Richard Nixon   Henry Kissinger

△ NGUYEN PHU DUC *was sent to Washington as an emissary by South
Vietnamese President Nguyen Van Thieu in November 1972, to approve the
cease-fire agreement Henry Kissinger had negotiated with the North Vietnamese.*

△ ALTHOUGH NIXON *was raised in the
pacifist Quaker faith and attended a Quaker
college, he always advocated a strong military.*

LYNDON BAINES JOHNSON
(1908–1973)

LYNDON BAINES JOHNSON was a powerful congressional leader during the 1950s and played an important role in the political upheavals of the 1960s as the 36th president of the United States.

△ JOHNSON'S DEEPENING *involvement in Vietnam compromised his ability to continue with his aggressive domestic agenda. Still, his "Great Society" proposals established Medicare, provided increased aid for the poor and for education, and passed the Civil Rights Act.*

LBJ

Born in southwest Texas, Johnson worked as a teacher and a legislative assistant before being elected as Representative from Texas in 1938. Known for his no-holds-barred approach to politics, he worked Washington's corridors and served briefly in the Navy during World War II before he was elected US Senator from Texas in 1948. Originally a New Deal Democrat, he drifted to the right for a time and supported a strong military as Senate majority leader. In 1960, with a strong southern power base, presidential aspirations of his own, and rediscovered liberal leanings, Johnson was chosen by John F. Kennedy to be his running mate, and succeeded him as president after JFK's assassination on November 22, 1963.

> ### Did you know?
>
> ■ Johnson was sometimes seen as unrefined, and was known to hold meetings with his advisors while he was in the bathroom.
>
> ■ Johnson suffered profound feelings of inferiority, especially around the Kennedys, and complained of their constant disapproval of him as president.

When North Vietnamese gunboats attacked American destroyers in August 1964, Johnson ordered retaliatory air raids while publicly declaring that he had no intention of widening the conflict. Two days after the attack, Congress granted Johnson the constitutional authority to declare war independent of formal approval from Congress. After Viet Cong guerrillas attacked the US military base at Pleiku in February 1965, Johnson ordered Operation Rolling Thunder, a massive bombing campaign on North Vietnam, and dispatched 3,500 Marines to protect the border city of Da Nang. Johnson increased the number of US military personnel in Vietnam to 180,000 by the end of the year. That figure peaked at about 550,000 in 1968. As American casualties mounted, Johnson's public support declined. He ordered major reductions in the bombing of North Vietnam in March 1968 and asked for peace talks. He also announced that he would not seek reelection. His presidency ended, Johnson retired to his ranch in Texas.

◁ AN ANTI-WAR BUTTON *expresses widening public disapproval of US military involvement in Vietnam; between January 1966 and October of that same year, Johnson's approval rating dropped from 63 percent to 44 percent.*

△ THE ANTIWAR PROTESTS *of Johnson's early years in the White House swelled by 1968 into a general outpouring of unrest. Riots flared in cities across the nation.*

▷ JOHNSON'S TERM *ended in January 1969. His successor, Richard Nixon, treated Johnson with great respect and the two became good friends.*

LEONID BREZHNEV
(1906–1982)

SOVIET LEADER Leonid Ilyich Brezhnev offered moral, political, and political support to North Vietnam in the early years of the war—but later helped forge ties between the USSR and the US, precipitating the end of the Cold War seven years after his death.

The Generals

WILLIAM WESTMORELAND b. 1914 Army Chief of Staff during Vietnam.

VO NGUYEN GIAP b. 1912 Viet Minh victor at Dien Bien Phu.

NGUYEN NGOC LOAN (1931–1998) South Vietnamese general.

SOVIET POWER

Born to a working-class family, Brezhnev joined the Communist party at age 21, served in the Red Army during World War II, and then served under Stalin in the powerful Secretariat of the Central Committee until Stalin's death in 1953. He enjoyed the favor of Stalin's successor, Nikita Khrushchev, who in 1960 helped install Brezhnev as chairman of the Supreme Soviet. Four years later, Brezhnev allied with other leaders to oust Khrushchev, and replaced him as first secretary of the party's Central Committee. Although Brezhnev adopted a less belligerent attitude toward the US than his predecessors, he heightened tensions by creating the "Brezhnev Doctrine," which stated that the USSR had the right to intervene in the affairs of other communist nations. He also supported revolutionary wars, primarily the war in Vietnam. Beginning in 1964, the USSR supplied arms and diplomatic support to North Vietnam, making it a flashpoint between the two superpowers. During President Nixon's May 1972 visit to Moscow, he signed the nuclear-arms limitation treaties known as SALT. Brezhnev and Nixon continued to meet, easing tensions enough to allow a joint US-Soviet space mission in 1975 and a massive Soviet purchase of American wheat. Despite declining health, Brezhnev continued to oversee Soviet policy until his death.

△ UNDER BREZHNEV *the Soviet Union continued to support leftist governments in "wars of national liberation" worldwide. He is seen here with Cuban dictator Fidel Castro.*

△ IN HIS LATER YEARS, BREZHNEV *engaged Nixon and Kissinger's policy of detente, and eventually signed the SALT treaty on May 26, 1972 (above), which began the process of limiting the world's nuclear arsenal. He came to the United States for an official visit in June 1973, and delivered an address on national television.*

◁ REPORTEDLY, *Stalin saw Brezhnev at a Party Congress in November 1952 and remarked, "What a handsome Moldavian!" In the early 1960s, he developed a reputation as the best-dressed Soviet leader.*

Did you know?

■ Brezhnev had dreamed of becoming an actor.

■ He originally trained to be a metallurgical engineer and graduated from Kamenskoe Metallurgical Institute.

■ When Brezhnev's coffin was lifted to be put in state, the bottom broke and his body fell out. The replacement coffin was so heavy that attendants could not carry it.

HENRY KISSINGER
b. 1923

SCHOLAR AND STATESMAN Henry Kissinger, who shaped foreign policy under presidents Richard Nixon and Gerald Ford, is best known for his crucial—and controversial—role in US policymaking during the Vietnam War.

THE SECRETARY

Kissinger was born in Germany to a Jewish family who emigrated to the United States to escape Nazi persecution. After serving in the US Army during World War II and in the postwar US military government of Germany, Kissinger earned his Ph.D in political science from Harvard in 1954. He then joined the Harvard faculty while also serving as a security consultant to government agencies. His book *Nuclear Weapons and Foreign Policy* (1957) established him as a leading authority on military and diplomatic strategy, and his ideas influenced the Kennedy administration. In December 1968 he was appointed assistant for national security affairs under Nixon, and became Secretary of State in 1973. Kissinger originally advocated the heavy bombing and increase of US troop commitment in Vietnam. Later he was responsible for Nixon's policy of reducing US troops and replacing them with South Vietnamese forces backed by US supplies. He also supported the invasions of Cambodia and Laos and rapprochement with China. On January 23, 1973, he signed a cease-fire agreement that provided for the withdrawal of US troops and outlined a peace settlement. Kissinger shared the 1973 Nobel Peace Prize with the North Vietnamese negotiator, Le Duc Tho, who refused the honor. Since then, Kissinger has written on foreign policy and consulted to major corporations.

△ **KISSINGER** *developed the policy of detente through the Nixon and Ford administrations; he is also believed by many to have been involved in the ousting of Chilean President Allende in 1973.*

"Power is the ultimate aphrodisiac."

HENRY KISSINGER

◁ **KISSINGER**, *shown here with his younger brother Walter, and his Orthodox Jewish family left Germany and came to the US in 1938 as a result of increasing Nazi discrimination.*

Did you know?

■ As of 2002 Kissinger has written six books and more than forty articles on foreign policy, international affairs, and diplomatic history.

■ Growing up in New York City in the late 1930s, he attended high school at night and worked in a shaving-brush factory by day.

△ **PROTESTER DANIEL ELLSBERG** *(center) and four friends sent a letter to Father Phil Berrigan (far right) in 1970, suggesting they kidnap Kissinger to protest "war crimes" in Vietnam. The letter was intercepted. All were tried for conspiracy, but a mistrial resulted.*

HO CHI MINH

(1890–1969)

HO CHI MINH, founder of the Indochinese Communist party, claimed the independence of Vietnam from France and was North Vietnam's leader during the Vietnam War.

UNCLE HO

Born Nguyen Tat Thanh, his father was a local official who opposed the French occupation of Vietnam. After teaching briefly, at the age of 21 Ho Chi Minh left Vietnam to work as a cook on a French ship. He eventually settled in France and became an active socialist. In 1929 he founded the Vietnamese Revolutionary Youth Association (Thanh Nien), later renamed the Indochinese Communist Party (PartiCommuniste Indochinois in French, or PCI). Minh and a few comrades in January 1941 returned to Vietnam to form the League for the Independence of Vietnam, or Viet Minh. With assistance from the United States, the Viet Minh fought the Japanese, who had temporarily driven out the French in World War II. Ho Chi Minh proclaimed the establishment of the Democratic Republic of Vietnam. France, though, refused to grant Vietnam independence and faced the Viet Minh in a war that climaxed with a crushing French defeat at Dien Bien Phu. A 1954 conference in Geneva resulted in the partition of Vietnam. Ho Chi Minh established a socialist state in poverty-stricken North Vietnam, where his regime became increasingly totalitarian and repressive. He and his followers grew convinced that the success of socialism in North Vietnam was closely linked to unification with South Vietnam. War broke out in 1959 between North Vietnam and the US-sponsored regime in South Vietnam. As chief of state during the war, Ho Chi Minh directed a North Vietnamese government that consisted largely of his followers, now that Ho himself was in declining health. He lived another decade, until his death in 1969 of heart failure. Ho Chi Minh's loyal supporters continued to fight for Vietnamese independence, which was finally achieved in 1975, six years after his death. In 1975 Saigon was renamed Ho Chi Minh City in his honor.

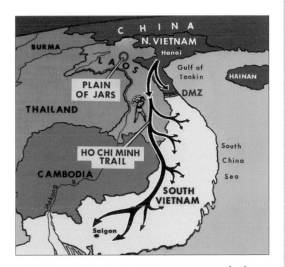

△ THE HO CHI MINH TRAIL *was a network of paths through the jungles of Cambodia, Laos, and Vietnam, used by the Viet Cong to infiltrate the south.*

△ HO CHI MINH *was too old to direct much of the war effort himself; his major contribution during the Vietnam War was to solicit help from the Soviet Union and China.*

Did you know?

■ In 1948, a biography was published of Ho Chi Minh, supposedly written by "Tran Dan Tien," who turned out to be Ho Chi Minh himself.

■ Ho Chi Minh means "He who enlightens." He began using this name around 1940, after using two other names.

■ To the North Vietnamese people, Ho Chi Minh was known as "Uncle Ho."

△ THE WAR RAVAGED VIETNAM, *leaving the civilians who survived to rebuild their country as best they could.*

▷ HO CHI MINH *traveled through Southeast Asia in the 1920s, creating revolutionary cells and working toward the eventual independence of his homeland.*

POP STARS OF THE '80s & '90s

AS THE WEST PROSPERED DURING THE ECONOMIC BOOM OF THE 1980s, the rough edges of late 1970s punk and new wave gave way to the visual gloss and accessibility offered by the emergence of music videos. Radio became less important as kids around the world demanded their MTV.

Along with rock's new look came mainstream approval. Ronald Reagan quoted Bruce Springsteen in his speeches, while Tina Turner and Cher scored smash hits that attracted both kids and parents alike. Hundreds of musicians gathered at all-star benefits to raise money for famine-stricken countries, and even the once spikey Elvis Costello settled down to croon with the likes of Burt Bacharach. Above them all hovered the enigmatic figure of Michael Jackson, a musical genius whose eccentricities could not mask the corporate mind behind them. Rock stars, once the scourge of society, were turning into grandparents, and it was left to the grunge rockers of Seattle and the evolving urban sounds of hip hop and rap to annoy the grown-ups.

△ THE ADVENT OF MUSIC VIDEO *around 1980 changed the world of pop music forever. While radio airtime had once decided the success of a recording artist, suddenly their "look" became as important as their sound.*

MICHAEL JACKSON
b. 1958

MICHAEL JACKSON HAS BEEN A STAR for most of his life, beginning with his success as the 11-year-old lead singer of the Jackson Five and continuing as a solo artist throughout the 1980s and '90s.

THE GLOVED ONE

Born in Gary, Indiana, Jackson began performing when he was age five. At the insistence of his father, Jackson and his four brothers began singing together as the Jackson Five. They were a huge success for Motown mogul Berry Gordy, Jr., scoring four number-one hits in a row. Jackson's first major solo success was the album *Off the Wall* in 1979, which featured several pop-disco anthems. In 1982 he released *Thriller*, the second best-selling album ever, featuring pop smashes like "Billie Jean" and "Beat It." Its popularity was enhanced by his distinct fashion sense, brilliant dance moves, and slickly produced videos. Subsequent albums *Bad* (1987) and *Dangerous* (1992) continued the run of hits. As Jackson's notoriety grew, his behavior became more eccentric. He built a roller coaster at his estate, Never Land Ranch, and bought a pet chimpanzee. Allegations of sexual misconduct with a minor were brought against him in 1993, but were eventually dropped. Jackson married Elvis Presley's daughter, Lisa Marie, in 1994; they separated in 1996. He had two children, Prince Michael and Paris Michael Katherine, with Debbie Rowe, his wife from 1996 to 1999. He continued to tour and record, staging a 30th anniversary concert in 2001. In 2002 Jackson released a new album, *Invincible,* and was named Artist of the Century at the American Music Awards.

△ JACKSON *debuted the single glove look in the* Motown 25 *show, his solo breakthrough.*

△ JOHN LANDIS, *director of* National Lampoon's Animal House *and* The Blues Brothers, *directed the* Thriller *video, a 14-minute-long mini-film and the high-water mark of music video production.*

BRUCE SPRINGSTEEN

b. 1949

No single performer of the 1980s embodied the social and cultural idealism of America better than Bruce Springsteen. His epic, high-energy live performances and straightforward rock songs, which addressed working-class hopes and fears, provided a vital alternative to the banality of Reagan-era pop music.

Nils Lofgren

Bruce Springsteen

Steve Van Zandt, later of Sopranos fame

"THE BOSS"

Springsteen was born in the small working-class town of Freehold, New Jersey. He played with a number of Jersey-shore bar bands before releasing his debut album *Greetings from Asbury Park, N.J.* in 1973. Hailed as America's "next great songwriter," Springsteen landed on the covers of both *Time* and *Newsweek* following his 1975 release, *Born to Run*. It would be three years before his next album, *Darkness at the Edge of Town*, which paved the way for a series of records that offered powerful anthems and plaintive ballads about the American dream gone awry. In 1984 he released his most successful record to date, *Born in the USA*, which became one of the best-selling records of the decade. The record established Springsteen as more than the savior of rock 'n' roll, but as the voice of millions of ordinary Americans. He kept recording throughout the 1990s, and in 2000 launched a successful tour with his backup group, the E-Street Band.

△ BRUCE SPRINGSTEEN AND MEMBERS OF HIS E-STREET BAND *at New York's Madison Square Garden on the last night of his summer 2000 tour.*

Did you know?

- Bruce Springsteen co-wrote Patti Smith's 1978 hit "Because the Night."

- Springsteen won an Oscar in 1994 for Best Original Song with "Streets of Philadelphia" from *Philadelphia*.

- Springsteen was inducted into the Rock and Roll Hall of Fame in 1999.

△ DESPITE DRAMATIC *changes in his appearance since he was a child, Jackson maintains that he has had only two plastic-surgery operations and that the progressive lightening of his skin is due to a pigmentation condition.*

Did you know?

- Michael Jackson owns the lucrative publishing rights to the entire catalog of Beatles songs.

- The "Scream" video, Jackson's collaboration with his sister Janet, is the most expensive music video ever made.

- Rapper MC Hammer once challenged Jackson to a dance contest.

"Mister, I ain't a boy, no, I'm a man, and I believe in a promised land."

BRUCE SPRINGSTEEN

▽ MILLIONS OF AMERICANS *made "Born in the USA" (1984)—Springsteen's working-class anthem— their theme song.*

◁ HIS FIRST ALBUM, Greetings from Asbury Park, N.J., *was released in 1973. Sales were minimal, even though Springsteen was touted as "the new Bob Dylan."*

221

CHER
b. 1946

ONE OF ENTERTAINMENT'S TRUE
CHAMELEONS, Cher has moved
effortlessly from 1960s pop to 1970s
singer-songwriter stylings to the
bombastic power-ballads that made
her an enormous success in the
1980s, and on to Grammy-
winning techno-pop in the '90s.

IF YOU BELIEVE
Born Cherilyn Sarkisian in El Centro,
California, Cher began her career as a duo
with her first husband, Sonny Bono. The
two released several hit songs during the
1960s, including "I Got You Babe," and
were stars of a hugely successful TV
variety show, "The Sonny and Cher
Comedy Hour"(1971 to 1974). Cher had several
solo hits in the '70s, and in 1987 she released
the self-titled album, *Cher*. Filled with slick,
rock anthems and emotional ballads, the album
was a success and scored two Billboard chart
hits. Cher's success as an actress helped
promote her music career. After garnering critical acclaim for her work in
films such as *Mask*, *Silkwood*, and *The Witches of Eastwick*, Cher went on
to win a Best Actress Oscar for her performance
in *Moonstruck*. Although Cher focused on film
for most of the '90s, in 1998 she released the
techno-pop anthem "Believe," which eventually
became a Billboard number-one hit and a
Grammy winner.

△ CHER'S TASTE *for extreme
fashions, though attention-
getting, has sometimes obscured
the depth of her talent.*

Did you know?

■ At 52, Cher became
the oldest woman ever to
have a number-one
Billboard pop song when
she hit with "Believe."

■ Cher was married to
southern-rocker Gregg
Allman in the 1970s.

■ Both Sonny and Cher
starred in short-lived
variety shows after their
television show ended.

△ SONNY AND CHER *had
a daughter, Chastity, in
1969, who has since become a
vocal spokeswoman for gay
and lesbian causes.*

ELVIS COSTELLO
b. 1955

BEGINNING AS ONE OF BRITAIN'S NEW WAVE
artists of the late 1970s and early '80s, Elvis
Costello wrote and recorded a string of albums
that challenged not only the musical style of the
era, but the myriad styles of popular music.

FROM NEW WAVE TO BACHARACH
Inspired by the musical freedom left in the wake of the
Sex Pistols, Costello (born in London as Declan McManus)
threw off the shackles of his workaday office job as a
computer programmer and released a stellar debut album,
My Aim Is True (1977), on the small British label Stiff. Far
more conscious of pop song-craft than other bands of the
era, Costello, along with his
backup group, the
Attractions, recorded a series
of meticulously composed
yet edgy albums that ranged
in style from straightforward
power-pop to soul and
country. He scored his first
US Top-40 single in 1983
with "Everyday I Write the
Book." Known for inventive
collaborations, Costello
has recorded with Paul
McCartney and composer
Burt Bacharach, with whom
he won a Grammy in 1999.

Did you know?

■ Costello's father was
British big-band singer
Ross McManus and his
mother was the manager
of a record store.

■ Costello has produced
for bands including the
Pogues, Squeeze, and
the Specials.

■ He played his first gig
in 1970, performing his
own compositions in a
London folk club.

◁ COSTELLO *on the cover of*
This Year's Model *(1978).
He was joined on the
album—his second—by
The Attractions, a three-
piece group that would
work with him on most
of his albums for the
next eight years.*

▷ COSTELLO
named this album
Spike *in reference
to the wacky
1940s band leader
Spike Jones.*

▽ COSTELLO IN CONCERT
in 1981, four years after he was
first introduced to America on
Saturday Night Live in 1977 .

Other key players

DAVID BYRNE b. 1952
Cerebral frontman of
Talking Heads

JOHNNY ROTTEN
b. 1956 Lead "singer"
of the Sex Pistols

DEBBIE HARRY b.
1945 Sultry siren of
Blondie fame

TINA TURNER
b. 1939

TINA TURNER IS THE ULTIMATE pop music survivor. Despite a difficult past and speculation that her career was over, Turner released a series of pop-rock records in her mid-40s that stunned the music world.

△ TURNER WON *three Grammys for her 1984* Private Dancer *album.*

THE COMEBACK ARTIST

Born Anna May Bullock in Brownsville, Tennessee, Tina Turner and her husband Ike made up one of the most popular soul/rhythm-and-blues duos of the 1960s and early '70s. Renowned for turning out exhilarating live performances steeped in raw sexual energy, the duo scored hits such as "River Deep Mountain High" and a blistering cover of Creedence Clearwater Revival's "Proud Mary." The duo stopped performing together in 1976, and after several years Turner emerged from her abusive marriage with a string of pop hits that included "Private Dancer" and "What's Love Got to Do With It." She also starred alongside Mel Gibson in *Mad Max: Beyond Thunderdome* (1985). With the help of manager Roger Davies, Turner's work during that period reestablished her as a pop diva. Now in her sixties, she continues to tour and record as one of pop music's most respected female singers.

Did you know?

■ Tina Turner appeared as the Acid Queen in Ken Russell's film version of The Who's 1975 rock opera *Tommy*.

■ Turner's 2000 concert tour was the highest-grossing tour of the year, beating out such mega-stars of the day as the Backstreet Boys and *NSync.

△ NOT ONLY DID *her appearance in* Mad Max: Beyond Thunderdome *prove to be Turner's biggest movie role, but the film also featured the song* "We Don't Need Another Hero," *which earned her three more Grammy Awards.*

◁ FOR A TIME TURNER *held the record for drawing the largest live audience for a solo performer—180,000 for a 1988 date in Brazil.*

"My ultimate vocation in life
is to be an irritant."

ELVIS COSTELLO

ASSASSINS

ASSASSINS HAVE PLAYED A CRITICAL ROLE IN SHAPING HISTORY. Their actions have shifted political landscapes and also thrust killers, who in many cases lived on society's fringes, into the public eye.

Some of history's assassins have inspired wars: the murder of Archduke Franz Ferdinand by Gavrilo Princip created the international crisis that led to World War I. Other assassins have acted in the context of larger conflicts: Charlotte Corday killed French leader Jean-Paul Marat over what she perceived as the corruption of the French Revolution, and John Wilkes Booth shot Abraham Lincoln days after the Confederacy surrendered to end the American Civil War. The social turbulence of the 1960s fomented—and was exacerbated by—high-profile assassinations that still remain controversial. Lee Harvey Oswald's assassination of President Kennedy and James Earl Ray's killing of Martin Luther King, Jr. are still discussed today.

△ A GUN-SIGHT VIEW *from the Texas School Book Depository, part of a reenactment used as evidence during the inquiry into JFK's assassination— the first of several assassinations during the turbulent 1960s in America.*

LEE HARVEY OSWALD
(1939–1963)

LEE HARVEY OSWALD IS THE ONLY PERSON ever charged with what is arguably the most infamous crime in American history—the murder of President John F. Kennedy.

△ LEE HARVEY
*Oswald's passport.
In his 1960 application he said he planned to attend the University of Turku in Finland.*

LONE GUNMAN?

Oswald was born in New Orleans soon after his father died of a heart attack, then moved around the country with his mother, eventually returning to New Orleans in 1954. He joined the Marines in 1956; although considered an unruly loner (Oswald was court-martialed twice) he was known as a proficient rifleman. During his Marine tour, Oswald developed an interest in communism. He left the US for the Soviet Union after his discharge in 1959, and returned in the early 1960s to become active in socialist organizations. On November 22, 1963, John F. Kennedy was shot twice in the head while traveling in an open motorcade through downtown Dallas, Texas. The shots were traced to the book depository located nearby, where a rifle was discovered and eventually linked to Oswald, who was tracked down later that day in a movie theater and charged with killing President Kennedy. His repeated claims that he was not the culprit were silenced when local strip-club owner Jack Ruby shot and killed Oswald two days later. Ruby died in prison in 1967 while awaiting a retrial. The Warren Commissions's initial inquiry and a 1979 investigation on the possibility of multiple killers offered no conclusive evidence to identify Oswald as the sole killer—or to exonerate him.

△ THE TEXAS SCHOOL BOOK DEPOSITORY—*there is a dispute as to whether shots were fired from this building or from a nearby knoll.*

JOHN WILKES BOOTH

(1838–1865)

ACTOR, CONFEDERATE SYMPATHIZER, and white supremacist John Wilkes Booth assassinated Abraham Lincoln.

PRESIDENTIAL ASSASSIN

Born in Maryland, Booth was raised in a family of well-known actors—his father was one of the most celebrated Shakespeareans of the day. Booth became a popular actor in his own right, and also was a devout supporter of the Southern states during their struggle against the North. As a member of the Virginia militia, he participated in the execution of radical abolitionist John Brown in 1859.

Increasingly angered by the progressive politics of President Lincoln and the precarious state of the South in the last days of the Civil War, Booth and several cohorts hatched a plot to kidnap the president. The plan fell through, and Booth instead plotted to assassinate Lincoln. On April 14, 1865, just days after Confederate forces surrendered to General Grant, the president was attending a performance at Ford's Theater in Washington, D.C. when Booth shot Lincoln in the back of the head. Booth escaped, but was tracked down and killed 12 days later. Most agree that Booth was shot by one of the officers involved in his arrest, but questions as to whether Booth was actually dead—or even arrested—persisted for some time.

△ THIS PHOTOGRAPH OF OSWALD *was taken on November 24, 1963, just moments before Jack Ruby shot Oswald on live television as he was about to be handed over to state police.*

△ LINCOLN'S ORIGINAL *theater program stained by his blood. Two years earlier in the same theater, Lincoln admired Booth's performance and asked to meet him. Booth declined.*

"So help me holy God! My soul, life, and possessions are for the South."

JOHN WILKES BOOTH, TO ASIA BOOTH CLARK, HIS SISTER

△ LINCOLN'S PRIVATE BOX *in Ford's Theater, 1865. After shooting Lincoln, Booth leapt to the stage, breaking his leg. As he limped away, he reputedly cried, "Sic semper tyrannis"— "Such is the fate of tyrants."*

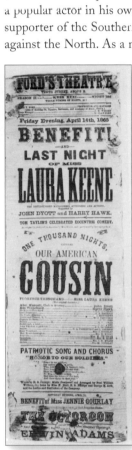

◁ AS AN ACTOR, *Booth was known to sometimes go overboard during dueling scenes, more than once actually injuring his fellow performers.*

GAVRILO PRINCIP
(1894–1918)

SERBIAN NATIONALIST Gavrilo Princip shot and killed Archduke Franz Ferdinand, heir to the Austro-Hungarian crown, helping ignite World War I.

AGITATOR

The son of a postal worker, Princip was born in Bosnia, but moved to Serbia in 1912 to attend school in Belgrade. As a student, Princip became involved with several nationalist organizations dedicated to winning independence for Bosnia-Herzegovina and Serbia, which were then provinces of the Austrian-Hungarian Empire. One such group, the secret Black Hand society, developed a plot to assassinate Archduke Ferdinand. Princip and two others were recruited to enact the plot, and on June 28, 1914, during the Archduke's visit to Sarajevo, Princip shot and killed him. Princip was arrested and sentenced to death, but his life was ultimately spared because he was believed to be younger than 20 years old. Ferdinand's murder aggravated the already unstable region, and Austria-Hungary declared war on Serbia one month later. Other countries quickly followed suit, and World War I had begun. Princip died of tuberculosis in prison four years later.

△ THE BLACK HAND *terrorists had placed several assassins along the Archduke's route, including two bomb throwers, one of whom did not throw his bomb.*

Did you know?

■ Princip attempted suicide twice following the assassination: once with his own gun (a bystander knocked the gun from his hand) and once with cyanide provided to him by the Black Hand.

■ Princip also shot and killed Ferdinand's wife, Countess Sophia.

■ Six of Princip's eight brothers and sisters died in infancy.

▷ THROUGHOUT PRINCIP'S *trial, he denied that the Black Hand had any role in Ferdinand's assassination, even though Princip and the two others had been trained by the group for exactly that purpose.*

JAMES EARL RAY
(1928–1998)

JAMES EARL RAY PLEADED GUILTY to the murder of civil rights leader Martin Luther King, Jr., then spent the rest of his life proclaiming innocence.

△ THE FBI'S WANTED *poster for Ray, who was on the run in Europe, stopping in Atlanta and Portugal en route to London, England.*

RACIST KILLER

Ray, a native of Alton, Illinois, dropped out of high school and was jailed for armed robbery in 1960. After serving seven years of his sentence, he escaped. On April 4, 1967, Martin Luther King, Jr., was shot and killed at the Lorraine Motel in Memphis, Tennessee. Ray's fingerprints were linked to the murder weapon, and he was tracked down in England, where he had fled. Ray pleaded guilty to murder in 1969, and although he quickly retracted his plea, he was sentenced to 99 years in prison. Ray spent the next 30 years attempting to prove his innocence until his death in prison, of liver failure. While some, including the family of Martin Luther King, Jr., believe Ray's claim that he was innocent or part of a larger conspiracy, most historians strongly disagree.

Did you know?

■ Ray escaped from prison in 1977; he was apprehended three days later by dogs.

■ Ray's room in Memphis contained binoculars, a rifle, two cans of beer and a prison radio with his convict number on it.

■ James Earl Ray was never actually put on trial for the murder of King.

△ DEXTER KING, *son of Martin Luther King, Jr., met with Ray on March 27, 1997. He told Ray that he believed he was innocent.*

> "If this case is such an open-and-shut case, why are we still being asked the question: Do you believe Mr. Ray killed your father?"

DEXTER KING, SON OF MARTIN LUTHER KING, JR.

△ **DESPITE HIS** *claims of innocence and the seeming acceptance of those claims by the King family, the evidence of Ray's guilt remains strong. He was a vicious racist with ties to J. B. Stoner, a Klan leader convicted of a church bombing. He followed King in Memphis, took a room across from the hotel, and his fingerprints were on the rifle used to kill King.*

Key Political Victims

YITZHAK RABIN (1922–1995) Prime minister of Israel and peace advocate.

MEDGAR EVERS (1925–1963) His death spurred JFK to act on civil rights.

ANWAR SADAT (1918–1981) Egyptian leader and Nobel Peace Prize winner.

CHARLOTTE CORDAY
(1768–1793)

SELF-STYLED PATRIOT Charlotte Corday murdered Jean-Paul Marat, a leader of the French Revolution.

REBELLIOUS ARISTOCRAT

Born into the French aristocracy, Corday supported the monarchy at the onset of the revolution, but soon became a supporter of the revolutionary government. She joined forces with the moderate Girondists following their expulsion from Paris to Caen at the hands of Marat's more radical Jacobins. Corday decided that Marat was the new scourge of France and believed it was her patriotic duty to eliminate him. She managed to arrange a meeting with Marat, under the guise of being a spy for the Jacobins, and stabbed him to death while he was taking a bath. Corday was quickly apprehended and sentenced to death by guillotine. Despite attempts to create a conspiracy around her, Corday resolutely protested that she had acted alone. "I told my plans to no one," she said at her trial. "I was not killing a man, but a wild beast that was devouring the French people."

△ **FOR WEEKS BEFORE CORDAY** *attacked Jean-Paul Marat with a butcher knife, she wrote "Shall I or shall I not?" on small pieces of paper.*

Did you know?

■ Corday had her portrait painted by a prison guard as she awaited execution.

■ *Marat/Sade*, a well-known 1964 play by Peter Weiss, is about a group of asylum patients who reenact Corday's murder of Marat.

■ Singer-songwriters Tori Amos and Al Stewart co-wrote the 1993 song "Charlotte Corday" about the young rebel assassin.

◁ **CORDAY'S EXECUTION** *was marked by her impressive composure in the face of her impending fate. Some French people see her as a martyr to liberty; others call her a traitor who helped derail the revolution.*

DANCERS

MANY PEOPLE BELIEVE THAT DANCE WAS THE FIRST ART FORM CREATED BY HUMANS. To shape the body into pleasing or meaningful forms for the pleasure of the performer and of the audience demanded no brushes or pens.

It is this primal appeal to the body, to the deeper rhythms of what we might call the soul, that gives dance its power over us. At the same time, dance offers perhaps the most elegant presentation of the human form. The discipline of dance encompasses an array of styles and techniques, from ballet to tap to tango—some based on subtle movements, others calling for intricate maneuvers. Certain men and women have come to define various dance styles. Our collective image of a ballerina comes directly from the work of Anna Pavlova; the image of a couple dancing elegantly across a ballroom floor calls to mind the grace of Fred Astaire and Ginger Rogers. The Nicholas Brothers defined the pyrotechnics of popular tap, and the significance of ballet and modern dance is due in no small part to the groundbreaking artistry of Vaslav Nijinsky and the prowess of Mikhail Baryshnikov.

△ DESPITE THE LONG HISTORY *of dance, classical ballet is a relatively modern invention. Until the 18th century, ballet sequences were usually a small segment within larger operatic performances.*

MIKHAIL BARYSHNIKOV
b. 1948

MIKHAIL BARYSHNIKOV'S BREATHTAKING dancing made him one of the most influential and celebrated dancers of his era. His daring defection to the United States during the Cold War only increased his fame.

Choreographers

GEORGE BALANCHINE (1904–1983) Genius of 20th-century ballet.

MARTHA GRAHAM (1894–1991) Luminary of modern dance.

MICHEL FOKINE (1880–1942) Founder of modern ballet.

MISHA

Born in the Riga, Latvia, the son of a Soviet colonel, Baryshnikov started studying dance in his early teens. He began training with distinguished choreographer Alexander Pushkin in 1963 at the Vaganova Choreographic Institute, and made his stage debut in a 1966 performance with the Kirov Ballet. Baryshnikov's fame quickly grew, and by the late 1960s he was one of the Soviet Union's most heralded dancers. Dancing the lead in Kirov Ballet productions, Baryshnikov dazzled audiences with his astounding physical and technical prowess as well as his emotional expressiveness. He grew tired of the stifling atmosphere in communist Russia, however, and in 1974, following a performance of the Bolshoi Ballet in Toronto, defected from the Soviet Union.

Baryshnikov's career in the West has included stints with several top American ballet companies, including George Balanchine's New York City Ballet and the American Ballet Theater, which he directed from 1980 to 1989. He has also experimented with modern choreography, and in 1990 founded the avant-garde White Oak Dance Project.

◁ BARYSHNIKOV *in the 1985 movie* White Nights, *in which he plays a dancer who defects—a role he duplicated in real life.*

Did you know?

- Baryshnikov was nominated for an Oscar for his acting in the film *The Turning Point* (1977).

- He also starred in *White Nights* (1985) with Gregory Hines.

- Baryshnikov started his own perfume line, called Misha (his nickname).

△ THE 1977 FILM, *The Turning Point, starring Shirley Maclaine, Anne Bancroft, along with Baryshnikov, ignited popular interest in ballet. Colorful personalities such as Gelsey Kirkland and Rudolf Nureyev also fueled an international passion for dance in the late 1970's.*

△ BARYSHNIKOV'S DAUGHTER, ALEXANDRA, *was born in 1981 to her father's then-lover, the actress Jessica Lange.*

▷ BARYSHNIKOV LIFTS *ballerina Gelsey Kirkland, as they rehearse for a 1978 television special. Kirkland left the New York City Ballet company in 1974 to dance regularly with Baryshnikov at the American Ballet Theater, but drug addiction and emotional problems would largely end her career by the mid-1980s.*

Placido Domingo

Angela Lansbury

Clint Eastwood

Chuck Berry

Mikhail Baryshnikov

"Be yourself and dance with your mind and your body, the way it is right now."

MIKHAIL BARYSHNIKOV

◁ KENNEDY CENTER HONOR AWARDS CEREMONY. *December 2000. Baryshnikov, along with other cultural luminaries, was recognized for a lifetime of extraordinary artistic achievement.*

ANNA PAVLOVA
(1881–1931)

ANNA PAVLOVA WAS THE FIRST internationally recognized ballerina, and one of a handful of dancers responsible for bringing ballet into the popular arena.

PRIMA BALLERINA

Born the illegitimate daughter of a washerwoman, Pavlova was brought to St. Petersburg's ballet academy on Theater Street at the age of eight and by her teens was already a sensation, breaking into the Imperial Ballet Russia in 1901 without having to put in time in the corps. A prima ballerina by 1905, she began to travel. Choreographer Michel Fokine created for her the role of the Dying Swan, which became her trademark. Involved in a scandal with an aristocratic lover, she left the Imperial Ballet in 1912 and moved to London, where she formed her own company. Pavlova toured the world, becoming one of the first ballerinas to win fame in the US. Not a physically powerful dancer, she did not perform complex acrobatics; instead she developed a gentle, fluid technique, expressive in its subtleties, which she also used when she turned to choreography. Pavlova contracted pneumonia in 1931 and died later that year.

△ THOUGH SHE BEGAN *dancing in pieces such as* Don Quixote *for the Imperial Ballet (seen here), Pavlova made her fame dancing works by Fokine such as* Les Sylphides.

Did you know?

■ Anna Pavlova was the first dancer to use the broad-toed point shoe that is ubiquitous among dancers today.

■ Pavlova starred in *The Dumb Girl of Portici*, a 1916 silent film made in the US.

■ Pavlova's last words were "Get my swan costume ready."

◁ PAVLOVA WITH MIKHAIL MORDKIN *in 1920.*

◁ PAVLOVA WITH CHARLIE CHAPLIN, *Hollywood, 1925. For two decades Pavlova crossed the globe, spreading the beauty of dance.*

"I beg you never to try to imitate those who are physically stronger than you. You must realize that your daintiness and fragility are your greatest assets."

PAVEL GREDT, PAVLOVA'S TEACHER

HAROLD LLOYD NICHOLAS 1921–2000
FAYARD NICHOLAS b. 1914

TAP-DANCING BROTHERS Fayard and Harold Nicholas broke through the color barrier to become one of the most popular show business acts of the 1930s and '40s.

THE KINGS OF TAP DANCING

Born to college-educated, musician parents, Fayard and Harold began performing together as children.

They first appeared at New York's famous Cotton Club in the early 1930s, attracting notice for their intricate, high-flying song-and-dance routine. They made their Broadway debut in 1936 alongside the likes of Bob Hope and Ethel Merman, in a version of the Ziegfeld Follies. By the start of the 1940s, the two men were international celebrities. They starred in several hit films, including *Stormy Weather* (1943) with Cab Calloway and Lena Horne, and acquired a reputation as the finest dance team in America.

The brothers continued to perform together for five more decades. Fayard received a Tony award in 1989 for his choreography in the musical *Black and Blue*. The act came to an end in 2000, when Harold died of heart failure.

△ SEEN HERE IN JUNE 1936, *the brothers were photographed arriving at London's Waterloo Station, en route to Manchester, where they would join the cast of the touring show* Blackbirds.

△ THE NICHOLAS BROTHERS, *posing on the Eiffel Tower in 1955. Fayard and Harold popularized tap dancing—which derived from Irish jigs and earlier forms of West African dance—around the world.*

> "They are probably the most amazing dancers I've seen. Those guys are perfect examples of pure genius."
>
> MIKHAIL BARYSHNIKOV

Did you know?

■ Harold Nicholas was married to screen legend Dorothy Dandridge.

■ In 1994 the brothers were presented with a star on the Hollywood Walk of Fame.

■ Harold Lloyd Nicholas was named after the acrobatic silent film star Harold Lloyd.

◁ THE NICHOLAS BROTHERS *inspired many tap dancers who followed them, such as Savion Glover and Gregory Hines, pictured here with Fayard Nicholas.*

△ THE NICHOLAS BROTHERS *with Bob Hope, during a USO show on the aircraft carrier* Ticonderoga, *1965. Hope tried to keep up with the flying feet of Fayard and Harold Nicholas.*

FRED ASTAIRE
(1899–1987)

WITH HIS DANCING ON SCREEN—especially with partner Ginger Rogers—Fred Astaire defined an elegant and sophisticated approach to popular dance.

△ ASTAIRE'S SHOES. *He refused to dance the same steps in any of his films, always working with choreographer Hermes Pan to come up with new moves.*

TOP HAT AND TAILS

The son of Austrian immigrants, Astaire was born Frederick Austerlitz II in Omaha, Nebraska. After his father lost his job, Astaire moved with his sister Adele and mother to New York City, where they found work in vaudeville. As a song-and-dance act, Fred and Adele shifted from comedy to a more artistic performing style, eventually becoming a top draw during the early 1920s. Though considered more talented than her brother by some, Adele retired from show business in 1931, forcing Fred to develop his own routine. Leaving vaudeville, Astaire went to Hollywood already a star and appeared in the musicals *Dancing Lady* (1933) and *Flying Down to Rio* (1933), which included his first pairing with Ginger Rogers. The duo went on to make more immensely popular musicals, including *The Gay Divorcee* (1934), *Swing Time* (1936), and *Shall We Dance* (1937). Fred and Ginger brought to their performances a sexually charged perfectionism that captivated Depression-era audiences. Offering a counterpoint to one another—Astaire witty and sophisticated, Rogers gutsy and effervescent—the couple was one of the finest dance teams ever. Following his run with Rogers, Astaire partnered with a variety of actresses, but never achieved the spark with these women that he had with Rogers. Nevertheless, he continued to dazzle audiences with his technique and dapper character. He danced less in his later career, instead taking dramatic roles in television and film—most notably *The Towering Inferno* (1974).

△ ALTHOUGH HE WAS MOST *famous for his dancing, popular composers worshiped Astaire. He debuted songs for the likes of Cole Porter, Jerome Kern, and the Gershwins.*

Did you know?

■ During World War II, Astaire started a chain of dance studios in New York City bearing his name.

■ Astaire married jockey Robyn Smith in 1980, and lived with her until his death.

■ Fred Astaire's first wife, Phyllis Potter, wouldn't allow Astaire and Rogers to kiss on screen.

"People think I was born in a top hat and tails."

FRED ASTAIRE

▷ ASTAIRE AND RITA HAYWORTH *in* You Were Never Lovelier *(1942). Though the dancing may not have been quite the same as it had been with Rogers, his two pairings with Hayworth were major hits.*

◁ JUST AS THE FILM Swing Time *made Astaire and Rogers the number-one box-office draw in the US in 1936, Astaire was considering an end to their partnership.*

FRED ASTAIRE GINGER ROGERS IN Swing Time

WITH VICTOR MOORE
HELEN BRODERICK
ERIC BLORE
BETTY FURNESS
GEORGES METAXA

Music by JEROME KERN

DIRECTED BY GEORGE STEVENS
A PANDRO S. BERMAN PRODUCTION
LYRICS BY DOROTHY FIELDS

VASLAV NIJINSKY

(1890–1950)

CONSIDERED THE GREATEST BALLET DANCER of the 20th century and a legendary performer whose gravity-defying leaps left audiences gasping, Nijinsky was also a revolutionary choreographer.

Other Ballet Stars

MARGOT FONTEYN (1919–1991) Grand dame of British dance.

RUDOLF NUREYEV (1938–1993) Expressive Russian inheritor of Nijinsky's mantle.

SUZANNE FARRELL b. 1945 Balanchine's favorite ballerina.

THE FOUNDER OF MODERN DANCE

Born in Kiev while his Polish dancer parents were on tour, Nijinsky was trained at Russia's legendary Imperial Ballet School despite his inability to speak Russian. Already a star in 1909, he and his sister Bronislawa, also a dancer, traveled to Paris that year with Sergei Diaghilev's Ballets Russes. Celebrated for his astounding leaps across the stage, Nijinsky's fame grew with his 1911 appearance in the debut performance of Igor Stravinsky's *Petrouchka*, and he began creating choreography. His radical choreography of Claude Debussy's *L'Apres-Midi d'un Faune* and Stravinsky's *Rite of Spring*, controversial to the point of causing riots, were monumental steps forward in the evolution of modern dance.

Despite a lengthy love affair with Diaghilev, Nijinsky married a Hungarian countess named Romola de Pulszka in 1913, with whom he would have two children. Fired by the jealous Diaghilev in 1914, he had a nervous breakdown and eventually retired in 1919 because of his acute paranoid schizophrenia. Nijinsky's next thirty years were spent in various asylums throughout Europe. He died in London at the age of 60.

△ **NIJINSKY** *portrayed the lasting scent of a rose, wafting through the dreams of a girl just returned from a ball in* The Spectre of the Rose.

> ## "There is no great genius without a touch of madness"
>
> VASLAV NIJINSKY

◁ **A POSTER OF NIJINSKI**, *by the painter Leon Bakst. Bakst created Nijinski's sinuous look, overseeing the art direction and costuming of the Ballets Russes.*

Did you know?

■ Nijinsky was an accomplished painter.

■ His career began to slide after his marriage to the dominating Romola de Pulszka in 1913.

△ **NIJINSKY** *(far left) and other members of the Ballets Russes, created a sensation dancing in Igor Stravinksy's* The Rite of Spring *in Paris, 1913.*

▷ **NIJINKSY'S FRANKLY SEXUAL** *interpretation of his role as a mythical satyr in Debussy's* L'Apres-Midi d'un Faune *scandalized audiences in 1912.*

SEX ON THE MIND

STARTING WITH ADAM AND EVE, THE PHENOMENON OF SEX HAS SHAPED ALL ASPECTS of human society, from economics to popular culture, and from religion to politics.

Some have made a business out of studying sex and sexuality. The five men and women profiled here used various methods, some clinical, some commercial, some diabolical, to influence the world's thinking about sex and sexuality and the roles they play in our lives. Hugh Hefner and the Marquis de Sade approached sex in ways that many consider pornographic or exploitative, but enduring interest in their creations suggests that they appealed to a basic aspect of human nature. Dr. Ruth and Masters and Johnson used a more clinical approach, while Freud's theories put sexuality at the core of human behavior. Their legacies continue to be built upon today as we keep trying to understand this primal element of human existence. And while their teachings and findings may fall in and out of favor, it is certain that human beings will never stop being fascinated by sex.

△ WHILE HIERONYMOUS BOSCH *may have portrayed the Garden of Earthly Delights (c. 1500) as a place of decadence and excess, the detail and variety of acts depicted prove that preoccupation with sex is hardly modern.*

SIGMUND FREUD
(1856–1939)

THE FOUNDER OF PSYCHOANALYSIS, Austrian neurologist Sigmund Freud developed theories about the workings of the human mind that dominated the 20th century.

PSYCHOANALYSIS

Born into a large Jewish family in Freiburg, Moravia (now part of Czechoslovakia), Freud grew up in Vienna after his family moved there in 1860. He studied medicine at the University of Vienna, and was appointed lecturer in neuropathology there in 1885. Freud continued his studies in Paris, returning in 1886 to marry Martha Bernays, with whom he had six children. He established himself as a clinical neuropsychologist in partnership with physician Josef Breuer. Their *Studies in Hysteria* (1895) described the technique of "free association," which encouraged the patient to express random thoughts in the belief that unarticulated material would be uncovered from the part of the mind that Freud termed the unconscious. Freud and Breuer eventually parted and Freud continued his work. In 1900 he published *The Interpretation of Dreams*, which defined dreams as subconscious expressions of repressed desires. Freud developed a model of the mind consisting of three elements: the id, the source of instinctive and pleasure urges; the ego, the link between the id and the external world; and the superego, the societal norms we set for ourselves through instruction from our parents. At the same time he saw patients, Freud worked diligently and successfully to advance his ideas, which would in time saturate Western culture. For his last 15 years, Freud battled oral cancer developed from cigar smoking. Weary from his flight from the Nazis in 1938, and experiencing great pain, he fulfilled his wish to die in freedom—he asked his doctor to give him a fatal injection of morphine.

△ FREUD, *as interpreted by French artist Jean Cocteau, c. 1929.*

Sigmund Freud

Anna Freud

Heinz, his grandson

△ FREUD, HIS DAUGHTER ANNA, *and grandson Heinz, c. 1925. Anna, a psychoanalyst specializing in children, carried on Freud's work.*

HUGH HEFNER
b. 1926

HUGH HEFNER EMBODIES the ideals of hedonism, stylishness, and sexual freedom to millions of men (and some women) worldwide thanks to *Playboy*, the magazine he founded and publishes.

THE ULTIMATE PLAYBOY

Born in Chicago, Hefner dreamed of becoming a successful cartoonist. After two years in the Army, he graduated from the University of Illinois where he had worked on the newspaper. For a short time he was a copywriter at *Esquire* magazine but he quit after he was refused a raise. In 1953 he conceived of the idea of *Playboy*. He produced the first issue on a card table at home. Featuring a nude photo of Marilyn Monroe, it quickly sold out. As *Playboy*'s popularity grew, the magazine helped usher in a new sexual openness in America. The suave Hefner became the ultimate playboy, hosting extravagant parties at his mansion attended by celebrities and scores of women. He also built Playboy Enterprises into an empire that now includes magazines, television, and electronic media. Hefner began slowing down in the late 1980s after suffering a minor stroke. Christine Hefner, his daughter from an early marriage that ended in divorce in 1959, took over *Playboy*'s daily operations. Hefner, the longtime swinging single, then married former Playmate Kimberly Conrad in 1989. After nine years and two children, the couple separated and now "Hef," dressed in his trademark smoking jacket, once again holds soirées in his California mansion.

△ THE PLAYBOY *empire boasted 35 Playboy Clubs in cities from Tokyo to Des Moines. The nightclubs featured top-tier entertainment and Playboy Bunnies serving cocktails.*

Did you know?

■ *Playboy* was almost named *Stag Party*, but Hefner decided that *Playboy* conveyed a more sophisticated image.

■ A brass plate on the original Playboy Mansion in Chicago read *Si Non Oscillas, Noli Tintinnare*—"If you don't swing, don't ring."

■ Scientists who discovered a type of marsh rabbit gave it the classification *Sylvilagus palustris hefneri*, in honor of *Playboy*'s mascot.

△ PORTRAIT OF FREUD.
He published more than 20 volumes of theory and clinical studies, and coined concepts and terms such as libido, subconscious, and inferiority complex.

Did you know?

■ Early in his career Freud developed an interest in the pharmaceutical benefits of cocaine, which he pursued for several years with very limited results.

■ Freud believed that all dreams, even nightmares, fulfill our unconscious needs and desires.

■ Freud's books were among the first to be burned as examples of "Jewish science" when the Nazis took power in Germany.

"If you had to sum up the idea of Playboy, it is anti-Puritanism."

HUGH HEFNER

◁ HEFNER *celebrated his 75th birthday in 2001 with four of his reported seven girlfriends, all between the ages of 19 and 28.*

△ HEFNER SOLD *54,175 copies of the first issue of* Playboy. *It was 44 pages long and cost 50 cents. While it featured a naked picture of Marilyn Monroe, the real reason men bought it was for the Sherlock Holmes story and the piece on office design—or so they said.*

MARQUIS DE SADE
(1740–1814)

THE FRENCH AUTHOR known as the Marquis de Sade is commonly viewed as the embodiment of perverted sexual cruelty: The word "sadism"— a tendency to find sexual gratification through the infliction of pain— is derived from his name.

△ THOUGH DE SADE *had shed blood for "pleasure," he was repelled by the Reign of Terror that freed him.*

THE PLEASURES OF PAIN
Sade, born Donatien Alphonse Francois, Comte de Sade, was a French aristocrat notorious for sexually abusing a long string of lovers—including his wife, female prostitutes, and other men. His brutal and violent sexual behavior resulted in several arrests and eventually a death sentence for attempted murder—after two prostitutes became sick from his aphrodisiac-laced candy. De Sade escaped to Italy for a short time, during which he was sentenced to death in absentia, beginning a cycle of captures and escapes that lasted until 1778, when he was finally imprisoned in the Bastille for eleven years. While in prison, de Sade wrote the infamous novels *Justine* and *The 120 Days of Sodom*, both of which contain graphic sexual and violent content that continues to shock readers. Freed from prison by the French Revolution, he spent a few years in public life before sinking into poverty. He was ultimately sent to the insane asylum Charenton, where he died in 1814.

Did you know?

■ As a boy, de Sade was a student at a Jesuit school in Paris, where he was often whipped.

■ His sexual exploits were so notorious that French police once ordered brothels not to accept de Sade's business.

■ The Marquis de Sade was the subject of two recent films—*Sade*, a documentary, and *Quills*, starring Geoffrey Rush and Kate Winslet.

△ THE RUINS OF DE SADE'S *chateau, La Coste, in Provence, where he often took refuge after time spent in prison or when his depravities had made him* persona non grata *in Paris, even among the debauched courts of the French kings.*

DR. RUTH WESTHEIMER
b. 1928

THE DIMINUTIVE (four-foot-seven-inch) Dr. Westheimer is perhaps the world's most popular authority on matters of sex.

GOOD SEX
Born in Frankfurt, Germany, to a wealthy Jewish family, Westheimer fled Germany as a young girl when her father was arrested by the Nazis. As a student at a Swiss school and orphanage she created controversy by sharing her thoughts on sex and other taboo subjects with her classmates. At the age of 16, she moved to Israel, where she lived on a kibbutz. Westheimer eventually studied psychology at the Sorbonne in Paris, and then in 1956, she moved to New York to study sociology at the New School for Social Research and then family and sex counseling at Columbia University. She then became an associate professor of sex counseling at Lehman College in the Bronx. Her rise to national prominence came when her popular New York radio call-in show, "Sexually Speaking," was syndicated nationally in 1984. Since then, she has dispensed sexual advice and information in newspapers across the country and on numerous talk shows, as well as through her own cable TV series. She has written several books, including *Dr. Ruth's Guide to Good Sex*.

Sex Doctors

RICHARD VON KRAFFT-EBING (1840–1902) Catalogued sexual abnormalities.

WILHELM REICH (1897–1957) Advocate of the power of the orgasm.

HAVELOCK ELLIS (1859–1939) First to study sexuality scientifically.

Dr. Ruth Westheimer

Gloria Steinem, publisher of MS *magazine*

Feminist actress Marlo Thomas

△ WESTHEIMER'S CANDOR *extends to feminist issues; she appears here in 1987 with two of the movement's leading voices.*

△ AFTER TWO BRIEF EARLY MARRIAGES, *Dr. Ruth initially raised her daughter Miriam alone. She and her third husband, Fred Westheimer, also have a son and two grandchildren. The National Mother's Day Committee has honored her as Mother of the Year.*

Did you know?

■ Westheimer never saw her family again after she fled to Switzerland.

■ Her birth name was Karola Ruth Siegel.

■ When Westheimer lived in Israel in the late 1940s, a bomb exploded outside her residence and blew off the top of one of her feet.

"She has become the Julia Child of sex."

GLORIA STEINEM

▷ DR. RUTH'S *outgoing personality and her outspokenness on sexual issues has made her as much a celebrity as an educator and counselor. Here she is seen with socialite Ivana Trump, former wife of real estate tycoon Donald Trump.*

WILLIAM MASTERS (1915–2001)
VIRGINIA JOHNSON b. 1925

WILLIAM MASTERS AND VIRGINIA JOHNSON pioneered research on sexuality by observing human sexual activity in a laboratory environment.

THE SCIENCE OF SEX

Masters, who was a gynecologist, began his work on sexual research in 1954. Johnson, a psychologist, joined him in 1957 as a research associate. Together in 1964 they began the Reproductive Biology Research Foundation, where the team conducted research on the psychology and physiology of human sexual activity—often by observing volunteers engaging in sexual intercourse. Masters and Johnson used medical equipment such as electroencephalographs to record the sexual reactions of their subjects. They released their findings in a groundbreaking, best-selling book, *Human Sexual Response* (1966). The couple married in 1971, and continued to publish studies and books based on their research on sexuality. They divorced in 1993, and in 2001 Masters died of complications from Parkinson's disease.

△ MASTERS AND JOHNSON, *as well as popularizing the study of sex, also authored a textbook on sexuality.*

Did you know?

■ After his death Masters was found to have amassed one of the world's largest collections of pornography for research purposes.

■ Their book, *Homosexuality in Perspective,* debunked the notion that homosexuality is a mental illness. However, the pair also claimed they could "cure" homosexuals who wished to become heterosexuals.

"When things don't work well in the bedroom, they don't work well in the living room, either."

MASTERS AND JOHNSON

Virginia Johnson

William Masters

△ MASTERS AND JOHNSON *identified four phases in the human sexual response cycle: excitement, plateau, orgasm, and resolution.*

THE FALL OF THE IRON CURTAIN

In 1946, Winston Churchill gave a speech at Westminster College in Fulton, Missouri, in which he used the term "Iron Curtain" to describe the division of Post-World War II Europe into communist and democratic states.

The phrase stuck, and so did the division, which dominated global relations for over 40 years. The curtain did not come down until the late 1980s, when reform efforts of Soviet and Chinese heads of state, the collapse of communist economies and popular unrest met strong Western leadership. British prime minister Margaret Thatcher and US president Ronald Reagan took strong anticommunist stances, and Lech Walesa led the peaceful overthrow of the Soviet-backed Polish government. Mikhail Gorbachev created an alternative to rigid communist ideology in the Soviet Union while in China, Deng Xiaoping worked free-market principles into Maoism.

△ A SOVIET PROPAGANDA *poster, c. 1944.*

△ THE MUCH-HATED *Berlin Wall, for decades the most potent symbol of the Cold War, was finally torn down on November 9, 1989, and the long-divided former capital of Germany became one.*

MIKHAIL GORBACHEV
b. 1931

As GENERAL SECRETARY of the Soviet Communist party, Mikhail Gorbachev brought down the Iron Curtain.

PERESTROIKA

Gorbachev grew up in Privolnoye in southwestern Russia. Though the region was sent into famine by Stalin's collectivization, both his father and grandfather were members of the Communist party. He became a party member in 1952, and in 1955 received a law degree from Moscow State University. He worked in various party organizations before becoming first secretary of the regional party in 1970. In 1985 Gorbachev was elected secretary of the Central Committee of the Communist Party of the Soviet Union. His immediate task was to reinvigorate the stagnant Soviet economy, which he accomplished by initiating reforms he called *glasnost* (openness) and *perestroika* (restructuring). Glasnost expanded freedom of expression and information. Part of this policy was Gorbachev's willingness to interact with the Soviet people which won him many admirers. Perestroika attempted to democratize the Soviet political and economic systems through open contests, some use of the secret ballot, and limited free-market mechanisms. These reforms encountered resistance from communist hard-liners unwilling to relinquish control.

Gorbachev supported the reformist communists in the Soviet-bloc countries of Eastern Europe, and gradually withdrew Soviet troops from Poland, Hungary, and Czechoslovakia. In the summer of 1990, he agreed to the reunification of East and West Germany. Later that year, he received the Nobel Peace Prize. As the party's power waned, Gorbachev was elected to the newly created post of president of the USSR. The Communist party's constitutionally guaranteed monopoly of political power was abolished, paving the way for the legalization of other political parties. A short coup in August 1991 by communist hard-liners left Gorbachev and his family under house arrest for a week. His presidency weakened, Gorbachev resigned on December 25, 1991.

▷ RAISA GORBACHEV, *an elegant and intelligent partner for her husband, helped to create a new vision of a Russia open to the West.*

> "Every part of our program of perestroika . . . is fully based on the principle of more socialism and more democracy."
>
> MIKHAIL GORBACHEV

△ COMMUNIST HARD-LINERS, *in Moscow on March 5, 1995, carrying red flags and portraits of Stalin and marching to Stalin's grave to commemorate his death on March 5, 1953.*

◁ JOURNALISTS IN FRONT *of a giant poster of Gorbachev in Cuba in 1999.* Time *magazine named Gorbachev not just Man of the Year in 1987, but Man of the Decade in 1989. Unlike his predecessors, he did not encourage a cult of personality.*

The White House *(parliament building)*

Soviet soldiers took the side of reformers in 1991.

△ GORBACHEV AND REAGAN
signed a treaty limiting short and intermediate range missiles on December 8, 1987.

Did you know?

■ Gorbachev joined the youth wing of the Communist party when he was 15.

■ Gorbachev appeared in a 1997 ad for Pizza Hut in Moscow.

■ When Gorbachev was elected secretary of the CPSU's Central Committee, some of his countrymen believed his success had been foretold in the Bible, and that the birthmark on his forehead was a symbol of his destiny.

◁ HARD LINE COMMUNISTS *tried to take over the Soviet government in August of 1991. The USSR was officially dissolved four months later, when Mikhail Gorbachev stepped down and Boris Yeltsin took over as president of the new Russian Federation.*

RONALD REAGAN
b. 1911

RONALD REAGAN, the 40th president of the United States, was noted for his conservatism and credited by many with helping end the Cold War through his strong stance against communism.

THE GREAT COMMUNICATOR

Raised in Illinois by his devout mother and alcoholic father, Reagan earned a bachelor's degree in economics and sociology at Eureka College before beginning a job as a sportscaster in Iowa. He soon turned to acting, and went on to appear in more than 50 films, often playing easygoing "good guys." As Reagan's acting career wound down, he shifted into conservative politics. He served two terms as governor of California (1966–74), and in 1980 was elected president as the Republican candidate. Reagan's aggressive anti-communist stance and harsh anti-Soviet rhetoric contributed to poor relations with the Soviet Union in the first years of his presidency, yet his substantial military spending imposed a strain on the Soviet economy that many believe contributed in large part to the collapse of the Soviet Union. During his second term, Reagan was more accommodating to the Soviets. He supported Gorbachev's policies of *glasnost* and *perestroika* after 1985. Among the achievements of this period was the 1987 Intermediate-range Nuclear Forces (INF) Treaty, the first arms-control pact to require an actual reduction in nuclear arsenals. Reagan's second term ended in 1988. In 1994, the former president revealed that he was suffering from Alzheimer's disease, and has since avoided all public appearances.

Did you know?

■ Reagan is the only divorced president thus far. His ten-year marriage to costar Jane Wyman ended in 1948. He married Nancy Davis in 1952.

■ Reagan landed a job as a sportscaster at station WOC in Davenport, Iowa, by delivering an exciting play-by-play description of a Eureka College football game— entirely from memory.

△ **THE REAGANS** *reestablished a pride and formality in the White House, but many Americans found fault with the First Lady's preoccupation with style and celebrity, especially during the economic downturn of the early 1980s.*

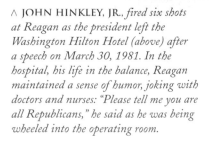

∧ **JOHN HINKLEY, JR.,** *fired six shots at Reagan as the president left the Washington Hilton Hotel (above) after a speech on March 30, 1981. In the hospital, his life in the balance, Reagan maintained a sense of humor, joking with doctors and nurses: "Please tell me you are all Republicans," he said as he was being wheeled into the operating room.*

▷ **WHILE MANY OF** *his films were well-reviewed, and he was an A-list Hollywood celebrity, Reagan is also remembered for the comedy* Bedtime for Bonzo, *in which he and Diana Lynn try to teach a chimp right from wrong.*

MARGARET THATCHER

b. 1925

MARGARET THATCHER served Britain's Conservative party as Europe's first female prime minister from 1979 to 1990, earning both praise and blame for toppling Britain's welfare state and promoting capitalism.

△ THATCHER'S DECISION *to accept US cruise missiles at the Greenham Common Royal Air Force Base in the early 1980s stirred vigorous dissent among the British population.*

THE IRON LADY

Thatcher studied chemistry at Oxford University and worked briefly as a chemist before becoming a barrister in 1954. She married wealthy industrialist Denis Thatcher, who supported her political ambition. In 1959, Thatcher was elected to the House of Commons, and rose steadily to hold many positions in Parliament, including secretary of state for health and education in the Conservative government of Edward Heath. As prime minister starting in 1979, she advocated greater independence of the individual from the state and a smaller government role in the economy. Her policies included privatization of state-owned enterprises and reductions in expenditures on social services such as health care, education, and housing. Thatcher shared Ronald Reagan's view of the Soviet Union as an "evil empire," and encouraged him to heavily fund military spending as a means of bringing Russia to the negotiating table. When Mikhail Gorbachev rose to power in the Soviet Union in 1985, Thatcher joined Reagan in encouraging Gorbachev to push his free market–based policy of perestroika to its limits. In 1990, Thatcher resigned as prime minister after losing the support of the Conservative party, whose members objected to her stance against a European union and her attempt to institute a widely unpopular poll tax—a per capita tax to pay for local government.

△ THATCHER'S *initial willingness to oppose communism in the late 1970s—as America still reeled from Vietnam—is believed to have set the stage for the final phase of the Cold War.*

Did you know?

■ Thatcher eliminated a program providing free milk to schoolchildren—prompting opponents in the Labour Party to call her "Thatcher the milk snatcher."

■ She was the only British prime minister in the 20th century to win three straight terms, and was, at her resignation, Britain's longest continuously serving PM since 1827.

∧ TAKING HER PLACE *at 10 Downing Street in 1979, Thatcher would soon prove to be a major influence on America, as Reagan imitated many of her domestic initiatives.*

"If you want anything said, ask a man; if you want anything done, ask a woman."
MARGARET THATCHER

▷ THATCHER GAVE BIRTH *to twins, Mark and Carol on August 15, 1953. Here the family celebrates the Thatchers' 25th wedding anniversary in December 1976.*

DENG XIAOPING
(1904–1997)

THE MOST POWERFUL FIGURE in the People's Republic of China from the late 1970s until his death, Communist party leader Deng Xiaoping incorporated elements of capitalism into the Chinese economy.

△ **STAMPS WERE ISSUED** *from Togo (above) and more than 20 other nations were issued to commemorate the return of Hong Kong from the UK to China on July 1, 1997.*

CHAIRMAN DENG

Born in the Sichuan province of China, between 1921 and 1924 Deng was a student in France, where he became active in the communist movement. He then studied for a year in the Soviet Union before returning to his native China, where he became a leading political and military organizer.

In 1952 Deng was summoned to Beijing. He first served as vice premier and in 1954 became general secretary of the Chinese Communist Party (CCP). In 1955 he was made a member of the ruling Political Bureau. During the Cultural Revolution (1966–76) Deng lost these positions, but he was reinstated in the late 1970s.

As vice chairman of the CCP and a member of its powerful Political Bureau Standing Committee, Deng engineered important reforms to help China move from a managed economy to free markets. He stressed individual responsibility in economic decisions and material incentives as the reward for industry and initiative. He freed many industries from excessive government regulation and encouraged managers to pursue the profit motive. Perhaps most significant, Deng strengthened China's trade and cultural ties with the West and opened up China to foreign investment. He continued to be the ultimate authority in Chinese government until the early 1990s, and maintained an influence on China's policy until his death.

△ **DENG REFORMED** *the Chinese economy after decades of brutal mismanagement by Mao, thereby lifting the standard of living for hundreds of millions in the 1980s.*

> ## "Marx sits up in heaven, and he is very powerful. He sees what we are doing, and he doesn't like it."
>
> DENG XIAOPING

Did you know?

■ Deng Xiaoping supported the use of force to suppress the 1989 student protests in Tiananmen Square. The clash resulted in an estimated 7,000 deaths and more than 20,000 injuries.

■ Deng's birth name was Deng Xixian, a two-character Chinese name that means "First Saint." Later, he took the name Deng Xiaoping, which means "Little Peace."

◁ **AS COMMUNIST CHINA** *celebrated its 50th birthday in 1999, it was Deng Xiaoping's portrait that overshadowed Mao Zedong's during this parade through Tiananmen Square in Beijing.*

▷ **WHILE STUDYING** *in France in the 1920s, Deng worked in an iron plant, as a kitchen helper, and at the Renault auto factory.*

LECH WALESA

b. 1943

LABOR ACTIVIST Lech Walesa led the movement that ended communist rule in Poland and served as president from 1990–1995.

SOLIDARITY

△ WALESA has eight children. Here he holds his daughter, Maria Victoria, while picnicking near Gdansk on May 21, 1983. He is a devout Roman Catholic.

The son of farmers in Popowa, Poland, Walesa had only a primary and vocational education when he began work as an electrician in the Gdansk shipyard in 1967. In 1976 he was fired from his job for being an antigovernment union activist. Walesa went on to take charge of the Interfactory Strike Committee that united the enterprises of the Gdansk-Sopot Gdynia area. In August 1980 this committee declared a general strike and issued a set of what were considered audacious political demands, including the right to strike and to form free trade unions. The communist authorities yielded to the workers' principal demands, and on August 31 Walesa signed an agreement with Poland's deputy premier giving workers the right to organize freely and independently. The Interfactory Strike Committee was reorganized into a national federation of unions under the name "Solidarity," with Walesa as its chairman. However the communist government of Poland imposed martial law in December 1981 and Solidarity was outlawed. But a new wave of unrest in 1988 forced the Polish government to renegotiate with the group. Walesa meanwhile had been awarded the 1983 Nobel Peace Prize and had kept his organization active underground. In 1988 the organization regained its legal status and the right to compete for a limited number of seats in the newly established Polish parliament. Solidarity won the majority of those seats, and began to lead the Polish government. In 1990 Walesa won Poland's first direct presidential election by a landslide, becoming the country's first non-communist leader in 40 years. As president, he oversaw the conversion of Poland's economy into a free market system. His support slipped in the early 1990s, however, in part because he refused to relax strict prohibitions on abortion, and in 1995 he lost his bid for reelection.

△ WALESA ADDRESSED shipyard workers on August 8, 1980 after emerging as the leader of the first free trade union in a Soviet bloc country—though he had already been fired for his labor agitation.

Did you know?

■ Walesa feared involuntary exile if he traveled to Norway to accept the Nobel Peace Prize, so his wife, Danuta, went to accept the award on his behalf.

■ Walesa is an avid Ping-Pong player.

■ Walesa once claimed he had never read a serious book in his life.

Deposed Leaders

WOJCIECH JARUZELSKI b. 1923 Polish general, kept Soviets at bay.

ERICH HONECKER (1912–1994) East German leader, escaped to Chile.

NICOLAE CEAUSESCU (1918–1989) Despised Romanian dictator.

△ IN 1989, SOLIDARITY NEGOTIATED NATIONAL ELECTIONS. Lech Walesa was elected the first non-communist Prime Minister of Poland since the 1950s. This began the so-called "velvet revolution" among Eastern European nations.

PHOTO CREDITS

Cover	Credit
Row I	
1	CORBIS
2	Bettmann/CORBIS
3	CORBIS
4-7	Bettmann/CORBIS
Row 2	
1	CORBIS
2	Bettmann/CORBIS
3	Reuters NewMedia Inc./CORBIS
4	Francis G. Mayer/CORBIS
5	Bettmann/CORBIS
6	Bettmann/CORBIS
7	Getty Images/Hulton Archive
Row 3	
1-2	Bettmann/CORBIS
3	Underwood & Underwood/CORBIS
4-5	Getty Images/Hulton Archive
6	Archivo Iconografico, S.A./CORBIS
7	Bettmann/CORBIS
Row 4	
1	Mitchell Gerber/CORBIS
2	Bettmann/CORBIS
3	Getty Images/Hulton Archive
4	Bettmann/CORBIS
5	Underwood & Underwood/CORBIS
6	Getty Images/Hulton Archive
7	Catherine Karnow/CORBIS
Row 5	
1	David & Peter Turnley/CORBIS
2	Bettmann/CORBIS
3	Reuters NewMedia Inc./CORBIS
4	Flip Schulke/CORBIS
5	Lynn Goldsmith/CORBIS
6	Getty Images/Hulton Archive
7	Bettmann/CORBIS
Row 6	
1	CORBIS
2-3	Bettmann/CORBIS
4	Neal Preston/CORBIS
5	Bettmann/CORBIS
6	Underwood & Underwood/CORBIS
7	Bettmann/CORBIS
Row 7	
1	CORBIS
2-3	Bettmann/CORBIS
4	Hulton-Deutsch Collection/CORBIS
5	Bettmann/CORBIS
6	CORBIS
7	Doug Wilson/CORBIS

Page #/Position		Credit
ii	Row 1	
ii	l	CORBIS
ii	c	Getty Images/Hulton Archive
ii	r	Bettmann/CORBIS
ii	Row 2	
ii	l	CORBIS
ii	c	AP Photo/Emile Wamsteker
ii	r	Getty Images/Hulton Archive

Page #/Position		Credit
ii	Row 3	
ii	l	Douglas Kirkland/CORBIS
ii	c	Courtesy of Showtime Archives {Toronto}
ii	r	Mitchell Gerber/CORBIS
ii	Row 4	
ii	l	CORBIS
ii	c	Bettmann/CORBIS
ii	r	Courtesy of Showtime Archives {Toronto}
ii	Row 5	
ii	l	Bettmann/CORBIS
ii	c	Getty Images/Hulton Archive
ii	r	Norman Parkinson Limited/Fiona Cowan/CORBIS
ii	Row 6	
ii	l	Bettmann/CORBIS
ii	c	AP Photo
ii	r	Hulton-Deutsch Collection/CORBIS
ii	Row 7	
ii	l, c	Hulton-Deutsch Collection/CORBIS
ii	r	Leonard de Selva/CORBIS
8bl		Photos 12.com-ARJ
8tc		David Lees/CORBIS
8-9		Bettmann/CORBIS
9tl		Bettmann/CORBIS
9c		National Gallery Collection; By kind permission of the Trustees of the National Gallery, London/CORBIS
9b		E_imédia/CORBIS
9cr		Elio Ciol/CORBIS
10tl		Stapleton Collection, UK/Bridgeman Art Library
10bl		Bibliotheque Nationale, Paris/Giraudon-Bridgeman Art Library
10tr		Private Collection/Bridgeman Art Library
10br		Archivo Iconografico, S.A./CORBIS
11cl		Seattle Art Museum, Seattle, USA/Giraudon-Bridgeman Art Library
11tr		Bettmann/CORBIS
11br		Reuters NewMedia Inc./CORBIS
12tl		Ali Meyer/CORBIS
12bl, cr		Photos 12.com-ARJ
13bl		Musee Guimet, Paris, France/Bridgeman Art Library
13bc		David & Peter Turnley/CORBIS
13tr, br		Photos 12.com-ARJ
14bl		Dean Conger/CORBIS
14tc		Photos 12.com-Oasis
14-15		Photos 12.com-ARJ
15bc		Michael Nicholson/CORBIS
15tr		British Museum, London, UK/DK Picture Library
15cr		North Carolina Museum of Art/CORBIS
16bl		Chris Hellier/CORBIS
16tc, br		Getty Images/Hulton Archive
16tr		Gianni Dagli Orti/CORBIS

Page #/Position	Credit
17tl, bc	Getty Images/Hulton Archive
17tr	Itar-Tass from Sovfoto/EastfotoFOTO X-341984
18bl	AP Photo Horace Court
18c	AP Photo/Butterfield and Butterfield via New York Post)
18br	Bettmann/CORBIS
18-19	Getty Images/Hulton Archive
19c	David J. & Janice L. Frent Collection/CORBIS
19bc	AP Photo
19tr	Flip Schulke/CORBIS
20tl	Bettmann/CORBIS
20c	David J. & Janice L. Frent Collection/CORBIS
20bl, br, tl	Getty Images/Hulton Archive
21c	David Murray/DK Picture Library
21tr	AP Photo
21br	AP Photo/Gene Herrick
22bl, br	Photos12.com-ARJ
22c	The Musee Marmottan/DK Picture Library
23bl	Private Collection/Roger-Viollet, Paris/Bridgeman Art Library
23tc	Bridgeman Art Library
23bc	Susanna Price/DK Picture Library
23tr	Getty Images/Hulton Archive
23cr, br	Susanna Price/The Musee Marmottan/DK Picture Library
24tl, br	Photos12.com-ARJ
24bc	Private Collection/Roger-Viollet, Paris/Bridgeman Art Library
25tl	Musee D'Orsay/DK Picture Library
25bc	Private Collection/Christie's Images/Bridgeman Art Library
25tr	Getty Images/Hulton Archive
25br	Photos12.com-ARJ
26tl	Geoffrey Clements/CORBIS
26br	Photos12.com-ARJ
27bl	Getty Images/Hulton Archive
27tr	Photos12.com-ARJ
27br	Musee de la Revolution Francaise, Vizille, France/Visual Arts Library, London, UK/Bridgeman Art Library
28	Bettmann/CORBIS
28-29	CORBIS
29c, bc	Photos 12.com-ARJ
29br	Bettmann/CORBIS
30bl, tc	Bettmann/CORBIS
30br	AP Photo
30-31	Bettmann/CORBIS
32bl	Courtesy NASA
32tc	Cathy Crawford/CORBIS
32br	Getty Images/Hulton Archive
32-33	Bettmann/CORBIS
33bc	Sovfoto/Eastfoto
33cr,	
34bl	Itar-Tass from Sovfoto
34tc	Bettmann/CORBIS
34bc	Sovfoto/Eastfoto
34-35	Bettmann/CORBIS
35tl	AFP/CORBIS
35bl, tr	Courtesy NASA

Page #/Position	Credit	Page #/Position	Credit	Page #/Position	Credit
35br	Bettmann/CORBIS	50bl	Werner Forman/CORBIS	66	Bettmann/CORBIS
36bl	Bob Krist/CORBIS	50br	CORBIS	66-67	CORBIS
36tc	Ashmolean Museum, Oxford, UK/Bridgeman Art Library	50-51	Bettmann/CORBIS	67bl	Photofest
		51c	Underwood & Underwood/CORBIS	67tr	Bettmann/CORBIS
36br	Gianni Dagli Orti/CORBIS			67br	CORBIS
37tl	Adam Woolfitt/CORBIS	51bc	Paul A. Souders/CORBIS	68bl	AP Photo/Peter Dejong
37tc	Bettmann/CORBIS	51cr	Bettmann/CORBIS	68tc	David J. & Janice L. Frent Collection/CORBIS
37bc	Yale Center for British Art, Paul Mellon Collection, USA/Photo: Bridgeman Art Library	52tl	Bettmann/CORBIS		
		52bl	Getty Images/Hulton Archive	68br	Sovfoto/Eastfoto
		52br	Tom Bean/CORBIS	69bl	Getty Images/Hulton Archive
37cr	Archivo Iconografico, S.A./CORBIS	53tl	Reuters NewMedia Inc./CORBIS	69tc	Hans Halberstadt/Sovfoto
		53tr	Private Collection/Bridgeman Art Library	69tr	Shepard Sherbell/CORBIS
37br	Private Collection/Bridgeman Art Library			69cr	Itar-Tass from Sovfoto
		53br	Library of Congress, Washington D.C., USA/Bridgeman Art Library	69br, 70tl	Sovfoto/Eastfoto
38tl, br	Getty Images/Hulton Archive			70bc	Getty Images/Hulton Archive
38bl	Private Collection/The Stapleton Collection/Bridgeman Art Library			70cr, br	Sovfoto/Eastfoto
		54bl	Jan Butchofsky-Houser/CORBIS	71bl	Bettmann/CORBIS
39bl	Private Collection/Bridgeman Art Library	54tc	Geoff Brightling/DK Picture Library	71tr	Leonard de Selva/CORBIS
				71cr	Sovfoto/Eastfoto
39tr	Private Collection/The Stapleton Collection/Bridgeman Art Library	54br	CORBIS	72tl, br	Sovfoto/Eastfoto
		55tl	Medford Historical Society Collection/CORBIS	72bl	Tim Page/CORBIS
39br	Bettmann/CORBIS			72cr	Amos Nachoum/CORBIS
40tl	Yale Center for British Art, Paul Mellon Collection, USA/Photo: Bridgeman Art Library	55bl, tc	CORBIS	73cl	Cathy Crawford/CORBIS
		55bc, br	Bettmann/CORBIS	73bl, tr	Getty Images/Hulton Archive
		56tl, tr	Bettmann/CORBIS	73br	The Illustrated London News Picture Library, London, UK/Bridgeman Art Library
40bc	British Museum, London, UK/Bridgeman Art Library	56bc	Getty Images/Hulton Archive		
40br	Archivo Iconografico, S.A./CORBIS	57tl	Private Collection/Bridgeman Art Library	74bl	Reuters NewMedia Inc./CORBIS
				74c	AP Photo/Steve McHenry
41bl	Bridgeman Art Library, London, UK/Bridgeman Art Library	57bl	Joseph Sohm; ChromoSohm Inc./CORBIS	74-75t	AP Photo/Danny Johnston
				74-75b	AP Photo/Robert Button
41tr	Private Collection/Bridgeman Art Library	57tr	Bettmann/CORBIS	75bc	Getty Images/Hulton Archive
		57br	Getty Images/Hulton Archive	75tr	Horace Bristol/CORBIS
41br	Bettmann/CORBIS	58tl, c, bc, cr	Jonathan Blair/CORBIS	76bl	Doug Wilson/CORBIS
42bl	O'Brien Productions/CORBIS	58br	Dave G. Houser/CORBIS	76tc	Ed Kashi/CORBIS
42c	Associated Press, AP	59cl, tr	Bettmann/CORBIS	76c	CORBIS
42br	Larry Downing Getty Images News Services	59br	Richard Cummins/CORBIS	76-77t	Hulton-Deutsch Collection/CORBIS
		60bl	Bettmann/CORBIS		
42-43	CORBIS	60tc	Getty Images/Hulton Archive	76-77b	Joseph Sohm; ChromoSohm Inc./CORBIS
43bc, cr	Bettmann/CORBIS	60br	Vatican Museums and Galleries, Vatican City, Italy/Bridgeman Art Library		
43tr	Digital Art/CORBIS			77tr	Getty Images/Hulton Archive
44cl, bl, tc 44br,	AFP/CORBIS			77br	Joseph Sohm; ChromoSohm Inc./CORBIS
		60-61	Galleria dell'Accademia, Florence, Italy/Bridgeman Art Library		
44-45	Getty Images/Hulton Archive	61c	British Museum, London, UK/Bridgeman Art Library	78bl	Bettmann/CORBIS
45bl, bc	Getty Images/Hulton Archive			78tr	Gallo Images/CORBIS
45tr	Private Collection/Bridgeman Art Library	61bc	Archivo Iconografico, S.A./CORBIS	78br, 79 bl	David & Peter Turnley/CORBIS
				79bc	Hulton-Deutsch Collection/CORBIS
46bl	Seattle Post-Intelligencer Collection; Museum of History & Industry/CORBIS	61tr	National Galery of Victoria, Melbourne, Australia/Felton Bequest/Bridgeman Art Library		
				79tr	Getty Images/Hulton Archive
		62tl	Leonard de Selva/CORBIS	79br	Bettmann/CORBIS
46tc	Courtesy of Showtime Archives (Toronto)	62bl	Victoria & Albert Museum, London, UK/Bridgeman Art Library	80tl	Catherine Karnow/CORBIS
				80bl	Reuters NewMedia Inc./CORBIS
46br	AP Photo/White House Photo			80br, 80-81, 81tc, bc, tr	Bettmann/CORBIS
46-47	CORBIS	62c	Leonard de Selva/CORBIS		
47c, bl	Courtesy of Showtime Archives (Toronto)	62br	Galleria dell'Accademia, Venice, Italy/Bridgeman Art Library	82c	Joseph Sohm; Visions of America/CORBIS
		62-63	Bettmann/CORBIS	82-83t	Bettmann/CORBIS
47cr	Contemporary African Art Collection Limited/CORBIS	63bl	Louvre, Paris/Bridgeman Art Library	82-83b	Buddy Mays/CORBIS
				83bc	Museum of the City of New York/CORBIS
48cl	Courtesy of Showtime Archives (Toronto)	63bc	Santa Croce, Florence, Italy/Bridgeman Art Library		
				83tr	Bettmann/CORBIS
48tc	Bettmann/CORBIS	63tr	Palazzo Vecchio (Palazzo della Signoria) Florence, Italy/Bridgeman Art Library	83br	Metropolitan Museum of Art, New York, USA/Bridgeman Art Library
48bc, tr	Courtesy of Showtime Archives (Toronto)				
		64bl	Photofest	84cl	David J. & Janice L. Frent Collection/CORBIS
48-49	Neal Preston/CORBIS	64br, 64-65	Reuters NewMedia Inc./CORBIS		
49tl	Courtesy of Showtime Archives (Toronto)	65tr	Photofest	84bc	Bettmann/CORBIS
49bc	Bettmann/CORBIS	65br	Photofest	84tr, 84-85 t	Joseph Sohm; Visions of America/CORBIS
49tr, br	Courtesy of Showtime Archives (Toronto)				

Page #/Position	Credit	Page #/Position	Credit	Page #/Position	Credit
84-85b	Museum of the City of New York/CORBIS	102bl	Richard Bickel/CORBIS	123bc	Bettmann/CORBIS
85bc	David J. & Janice L. Frent Collection/CORBIS	102tc	Bettmann/CORBIS	124bl	Musee de la Revolution Francaise, Vizille, France/Visual Arts Library,London, UK/Bridgeman Art Library
		102-103t	Reuters NewMedia Inc./CORBIS		
		102-103b	Bettmann/CORBIS		
85tr	Bettmann/CORBIS	103bc	Reuters NewMedia Inc./CORBIS		
86bl	Mosaic Images/CORBIS	103tr	Getty Images/Hulton Archive	124tc	Getty Images/Hulton Archive
86-88, 89cl, tr, 89tr, 90tl, tr, cr	Courtesy of Showtime Archives {Toronto}	10 bl	CORBIS	124bc	Nationalmuseum, Stockholm, Sweden/Bridgeman Art Library
		104br, 105c	Bettmann/CORBIS		
		105tr ,br	AP Photo	124-125	Chateau de Versailles, France/Lauros-Giraudon-Bridgeman Art Library
89bc	FDR/Michael Ochs Archives.com	106tl	CORBIS		
90bl	Michael Ochs Archive.com	106c, br	Bettmann/CORBIS-		
91bl	Lynn Goldsmith/CORBIS	107bl	Bettmann/CORBIS	125bc	British Library, London, UK/Calmann & King Ltd./Bridgeman Art Library
91tr	The Schomburg Center for Research in Black Culture/ The New York Public Library	107tr	CORBIS		
		107cr	Photofest	125tr	Pushkin Museum, Moscow, Russia/Bridgeman Art Library
		108tl	Photofest		
91br	Courtesy Eric Haugesag	108bl	Hulton-Deutsch Collection/CORBIS	125br	Getty Images/Hulton Archive
92bl	Private Collection/Bridgeman Art Library			126cl	Musee de la Revolution Francaise, Vizille, France/Visual Arts Library, London, UK/Bridgeman Art Library
		108br, 109bl, bc	Photofest		
92c	DK Picture Library	109tr	Getty Images/Hulton Archive		
92bc	Bettmann/CORBIS	110bl	Private Collection/Bridgeman Art Library		
92-93	Underwood & Underwood/CORBIS			126bc	Leonard de Selva/CORBIS
		110c	James Marshall/CORBIS	126tc	Archivo Iconografico, S.A./CORBIS
93c	Bettmann/CORBIS	110-111t, b	Bettmann/CORBIS		
93bc	Archivo Iconografico, S.A./CORBIS	111bc	Francis G. Mayer/CORBIS	126-127	Musee de la Ville de Paris, Musee Carnavalet, Paris, France/Lauros-Giraudon-Bridgeman Art Library
		111cr	Royal Geographical Society, London, UK/Bridgeman Art Library		
93tr	Getty Images/Hulton Archive				
93br	Royal Society, London, UK/Bridgeman Art Library	112cl, br	Hulton-Deutsch Collection/CORBIS	127tl	Leonard de Selva/CORBIS
				127bc	Photos12.com-ARJ
94tl	Gustavo Tomsich/CORBIS	112bl	Bettmann/CORBIS	127tr	Getty Images/Hulton Archive
94bl	Biblioteca Nazionale Centrale, Florence, Italy/Bridgeman Art Library	112c	Commonwelth Institute, London, UK/Bridgeman Art Library	127cr	Musee de la Revolution Francaise, Vizille, France/Visual Arts Library, London, UK/Bridgeman Art Library
		112-113	Bettmann/CORBIS		
94c, bc	Bettmann/CORBIS	113tc	James Marshall/CORBIS		
94br	Stuart Westmorland/CORBIS	113bc	Private Collection/The Stapleton Collection/ Bridgeman Art Library	128bl	Hulton-Deutsch Collection/CORBIS
94-95	Bettmann/CORBIS				
95bl	Michael Nicholson/CORBIS			128tc	Bettmann/CORBIS
95tr	Hulton-Deutsch Collection/CORBIS	113tr	CORBIS	128-129	Getty Images/Hulton Archive
		114bl	Joseph Sohm; ChromoSohm Inc./CORBIS	129tl	Photofest
95br	Associated Press, AP			129bc	Kelly-Mooney Photography/CORBIS
96bl	British Library, London, UK/Bridgeman Art Library	114tc	AP Photo/Bebeto Matthews		
		114-115	Getty Images	129tr, 130tl, bl, bc	Getty Images/Hulton Archive
96c	Ashmolean Museum, Oxford, UK/Bridgeman Art Library	115tc	Michael Neveux/CORBIS		
		115tr	Underwood & Underwood/CORBIS	130tr, br	Photofest
96br	Getty Images/Hulton Archive			131cl	Reuters NewMedia Inc./CORBIS
96-97,97c	Archivo Iconografico, S.A./CORBIS	115br	Bettmann/CORBIS	131bc	Bettmann/CORBIS
		116tl	Dave King/DK Picture Library	131tr	CORBIS
97br	Bettmann/CORBIS	116tc	IHA/Icon SMI	132bl	AP Photo
98bl	Woburn Abbey, Bedfordshire,UK/ Bridgeman Art Library	116bc	AP Photo	132tc, 133tl	Bettmann/CORBIS
		116br	AP Photo/McDonald's	133bl	Getty Images/Hulton Archive
98tc	Victoria & Albert Museum, London, UK/Bridgeman Art Library	116-117	John Biever/SI/Icon SMI	133tc	Bettmann/CORBIS
		117tr	Leonard de Selva/CORBIS	133bc	AP Photo/Marty Lederhandler
98cr	British Library, London, UK/Bridgeman Art Library	117br	AFP/CORBIS	134tl	AP Photo
		118bl	Bettmann/CORBIS	134bl	Bettmann/CORBIS
98br	Private Collection/Bridgeman Art Library	118tc	Duomo/CORBIS	134tr	AP Photo/Jim Pringle
		118br	Getty Images/ HultonArchive	134br	AP Photo/The Metropolitan Museum of Art
98-99	Bettmann/CORBIS	119cl, ccr	Hulton-Deutsch Collection/CORBIS		
99bc	Private Collection/Bridgeman Art Library			135tl	Getty Images/Hulton Archive
		119tc	Bettmann/CORBIS	135bl	CORBIS
99br	National Portrait Gallery of Ireland, Dublin, Ireland/Bridgeman Art Library	119bc	Reuters NewMedia Inc./CORBIS	135tr	Getty Images/Hulton Archive
		120tl	Getty Images/Hulton Archive	136tl	Bettmann/CORBIS
100bl, tc	Bettmann/CORBIS	120bl, br	Bettmann/CORBIS	136bc	Wally McNamee/CORBIS
100br	Getty Images/Hulton Archive	121tl	Janet Wishnetsky/CORBIS	136cr	Henry Diltz/CORBIS
100-101	Bettmann/CORBIS	121bl, tr	Bettmann/CORBIS	137bl	Mitchell Gerber/CORBIS
101c	Layne Kennedy/CORBIS	121br	Steven Chernin/CORBIS	137tr	Bettmann; Stanley Tretick, 1963/CORBIS
101tr, cr	Bettmann/CORBIS	122tl, bl	Bettmann/CORBIS		
101br	AP Photo	122bc	AFP/CORBIS	137br	AFP/CORBIS
		122br	Getty Images	138bl	Hulton-Deutsch Collection/CORBIS
		123cl, tr	Photofest		

Page #/Position	Credit
138c, br,	
138-139	Bettmann/CORBIS
139c	Hulton-Deutsch Collection/CORBIS
139tr	Photofest
139br	Gustavo Tomsich/CORBIS
140tl	Leonard de Selva/CORBIS
140bl	Hulton-Deutsch Collection/CORBIS
140-141	Bettmann/CORBIS
141tl	Rykoff Collection/CORBIS
141bl, br	Hulton-Deutsch Collection/CORBIS
141tr	Bettmann/CORBIS
142bl	Henry Diltz/CORBIS
142c	Courtesy of Showtime Archives {Toronto}
142br	Stephen Paley/MICHAEL OCHS ARCHIVES.COM
142 spread	Neal Preston/CORBIS
143bc	Photodisc
143tr	Bettmann/CORBIS
143br	Getty Images/Hulton Archive
144c	Walter Iooss/Globe Photos Inc.
144bc	Posters.com
144cl	DK Picture Library
144cr	Hulton-Deutsch Collection/CORBIS
144br	Bettmann/CORBIS
144-145	Lynn Goldsmith/CORBIS
145c	Sandy Felsenthal/CORBIS
145bc, cr	Baron Wollman
146bl, br,	
147tl	Getty Images/Hulton Archive
147bl	Dave Bartruff/CORBIS
147tc	CORBIS
147tr	Bettmann/CORBIS
147cr	Getty Images/Hulton Archive
148tl, cr	Bettmann/CORBIS
148br	Medford Historical Society Collection/CORBIS
149tl	Getty Images/Hulton Archive
149bl, br	Dave King/DK Picture Library
149cr	Private Collection/ Bridgeman Art Library
150tl	Bettmann/CORBIS
150bc	CORBIS
150br	Getty Images/Hulton Archive
151tl	AP Photo
151bl, tr	Getty Images/Hulton Archive
151br	AP Photo/The Daily Journal, Dennis Reavis
152bl	Bettmann/CORBIS
152c	National Army Museum/DK Picture Library
152-153t	Bettmann/CORBIS
152 153b	Private Collection/Bridgeman Art Library
153bc	Getty Images/Hulton Archive
153tr	Bettmann/CORBIS
153cr	CORBIS
154tl	Time Magazine, Copyright Time Inc.
154bc	Ted Thai/TimePix
154tr	Bettmann/CORBIS
154-155t	Bettmann/CORBIS
154-155b	Catherine Karnow/CORBIS
155tr	Getty Images/Hulton Archive
155br	Bettmann/CORBIS
156bl	Reuters NewMedia Inc./CORBIS
156c, br,	
157tl	Getty Images/Hulton Archive
157bl	AP Photo/Emile Wamsteker
157tc	Liba Taylor/CORBIS
157bc	AP Photo/PA
157br	AP Photo/Hans Deryk
158tl, bl, br,	
159cl	Getty Images/Hulton Archive
159bl	AP Photo/Martin Cleave
159tr, br	Getty Images/Hulton Archive
160bc	AP Photo
160tl, cr	Getty Images/Hulton Archive
160br	AP Photo
161bl	AP Photo/Ed Bailey
161tr	AFP/CORBIS
161br	AP Photo
162bl	Bettmann/CORBIS
163	Archivo Iconografico, S.A./CORBIS
164tl	Getty Images/Hulton Archive
164bl	Wolfgang Kaehler/CORBIS
164br	AP Photo/Jeff Widener
164-165	Bettmann/CORBIS
165	AFP/CORBIS
166bl	Kelly Harriger/CORBIS
166tc	Farrell Grehan/CORBIS
166br	CORBIS
166-167	Angelo Hornak/CORBIS
167bc	Museo Gaudi, Barcelona, Spain/Index/Bridgeman Art Library
167tr	Stephanie Colasanti/CORBIS
167c	Ramon Manent/CORBIS
167br	Archivo Iconografico, S.A./CORBIS
168tl	Sarah Quill/The Bridgeman Art Library
168bl	Michael Nicholson/CORBIS
168bc	CORBIS
168-169	AP Photo/Richard Drew
169tl	AP Photo/Barry Sweet
169bc	Francesco Venturi/CORBIS
169tr	Bettmann/CORBIS
169br	Angelo Hornak/CORBIS
170bl	Ann Hawthorne/CORBIS
170tc	AFP/CORBIS
170br	Bettmann/CORBIS
170bl	Ann Hawthorne/CORBIS
171tl	Hulton-Deutsch Collection/CORBIS
171bl	Ann Hawthorne/CORBIS
171tr	Underwood & Underwood/CORBIS
171br	Hulton-Deutsch Collection/CORBIS
172tl	Bettmann/CORBIS
172b	Galen Rowell/CORBIS
172cr	Underwood & Underwood/CORBIS
172tl	Bettmann/CORBIS
172bc	Galen Rowell/CORBIS
173tl	Bettmann/CORBIS
173tr	Paul A. Souders/CORBIS
173br	Hulton-Deutsch Collection/CORBIS
174tl	Bettmann/CORBIS
174bl	Bettmann/CORBIS
174tr	Leonard de Selva/CORBIS
174br	Underwood & Underwood/CORBIS
175tl	CORBIS
175bl	Underwood & Underwood/CORBIS
175tr	Leonard de Selva/CORBIS
175br	Bettmann/PA
176bl	Museo di San Marco dell'Angelico, Florence, Italy/The Bridgeman Art Library
176c	Getty Images/Hulton Archive
176-177	Phillips, The International Fine Art Auctioneers, UK/Bridgeman Art Library
177tl	Duomo, Siena, Italy/Bridgeman Art Library
177bc	National Gallery Collection; By kind permission of the Trustees of the National Gallery, London/CORBIS
177tr	Archivo Capitular, Tortosa, Spain/Index/Bridgeman Art Library
177br	National Gallery Collection; By kind permission of the Trustees of the National Gallery, London/CORBIS
178tl	Museo de Santa Cruz, Toledo, Spain/Bridgeman Art Library
178bc	Biblioteca Medicea-Laurenziana, Florence, Italy/Bridgeman Art Library
178c	Louvre, Paris, France/Peter Willi/Bridgeman Art Library
178br	San Francesco, Upper Church, Assisi, Italy/Bridgeman Art Library
178-179	Dulwich Picture Gallery, London, UK/Bridgeman Art Library
179bc	Archivo Iconografico, S.A./CORBIS
179tr	Getty Images/Hulton Archive
180bl	Sovfoto/Eastfoto
180-181	Nationalmuseet, Copenhagen, Denmark/Bridgeman Art Library
180br	Photos12.com-Collection Cinema
181tl	Bettmann/CORBIS
181bl	Private Collection/Bridgeman Art Library
181cr	Sovfoto/Eastfoto
181br, tl	Bettmann/CORBIS
182bl	Sovfoto/Eastfoto
182br	Itar-Tass from Sovfoto/Eastfoto
183bl	Getty Images/Hulton Archive
183tr	Bettmann/CORBIS
183br	Underwood & Underwood/CORBIS
184tl	Private Collection/Bridgeman Art Library
184bl	Photos12.com
184tr	Private Collection/Bridgeman Art Library
184br	Photos12.com
185cl	Private Collection/Topham Picturepoint/Bridgeman Art Library
185bl	Photos12.com-coll. DITE-USIS
185tr	Bettmann/CORBIS
185cr	Photos12.com
186bl	AP Photo/stf

Page #/Position	Credit	Page #/Position	Credit	Page #/Position	Credit
186c	CORBIS	208-209	AP Photo	229bl, c	AP Photo/Stephen J. Boitano
186-187t	Bettmann/CORBIS	209bl, br	Bettmann/CORBIS	229tr	Photofest
186-187b	AP Photo/The Eisenhower Library	209tr	Hulton-Deutsch Collection/CORBIS	229br	AP Photo/Carlos Rene Perez
187c	AP Photo	210bl	Private Collection/Bridgeman Art	230tl	Sovfoto/Eastfoto
187br	Photos12.com-Bertelsmann Lexikon Verlag		Library	230bl	Hulton-Deutsch Collection/CORBIS
188tl, bl	Photos 12.com-coll. DITE-USIS	210c	Reuters NewMedia Inc./CORBIS	230c	Bettmann/CORBIS
188br	Bettmann/CORBIS	210-211t	Vittoriano Rastelli/CORBIS	231tl, tr	Bettmann/CORBIS
188-189	CORBIS	210-211b	Michael T. Sedam/CORBIS	231bl	Reuters NewMedia Inc./CORBIS
189bc	AP Photo/stf	211bl	Bristol City Museum and Art	231br	CORBIS
189tr	Photos 12.com-coll. DITE-USIS		Gallery, UK/Bridgeman Art	232tl	AP Photo
190bl	Bettmann/CORBIS		Library	232 bl, br	Photofest
190c	Picture Press/CORBIS	21 tr	Bible Society, London,	232tr	AP Photo/Angela Rowlings
190br	Bettmann/CORBIS		UK/Bridgeman Art Library	233cl	Bibliotheque Nationale, Paris,
191tl	Getty Images/Hulton Archive	211br	Christel Gerstenberg/CORBIS		France/Bridgeman Art Library
191tr	Photofest	212-213	Bettmann/CORBIS	233bl	Private Collection/Roger-Viollet,
191cr	AFP/CORBIS	213tl	Stefano Bianchetti/CORBIS		Paris/Bridgeman Art Library
191br	Bettmann/CORBIS	213bc	Gustavo Tomsich/CORBIS	233tr	Haags Gemeentemuseum,
192tl	Photos12.com-Oasis	213tr	Getty Images/Hulton Archive		Netherlands/Bridgeman Art
192bl	Photos12.com-Collection Cinema	214bl, br	CORBIS		Library
192cr	Getty Images/Hulton Archive	214c	Private Collection/Bridgeman Art	233br	Sovfoto/Eastfoto
193cl, tr	Bettmann/CORBIS		Library	234bl	Francis G. Mayer/CORBIS
193br	Getty Images/Hulton Archive	214-215	Bettmann/CORBIS	234tc,	
194tl, bl	Reuters NewMedia Inc./CORBIS	215bc	Bettmann/CORBIS	234-235	Bettmann/CORBIS
194bc	Henry Diltz/CORBIS	215tr	David J. & Janice L. Frent	234br	CORBIS
194cr	Reuters NewMedia Inc./CORBIS		Collection/CORBIS	235bc	AFP/CORBIS
195bl	Photofest	215cr	Owen Franken/CORBIS	235tr	Bettmann/CORBIS
195bc	Photos12.com-Collection Cinema	215br	Bettmann/CORBIS	235br	AP Photo/Playboy,Inc.
195tr, bl	Underwood & Underwood/CORBIS	216tl	Getty Images/Hulton Archive	236tl	Photos12.com
		216cl	David J. & Janice L. Frent	236bl	Franz-Marc Frei/CORBIS
196-197	Bettmann/CORBIS		Collection/CORBIS	236br	Francis G. Mayer/CORBIS
197bc	AP Photo/Jean-Jacques Levy	216bl, br	Bettmann/CORBIS	237tl	Getty Images/Hulton Archive
197tr, tc	CORBIS	217bl, tr	Getty Images/Hulton Archive	237bl	Mitchell Gerber/CORBIS
198bl	Bettmann/CORBIS	217cr	Bettmann/CORBIS	237br	Bettmann/CORBIS
198br	The Schomburg Center for Research in Black Culture/The New York Public Library	218tl	Getty Images/Hulton Archive	238bl	AFP/CORBIS
		218bl, br	Bettmann/CORBIS	238tc	Leonard de Selva/CORBIS
		219cl	Bettmann/CORBIS	238br	AFP/CORBIS
199tl	CORBIS	219bl	Tim Page/CORBIS	238-239	AP Photo/Pavel Gorshkov
199tr	The Granger Collection, New York	219tr	Bettmann/CORBIS	239bl, c	David & Peter Turnley/CORBIS
199br	The Schomburg Center for Research in Black Culture/The New York Public Library	219br	Getty Images/Hulton Archive	239br	Sovfoto/Eastfoto
		220bl	Jan Butchofsky-Houser/CORBIS	240tl	Norman Parkinson Limited/Fiona
		220c	Layne Kennedy/CORBIS		Cowan/CORBIS
200bl	Science Museum, London, UK/Bridgeman Art Library	220br	Photofest	240bl	CORBIS
		220-221	Neal Preston/CORBIS	240br	Bettmann/CORBIS
200-201	Bettmann/CORBIS	221bc, br	Courtesy of Showtime Archives {Toronto}	241tl	Norman Parkinson Limited/Fiona Cowan/CORBIS
202tl	Getty Images/Hulton Archive				
202bl	Photos12.com	221tr	Reuters NewMedia Inc./CORBIS	241bl, br	Getty Images/Hulton Archive
202bc	Lester V. Bergman/CORBIS	222bl	Bettmann/CORBIS	241tr	Bettmann/CORBIS
202br	Bettmann/CORBIS	222tc	Photofest	242tl, br	Xinhua from Sovfoto/Eastfoto
203tl	Underwood & Underwood/CORBIS	222-223	Lynn Goldsmith/CORBIS	242bl	AFP/CORBIS
		223tc	Courtesy of Showtime Archives {Toronto}	242tr	AP Photo
203bl, tr	Bettmann/CORBIS			243tl	Bettmann/CORBIS
203br	CORBIS	223bc	Mitchell Gerber/CORBIS	243tr, br	Reuters NewMedia Inc./CORBIS
204tl, br	Bettmann/CORBIS	223cr	Photofest		
204cl, bc	CORBIS	224bl	Bettmann/CORBIS		
204cr	Jay Syverson/CORBIS	224tc	CORBIS	Back Cover (from left to right)	
205cl, tr	Bettmann/CORBIS	224br	Joseph Sohm; ChromoSohm Inc./CORBIS	Chas Howson/British Museum/DK Picture Library	
205cr	Hulton-Deutsch Collection/CORBIS			Bob Guthany/Space and Rocket Center, Alabama/DK Picture Library	
		224-225	CORBIS		
205bc	Bettmann/CORBIS	225c	AP Photo	Geoff Brightling/DK Picture Library	
206tl	Roger Ressmeyer/CORBIS	225tr	AP Photo/Matthew Brady	DK Picture Library	
206bl	Papilio/CORBIS	225br	CORBIS	Dave King/DK Picture Library	
206br	AP Photo/Jim Rogash	226tl, bc	Getty Images/Hulton Archive	Philippe Sebert/Musée de Louvre/DK Picture Library	
206-207	AP Photo/EliseAmendola)	226tr	Bettmann/CORBIS		
207bc	Douglas Kirkland/CORBIS	226br	AP Photo/Earl Warren/State of Tennessee		
207tr	Roger Ressmeyer/CORBIS				
208tl	The Granger Collection, New York	227cl, bc, tr	Bettmann/CORBIS		
208bl	CORBIS	228bl	Left Lane Productions/CORBIS		
208br	Bettmann/CORBIS	228br	Photofest		
		228-229	AP Photo/Marty Lederhandler		

INDEX

ACKNOWLEDGEMENTS

DK PUBLISHING WOULD LIKE TO THANK the following people and organizations for their invaluable help: we are grateful to Carrie Trimmer and Cindy Berenson at A&E Television Networks for making this incredible project a possibility; and Harry Smith for his insightful foreword. Special thanks go to our publishing partners at Avalon for their hard work and good humor throughout: f-stop Fitzgerald and Will Balliett for organizing the project; Tom Dyja for his herculean efforts and boundless enthusiasm; Tracy Armstead for her tireless picture research; and Lisa Vaughn for her design work. Thanks also to Katherine Yam at Colourscan, researcher Adam Park, editorial assistant Joanna Roy, and proofreader Rachel Weiss.

AVALON PUBLISHING GROUP WOULD LIKE TO THANK Donna Stonecipher, Richard Willett, and Nanette Cardin for their efforts on this project, as well as the kind cooperation of Hanna Edwards at CORBIS, Marcus Morrell and Ed Whitley at the Bridgeman Art Library, New York, Meredith Brosnan at Sovfoto, Dave Booth with Showtime Archives, and Michael Shulman at Hulton/Getty. At DK, Chuck Lang for his support; Chuck Wills for his dogged pursuit of accuracy and good writing; Michelle Baxter for her great design eye and Barbara Berger for keeping things moving with patience and understanding. At AETN, Juan Davila, Chey Blake, Charles Wright, Liz Durkin and David Walmsley all helped put the pieces together,. Cindy Berenson kept the ball rolling with her graceful professionalism and, most of all, thanks to Carrie Trimmer, who came up with the idea for this book and has contributed to it in so many ways above and beyond the call.